*Truth, Love and a
Little Malice*

Truth, Love and a Little Malice: An Autobiography

KHUSHWANT SINGH

VIKING

in association with

RAVI DAYAL Publisher

VIKING

Penguin Books India (P) Ltd., 11 Community Centre, Panchsheel Park, New Delhi 110 017, India
Penguin Books Ltd., 80 Strand, London WC2R ORL, UK
Penguin Putnam Inc., 375 Hudson Street, New York, NY 10014, USA
Penguin Books Australia Ltd., Ringwood, Victoria, Australia
Penguin Books Canada Ltd., 10 Alcorn Avenue, Suite 300, Toronto, Ontario M4V 3B2, Canada
Penguin Books (NZ) Ltd., Cnr Rosedale & Airborne Roads, Albany, Auckland, New Zealand

First published by Ravi Dayal Publisher and Penguin Books India 2002

Copyright © Khushwant Singh 2002

10 9 8 7 6 5 4 3 2 1

Typeset in Caslon by Asterisk, New Delhi

Printed at Ajanta Offset Press, New Delhi

Publisher's Note

This volume was to have been published in January 1996, but for reasons briefly explained in the postscript, that did not come to pass. Apart from the postscript, which the author added in November 2001, the text of *Truth, Love and a Lilttle Malice: An Autobiography* remains substantially as it was when originally completed in 1995.

Contents

	Prologue	1
1	Village in the Desert	3
2	Infancy to Adolescence: School Years	11
3	College Years in Delhi and Lahore	30
4	Discovering England	53
5	Lahore, Partition and Independence	87
6	With Menon in London, with Malik in Canada	116
7	Purging the Past and Return to India	154
8	Parisian Interlude	164
9	Discovery of India	192
10	Sikh Religion and History	205
11	Bombay, The Illustrated Weekly of India, 1969–79 and the Aftermath	229
12	With the Gandhis and the Anands	279
13	1980–86, Parliament and The Hindustan Times	301
14	Pakistan	346
15	Oddballs and Screwballs	359
16	Wrestling with the Almighty	369
17	On Writing and Writers	384
18	The Last but One Chapter	403
	Postscript: November 2001	413

Prologue: An Apology for Writing an Autobiography

I STARTED ON this autobiography with some trepidation. It would inevitably be my last book, my swansong penned in the evening of my life. I am fast running out of writer's ink. I do not have the stamina to write another novel; many short stories remain half-written and I do not have the energy to finish them. I am eighty-seven. I am made daily aware of old age creeping over me. My memory, of which I was once very proud, is fading. There was a time when I rang up old friends in Delhi, London, Paris and New York without bothering to re-check their numbers from telephone directories. Now I often forget my own number. I may soon decline into senility and try to get myself on the phone. I have cataracts developing in both eyes, I suffer from sinus headaches, I am slightly diabetic and have blood-pressure problems. I also have an enlarged prostate; at times it produces illusions of youth in the form of massive erections in the mornings; at others, it does not give me enough time to undo my fly to urinate. I will have to get the prostate out soon; with it will go fake erections and youthful fantasies. I have been on the hit list of terrorist organizations for almost two decades. Till recently my home was guarded by soldiers and three armed guards took turns to accompany me wherever I went — to play tennis, to swim, for walks and to parties. I don't think terrorists will get me. But if they do, I will thank them for saving me from the agonies of old age and the indignity of having to shit in bed pans and having nurses wipe my bottom. Both my parents were long-lived. My father died at ninety — a few minutes after he had his last sip of Scotch. My mother followed him eight years later when she was ninety-four. Her last request, made in a feeble, barely audible voice, was 'Viskee'. It was given to her. She threw it up and spoke no more. I hope that when my time comes, I too will be able to raise my glass to take one for the long road.

When I started on my memoirs, I gave myself another four or five years of creative activity. I proposed to devote them in recording whatever I could recollect of my past. I have never disclosed my past to anyone. As the Urdu poet Hakeem Makhmoor wrote:

> I told no one the story of my life
> It was something I had to spend;
> I spent it.

I reveal myself without shame or remorse. Benjamin Franklin wrote:

> If you would not be forgotten
> As soon as you are dead and rotten
> Either write things worth reading
> Or do things worth writing.

I have not done things which anyone else may feel are worth recording. My only chance of not being forgotten when I am dead and rotten is to write about things worth reading. I have been witness to many historical events, and as a journalist, I have interviewed many characters who played decisive roles in shaping them. I am not an admirer of great people. The few I got to know at close quarters turned out to have feet of clay: they were pretentious, feckless, lying and utterly commonplace.

I have no pretensions to being a craftsman of letters. Having had to meet deadlines for the last five decades, I did not have the time to wait for inspiration, indulge in witty turns of phrase or polish up what I wrote. I have lost the little I knew of writing good prose. All said and done, this autobiography is the child of ageing loins. Do not expect too much from it: some gossip, some titillation, some tearing up of reputations, some amusement — that is the best I can offer.

My daughter, Mala Dayal, to whom this book is dedicated, bullied me into writing it. She may have good reason to regret her persistence in reminding me to get on with it. Special thanks are due to my niece, Geetanjali Chanda, who typed the MS many times, pointed out flaws in the text and often corrected them herself.

1 Village in the Desert

IT IS SAFEST to begin with the beginning.

Where I was born I have been told by people who were present at my birth. When I was born remains a matter of conjecture. I am told I was born in a tiny hamlet called Hadali, lost in the sand dunes of the Thar desert some thirty kilometres west of the river Jhelum and somewhat the same distance southward of the Khewra Salt Range. Hadali is now deep inside Pakistan. At the time I was born, my father, Sobha Singh, was away in Delhi with his father, Sujan Singh. When the news was sent to him, he did not bother to put it down in his diary. I was his second son. At that time records of births and deaths were not kept in our villages. Unlike Hindus who noted down the time of birth of their offspring so that their horoscopes could be cast, we Sikhs had no faith in astrology, and therefore attached no importance to the time and place of nativity. Several years later, when he had to fill a form for our admission to Modern School in Delhi, my father gave my elder brother's and my date of birth out of his imagination. Mine was put down as 2 February 1915. Years later, my grandmother told me that I was born in *Badroo* — some time in August. I decided to fix it in the middle of the month, to 15 August 1915 and made myself a Leo. Thirty-two years later in 1947, 15 August became the birthday of independent India.

Some time after I had been weaned, my father came to Hadali to take my mother and elder brother to Delhi, where he and his father had secured some building contracts. I was left with my grandmother. For the first few years of my life she was my sole companion and friend. Her name I later discovered was Lakshmi Bai. We called her Bhaabeejee. Like her, my mother also had a Hindu — Maharashtrian — name, Veeran Bai. The children knew her as Baybayjee.

I have hazy recollections of my childhood years in Hadali.

The village consisted of about three hundred families, most of them Muslims of Baluch extraction. They were enormous men, mostly serving in the British Indian army, or having retired from it. A fair proportion of the Viceroy's bodyguard came from Hadali. Till recently, a marble plaque on a wall alongside the railway Station Master's office stated that Hadali had provided proportionately more soldiers from its population for World War I than any other village in India. There were about fifty Hindu and Sikh families engaged in trade, shopkeeping and moneylending. My ancestors — I can only trace them back to my great-grandfather, Inder Singh, and his father, Pyare Lal, who converted to Sikhism and became Sohel Singh — were tradesmen. They had camel caravans which took rock-salt from the Khewra mines, and dates, the only fruit of our desert homeland, to sell in Lahore and Amritsar. They brought back textiles, kerosene oil, tea, sugar, spices and other items to sell in neighbouring towns and villages. Later, my grandfather and father got into the construction business. They laid a part of the small-gauge railtrack and tunnels on the Kalka-Simla railway.

We were the most prosperous family of Hadali. We lived in a large brick-and-mud house with a spacious courtyard enclosing a buffalo shed and had a well of our own. The entrance was a massive wooden door which was rarely opened. It had a small aperture to let people in. A number of Hindus and Sikhs served us as clerks, and hired Muslim camel-drivers took our wares to the markets. Many Muslim families were our debtors.

Our family's prosperity was ascribed to a legend. It is said that one year, when it rained heavily on the Salt Range, flood waters swept down the rocky ridge, carrying with them a Muslim holy man named Shaida Peer, who had climbed on to the thatched roof of his hut. By the time he floated down to Hadali, he had nothing on him except his loin cloth. My grandfather, Sujan Singh, gave him clothes, made a hut for him near the Muslim graveyard and sent him food. Shaida Peer blessed him: 'I will give your two sons the keys of Delhi and Lahore. They will prosper.' And prosper they did — my father as a building contractor in Delhi; and his younger brother Ujjal Singh as one of pre-Partition Punjab's biggest landowners. He later became a Member of the Legislative Assembly and, after Independence, Finance Minister of Punjab and still later its Governor. He ended his career as Governor of Tamil Nadu.

We Sikhs and Hindus of Hadali lived with the Muslims in an uneasy but peaceful relationship. Though we addressed their elders as uncles or aunts as they did ours, we rarely went to each other's homes except on marriages and deaths. We lived in slight awe of the Muslims because they were more numerous and much bigger built than us. Fortunately for us, they were split into different clans — Waddhals, Mastials, Awans, Janjuas, Noons and Tiwanas — and were often engaged in litigation over land, frequently murdering each other. We kept ourselves at a safe distance from them.

I recall passing their men striding down the village lanes. Most of them were over six feet tall and made as if of whipcord. They wore their well-oiled hair curling out behind their ears, stuck with small wooden or ivory combs. They normally twirled spindles with the fleece of sheep or camels to make yarn, or took their hooded falcons out for airing. Their women were also tall, slender and well proportioned. They could carry two pitchers full of water balanced on their heads, and one pitcher caught between the right arm and waist. Water splashed on their muslin shirts and ankle-length lungis, displaying the outlines of their taut, shapely, black-nippled breasts as well as their muscular, dimpled buttocks. They never looked up from the ground as they glided past, aware of men eating them up with their eyes. Though barely four years old, I became an inveterate voyeur.

Nothing very exciting happened in Hadali. Life had a soporific routine. My grandmother rose well before dawn to milk the buffaloes and put the milk in an earthen pot over smouldering embers of pats of buffalo dung. She went out into the open with neighbouring women to defecate. She pulled up a couple of buckets of water from the well and bathed herself under starlight as she mumbled the morning prayer, *Japji*. She spent the next half hour churning butter and butter-milk, reciting her prayers as she did so. Then she woke me up. I was allowed to defecate on the roof-top where the hot sun burnt up everything exposed to it. I washed myself. She combed my long hair and plaited it: being Sikhs we did not cut our hair. I got out my wooden *takhti* (slate) smeared over with yellow *gaachnee* (clay), my reed pen and earthen soot-inkpot. She got a bundle of stale chappatis left over from the previous evening's meal and wrapped them in her *dupatta*. We set out together for the Dharamsal-cum-school. Pi dogs awaited us at our threshold. We took turns tearing up pieces of chappati and throwing them to the dogs. We kept a few in reserve for our return journey.

The Dharamsal was a short distance from our home. I was handed over to Bhai Hari Singh who was both Granthi and teacher. I sat on the floor with other Hindu and Sikh boys and chanted multiplication tables in sing-song. My grandmother went to the large hall where three copies of the Granth Sahib were placed side by side on a low table. Beneath the table was an assortment of spectacles discarded by worshippers for the use of anyone they fitted. After chanting the tables, Bhai Hari Singh wrote the letters of the Gurmukhi alphabet on a board for us to copy. Though bent with age, he had a terrible temper. Any mistake he spotted on our wooden slates was rewarded with resounding kicks on our backsides. Mercifully, the lesson did not last more than an hour. My grandmother and I walked back, giving the village dogs all that remained of the chappatis. While she busied herself sweeping the floor, rolling up beds and cooking the midday meal, I went out to play hop-scotch or tip-cat (*gullee-dundaa*) with boys of my age.

What we did in the afternoons depended on the time of the year. Desert winters could be very cold and the days very short. There was more to do and less time to do it in. But the real winter lasted barely forty days. After a brief spring, the long summer was upon us. It became hotter day by day with temperatures rising to 125°F. We hardly ever had any rain. Our *tobas* (ponds) were filled with brackish rain-water coming down the Salt Range. Some of it percolated into the wells. Only a few of these wells, which were brick-and-cement lined, yielded potable water fit for human consumption. For some reason brackish wells were referred to by the male gender as *khaara khoo*; those which yielded sweet water were known by the diminutive, feminine gender as *mitthee khooee*. Most of us had pale yellow teeth with a brown line running horizontally across the upper set. This was ascribed to the impure water we drank. No matter what time of year it was, my grandmother spent her afternoons plying the charkha while mumbling Guru Arjun's *Sukhmani* — the Psalm of Peace. My memories of my grandmother are closely linked with the hum of the spinning wheel and the murmur of prayers.

The long summer months were an ordeal. The hot sands burnt the soles of one's feet. Going from one house to another we had to hug the walls to walk in their shadows, deftly avoiding blobs of shit left by children who too had found the shadows the coolest places in which to defecate. We spent most of the day indoors gossiping, or drowsily fanning away flies. It was only late in the afternoon that camels and buffaloes were taken to the *tobas* for watering. The buffaloes were happiest wallowing in the stagnant ponds. Boys used them as jumping boards. At sunset the cattle were driven back, the buffaloes milked and hearths lit. The entire village became fragrant with the aroma of burning camel-thorn and baking bread. Boys formed groups to go into the sand-dunes to defecate. While we were at it, dung beetles gathered our turds into little marble-sized balls and rolled them to their holes in the sand. We had a unique way of cleansing ourselves. We sat on our bottoms in a line. At a given signal we raised our legs and propelled ourselves towards the winning post with our hands. By the end of the race called *gheesee*, our bottoms were clean but full of sand. Later, in the night and during the early phases of the moon, we played *kotla chapakee*, our version of blind-man's buff. Full-moon nights on the sand-dunes remain printed in my memory. We ran about chasing each other till summoned home for supper. The one threat that worked was that we might be kidnapped by dacoits. We were familiar with the names of notorious outlaws like Tora and Sultana who had spread terror in the countryside because of the number of murders and abductions they had committed.

Next to dacoits we most feared sand storms. We were used to living with dust-raising winds and spiralling dust-devils, but *haneyree* or *jhakkhar* were something else. They came with such blinding fury that there was little we could do besides crouching on the ground with our heads between our knees to prevent sand getting into our nostrils, eyes and ears. There were times when so much sand was blown that the rail track was submerged under it, and no trains ran till it was cleared. But it purged the air of flies and insects, and for the following day or two the air would be cleaner and cooler.

After the evening meal we went to our roof-tops to sleep. My grandmother, who had already said her evening prayer, *Rehras*, recited the last prayer of the day, *Kirtan Sohila*. She rubbed clotted cream on my back. If her gentle ministrations did not put me to sleep, she would tell me anecdotes from the lives of our Gurus. If I was still wide awake, she would point to the stars and reprimand me: 'Don't you see what time it is? Now *chup* — shut up.'

The nicest time in the summer was the early morning. A cool breeze blew over the desert, picking up the fragrances of roses and jasmine which grew in our courtyards. It was the time for half sleep and fantasizing. It was all too brief. The sun came up hot, bringing with it flies and the raucous caw-cawing of crows. The blissful half hour that Urdu poets refer to as the *baad-e-naseem* — zephyr of early dawn — came to an end all too suddenly.

Little happened in Hadali to relieve the tedium of our daily routine. There was a murder or two every other year. But since murders were confined to the Muslims, we never got over-excited about them. Once a year there were tent-pegging competitions on the open ground near the railway station. Competitors lined up on their horses and, at a given signal, galloped towards the stakes waving their spears and yelling *'Allah Beli Ho'* — Oh Allah is my best friend. After piercing the stakes they waved their spears triumphantly for all to see. They often raced passing railway trains and kept pace with them till their horses ran out of breath. I remember the first time a Sikh brought a bicycle to Hadali. He boasted that he would outrun any horse. Before a horseman could take up his challenge, we boys decided to take him on. Hadali had no metalled road and the cyclist was still wobbly on the wheels. He fared very poorly as his cycle got stuck in the sand. He became the laughing stock of the village and was thereafter mocked with the title 'Saikal Bahadur' — brave man of the bicycle.

I returned to Hadali three times after shifting to Delhi. The first time, to be initiated into reading the Granth Sahib. My elder brother, a cousin and I were made to read aloud the *Japji* in front of the congregation and asked to swear that we would read at least one hymn every day. None of us was able to keep our promise for very long. I went there next when practising law in Lahore. I drove to Hadali with a friend whose cousin was the manager of the salt mines. As we pulled up near the railway station tears welled up in my eyes. I resisted the urge to go down on my knees and kiss the earth. I walked up to the Dharamsal and to the house where I was born. A man who was Risaldar in the Viceroy's bodyguard recognized me and spread the news to the village. By the time I left, there was a crowd to see me off.

My last visit to Hadali was in the winter of 1987. The partition of India in 1947 had brought about a complete change in its population. Not a single Sikh or Hindu remained. Our homes were occupied by Muslim refugees from Haryana. Our family haveli was divided into three equal parts, each shared by Muslim refugees from Rohtak. A new generation of Hadalians who had never seen a Sikh were then in their forties. I was uncertain of the reception they would give me. My only contact with this generation was through meeting a few young soldiers taken captive in the Indo-Pakistan war of 1971 in the prisoner-of-war camp in Dhaka. I had sought them out and written to their parents that they were safe and in good health.

I drove from Lahore and reached Hadali early in the afternoon. Village elders awaited me on the roadside with garlands of silver and gold tassels with the words *Khoosh Amdeed* — welcome — inscribed on them in Urdu. I did not recognize any of the men whose hands I shook. I was escorted to the High School ground where a dais with the Pakistan flag fluttering over it had been put up. Over 2,000 Hadalians sat in rows on chairs and on the ground. Speeches in badly pronounced, florid Urdu were delivered acclaiming me as a son of Hadali. My heart was full of gratitude. I sensed that I would make an ass of myself. I did. I started off well. I spoke to them in the village dialect. I said that just as they looked forward to going on pilgrimage to Makka and Madina, coming back to Hadali at the time of the *Maghreb* (evening prayer) of my life was my *Haj* (big pilgrimage) and my *Umra* (small pilgrimage). And as the Prophet on his return to Makka as Victor had spent his first night wandering about the streets and praying beside the grave of his first wife, I would have liked nothing better than to be left alone to roam about the lanes of Hadali and rest my head on the threshold of the house in which I was born. Then I was overcome by emotion and broke down. They understood and forgave me. I was escorted to my former home with the entire village following me. Fireworks were let off; women standing on rooftops showered rose-petals on me. Who was the author of the perfidious lie that Muslims and Sikhs were sworn enemies? No animosity had soured relations between the Muslims, Hindus and Sikhs of Hadali. Muslims had left the Sikh-Hindu Dharamsal untouched because it had been a place of worship for their departed cousins.

The Rohtak families living in what was once our home had done up the haveli with coloured balloons and paper buntings. The elders of the village who once knew my father had a feast laid out in my honour. There was little that I saw of Hadali that I recognized. The sand-dunes which had been the playgrounds of my childhood years were gone. A canal had greened the desert. The *tobas* had become swamps full of reeds. The marble plaque commemorating the services of the men who had fought in World War I had been removed. I left Hadali a little before sunset, aware that I would never return to it again.

2   *Infancy to Adolescence: School Years*

THE TEN YEARS between the ages of five and fifteen are probably the most formative in the shaping of a person's mind and body. Family members who once provided emotional sustenance are gradually replaced by outsiders who become increasingly more important in moulding one's personality. Sexual desire becomes stronger day by day. You grope about to give it expression. You are confused, and unsure of how to go about doing so. Schoolmates, teachers, domestic servants, cousins and older relations direct or misdirect you. You go through homosexual and incestuous desires. With alarm you notice pubic hair sprouting round the genitals. And suddenly one day, while you are amusing yourself, a strange thrill builds up in your body. It is ecstatic, it is agonizing. If you are a male, you are convulsed from head to foot as semen gushes out of your phallus. You have become a man, capable of impregnating women and becoming a father.

It is about these formative years that I will write in this chapter.

I do not recall the exact year when my grandmother and I joined my parents, my brothers and sister in Delhi. My mother had by then given birth to another son and daughter. World War I had raised our family from trading, landowning and contracting to dabbling in industry. For its efforts in recruiting soldiers and raising donations for the war chest, it was rewarded with extensive tracts of land irrigated by canals. There was one large block between Mian Channu and Khanewal (now in the Multan district of Pakistan). A small railway station named Kot Sujan Singh between the two still marks the family's presence there. There was another tract of land given to them near Jaranwala in Lyallpur district (now Faisalabad, Pakistan). My grandfather and his two sons put up cotton ginning and spinning mills and oil presses in these towns. My uncle Ujjal Singh, who was the first in the family to go to college and get a Master's degree, was put in charge of the lands and mills in the Punjab. My father became a building contractor. As if this was not enough, they went into the textile business as well. They bought a cotton mill near Delhi's Subzi Mandi. Originally named Jumna Mills, it was given a recognizably Sikh name: Khalsa Cotton Spinning and Weaving Mills. We moved into an apartment above the entrance gate. The mill had been doing poorly under its previous owners; it did worse under my grandfather and father's management. They had no experience of running a large mill and did not have enough liquid cash to replace old machinery with new. It was often closed down. The money they made in their contracting business was swallowed up by losses incurred by this mill. It brought the family to the verge of bankruptcy. In 1919 a fire reduced most of it to ashes. It is more than likely that the fire was contrived to claim insurance money.

The end of the textile venture ended our connection with the Old City. We moved to a site close to the buildings my father had undertaken to construct in what was to become New Delhi. However, we were still living above the entrance of the mill when I joined school.

I do not know what made my father choose that particular school for us. He had got to know some old, well-to-do residents of Delhi. Amongst them was a Jain family consisting of Rai Bahadur Lala Sultan Singh and his son, Raghubir Singh. They owned considerable real estate in the city. Raghubir Singh was not interested in business. He had taken an arts degree from St Stephen's College and became an ardent admirer of its Christian Principal, S.K. Rudra. While in college, he had been coached by a private tutor who had links with terrorists. This teacher was later convicted and hanged for conspiring to murder the Viceroy, Lord Hardinge, in 1912. Young Raghubir Singh turned nationalist and decided to devote his life to rearing a new breed of Indians who would be both patriotic and westernized. He persuaded his father to let him take over the sprawling mansion they owned in Daryaganj alongside the old Mughal city-wall and convert it into a school. About the same time, he ran into a Bengali Christian lady, Kamala Bose, who agreed to come over from Calcutta to take over as Principal of the school. He soon developed a deep emotional attachment for Kamala Bose. His own wife, who had borne him two sons and a daughter, was a short, squat woman of little education and provided him no companionship. Though Kamala Bose was no beauty, being as short and squat as his wife and much darker, she was better educated. She gave him what he was looking for in a woman — intellectual stimulation and meaningful friendship. Between the two, they gave birth to a school destined to be rated among the best in India: it was more Indian than the imitation public schools set up by the British for sons of the aristocracy, and more liberal than other educational institutions.

To this school came nationalists like Mahatma Gandhi, the poet Rabindranath Tagore, Dr Ansari, Maulana Azad, Sarojini Naidu and Pandit Nehru. The Commander-in-Chief, Lord Chetwode, the Reverend C.F. Andrews and many other distinguished Englishmen also visited the school. There were some English women on the staff as well. It was the first co-educational school in Delhi. Although English was the medium of instruction, Indian languages like Sanskrit, Hindi and Urdu were also taught. Besides the normal courses of study, the school provided facilities to learn music, painting, carpentry, horse-riding, scouting, military drill under the supervision of a British sergeant, and team games like hockey and football. Instead of giving their child a grandiose name, Raghubir Singh and Kamala Bose gave it one more descriptive of its being ahead of its times, Modern. Against the wishes of my grandfather who held strong views about boys being taught by women, my father registered both his elder sons in this school. The one and only time my grandfather came to the school was for an annual function. When he saw his grandsons play the sitar and esraj he left in disgust. 'You want your sons to become *miraasees* [folk-singers]?' he angrily demanded. Thereafter he always referred to us as *rann-mureed* — disciples of lowly women.

We were fitted out for school uniforms. This was something unknown in the India of those times. We wore dark blue jackets and shorts. The jacket bore the insignia of the school — a banyan tree spreading over a pool of water with a swan floating beside a lotus in full bloom. Beneath it was the school motto in Sanskrit — *'naim aatma bal heenay na labhya'* — a timid mind can never discover the truth.

It took me quite some time to adjust myself to school and city life. It loosened my close relationship with my grand-mother, and my reliance on her. Although I still shared a room with her, I was hurried through my toiletry, bathing, dressing and breakfast by servants. Then, accompanied by a servant we two brothers took a tram from the Subzi Mandi terminal and rode in it through congested bazaars up to the Jama Masjid. There we were transferred to a tonga which took us to our school in Daryaganj. We returned home late in the evening. My grandmother sat by me while I ate supper and asked what I had learnt. But she could not help me with my homework or cajole me to say my prayers.

Modern School started with only thirty students, twenty-seven boys and three girls. Of the girls, the oldest was the daughter of a Sikh engineer. Her elder brother and two cousins came with her. This girl, Kaval Malik, was to re-emerge in my life two decades later in England to become my fiancée and then my wife when we returned to Delhi. The second girl, Rita, was the daughter of Raghubir Singh. She joined the school with her two older brothers. The eldest, Pratap Singh, was in my class. Of the third girl I recall nothing except her name, Kaushalya. In my ten years in this school some other girls joined with their brothers and left after a few months. Modern School was co-educational only in name.

It is commonly believed that the years at school are the most carefree and the happiest in a person's life. This was not true of my time in Modern School. I lived in dread of Kamala Bose, of recurring examinations and of school bullies who found me an easy target. I made a bad start. Most boys were from large cities and had a smattering of English. I came from a tiny hamlet and could only speak in my village dialect. The boys found the name Hadali very funny and kept reminding me of it: 'Where did you say you were born? Tell us again'. Then there was the name my grandmother had given me, Khushal Singh. I disliked it and had it changed to Khushwant, to rhyme with my brother's name, Bhagwant. The boys got to know about my first name — as well as its shortened version, Shaalee, used by my parents as my nick-name. They made a doggerel of it: *'Shaalee shoolee baagh dee moolee'* — a chap called Shaalee or Shoolee is like a radish in some garden. Or they changed it to Khushy, Khusro, or worse, Khusra, meaning eunuch. They also got to know that my grandmother washed my hair with yoghurt and, instead of scented oil, rubbed butter into my scalp. After exposure to the sun it smelt of rancid ghee and attracted hordes of flies. They would take turns to sniff at my head, shut their nostrils and run off shouting, 'Uff ! How he stinks! His head must be full of lice.' Just to oblige them, Miss Bose spotted one crawling down my neck one day. I was sent home with a note saying that I was not to return to school till my head was free of lice and asking my grandmother to stop washing my hair with curd and rubbing butter into it.

Having come to Delhi earlier, my elder brother was spared these humiliations. I sometimes hated my mother and grand-mother for exposing me to ridicule. To add to my troubles, I was no good at either studies or sports. The only subjects I did well in were English and geography. I scraped through science, algebra and geometry. Arithmetic remained my undoing. I scored a zero many times in my term examinations. I played truant as often as I could. Using the pretext of imaginary ailments, I would go to a dispensary run by a friendly doctor in Lalkuan to consume medicines and miss the morning classes. When this was found out I was severely reprimanded.

Modern School boasted that it had abolished corporal punishment. But Miss Bose did not believe in sparing the rod. She would make errant boys put out the palms of their hands and hit them hard with her foot-ruler — at times she made us turn our hands and hit them with its sharp edge on the back of our palms. Her example was followed by other teachers. Some believed in slapping, others in boxing our ears. The more anglicized, like our drill master, would make us bend and smack our bottoms with a cane. I had more than my share of corporal punishment. It did not leave any scars on my mind save the one time I was punished for an offence I did not commit. Something obscene was found written in one of the lavatories. Boys who had been to the loo that afternoon were questioned and asked to write a sentence on the blackboard. We knew the culprit was Amarjit Singh of my class. He was cunning enough to write the sentence in capital letters. I wrote it in my usual running hand. The panel of teachers decided that my handwriting had the closest resemblance to the one in the loo. I was caned in front of the entire school. Amarjit Singh left school after a few months. He reappeared in my life at St Stephen's College where he was caught cheating at a term exam and debarred for a year. Nevertheless, he made it to Cambridge University and landed a good job. His sister married the eldest brother of the girl who became my wife.

It took three or four years to sort out students into different classes according to their ages. My elder brother was in the first batch of three. The next batch had four. I was in the third batch of five, including Pratap, the elder son of Raghubir Singh, and Ashok Sen, son of the Registrar of Delhi University. Then there were Anand Nath who became a dentist, Satinder who later did medicine when I was in London and M____, who was the son of a friend of Kamala Bose's and also her favourite. He was the school bully. The only good student in our class was Anand Nath. The others were no better than I in studies or games. Pratap excelled in memorizing railway train time-tables but nothing else. Ashok always got a zero in arithmetic and did marginally worse than me in other subjects. M____ didn't give a damn for studies or sports and believed in having a good time endlessly. He was a tough fellow — we called him *Mota* (fat), and were scared of him. He was sexually more advanced than the rest of us. Although he had a tiny penis, he did not hesitate to haul it out of his shorts when erect and show it off. At times during our English lesson, taken by Kamala Bose's niece, who was then in her early twenties, he would put his hand inside his shorts and gaze intently at her while he yanked his tool. At the time none of us could comprehend what he was up to, but he succeeded in getting our lady teacher very flustered. Mota had a code of morality all his own. If anybody wanted to be buggered, he buggered him. If they wanted to bugger him, he was equally accommodating. Amongst those he obliged was our scout master, a young Parsi studying at St Stephen's. After he had seduced some other boys the scout master was hauled up for disciplinary action. Among the boys who gave evidence against him was Mota. Although Mota was into everything, he did not tell lies.

Mota's principal target was Ashok Sen, whom he accused of being a farter. He tormented him throughout school hours. He would push him, trip him and exclaim, 'Sorry, old farter! Didn't see you.' He would pull Ashok's shirt out of his shorts, punch him without provocation and say, 'No harm intended, old boy!' Poor Ashok was too frail to retaliate. After squeaking 'Stop it!' a few times he would run to the teachers for help.

Mota's day of reckoning came a couple of years later. One summer a group of six boys including him were sent to Kasauli, the hill resort off the route to Shimla, for a week's holiday. We were put up in Lala Raghubir Singh's house, 'Shantikunj'. Since Ashok had wisely stayed back, Mota had to find another victim. He picked on me. Although he was much stronger, I could run faster than him. When he hit me, I hit back and ran him out of breath. He turned his attention to the others till we couldn't take it any more. We decided that if he touched any of us we would take him on together. We did not have to wait long, because Mota was a compulsive bully. On our last morning in Kasauli he knocked me down on the lawn. I shouted for help. Four boys pounced on him and had him flat on the ground. One sat on his legs, one on his tummy, the other two pinned down his arms. Then we slapped and punched him till our hands and his cheeks were sore. He called us bloody bastards and spat on the boy sitting on his belly. All of us spat on his face in turn. He began to cry. We let him off with a warning that if he dared touch any of us he would get the same treatment again.

He left Kasauli crying and swearing vengeance. The same evening we took the bus for Kalka to catch the train for Delhi. Mota had got there before us by taxi and was strolling about the platform. He refused to recognize us. We got into a third-class compartment; he bought himself a second-class ticket. We did not see him at Delhi railway station. He complained to Kamala Bose. We gave her our version of the incident. Though he was her favourite, she could do no more than give us all a severe scolding: it was four against one. The treatment cured Mota of bullying. The whole school heard of what had happened at Kasauli and word went round that anyone molested by Mota was to call on us for help. Thereafter, the best he could do was swear at us under his breath and call us bloody cowards for ganging up against him. After I returned from England we became friends and shared many experiences, including a visit to a brothel. Of that adventure in its proper place.

School days were long. We were woken up when it was still dark, hurried through breakfast, and sent away by train, tonga, phaeton, or bicycles as we grew older. We started off in school with the singing of a morning prayer, usually *Jana Gana Mana*, which later became India's national anthem. Then there was the reading of some passages from the writings of sages: Rabindranath Tagore's 'Where the mind is without fear' was often repeated. It was followed by five minutes of silent meditation. Important subjects like mathematics, English, history and science were taught in the mornings. There was a short break for P.T. Then we ate our midday meal in a cavernous hall used as a refectory. My aversion to oatmeal porridge and aubergines began with these meals where you had to eat everything that was served. We were allowed an hour of rest. The habit of taking a siesta was formed at school. In the afternoons we usually did drawing, music and carpentry. The last item was team games like hockey or football. We rarely got home before dark. We were given a lot of homework and were left little time to play or relax at home.

Some trivial incidents have stuck in my memory. One took place during the five-minute meditation following prayers. Two boys from Almora had recently joined school. We had hardly got to know their names when one morning the elder boy blew up the period of silence by letting out a resounding fart. This is something no children anywhere in the world can take with a straight face. Some sniggered, some choked trying to suppress their laughter. Even Kamala Bose's stern rebuke of 'silence!' ended in a giggle. The boy was promptly endowed with the title *paddoo* — the great farter. He did not return after the summer vacation.

Though I was no good at either studies or games, I showed some ingenuity in playing pranks. One of my favourites was to put a basin of water or pairs of shoes on half-opened doors. Anyone who pushed them apart received a shoe beating or a shower. In the summer months we slept at home in the open, usually on the road connecting the 'in' and 'out' gates of our new home in New Delhi. At one time a distant relation from Hadali who came to stay with us had his charpoy next to mine. He snored loudly throughout the night and got up in the early hours of the morning. He could not get used to flush toilets and preferred to defecate behind the bushes in the garden. Before retiring for the night he would keep a brass *lota* full of water under his bed to wash his bottom in the morning. One night as he slept I poured gum into his *lota*. The next morning he looked unwell. He complained of a mucous discharge from his bowels which made his *tehmad* stick to his buttocks. I repeated the prank the next two nights. He went to consult a doctor and had his stools examined. By then I was unable to keep the secret to myself. My parents reprimanded me, but could not help going into fits of laughter when telling others of what I had done.

Another time we brothers spotted a cobra in our garden. After beating it to a pulp, but leaving its head untouched, we put it in a biscuit tin, tied the cover with a string and took it to school as a present for our chemistry teacher, Dr Chaubey. He had quite a collection of snakes in jars of methylated spirit in the laboratory: vipers, adders, banded kraits, grass-snakes, and other varieties. But no cobra. He brought a jar of spirit and placed it on the table beside the biscuit tin. As he undid the cord, the lid flew into the air and a very angry cobra with its hood spread out lunged at him, missing his face by a fraction of an inch. Many years later I turned this incident into a short story, '*The Mark of Vishnu*', the first of mine to be accepted by *Harpers Magazine* of New York.

In those days snakes were not uncommon in Delhi. Being close to the river and old Mughal fortifications, Modern School had quite a few around during the summer months. There was never a monsoon when some were not flushed out of their holes and beaten to death. There were also scorpions, bee-hives and hornets' nests. Once Charat Ram, the third son of Shri Ram (who became one of India's biggest industrialists), was stung in the ankle by something which he promptly wailed was a poisonous snake. With tears running down his cheeks he bade farewell to his elder brother, Bharat, and his friends. There was a lot of sobbing and crying before the doctor arrived on the scene armed with anti-snake bite serum. 'It is too late,' howled Charat, 'I am going to die.' The doctor examined the site of the sting and plucked out a tiny black piece. Charat had been stung by nothing more lethal than a wasp.

It was during my school days that I picked up a terrible phobia about ghosts. We were fed with ghost stories by our servants. While holidaying in Shimla they told us about gangs of *mumiaaee vaaley* who roamed about looking for victims whom they hung upside down over a slow fire to extract human oil *(Ram Tel)* which could join cut-off limbs. They were said to be agents of the British who needed this valuable oil for their army. The only way of recognizing a *mumiaaee vaala* was to look at his feet: they were turned backwards — heels in front, toes at the back. No one ever caught one, but periodically when there were scares that they were about, people did not venture out of doors after dark.

My fear of ghosts had a more substantial basis. I was exposed to death as a child. I was in Mian Channu when my grandfather, Sujan Singh, then in his sixties, was taken ill. Village doctors were summoned to his bedside. He kept gasping and calling for more medicine every five minutes. Then he opened his mouth wide as if to yawn, gasped and collapsed on his pillow. My grandmother set up a loud wail, chanting the hymn of death: '*Deeya mera ek naam dukh vich paya tel*' — my lamp is the name of the Lord filled with the oil of sorrow. She slapped her forehead with both her palms and smashed the glass bangles on her arms. I was frightened by the sight of my parents, uncles and relations crying like children. Servants told me that they had seen my grandfather's spirit fly out of the room like a puff of smoke and disappear in the sky.

Even more gruesome was watching my aunt, the first wife of my uncle Ujjal Singh, die. This was also in Mian Channu. She was expecting her second child. I accompanied my mother who was sent to look after her during her confinement. The foetus died in her womb and spread poison in her body. Every evening when her bed was brought into the courtyard she had hallucinations. 'Look!' she would scream pointing towards her feet, 'There she is, the *dayn* — witch.' My grandmother and mother assured her that there was no one there and chanted prayers loudly to dispel evil spirits. It was whispered around that she had brought evil on her own head by plucking a lemon off a tree in the garden after sunset. It was a common belief that anyone who did so was possessed by a witch who could only be got rid of by exorcism. A prayerbook and a kirpan were placed under her pillow. Nothing helped. The *dayn* continued to possess her. One afternoon she had terrible convulsions. Her eyes turned till only the whites could be seen. She bit her tongue till blood flowed out of her mouth. She died in great agony. Once again, there was a loud wailing and slapping of foreheads. As news reached the town, women came in droves, beating their breasts in unison and crying '*hai! hai!*' They sat round the corpse and chanted praises of the dead woman they had never known. The *veyn* — praises of the departed — were heart-rending. Since her own son, Narinder, was away I had to light her funeral pyre. I never understood why children of my age were exposed to such ghastly scenes.

Another time in Shimla, while returning home in the evening, my sister and I saw a road-roller topple into a *khud*.

Both the driver and his assistant had their heads and limbs ripped off their bodies. We could not tear ourselves away from the gory scene and watched their limbs being collected and put together and their bloodied corpses borne away on stretchers. That night we slept in the same bed because we were too frightened to be by ourselves.

The fear of ghosts has never left me. I am drawn to the dying as iron filings to a magnet. I visit cremation grounds and cemeteries to purge myself of this phobia. But no sooner is it dark than I am at the mercy of the spirits of the dead. As a child I envied people who lived in crowded bazars and slept alongside each other on pavements. Ghosts do not haunt crowded places. I still find it difficult to sleep soundly if I am alone in a house.

There were some positive gains in my otherwise undistinguished years at school. I learnt to love the English language. And poetry, both in English and Urdu. My eyes also became more receptive to things of beauty. I picked up English quite rapidly on my own. Since there was no one to guide me at home, it was acquired haphazardly by reading and rereading strip cartoons in the English children's weekly *Puck*, poring over pictures of World War I, illustrated stories from the Bible and volumes of *The Book of Knowledge*. On my own, I went on to Edgar Rice Burrough's series, *Tarzan the Ape Man* and Rider Haggard's novels on Africa. Very often I got the meanings of words wrong and mispronounced them. I made doggerels of mispronunciations.

One of my compositions was based on an opening line given by our chauffeur in Mian Channu. He told us how Indian whores solicited Tommies: '*O Sahab! O Sahab! Come haeyyur.*' Then my cousin mispronounced youth as *yath* and put as *putt*. A brother, while shouting for a ball at the tennis court, yelled out '*Sut goli gul*' instead of just asking for the *goli* (ball). He also pronounced tyre as *taiyyar*. The words meant nothing but gave birth to our private doggerel:

> O Sahab! O Sahab! come haeyyur,
> Yath, patt, gul, taiyyar.

My interest in English became more organized when a young English lady, Miss Budden, took over English classes. Instead of going over boring textbooks, she read us *Ivanhoe, Last of the Barons*, and *Tess*. She read us children's stories by Oscar Wilde and short poems by Shakespeare. One day she recited 'Under the greenwood tree . . . ' The verse touched a cord in my heart. I memorized it and many others that she read to us from Wordsworth, Tennyson and other poets. On Saturdays we played a word game devised by her. We were given small dictionaries. She called out a word; the first to spot it in the dictionary was declared the winner. It taught me the habit of consulting a dictionary whenever in doubt about the exact meaning of a word.

The love of Urdu poetry was instilled in me by Moulvi Shafiuddin Nayyar. I was his only student. He had to get me through the matriculation examination in four years. I had to often go to his home to be coached. I found Urdu prose very uninspiring, but its poetry had more music and message packed in a few words than English verse. Moulvi Sahib was himself a poet and wrote a lot of children's verse. When the lesson was over, he read passages from poets like Ghalib, Zauq, Zafar and Akbar Ilahabadi. He made me memorize several of them. They have remained with me ever since.

Once a month we were taken out for a picnic to the old monuments of Delhi. We were told about their history and left to roam about tombs, mosques and palaces. Twice a year we went on excursions to different parts of India. Some experiences remain in my mind. One is of my first look at the ocean. This was during a scout jamboree in Bombay. I was awe-struck and dumb-founded on seeing the endless expanse of water. I ran to meet an oncoming wave and took a palm-full to see how it tasted. And at once spat it out. More spectacular was our visit to Rajasthan. Amongst the places we were taken to was the enormous Rajput fort of Chittor, standing on top of a hill. After walking round the ruins of palaces and temples we came down the hill to await our bus. As the sun was about to set, hundreds of peacocks lined up on the parapet of the fort. Then, as if on a signal given by their leader, the entire flock floated down crying *paon paon* with their long gold, green and blue tails gleaming in the last rays of the setting sun. How can one ever forget such a scene! During the same visit we were taken to Ajmer and Udaipur. We saw the forts, palaces and lakes. One evening somebody brought a cob of *Rewra* cactus and hung it on the lamp in the room. All at once, the room was full of its pungent, sweet fragrance. *Kewra* and *Khus*, which smell of the parched earth after the first drops of rainfall, remain my favourite perfumes. And I have never tired of visiting and writing about monuments.

The most memorable of these excursions was to Fatehpur Sikri and Agra. After hours of trudging through red sandstone palaces and mosques at Sikri we were taken to the Agra Fort. It was another succession of red and beige stone and white marble. I was tired and getting bored. Then we were lined up in front of the entrance gate of the Taj Mahal. And another lecture: 'Now children, you will see one of the seven wonders of the world. It was built by the Emperor Shahjehan as the final resting place of his Empress, Mumtaz Mahal.' At that moment of tedium I could not have cared less for any of the world's wonders or for the love of an emperor for his woman. The lecture over, we were ordered to march in single file. The Taj burst into view. I was stupefied by its gigantic magnificence and stood gaping at it with my mouth wide open. I didn't want to go any further. I just sat on the steps of the gates and took it all in.

Though I spent ten years at Modern School and years later married the girl I set my heart on when I saw her first at the age of five, I made no lasting friendships in the school. Some teachers like Moulvi Shafiuddin Nayyar kept in touch with me. Roma Biswas, one of the younger lady teachers, came back into my life when I was in college in Lahore and briefly when I first went to England. I saw a lot of Satinder in London and we spent our vacations together in Paris. I lost sight of him when he migrated to Canada. Mota was about the only classmate I ran into off and on in later years.

Despite having competent teachers and small classes, Modernites did not make the top grades in the matriculation examinations. There were no failures, but there were no 'toppers' either. This was a great disappointment to the school authorities. The emphasis in the Indian examination system was (and is) on cramming answers to likely questions. This was rightly frowned upon in Modern School and, even though their performances in exams were indifferent, most of the students did well in later life. An annual prize instituted in the name of S.K. Rudra (Principal of St Stephen's College) for the most outstanding student in 'character combined with learning' went to my elder brother Bhagwant Singh in its first year. There were five in my class when we took the matriculation examination in 1930. Of the five, the most mediocre in studies who also took no part in games because of his weak eyesight was Pratap Singh. If anything, his learning was less than that of the other four. Unknown to us, he must have possessed a sterling character. The teachers unanimously chose him for the Rudra Prize. His father was the founder of the school.

As expected, I passed the matriculation in the second division. The greatest worry of the school was Ashok Sen who had maintained an unbroken record of zeroes in arithmetic. Arithmetic was a compulsory subject in which you had to secure pass marks — or fail the entire examination. Ashok also passed the matriculation with a second division. His father was then Registrar of the University of Delhi. Modern School made me aware of the ways of the world.

The years at Modern School (*circa* 1920–30) saw many changes in our family fortunes and in my person. After abandoning the futile venture of trying to become a textile magnate, my father decided to concentrate on making buildings. We had moved out of the rooms we occupied above the entrance gate of Khalsa Mills to Raisina, destined to become New Delhi. For the first year or two we lived in a largish shack on what came to be known as Old Mill Road (now Rafi Marg) because of a flour mill located there. This faced what is today Sansad Marg (Parliament Street), close to the site where the two Secretariats, North and South Block, were to be built. My father got the contract to build South Block; Basakha Singh, who became his closest friend, got the contract for North Block. In front of our shack ran a narrow-gauge railway track from the village of Badarpur, about twelve miles south of Delhi, to what is now Connaught Circus. It had been laid to bring stone, gravel and rubble from Badarpur to the building sites. Huge sheds to house stone-cutting machines and masons employed to sculpt the stones into patterns given to them were set up right in front of our new home. In the morning we were roused by the roar of stone-cutting machines starting up and the pit-pat, pit-pat of masons hammering chisels on sandstone. This went on from dawn to dusk. On holidays we awaited the arrival of the midget Imperial Delhi Railway to off-load its cargo of stone and rubble so that we could take free rides to Connaught Circus and back.

At the peak of his contracting business my father had over 6,000 labourers and dozens of supervisors, clerks and accountants on his pay rolls. The labourers were Bagadis from Rajasthan. The men got 8 annas (half a rupee) per day, and their women 6 annas for carrying bricks, cement and mortar on their heads. They had to pull heavy blocks of stone to their proper locations: as they heaved them they chanted in unison: *'Haee sah! Haee sah! Ram bharosey, haee sah! Jore lagaa dey, haee sah!'* It was sweated labour. They never complained. There were no labour unions to fight for their rights. What they earned was barely enough to fill their bellies. But every evening while my father and his clerks were computing their gains and quarrelling with each other, the Bagadis went home singing lustily and dancing all the way to their hutments.

In those days there were no street lights. Since we slept in the open during the summer months we were more aware of the phases of the moon and movements of the stars than the time on the clock. Moonlit nights were often celebrated with picnics or after dinner strolls in the parks and roundabouts that were coming up. Every night jackals howled in the wilderness; we heard night-jars call and the chitter-chatter of owlets. We slept to the reassuring cries of chowkidars calling to each other, *'Khabardaar ho!'*

There was plenty of left-over government material for the contractors to use in their own private properties. They bought adjacent plots of land, three acres each on Jantar Mantar Road, to build their houses. All of them were Sikhs. Although they came from different parts of the Punjab and had not known each other before coming to Delhi, they became like members of one family. There was no dearth of opportunity and no need to undercut each other. Jantar Mantar Road became the rich Sikh contractors' colony. My father built himself a double-storeyed house. In the rear were clerks' and servants' quarters, cow and buffalo sheds and stables for horses to draw his phaeton, and a couple of garages. Near the exit gate of the house he had an annexe as an office with two rooms for guests. In the front was a large garden with a marble fountain; there was a tennis court on one side, a fruit-cum-vegetable garden on the other. He had cultivated a taste for flowers and sent for seeds from Calcutta and Bombay. He had a passion for roses and grew many exotic varieties in beds lining the road which ran from the 'in' gate through the portico to the 'out' gate. The other contractors built equally large houses. One Dharam Singh Sethi, who had the monopoly of supplying marble, granite and sandstone from quarries in Dholpur, built the biggest house here, in stone and marble. It is today shared by many political parties, including the Congress, for their offices. Without doubt, our house was the best designed in the new city and with the most attractively laid out garden. My father proudly named it *Baikunth* — paradise. Years later, he went on to build an even larger and more attractive house at the intersection of Janpath and Albuqurque Road (now Tees January Marg). He transferred the name *Baikunth* to it. The original paradise in which I spent most of my school years was sold to the Maharaja of Travancore. When he was divested of his state, it became the Kerala State Government Guest House.

More than changes in the family's fortunes were changes wrought in my body and mind. I grew from a granny-loving child to a sex-obsessed adolescent. This development was hastened by boys (*mundoos*) who worked in the kitchen. They were about the same age and were going through the same physical transformation. We learnt from each other how to amuse ourselves with our genitals. When a girl cousin came to spend her winter vacations with us, she was allowed to share my bed because we were little children and like 'brother and sister'. I pretended to be asleep while I lowered her pyjamas; she pretended to sleep through my ministrations. Neither of us had the foggiest notion what grown up men and women did when they slept together, but to us it seemed pleasant enough to press against the other. I developed a compelling desire to see women in the nude. Often Bagadi women came to bathe in a clerk's courtyard which had a hand-pump. I would climb up over a neem tree and from my perch watch them soaping their breasts; they never fully bared themselves. Whenever relatives had to catch an evening train from Delhi railway station I went to see them off. The ride back on the phaeton through Chauri Bazaar and Ajmeri Gate gave me the opportunity to ogle at the prostitutes who lined the balconies on either side of the bazaar. Once I was rewarded by a woman who gave me a wink and beckoned me with her hand. I fantasized about her for many nights. Till I was twelve I had no idea how the sex act between a man and a woman was performed. One moonlit night when our charpoys were laid alongside each other in the courtyard I saw my father come home from the club, change into his *tehmad* and go to my mother's bed. I heard her protest *sotto voce*: 'The children may be awake!' He was evidently high on drink and ignored her warning. I saw him remove his *tehmad* and lie on top of her, heave up and down a few times and collapse in a heap, and then go to his bed retying his *tehmad*. I didn't understand what he had been up to except that it was no good. My mind was disturbed for several days and I could not talk to him.

During our summer vacations in Mian Channu a young lad a few years older than us regaled us with stories of buggery in his school. The *mashook* — beloved — was always a pretty boy with a nicely rounded bottom. It seemed that all there was to sex was buggering effeminate boys. What were women for? He informed us that the only difference was that if you buggered a woman she became pregnant. Till fourteen I did not know what an adult woman's genitals looked like. The first time I saw, it was at an al fresco lunch given to Modernites on the lawn of a professor's garden in Varanasi. I happened to be sitting facing a line which had one of our senior teachers in the centre. As she lowered herself on the grass her sari got raised exposing a very hirsute something between her thighs. I was appalled.

It was after I had taken my matriculation examination and left Modern School that my mind was deflected from boys to girls. I went down with typhoid. I had two relapses which deprived me of the power of speech and movement. A young nurse was hired to look after me. All I can recall of her was that she was very dark, slightly built, had a small bosom and sparkling eyes. Besides taking my temperature every few hours and giving me medicine, she also sponged me in the mornings. It was during these sponging sessions that she lovingly took my penis in her hand and kissed it. 'You are beginning to have hair round your little *podnee*. Soon you will become a man and this fellow bigger and stronger.' I heard her but could not reply. She would also take my limp hands and rub her breasts with them. I liked the sensation but did not have the strength to fondle them. By the time I was able to react to her ministrations and mumble a few words, her services were dispensed with. It was that young nurse whose name I never got to know who turned my thoughts to women as objects of love and lust. Till then I did not believe women wanted sex as much as men, but had thought that they only put up with it to keep their men happy. My days of schooling were over.

3 College Years in Delhi and Lahore

S OME TIME AFTER my matriculation results were announced I put in an application for admission to St Stephen's College. It was then, as it is today, the most prestigious college in Delhi. At that time admissions were not as difficult as they became some years later. Boys from Modern School, coming from affluent families with a better command of English than others, were readily admitted. So was I. What I was apprehensive about was the ragging to which new entrants were subjected. It was said to be in the best tradition of British universities and designed to rub edges off boys who had fancy notions of themselves. Some of it was harmless but downright silly: asking newcomers to dance or sing, or to carry placards bearing the admission, 'I am a first year fool'. If new entrants resisted, it could get rough. In the hostels new boys were often subjected to humiliation like being made to strip and masturbate. There had been cases when effeminate boys were subjected to buggery. I was saved from ragging by missing the first term because of prolonged illness.

In those days not much was known about typhoid. There were no blood, sputum or other tests to determine the kind of fever you had. The only medicine prescribed was a foul-smelling bitter concoction. Solid food was forbidden. It was known to be one of a variety of *miyaadi* (periodical) fevers which lasted eleven or twenty-two days. If you had a relapse, you could have another bout of eleven or twenty-two days. I had two relapses. On the onset of the second, the doctors shook their heads and observed that my fate was in the hands of the Great Guru. I went into a coma. My parents had me touch trays full of rice, flour, ghee and sugar to be given away to beggars. They hired a day and a night nurse to look after me. When the battle to keep me alive seemed to have been lost, they sent for my grandmother who was then staying with my uncle at Mian Channu.

I became vaguely aware of her presence when she arrived. She took over my treatment. She tied a coloured string round the big toe of my left foot. Then she began to chant Guru Arjun's hymn *Sukhmani*. It went on all day and late into the night. She slept in the same room and began the chant again the next morning. By the afternoon I had come out of the coma. By the evening the fever mysteriously left me. Or perhaps it was a coincidence: the *miyaad* of the second twenty-two days was over.

Even before I could put my foot on the ground I was back at my pranks. I pretended to be asleep when the thermometer was slipped in my mouth and the doctor held my wrist to take my pulse beat. With my left hand, I quietly pressed the pulse on the inside of my elbow to stop its flow down the arm. The doctor frantically searched for my pulse, then turned up my eyelids to see if there was life in my eyes. I gave him a reassuring smile. In the three months that I spent lying in bed I gained almost two inches in height, but my liver was impaired for ever. Ever since I have slavered in the mouth while sleeping and have had to cajole my bowels into evacuating. Laxatives, purgatives and enemas became a part of my daily routine.

I had a long period of convalescence in the hills. It was pleasant to have people fussing over me, eager to do whatever I wanted. I spent two months in Shimla with my uncle and his second wife, a lovely, lotus-eyed woman who was spectacularly photogenic. It did me a world of good. I began to take long walks round Jacko Hill, ending on the Mall. It was then a most bewitching half mile of gaily-lit shop windows between two highly rated restaurants, Davico's at one end, Wenger's at the other. In the centre, where four roads intersected, was Scandal Point, the place for rendezvous. Here everyone who was anyone would spend some time exchanging gossip, ogling at beautiful women and inhaling the perfumed air they left behind. You could see senior English officials, the Governor of the Punjab, the Commander-in-Chief and others, taking a stroll or on their way to the Gaiety Theatre. Every evening you saw the tall, handsome Chief Minister of the Punjab, Sir Khizr Hayat Tiwana, in his plumed turban striding ahead of his rickshaw pulled by liveried flunkies. It was hard to drag oneself away from the Mall to go home.

Those summer months in Shimla made me aware of the beauty of the Himalaya. I began to write poetry — very bad poetry. I learnt to play the sitar. I desperately wanted to fall in love with somebody, it didn't matter who or of what age, provided she was a woman. Since I could not find anyone to respond to my yearnings, I wrote anonymous love letters to a girl from Amritsar whose parents had rented the neighbouring bungalow.

I returned to Delhi and made my appearance at St Stephen's College at the beginning of the second term. The season of ragging was over. I acquired the textbooks prescribed for English literature, history, philosophy and economics. They were the most popular subjects because they were the easiest for passing examinations. I also attended Bible classes, where attendance was optional: I went to them to ingratiate myself with my Christian professors, particularly K.M. Sarkar who also taught us English literature. His stress was on the New Testament. I found the Old Testament more interesting because of the sonorous sounds of its words. I memorized passages from the *Songs of Solomon* and the *Psalms*. The *Book of Job* became my favourite reading. I sensed that in order to write good English one should be familiar with the Bible as well as European fairy tales, nursery rhymes and even nonsense verse like the limericks of Edward Lear. I read them not for fun but as the basics of literature.

My comparative affluence, generous allowance of pocket money and the fact that, like my elder brother, I had a motorcycle to ride to college, made me sought after by my classmates who were eager to be treated to free lemonades and chicken patties and ride my A.J.S. Amongst them was E.N. Mangat Rai, who was later to play a very intrusive role in my life.

His full name was Edward Nirmal Mangat Rai. He was the third child and second son of a Punjabi Hindu father who had converted to Christianity, and a Bengali Christian mother. The father was in government service and ended his career as Commissioner of Income Tax. All the four Mangat Rai children were good looking and westernized. The eldest, Priobala, became a college professor and retired as Principal of Kinnaird College, Lahore. She chose to remain a spinster and spent her post-retirement years in Edinburgh. The second, Charles, went into the army, married an American and retired as a Brigadier. He settled in Canada, was a yoga teacher, and on the death of his wife married a Canadian girl much younger than himself. Edward Nirmal was the third. The fourth, Sheila, was a petite, cherry-blossom beauty who made a disastrous marriage with Arthur S. Lall of the ICS. She bore him a daughter, Tookie, who died of cancer in her thirties in California. After divorcing Arthur, Sheila took to the bottle and drugs. She lived with a succession of lovers before she returned to India to look after her apple orchard in Kulu. She was murdered by her own servants. I mention the Mangat Rais and the Lalls because all of them re-emerged in my life at different periods.

E.N., as I called him, and I hit it off as soon as we met. Though tall, he was somewhat effeminate. Effeminate boys were drawn towards me, perhaps because of my uncouth, rugged exterior. What initially drew me to E.N. were his academic achievements and his iconoclasm. He was much the best student in the class and usually got the top position in all the subjects in term examinations. On annual prize-distribution days his haul of presentation books and cups made an impressive pile. He was also a good conversationalist. He questioned every assumption and accepted norm of religion and social conduct. He cleared many cobwebs from the minds of boys brought up on traditional ideas and acquired a large number of admirers, among whom I was one. We began to argue like him and imitate his manner of speech. That he preferred my friendship to that of others flattered my vanity. We were always together in class and on the sports grounds. He often spent his weekends in my home. It was wrongly assumed that our relationship was unnatural. However,

Principal S.N. Mukherjee leant an ear to gossip and forbade Rai from leaving the hostel on holidays.

My two years at St Stephen's opened up an India I had not known in the enclosed atmosphere of Modern School. There were men with strange names like Sarkar, which meant government. Despite having spent the first few years of my life in a predominantly Muslim village, and given my admiration for my Urdu teacher, Moulvi Shafiuddin Nayyar, I was pained to discover that most Muslims in College regarded themselves as a community apart from other Indians. At that time the nationalist movement was on the upsurge. Gandhi had become the Mahatma and acknowledged as India's leader by all except the majority of Muslims and some Christians. It was during my second year at St Stephen's that three revolutionaries, Bhagat Singh, Raj Guru and Sukhdev, were hanged. All over India, schools and colleges closed as a mark of protest against the executions. Not St Stephen's. After the morning assembly another boy and I raised the slogan 'Bhagat Singh, Zindabad'. We hoisted the Indian tricolour on the college flagmast meant for the insignia of St Stephen's bearing a red cross and the college motto, *Ad Dei Gloriam* — to the glory of God. We were summoned by the acting Principal, an Englishman named Monk, to his office. He reprimanded us and warned us that if we did that sort of thing again we would be expelled from the College. I promised to behave myself and begged Monk not to report me to my father.

An incident that rankled in my mind for many years occurred while I was holidaying in Shimla with my uncle and aunt. He was a member of the Punjab Legislative Assembly and very eager to be made a minister or a deputy minister. He was always calling on the Governor, Chief Minister and members of the Punjab cabinet to plead his case. He was undoubtedly the ablest Sikh politician of his time, but he could not get ahead because, despite being a big landowner, he was not recognized as a Jat agriculturalist. At the time Punjab's politics was Jat-oriented. The only non-Jat minister was a Hindu; the Sikh minister was Sir Sunder Singh Majithia — a Jat with aristocratic pretensions. My uncle threw a large tea party at Davico's at its newly acquired premises above a cinema house between the Mall and Lakkar Bazar. Over three to four hundred of the elite of Shimla society, including ministers of the Punjab government, were present. I was then an avid collector of autographs and had in my album the signatures of Jawaharlal Nehru and Sarojini Naidu among others. I could not get the signature of Bhagat Singh, so I simply stuck a photograph of the young man in one of the pages. I went round the tea party asking celebrities for their signatures. They did so without comment. Last of all I approached Sir Sunder Singh Majithia. He began to turn over the pages of my album to see whose signatures I had and came upon the photograph of Bhagat Singh. 'Why have you got this fellow's picture here?' he demanded angrily. 'Because he is my hero,' I replied without flinching. 'Hero!' scoffed the knight. 'He is a renegade.' (Bhagat Singh, a Sikh, had cut off his long hair and shaved his beard.) 'I will not put my name in an album with the picture of a renegade,' he shouted. Then he flung my album across the hall. I was shaken and broke down. Sewa Singh and his wife who were close friends of my father shouted back at Majithia: 'How dare you treat this boy in this way? He has every right to admire Bhagat Singh. We all do.' Majithia stormed out of the room. The party was a fiasco. My uncle and aunt were understandably upset. I was never able to forgive Sir Sundar Singh Majithia for his boorish behaviour — nor even respond to gestures of friendship made by his sons and grandsons.

As for Muslims, except for one boy who wore a Gandhi cap and dressed in khadi, the others sported red Fez caps and wore distinctly Muslim dress. They did not speak the language of nationalism. On the staff was a history professor, Dr Ishtiaq Hussain Qureshi, who constantly harped on his Islamic heritage and supported separate electorates for Muslims. He was among the first to migrate to Pakistan and later became its education minister. This feeling of separateness on the part of the Muslims saddened me. I did my best to befriend them but had little success.

It is not quite accurate to say that I made no Muslim friends. A very happy and wholly unexpected bonus came through my sister, who was then studying in Lady Irwin College for women. She became friendly with a Muslim girl, Ghayoorunissa Hafeez from Hyderabad. She was invited for tea on Sundays. The first time she came she wore her burqa and had to be persuaded by my sister to take it off in our home. She was a frail, sallow-complexioned girl with curly, light-brown hair. Despite having been in purdah, she was quite saucy in her talk and behaviour with the boys she met in our home. I fell madly in love with her. I also realized that I had no hope of getting closer to her because of the distance that religion created between us, and was quite happy just to know a Muslim girl I could call a friend. She was bolder than I. One evening my sister and I took her to the pictures. She wore her burqa till the lights were dimmed. I sat between the two girls. As the film started, I felt her hand gently rest on mine. For a while I was not sure whether she was aware of where her hand had strayed or whether she had placed it there deliberately. To put my doubts at rest she pressed my hand gently and twined her fingers in mine. I was out of my wits with excitement and lost all interest in the film. In the interval, while my sister's attention was distracted elsewhere, I asked her whether I could write to her and take her out. She nodded her head. 'I have permission to go with your sister,' she said, 'you can come to fetch me and drop me back.'

Unknown to my sister, I began to pick up her friend every Sunday afternoon and take her out for long drives. At the time my father had two cars: a new one which he drove himself and an old Fiat for the use of the family. This Fiat had a small lever close to the clutch which could be turned off to stop the flow of petrol into the carburettor. With my left hand I used to hold hers, while the right was on the steering wheel. She would not let me take any further liberties. One evening I turned off the petrol lever in a secluded spot on the Ridge in the hope that I could draw her into my arms. She was familiar with such tricks and turned the lever on. 'If you don't behave, I will not see you again,' she warned me. I got no nearer Ghayoor than writing love letters to her from college in Lahore and in England. I was writing such letters to other girls as well.

More than thirty years later Ghayoor came back into my life and again through my sister, who was still unaware of what had gone on between us behind her back. By then Ghayoor had seen two husbands to their graves and was the mother of a lovely eighteen-year-old-girl, Fareesa, who was in the same college as her mother's, Lady Irwin. Ghayoor appointed me her local guardian. Fareesa turned out to be like her mother. On many occasions she left college on the pretext of visiting her local guardian but instead of coming to my home she went out partying. She had no problem extracting a letter from me to say that she had spent the day with us.

Ghayoor remained my friend into her eighties. Every time I went to Hyderabad I spent my spare time with her. It was Ghayoor's affection for me that made me an ardent lover of Muslims. For me an Indian Muslim could do no wrong. I came to the conclusion that all you have to do is to fall in love with one person to love his or her community.

I did not take Indian Christian aloofness from the freedom movement too seriously. To my prejudiced mind, most of them were converts from the lower castes. We made fun of their adopted English-Indian names, such as Robert Masih, Hubert Marr or, for that matter, Edward Nirmal. Their efforts to identify themselves with their English rulers could be ludicrous. Once, when I made some derogatory remark about the Union Jack flying over the College building on the King's birthday, Hubert Marr, a Punjabi Christian from Batala, protested: 'We don't mind your hoisting your flag; you should not object to our having our flag one day in the year.' Mangat Rai had no strong views on the subject. The son of a civil servant and with ambitions of his own, he never ventured into the 'for or against *Swaraj*' debate.

I did not achieve much in my two years at St Stephen's. I just about managed to pass my examinations. I spent more time playing tennis than on my books. But even in tennis I was unable to make the College B team. Being a Sikh, I felt I should know something about soldiering. I joined the U.T.C. (University Training Corps) which entailed bi-weekly drills in the Red Fort. In the heat of summer we had to wear prickly grey woollen shirts next to our skin, thick puttees around our legs and hob-nailed boots on our feet. I soon got bored with drilling and wanted to quit. Rules did not permit anyone leaving after having enlisted: it amounted to desertion and was punishable with imprisonment. There was no escape. We also had to spend one week every year in camp where attendance was compulsory. Our tents were pitched on what is today known as Kingsway Camp, where King George V and Queen Mary had laid foundation stones for New Delhi in 1911. In the 1930's Kingsway Camp was a wilderness of thorny scrub infested with snakes and scorpions.

At the U.T.C. Camp tents were allotted in alphabetical order according to surnames and I found myself with five other Singhs, all Sikhs who came from different colleges. Two were lance-corporals, two corporals and one a sergeant. I was the only private and the only Stephanian amongst them. They were a tough, hairy lot, determined to win the track and field events which were the main feature of the week in camp. The sergeant assured me that, if I did well at sports, he would recommend my being made a lance-corporal.

I found sharing accommodation with my fellow Sikhs very trying. They snored loudly and disturbed my siestas and my night's sleep. They were rustics who cracked bawdy jokes in their village dialects. My poor performance in sports made them more contemptuous of me — all of them having won some event or the other. 'Are you a Sikh or a bania?' they taunted me. When I had had enough of them, I decided to teach them a lesson: I bought a packet of snuff. One afternoon, while they were having their siesta, I dropped it on their moustaches close to their nostrils and ran to another tent where some boys from St Stephen's were staying. 'Watch the fun,' I told them. A few minutes later the five came out of the tent sneezing violently. They did not know how they had been overtaken by fits of sneezing at the same time. They found the entire U.T.C. contingent in roars of laughter. On discovering the source of mischief, they swore to get even with me.

Foolishly, I tried to repeat the prank two days later, but my tent-mates were only pretending to be asleep. They pounced on me, divested me of all my clothes and threw me out of the tent. Then they roared invitations to the entire encampment to watch the tamasha. We were quits. I made my peace with them. And found it very profitable.

Amongst the Stephanians was a wrestler named Z____, who was also into buggery. When we took our morning and afternoon showers in a tented enclosure Z____ eyed his possible victims. He picked on a Keralite named Ittiyara and me. 'It has to be one or the other,' he told us. 'You decide which of you it will be or I'll bugger both of you.' The Keralite and I decided to fight the wrestler together. I appealed for help to my tent-mates. The Sikh sergeant, who was tougher than Z____, offered his services to the sodomist. 'I believe in fair exchange — *vaaree vatta*. I take you first, then you can take me. But if you lay your hands on this Sikh boy, I'll bugger the life out of you.' That cured Z____.

One hot afternoon while we were snoozing a large cobra crawled over the neck of one of the boys to get over to the other side. The boy awoke with a cry of horror and flung the snake off his body. It fell on the chest of another, hissing and spitting angrily. We tried to run out of the tent. In our panic we knocked down the pole in the centre and brought the tent over our heads, with the cobra and us under it. We managed to wriggle out, but so did the snake. U.T.C. boys armed with rifles but no bullets gave chase to the snake. It proved faster on its belly than we on our legs. The cobra episode was the last straw as far as I was concerned. I put in a medical certificate stating that, due to my prolonged illness the year before, I should not be subjected to drills and parades. That ended my adolescent ambition of becoming a soldier.

I took my Intermediate arts examination in 1932. As expected, I just managed a second division. And, as anticipated, Mangat Rai topped the university in several subjects.

I am not sure why I decided to leave St Stephen's to join Government College in Lahore for my Bachelor's degree. My father had a decisive role in chalking out my future. Once, when I was still at school, Principal Kamala Bose, egged on by my English teacher Miss Budden, suggested to him that I might make a career as a writer. He pondered over the suggestion for many days but came to the conclusion that no one could make a living out of writing. At best, it could be a sideline which had to be combined with a profession. Since I talked too much — my mother often called me a *galaadher* (chatter-box) — and was always getting into arguments, my parents decided I was best suited for the law. We had no lawyer in the family and my father had had to pay large fees to advocates who looked after litigation connected with the family business and property. He probably had this in mind when he made me switch from Hindi to Urdu in Modern School, for court records were kept in Urdu. The Delhi courts were under the jurisdiction of the Lahore High Court. My father no doubt thought it best that I acclimatize myself to Lahore before setting up legal practice there. I had no strong views on what I would do with my life. I agreed to move to Lahore for undefined reasons of my own. I quickly tired of places and people, as I still do, and was forever looking for fresh pastures and wanting to know new people. I was then, as I am now, incapable of making lasting friendships.

Government College was much the most sought-after educational institution in northern India, for its achievements in both sports and in studies. At the time, four of India's Olympic hockey eleven, including the captain, were from this college. A large proportion of the Indian cricket and athletic teams were also drawn from it. Presiding over the college was a retired English Colonel, H.L.O. Garret, a tall and dour man who ran the institution as if it were a regimental centre. There were other Englishmen on the staff. Quite a few of the Indian lecturers had degrees from Oxford or Cambridge — among them were two distinguished scientists, Birbal Sahni and Dr Kashyap. Admission to the College was restricted. Merit counted for less than wealth, ancestry and political clout. The sons of the landed aristocracy coming from Aitchison Chief's College were admitted without fuss no matter how poorly they had fared at school. Others were interviewed along with their fathers or guardians. I was taken to face the board accompanied by my uncle, Ujjal Singh, who had captained the College hockey side in his days, taken his Master's degree from there and was now a member of the Punjab Legislative Assembly. None of the board members bothered to ask me any questions. My uncle was my passport and my visa for admission to Government College.

Mangat Rai was upset at my leaving St Stephen's. He wrote me long letters during the vacations preceding the opening of the new term and was almost in tears when I told him that I was determined to go to Lahore. I drove to Lahore on my A.J.S. motorcycle and did the 300 miles on the Grand Trunk Road from Delhi to Lahore in eight hours. In those days there was very little traffic on this highway.

For the first four months in Lahore I stayed with my uncle in a house he had rented on Jail Road. His wife had just borne him twin girls. He was also engaged in fighting elections to the Punjab Assembly. There was a lot of coming and going of politicians, supporters, campaign managers and the like. My cousin, who had also joined the College, and I decided to move to its hostel. Government College had two hostels: the Quadrangle for the *hoi polloi* and the more expensive New Hostel with special suites for sons of zamindars, some of whom had servants to look after them. We were allotted a suite in a corner overlooking D.A.V. College and the law courts. Beneath our window was the spot from where Bhagat Singh and Raj Guru had shot and killed the Anglo-Indian police inspector, Saunders, for having hit Lala Lajpat Rai during an anti-Simon Commission demonstration outside Lahore railway station. The law courts were not a very edifying sight. We saw black marias off-loading prisoners in handcuffs and foot chains in the mornings and taking them back in the evenings. Also, litigants and lawyers who lined up against the court walls to urinate.

Government College was a handsome building, looking very much like a Gothic cathedral atop a hill. In front, it had a large playing field; there were tennis courts on its western flank, a bathing pool and the Quadrangle on its eastern side. The College stood at one end of a circular park named Gole Bagh which led to the museum and a huge cannon, Bhangian di tope, captured from the Sikhs and later named Kim's Gun after the hero of Rudyard Kipling's novel. From there began The Mall, which ran past the High Court, the Legislative Assembly building and Lawrence Gardens to a canal which marked the eastern extremity of the city. Lahore's main bazar, Anarkali, was only a furlong away from the college. And not very far was Lahore's famous red-light district, Hira Mandi, named after Raja Hira Singh Dogra, a favourite of Maharaja Ranjit Singh. The locals knew it as Tibbi Bazar. Quite a few Government College boys lost their virginity to the whores of Tibbi.

Many of my contemporaries at Government College rose to eminence in different fields. One was the professor of English, A.S. Bokhari, who was an excellent after-dinner speaker, a writer of light prose in Urdu (*Pitras Kay Mazaameen*) and a celebrated connoisseur of women. He became Director General of All India Radio and then head of the Mass Communications Department of the United Nations. He died suddenly of a stroke. Shafqat Mahmud, who was then posted in the Pakistani Consulate in New York and was a close friend, went to Bokhari's apartment to make an inventory of his belongings. The housekeeper told Shafqat that Bokhari spent many hours in his study and never allowed anyone in it. She found the key in his pocket and gave it to Shafqat. He opened the study. It had hi fi equipment with shelves full of recorded tapes. They were of speeches delivered by Bokhari at different forums. He spent hours listening to his own voice and the applause he got.

Several eminent Urdu writers were associated with Bokhari, including Imtiaz Ali Taj, Mohammed Tahseer and Faiz Ahmed Faiz, Pakistan's greatest poet after Allama Iqbal. Tahseer had a Scottish wife whose younger sister, Alyce, later married Faiz. Theirs was a very close circle, consisting entirely of men who were well into Urdu or Persian poetry. Much as I tried, I failed to gain admittance into this charmed circle.

I did no better at Government College than I had at

St Stephen's. For one, our teachers were a singularly uninspiring lot. Bokhari took little interest in teaching and spent most of the forty-five minutes boasting of his exploits in England. M.G. Singh was more conscientious, but restricted himself to making pronouncements on poets and writers without allowing students to ask questions. Since my interest in English literature had turned into a passion, I memorized many poems in our textbook, as well as two Shakespeare plays, *A Midsummer Night's Dream* and *Richard II*, which were included in our course. What I did not understand remained un-understood. I did not like other people's analyses or criticism of the works of great writers, dramatists and poets. To me it was like dissecting a beautiful butterfly and killing it. My own efforts at writing were not appreciated. I sent two contributions to the College magazine, *Ravi*; both were rejected, with extracts taken from them published in the W.P.B. (Waste Paper Basket) column to prove they were junk.

Our history and economics teachers simply read out notes that they had compiled over the years. They did not encourage discussion or bother with new books published in their subjects. An anecdote which went round the College was of the visit of the distinguished scientist and Nobel Laureate, Sir C.V. Raman. Principal Garret took him round to see a new laboratory in the College. 'Sir C.V., what do you think of our laboratory?' asked the English colonel-turned-educationist. 'The marble flooring is very good,' replied the wily Tamilian. Garret who had not caught what C.V. Raman was driving at, repeated the question. He got the same answer.

My attempts to befriend Muslim students in Government College did not succeed. They kept mostly to themselves. They had their own mess where *halaal* meat was served, and their own tuck shop. Hindu and Sikh students had their vegetarian and non-vegetarian canteens as well as a separate tuck shop. Although we played table tennis, carom and other indoor games together and sat side by side in our classes, there were few instances of close friendship with Muslims. The few known became immediately suspect for allegedly homosexual overtones. An effeminate young Sikh who turned out to be a good boxer was known to be sodomized by the Muslim captain of the hockey eleven. After a couple of years, the Sikh himself befriended pretty new-comers. The usual comment on catamites turned sodomites was in Urdu: *Jab chabacchey bhar gaye, tootian behney lageen* — when cisterns are full, water overflows into pipes.

After a while, I resigned myself to befriending those I found congenial. One was a very good looking fellow, Chetan Anand — fair, girlish looking with curly hair and dreamy eyes. He had a hard time dodging older students who coveted his behind. He attached himself to me. He wrote poetry after the style of Rabindranath Tagore and often addressed sloppy, unrhymed verses to me. We went to classes together, sat next to each other, played tennis, and usually went to the pictures together. We met again in England for a short while. He spent a summer with me when I settled down in Lahore. He then went to Bombay to try his luck as a film producer, but did not get very far. He was a taker, not a giver. In our group there was also N. Iqbal Singh, a miniature Sikh no more than five feet four inches tall with a girlish, squeaky voice. He was nick-named Choochee. He too spent many months with me in Delhi, Lahore and London. Like Chetan, he also was a taker, not a giver. I tire of takers sooner than others and have never been able to sustain one-way traffic in hospitality. There were others in Government College who later became film celebrities, like Balraj Sahni, a very handsome and likeable fellow who was a couple of years senior to me. And a classmate, B.R. Chopra, who became a leading film producer in Bombay.

There was also Kirpal Singh Chawla, the eldest son of a prosperous businessman who, though he did not achieve much in life, I have good reason to remember. He befriended me because he too had a motorcycle and felt that the sons of the well-to-do should form a fraternity. He was always smartly turned out in well-cut suits, a bow-tie, a neatly-tied turban with a multi-coloured ribbon showing under its angle. He waxed his sparse beard, had his moustache twirled upwards and rode his motorcycle with his chest puffed out. He started by advising me to dress better and not sit hunched over my motorcycle. 'We who have four pice in our pockets should stick out our chests,' he told me. He began to invite me to his home. His father also dressed with meticulous care and wore silk ties imported from England. No one could see them because they were covered over by his long, grey beard which hung down to his navel. He had married a second time and had quite a few sons and nubile daughters from both wives. He encouraged his son to invite his Sikh friends to the house. Kirpal had a room to himself above a garage in the garden. He was an aesthete and had several records of Indian classical music. He took to playing the vichitra veena and became proficient enough to be invited to perform over the Lahore Station of All India Radio. He had an obsession about light-skinned women. 'No girls like daughters of Kashmiri Pandits,' he would say, holding an imaginary one in his arms. 'If ever I marry, it will be a Panditani virgin. But I won't marry because my life-line shows that I will die before I am thirty.' He would open the palm of his right hand to show how short his life-line was. His ambition of having a fair skinned woman was achieved while he was still at college. He told me how it happened.

One summer afternoon, while he was fantasizing about his Kashmiran beauty, he had a mighty erection. He was about to masturbate when the washerwoman came in with his bundle of clothes. She was a fat, middle-aged woman and the mother of a brood of children. She was also fair-skinned. Kirpal simply pushed her onto his bed and mounted her. The *dhoban* protested mildly before she let Kirpal do what he wanted. It didn't last long. He gave her a ten-rupee note as a tip. She was happy to take it. He checked the list of garments and made a pile of soiled ones to give her for washing. She taunted him saucily, 'You have lit a fire, now you must douse it.' So he had a second go, which pleased the old *dhoban* even more than the second note of ten rupees he gave her. It became an ongoing relationship. He looked forward to her weekly visits. He invited me to partake of the pleasure if I was willing to shell out a tenner. I did not relish having anyone privy to my sex escapades and politely declined his invitation. Kirpal died as a bachelor when in his forties.

I am not sure what rekindled my interest in poetry, music and the arts. It could have been Chetan's poems or listening to sitar maestros in Kirpal Chawla's room — I decided to resume my sitar lessons and try my hand at painting. When the first summer vacations were drawing near, I wrote to the Tagore university at Shantiniketan asking for admission to Kala Bhawan, its centre for music and the arts. I received an application form asking for a reference known to them. Ashok Sen's father had a plot of land in Shantiniketan and was known to many people there. I asked him to give me a letter of recommendation. 'You Akali! [he always called me Akali because I had taken to wearing a black turban during the Akali movement] what will you do in Shantiniketan?' I told him. He was a kindly old man and promptly wrote to the Registrar of Vishwa Bharati.

Going to Shantiniketan was the first train journey that I undertook on my own. I travelled third class, changing trains at Howrah to get to Bolpur. The monsoon had just set in. The countryside between Howrah and Bolpur was a vast expanse of water. I hired a bullock-cart, and an hour later reported my arrival to the administrator of the University. I was shown a large, unfurnished room which I was to share with a young Buddhist monk named Manjusri from Sri Lanka, and then taken round the dining halls and Kala Bhavan. By the time I had finished going round the campus, it had become dark and started to drizzle. I returned to my room and spread my bedding on the floor. Manjusri was reading by lamplight — there were no electric lights in our rooms. We exchanged information about each other in English as he spoke no Hindustani. He was working on some Pali manuscripts in the Shantiniketan archives and had taken a vow of celibacy which required him not to speak to women. His first questions to me were about the girls I had known.

I slept fitfully as I was not used to sleeping on a hard floor. It also began to rain heavily. I dozed off into a land of dreams. I heard voices singing in the distance draw closer to me. I

realized I was not dreaming. I arose from my bed and opened
the door. A misty moonlight filtered through the fine gauze of
drizzle. I saw a party of young men and women dressed in
spotless white bearing hurricane lanterns and candles come
down the path singing. I stood entranced till they had passed
my door. 'It is *Varsha Mangal*, to welcome the rains,' Manjusri
informed me. 'They will go round the campus singing Tagore's
songs.'

It was a very pleasant introduction to Shantiniketan. The
vision of song and beauty continued to haunt me for many
years. More was to follow after I registered as an arts student
under Surendra Nath Kar and was assigned a sitar teacher. I
spent the day buying equipment and familiarizing myself with
my surroundings. In the afternoon Tagore arrived at the campus
to introduce students to Uday Shankar and his French dancing
partner, Simkie, who had just returned from their first European tour. Tagore sat in a large armchair on a platform and
simply ordered Shankar, 'Let me see you dance!' There was no
make up, no equipment, no stage lights, no orchestra apart from
Timir Baran who played the sarod. Uday Shankar danced the
Tandava with Simkie as Parvati. I had never seen any Indian
dancing, except the crude gyrations of *hijdas* and renderings of
the Radha-Krishna theme by amateur Kathak dancers. I was
entranced by the sinuous movements of Shankar and Simkie as
they kept time to the notes of the sarod. That night I could not
sleep; the music and dance had deeply moved me.

Shantiniketan also opened my eyes to the beauties of the
Bengal countryside. I had spent my years in the pancake-flat
khaki plains of the Punjab and summers in Kasauli or Shimla.
Shantiniketan was different. It was Santhal country with
rolling, red gravel hills covered with sal forests and muddy,
fast-moving streams. Being monsoon time, most of the streams
were in spate. When it stopped raining, the place was littered
with small snakes and scorpions. At first they alarmed me and I
killed two snakes before I learnt that they were quite harmless.
(The favourite way of teasing women was to slip a few of these
hayla snakes under their bed sheets.) Once, during a heavy
downpour, I found myself in waist deep, muddy, swirling

water. I grabbed the branch of a thorny bush and found clustered round it snakes, scorpions, frogs and field mice. In common peril, they did no harm to each other. In these country walks I often came across semi-nude Santhal girls carrying firewood on their heads. They were ebony dark, had shapely figures and walked like dancers on a stage. Gurudev Tagore liked to be known as the Santhal Raja.

Once a week we were allowed to have darshan of Tagore at his palatial mansion, Uttarayan (Tropic of Cancer). He was usually seated in a large chair, very much like those of dentists. It was covered with a mosquito net and had a couple of cup holders with incense burning in them. Only the privileged like Nand Lal Bose and a few others were allowed to touch his feet. Students sat on the floor awaiting pearls of wisdom to drop from his heavily mustachioed and bearded mouth. He seldom had more than a few sentences to say to us. I thought the weekly exercise very phoney.

Once during my stay in Shantiniketan I decided to visit Calcutta and try to see Roma Biswas who spent her vacations there. Our correspondence had been getting somewhat amatory and I felt that seeing her alone might prove fruitful. I bought a weekend return ticket from Bolpur to Howrah. I had only two ten-rupee notes in an envelope. I proceeded on foot across the Howrah bridge into crowded bazars. It took me over three hours to find her apartment. I rang the bell. There was no answer. I banged on the door. No one opened it. A neighbour came out, eyed me suspiciously, and told me that she had gone out for the weekend. I tore a strip off an envelope to write my name, then discovered to my horror that, with the envelope, I had torn both my currency notes. I had no means of changing them as the banks were closed. I trudged back to Howrah not knowing what to do, where to spend the night or get a meal. I went to a Marwari dharamsala. The manager ordered me out: it was for Marwaris only. 'Go and stay in your own gurdwara,' he told me. I found the gurdwara in Howrah. The Granthi let me share a room with other travellers. I had a free daal-chapatti meal provided by the gurdwara kitchen and slept on the floor with my turban as my pillow. The next morning I took the first train back to Bolpur without having seen anything of Calcutta except the Howrah bridge and the city's congested bazars. The path of true love never ran smooth. This was not even true love: just the explosive lust of a teenager for an older woman who promised to be understanding about his problems.

It did not take me long to discover that I would never make a painter. After a few weeks of trying to sketch I gave up. I did better with the sitar. I bought an old instrument from the teacher, who evidently made a profit out of the deal. Thereafter he paid more attention to my lessons and often instructed me on rendering ragas in his home. I spent many hours practising the sitar in my room with the Sri Lankan monk as my only audience. I had also befriended a Parsee girl, Meher, who often dropped in to listen and chat with me. The monk never spoke to her, but no sooner would she leave than he would ask if I had made any progress. 'Have you held her hand? Kissed her?' He was disappointed at my failures.

My Shantiniketan sojourn came to an abrupt end. Despite the mosquito net around me and mosquito repellant creams smeared over my limbs, I was horribly bitten and came out with rashes all over my body. The doctor told me to get out of Shantiniketan as fast as I could. One morning, without bidding farewell to any of the people I had befriended, I touched Bhikku Manjusri's feet and left for Delhi. I was back in Lahore for the opening of the new term, this time with my sitar and a metronome.

My only achievement at Government College was in debating. I entered my name for the annual University debate. It was very hard for a Sikh to face an audience largely composed of non-Sikhs. His very appearance on the stage was greeted with hoots of derisive laughter and jeers, reminding him that at twelve noon all Sikhs went mad. I had the same reception when my turn came. But as soon as I began to speak they fell silent; when I ended they applauded. The panel of judges consisted of three professors presided over by A.S. Bokhari. The speakers included the best debaters from different colleges. Bokhari announced the unanimous decision of the panel: I was awarded the first prize. My triumph was somewhat diluted by the fate of my cousin and room-mate, Narinder. The poor fellow broke down halfway through his oration.

A few escapades in Government College remain in my memory. Being averse to studying, I tried to prevent others from swatting for their exams. I discovered an easy method of fusing lights. All I had to do was to insert a coin between the bulb and the socket and switch on my table lamp. It blew the fuse and plunged the hostel into darkness. Then I would go up to the roof and take a leisurely stroll in the starlight. One night, after having deprived the inmates of the hostel of light, I was joined by some other students on the roof. Suddenly the lights came on. And we had a good view of the warden, Professor Amolak Khanna, making love to his wife. His apartment was at the right angle of the L-shaped hostel. We shouted to others to come up and have a look, but the Khannas heard us and switched off their lights.

A few days later some students returning late to the hostel decided to empty their bladders in the petrol tank of Khanna's Baby Austin, alongside which I parked my motorcycle. I was not one of them, but Khanna proceeded to levy a heavy fine of Rs 50 on me on the presumption that, having a motorcycle, I alone knew the anatomy of a car. Actually, he had got to know that I was one of the students on the roof watching him with his wife.

Amolak Khanna was quite a character. He knew very little history, which he tried to teach, but he was a fiend for physical fitness. He was a very short man and played a vigorous game of tennis and hockey. On the coldest days of winter he spent half an hour every morning swimming in the college pool. I tried to emulate him and spent many hours after tennis doing lengths of the pool. I thus qualified for the College swimming and water polo teams.

An amusing incident took place at the College pool. A very hairy Sikh student who was in the wrestling team was in the habit of picking up anyone's cake of soap when he showered after swimming. A Muslim student decided to have fun at his expense. He got a cake of depilatory, hair removing soap and put it in the soap dish while towelling himself. The Sikh, as was his habit, picked it up and vigorously soaped his face, beard and body. The Muslim quietly slipped away. For the next four days a very angry Sikh, deprived of much of his hirsuteness, went hunting for the student who had played the dirty trick on him. The Muslim discreetly left Government College and joined Islamia.

I took my B.A. degree in 1934 — in the third division. I was lucky to have passed considering the amount of work I had put in. By then I had applied for admission to various British Universities. With a third division I had no chance of making it to either Oxford or Cambridge. I settled for London University. Of the three colleges open to me I chose Kings' simply because it sounded more regal than University College or the London School of Economics. I was registered for an L.L.B. degree and at the same time applied for membership of the Inner Temple to qualify as a Barrister.

I spent my last summer vacation in India at Shimla with the Gill family in their large house, Longwood, once owned by the grandson of Charles Dickens. Sewa Singh Gill lived in a style well beyond his means. My father had a soft corner for his wife and often went across the road at Jantar Mantar for his evening drink. The three had visited Europe together and apparently had a wonderful time. My father never tired of telling us of incidents that had occurred on the boat and in different cities in Europe. Sewa Singh's sister was married to Umrao Singh, Chief of Manauli. Umrao went on to acquire a second wife. Before he could consummate his second marriage, his first wife registered with the Resident, Punjab States the births of a daughter and a son born to her through Umrao Singh. Both children had been taken from a hospital. The elder girl was evidently a child of a European nurse; the son's paternity remained unknown. By the time Umrao Singh woke up to the fact, the children were grown up. He acquiesced and so did his second wife, who was a devoutly religious woman. Umrao Singh, his two wives and children shared Longwood with the Gills and lived in evident harmony.

Umrao Singh was a dipsomaniac and a voyeur. He would go

on binges, drinking steadily from morning to the late hours of the night. Then as suddenly he would go on the water wagon for a couple of months till the longing for liquor came upon him again. He was on one of these drinking bouts when I was staying with them. One night he forced a maid-servant into my room with orders to fuck me while he watched from behind the curtain. The poor girl stood by my bed for a long time waiting for me to make the first move. Despite her master's egging, she refused to divest herself of her salwaar-kameez. When Umrao Singh went to get another drink, she slipped out and I bolted my door behind her. Another time the chieftain of one of the hill principalities came to spend the night at Longwood. He got as uproariously tight as Umrao Singh. The Chief wanted Umrao to make love to him. Umrao got his chauffeur over and ordered him to bugger the chief. The chauffeur obliged. Umrao hopped about the couple watching them from different angles and cheering them on. It was said that he was quite impotent himself.

In the summer of 1934 I left Delhi for London. It was a tearful farewell, with my parents, relatives and friends at the station to garland and see me off. My elder brother and his wife Amarjit accompanied me as far as Bombay. There I boarded the Italian boat *Conte Rosso*. I knew no one on the ship, nor had I any friends in England. Only Roma Biswas had preceded me to do a course in higher education.

4   Discovering England

THERE IS SOMETHING about a ship voyage which binds fellow passengers in bonds of friendship for the rest of their lives. They will reminisce about little details as if they were never to be forgotten sagas of adventure. It is a carefree time between the world they have left behind and the new world yet to come. This state of limbo engenders a spirit of camaraderie of the kind that exists between men who have served in the same regiment. Whenever they meet in later life, their re-introduction to each other is: 'Weren't we on the same boat from Bombay to London?'

The sea voyage from Bombay to Southampton took eleven days, including a few hours' halt at Aden and Port Said. There was also a brief stop-over at Ismailia to off-load passengers who wished to visit the Pyramids and Cairo and rejoin the boat at Port Said. Quite often ships had to wait their turn at the entrance of the Suez Canal to take on pilots to steer them through the narrow seventy-mile long canal joining the Red Sea and the Mediterranean. It was slow going, with lines of ships in front and behind and a vast desert on either side, interspersed with nondescript, dusty habitations.

Most of the passengers in the economy class of the *Conte Rosso* were students from different parts of India. There were over a hundred males and about a dozen women. The only one I knew well was Arjan Singh, who had been in my class at Government College. He had been to England the year before and was travelling first class with his father, Bawa Dinga Singh, a prosperous timber contractor. Arjan had told me of the great time he had had on his earlier visit, how easy it was to lay white girls and the preparatory exercise one could get for a small sum of money in the brothels of Port Said.

The only other face familiar to me was that of Som Nath Chib, who had been recently appointed a lecturer in Dayal

Singh College, Lahore. A couple of weeks earlier he had married a well-known Lahore university beauty, Savitri Bhalla. For them it was a honeymoon voyage. They spent their time gazing into each others' eyes, kissing in front of everyone, then hurrying back to their cabin meant for two. Their amorous goings-on created much envy and gossip.

We were six males in one cabin. After the introductions were made, the gong sounded for lunch. Before going to the dining room, we went up to see the boat pull out of Bombay harbour and wave to our friends and relations who had come to bid us farewell. Then down the steps for our first repast on sea. No sooner had the soup been served than the ship began to heave and roll. It was monsoon time and the Arabian Sea was very turbulent. We left our soups unfinished and rushed down to our cabins. Some threw up in the wash basin; I managed to get on to my upper berth and overcome the nausea building up. I heard the ship groan and shudder as if it was about to break into pieces. For the next three days I left my bunk only to dash to the loo and back, to recover breath and equipoise. Occasionally the cabin steward brought me bread and fruit which I turned back. After three days and nights spent in agony, the *Conte Rosso* stopped rocking and rolling. We were out of turbulent waters. The next day the ship docked at Aden.

It was after spending some hours walking along Aden's bazars, largely owned by Indians, that I made the acquaintance of some of my fellow passengers. I will name only two who resurfaced in my life later. One was Lakshmi Kant Jha who made the I.C.S. and held many important positions in the government before he died at the age of seventy or so. He became Governor of the Reserve Bank of India, Ambassador to the United States, Governor of Jammu and Kashmir, and Chief Economic Adviser to Prime Minister Lal Bahadur Shastri. He also indulged in palmistry and horoscopy. Though big and flabby, he ardently wooed young and beautiful women. Jha and I lived in the same *pension* in London for some months and continued to see each other in later years. There was also a certain Miss Nehru, a distant relation of the first Prime

Minister of independent India. She always draped herself in handspun khadi and never missed an opportunity to sermonize us on how we should deport ourselves as 'ambassadors of India'. More about her later.

The voyage after Aden was sheer bliss. The Red Sea was placid as a lake. We played deck-tennis, quoits, table tennis or chatted with the girls. Warm winds blew over from the neighbouring deserts. At times migratory birds alighted on the ship; flying fish often landed on the deck. One evening as the sun went down the entire sea as far as the eye could see became alive with dolphins tumbling in and out of the water. At night the sky was brilliantly illuminated by a myriad stars. On moonlit nights the sea shimmered like a vast spread of quick-silver. Travelling by ship was so much more pleasurable than the non-stop flights I had to take later in life — getting drunk, over-eating hurriedly in cramped conditions and watching films to kill the hours.

After off-loading the party who wished to see the Pyramids, we entered the Suez Canal. It was like being on a massive chariot gliding slowly through the desert, with the water barely visible from the middle of the deck. On the Egyptian side a road ran along the canal, past small villas and an occasional township; on the other it was a stretch of barren, uneven, dusty wasteland. It was during this part of the voyage that Bawa Arjan Singh enlisted the names of young men who wanted to lose their virginity at Port Said. I was not one of them.

We docked at Port Said for six hours. As soon as we disembarked, we were surrounded by greasy looking men in red fez caps and jellabas trying to sell pornographic postcards and inviting us to savour the pleasures of Egyptian brothels! 'You no lublub?' they would ask poking their index fingers into a hole made by the thumb and the index finger of the other hand. We shook them off, only to be accosted by others who pursued us till we got to our destination, Simon Artz's Department Store. I had not seen a store of that size; it was then the biggest in Asia. It was Jewish-owned but much the most frequented by affluent Egyptians. I simply looked around in awe without buying anything. Then I set out on the narrow causeway which led to the statue of Ferdinand de Lesseps, the architect of the Suez Canal. By the time I got back there was only an hour left for the *Conte Rosso* to depart. Before going up the gangway I was persuaded to buy a carton of dates — they were longer, darker and more luscious-looking than those I had seen in Hadali. I was able to beat the vendor to half the price and triumphantly went up to the deck to savour them. I discovered that beneath the top layer of a dozen dates there was only saw-dust.

I warned fellow passengers who were buying things from boats tethered alongside the ship and having items sent up the baskets slung by ropes. Many bought boxes of chocolates only to discover there was nothing beneath the first layer; some bought perfumes with the names of French brands to discover the bottles contained scented oil. I have passed through Port Said and Cairo many times since then and have never bought anything in Egypt again.

That evening we heard of the adventures of the males who had visited the brothels. They had met no houris waiting to be deflowered by them: only middle-aged, fat, Arab and Black women. Once inside the brothels, they had no escape. They were made to part with more money in tips than they had bargained for. This being their first contact with female flesh, they came as soon as they entered — some even spent themselves before making contact. What bothered them was the fear of having contracted venereal diseases because none of them had as much as seen a contraceptive. They spent the next two days examining their penises for tell-tale signs of syphilis or gonorrhea. Word of what the males had been up to got to the Nehru girl's ears. One morning she summoned us to a meeting. Without disclosing what she had heard, she reprimanded us for our disgraceful behaviour. 'Would you like your country to be judged by what some of you have been up to in Port Said?' she asked.

The Mediterranean remained blue and sunlit throughout our passage. We passed through the Straits of Gibraltar into the Bay of Biscay, notorious for its turbulence. We were lucky. So also with the English Channel which was equally well-known for its roughness. We docked at Southampton and took the boat-train to London. I had no address to go to.

Roma Biswas was on the platform of Victoria Station waiting to receive me. As I have already noted, my letters to her from Government College had been getting amorous. Once on vacation in Delhi I had gone to see her in Modern School. She had a suite of rooms on the roof. We sat and talked late into the evening. When we came out, the moon was full. Instead of saying goodbye to her, I grabbed her in my arms and violently kissed her on her lips. She remonstrated, 'Really, how can you?' I fled downstairs. Back in Lahore I wrote to her apologizing for my behaviour. She generously forgave me. But thereafter her letters had become as warm as mine. I was not sure how she would receive me.

I was not left in doubt. As soon as we got into the taxi which was to take us to the Indian Students' Union Hostel on Gower Street she put her arms around me and glued her lips to mine. We continued to kiss each other passionately till the cab pulled up outside the hostel. There was no room available. The secretary pointed to a *pension* across the road and asked us to try there. We went across with my valise. L.K. Jha was already there. The pension was run by an Italian named Serafino — a small, wizened man and his much larger English wife who did the cooking. I was shown into a small room on the top by one of the two maids serving in the establishment. The terms for bed and breakfast were within my means. I decided to settle there for the first few months. No sooner were we left alone than Roma and I fell on the bed, passionately kissing each other. I had not known a woman at close quarters and was unsure of what I should or should not do. I went on kissing her till her lips were sore. I struggled wildly to undo her sari. I could not hold myself. It was a messy business. I felt thoroughly ashamed and did not want to see any more of her.

'That is not love, that is lust,' she scolded me. But she had been roused and was unwilling to let me go. As I lay in bed feeling sorry for myself she came over to me. 'Promise you won't try this again!' she demanded. The mauling began all over again. And again it ended the same way. I felt nauseated with her and myself.

I did not want to take any more chances with Roma. It was time for dinner. We went and ate in a small wayside cafe. Mercifully the rules of the *pension* did not allow women visitors after dark.

If Roma had been more experienced in dealing with teenagers, she might have become my mistress for the rest of her stay in England. What she succeeded in doing was to put me off her and off sex for many months. For the next few days she laid siege to the *pension*. I dodged every attempt she made to get me alone in my room. She gave up in disgust and went off with an older and more experienced student from Modern School. I lost track of her.

With London it was love at first sight. I fell in love with its streets, its beautifully done-up shop windows, its buses, tramcars, the Underground and its smells. Above all, its women and just about everything else. I spent the first few days getting to know it. I walked over to Tottenham Circus, down Oxford Street to Marble Arch, back to Oxford Circus and through Regent Street to Piccadilly Circus, Leicester and Trafalgar Squares. I sat on the steps of St Martin-in-the-Fields watching people feed pigeons; I listened to the chittering of millions of starlings. When the shades of twilight darkened I walked through the Stand to Holborn, Bloomsbury and back to the pension in time for supper.

In a few days life fell into a routine. The morning started with a lecture on Roman Law at University College. Our teacher was the very grim-faced, short tempered Dr Jolowicz. Then I took a bus to King's College on the Strand. There the Dean of Studies, Dr Potter, lectured to us on English Law. Then across Aldwych to the London School of Economics to hear bi-weekly orations on politics by Professor Harold Laski, lectures on the Law of Tort by Professor Davies and on Constitutional Law by Professor Ivor Jennings. I walked back in the evenings through gas-lit Holborn, with the organ grinders grinding out popular tunes, past the British Museum and to the Serafino establishment. Often I had my dinner at the Indian Students' Hostel because it was the cheapest place for curry and rice. Once in a while I went to an Italian restaurant where you could eat a filling meal of pasta for under five shillings. During term time there were also dinners at the Inner Temple. One had to be dressed in black and wear a black gown. There were two bottles of port or red wine for every four diners. English students, ever thirsty for an extra glass, sought me out to make up their four so that they could take my share.

In November it turned cold. Then came pea-souper fogs: brown-and-yellow and pestilential. You could hardly see beyond your out-stretched hand. I caught a chill, followed by a cough and fever. The doctor I consulted advised me to get out of London for a few days. I took a train to some place in Buckinghamshire and found a room in a pub deep in the heart of New Forest. The fresh air and long walks amidst elm, oak and pine soon cleared my chest of colds and coughs. I felt on top of the world and was not eager to return to London.

One night after a longish after-dinner walk in the woods I reluctantly retired to my room on the first floor. I heard voices in the entrance hall asking for a room for the night. The female voice sounded familiar. I tiptoed out of the room and looked down the balcony. It was the sermonizing Nehru woman with a young Englishman. She had apparently spotted the name Singh in the guest register, but at that hour she had no choice and could not escape. The couple were given the room next to mine and spent the night together. Early next morning they left the pub without breakfast, which was included in the fare. When I went down to the dining room, I took a quick look at the register: they had put themselves down as Mr and Mrs English something-or-the-other: A fitting epilogue to her sermons on how Indians abroad were ambassadors of their country and legends about the purity of Hindu womanhood! I ran into her at several Indian functions, like Gandhi's birthday and Diwali, and I was surprised that she had not rid herself of the habit of telling others how to behave in a foreign country.

There were times when I felt extremely lonely and

homesick. I had got to know quite a few English students at college but they lived in distant parts of London. The Indians I groups and, apart from playing table-tennis with me, did met every evening at the Students' Union Hostel had their own not wish to add me to their friends. Jha was too occupied preparing for the I.C.S. and only came to my room to borrow my notes. Occasionally, the two English maids of the pension who came to do my bed tried to flirt with me. I did not have the guts to respond. They found Jha more responsive.

Across from my room was the University College Hospital. On Saturday nights they had dances for doctors, students and nurses. From my window I could see them whirling around. I caught the strains of Viennese waltzes and current favourites like 'Red sails in the sunset', 'Music goes round and round and comes up here' and 'Lambeth Walk'. Seeing other people happy and enjoying themselves made me more acutely conscious of my loneliness.

Weekends were the worst. After playing tennis or hockey at the college grounds at Mitcham I had nothing to do except make fair copies of my lecture notes or read law books. The bolder Indian men would go to Piccadilly Circus and pick up women to take to their digs. They told me that it was easy and cost them nothing more than giving the women a drink or two in a pub and some sandwiches at home. Then they played strip poker. The person who drew the lowest card had to discard a garment. Fifteen minutes of the game and both were as naked as the day they were born. Then they got down to business. I would hear those tantalizing stories, get worked up but never acquired enough courage to follow their example. The best I could do was walk round the by-lanes of Piccadilly Circus, Shepherd's Market or Bayswater Road and ogle at prostitutes who frequented these areas. No one ever propositioned me. I got the feeling that, if I approached them, they would snub me for no other reason than that I was dark and wore a turban and a beard.

On Sundays I went to Hyde Park. I would hire a boat and row up and down the Serpentine from end to end several times to burn out the excess energy which seemed to be centred on one point in my middle. It did not prove very efficacious. Strewn about the stretches of green lay couples in tight embrace, oblivious of passersby. The English were too well-mannered to stare, but Orientals like myself could not keep our eyes off them. At times they lay one on top of the other with nothing more than a mackintosh or an overcoat over them. After a while such close proximity proved too much even for the cold-blooded English: their covering would start heaving rapidly and then collapse into a heap. If the copulation became too explicit, the police took the couple to a nearby station. They were let off after paying a small fine. The best I could do was re-create these scenes in letters to my cousin, Narinder. At times I would substitute myself in the letters for one of my friends at strip poker and tell him of the wonderful time I was having. The truth was that at the end of my first year in England I was still a virgin.

My one regret was that I had not been inside an English home. The one Englishman I knew well was C.H. Everett of the Indian Police, who was doing a course in law at University College. He was a shy, reticent man. Nevertheless, he invited me to his wedding to the daughter of a retired I.C.S. officer who had been Commissioner of Karachi. After his honeymoon, Everett asked me to spend a weekend in the country home of his wife's parents. They were gracious but ill-at-ease having a coloured man as their house-guest. So was I. They dressed for dinner and followed the strict discipline of upper-class English families. The next morning they took me with them for the county fox hunt. Since I could not ride, I asked to be excused. But I did get to see the ritual of dress, the hierarchy observed among hunting types, the blowing of horns, the handling of beagles, a poor fox being run to death and having its tail (brush) cut off. Having achieved their object, glasses of sherry were passed round like *prasad* after a religious service.

Instead of spending my summer vacations in England I decided to return to India. I went to Genoa by train and once again took a Lloyd Trestino boat, the *Conte Verde*, for Bombay. This time I pretended to be an experienced traveller. On the way out, I had picked up a dozen Italian words and added a few more during my visits to Italian restaurants: *buon giorno, buona sera, grazie, si, no, perfavore, quanto costa?* etc. Amongst the passengers were the Chibs returning home with their four-month-old daughter. They had got over the period of frenzied love-making. He was back at his books; she pre-occupied with her child. We were placed at the same table.

Our next stop was Brindisi, which was twenty-four hours by sea from Genoa. Before we docked at Brindisi, Savitri Chib, who had noticed my speaking to the Italian waiters asked me, 'You speak some Italian, don't you?'

I nodded my head.

'Could you get me a packet of glycerine suppositories for a child? My daughter is constipated and I don't want to give her a laxative orally.'

I readily undertook to do so.

I did not have much trouble in finding a drug store. I scanned the shelves to see if I could spot glycerine suppositories. I couldn't. I decided to explain what I needed in my vocabulary of a dozen words. The pharmacist understood the word constipation and produced some brands of laxatives. I shook my head saying 'no, no'. Then pointed to my bottom with a crooked index finger. The pharmacist understood and produced an enema apparatus. I knew I was getting close to my quarry. Suddenly the Italian word for child came to me. I patted my belly (I should not have done so) and triumphantly shouted 'bambino, pore bambino'.

'Ah, si Signor!' exclaimed the pharmacist with an understanding look. And slapped a packet of contraceptives on the counter. I returned to the *Conte Verde* not with suppositories to relieve a child of constipation but with an anecdote to enliven many parties.

The rest of the voyage was uneventful. At Port Said it was another long walk to De Lessep's statue. I bought nothing. We did not stop at Aden, and the Arabian Sea was calm. Soon I was back in India. I spent the day wandering about Bombay and took the evening train to Delhi.

This time only members of my family came to receive me at

the railway station. They were disappointed to see me as shabbily dressed as when I had left them. 'You must have come back from Aden,' my mother carped at me. It was the same when I went up to Shimla to spend a week with my uncle, aunt and their twin daughters. My uncle and aunt, who had been to the Round Table Conference in London some years earlier, had picked up a lot more in the few months they had spent there than I had in a year. He had a couple of Savile Row suits; she had learnt to speak English better, and cultivated a taste for English salads. Her favourite item was lettuce which she nevertheless pronounced as 'let oose'. My girl cousins, whom I accompanied on their evening walks, said that all I had learnt was Tarzan's cry when he summoned his monkey brigade by shouting *yoo hoo*. However, I had an ardent listener in Narinder, whom I regaled with made-up stories of my seducing English girls.

The two months went by faster than I expected. Once more I took the Frontier Mail to Bombay to catch the *S.S. Victoria* — another Lloyd Trestino liner (we Indians avoided P & O boats as we had been told that English stewards did not show the same courtesy to Indian passengers that they did to the English). I arrived in Bombay in the afternoon. My ship was to sail next morning. I found a room for the night in the Victoria Terminus station where I had detrained. It was not a fortunate choice, but for reasons personal, a memorable one.

I left my luggage in my room and locked it. I went out to explore the neighbourhood. I found myself in a narrow lane with mean-looking shops below and women sitting by open windows on the floor above. As I looked up, one of them smiled and beckoned to me. I ignored her solicitation and walked on. I discovered I was in the prostitute quarter, Kamatipura. I proceeded to the end of the lane and turned back. The woman who had beckoned me was still by her window. She again gestured to me to come up. 'Which way?' I asked her. She pointed to a staircase leading up to her room. I went up the dark flight of steps. There was a boy sitting there. The woman came to receive me. She was fat, dark, middle aged and dressed in a salwar kameez. Without a word of welcome, she said in

Punjabi: 'It will be ten rupees.' I pulled out a ten-rupee note and handed it to her. She gave the boy a five-rupee note and ordered him to give it to her landlord. She bolted the door from inside.

It was a dark, dingy room lit by a single oil lamp. It had no furniture save her charpoy covered over with a greasy durrie and a dirty pillow. There was a pitcher of water with a lota covering its mouth. She turned round to address me. 'You Sardars are such fine looking men, why do you grow this fungus round your chins?' she asked, running her hand over my beard. I did not reply. She sensed that I was a novice. 'Have you been to a woman before?' she asked. 'No,' I replied somewhat hoarsely. 'You are the first one.'

'You have nothing to worry,' she replied, 'I am quite clean.'

She slipped off her salwar and tucked her shirt above her waist, baring her fat bottom. She went to the pitcher, filled the lota and splashed water between her thighs and dried her middle with a dirty rag. She laid herself on her back on the charpoy and raised her legs bent at the knees to her chest. 'Come!' she said, stretching out both her arms towards me.

Till then I had not so much as had a good look at a woman between her thighs. A fleeting glimpse of Kamala Bose's hairy private parts had revolted me. My vision of a woman's lower portion was what I had seen on marble statues, none of which had pubic hair. This dark, fat woman who lay before me with her knees touching her chin had shaved herself. I was not sure where to enter her. As I undid my trousers and bent over her, she took my penis in one hand and directed it to its target. As I entered her, I spent myself.

She was a kindly whore. She realized I had got very little for my money. 'If you want to do it again, it will cost you only five rupees,' she said sitting up on her charpoy. I wasn't sure how long it would be before I would want to repeat the performance and excused myself. 'Come whenever you want to, you have nothing to worry about me,' she assured me. 'I will give you a much better time. You can touch my breasts and kiss me as well.'

I returned to my room at Victoria Terminus. The vision of

my brief encounter would not leave my mind. I decided to return to the whore to have a second and perhaps a more satisfying go. I found the gates of the station shut. The Gurkha guard told me that if I went out I would not be allowed in till the morning. Reluctantly I returned to my room and relieved myself of the tension that had built up. I was not sure if I could describe that all too brief act of sex as losing my virginity. However, during the return voyage to England, I spent many anxious moments examining my penis for syphilitic sores.

Before leaving for my vacation I had shifted from Serafino's pension to a boarding house kept by a Miss Whaley of Knolly's Road between Tulse Hill and Streatham in south-west London, not far from Crystal Palace. The three-storeyed pension was along a railway track over which trains passed every five minutes. It took me a couple of days to get used to them. The other residents of Miss Whaley's boarding house were an elderly Scotsman, Armstrong, who shared her bedroom, a middle aged lady who looked after a laundry establishment, an aged Scots brother and sister, the Dunsmuirs, two nurses, Miss Madge Barkham and Miss Lillian Booth, and a young English chemist.

The lodging had been found for me by Shoran Singha, Secretary of the Indian Students' Hostel, who had his house at the Streatham end of the same road, where he lived with his French wife and her daughter. I used to go to the Singhas twice a week to have lessons in French from his step-daughter. Also twice a week, I went to a young English girl to learn ballroom dancing.

I occupied an attic room next to Madge Markham's. She was a plain-looking woman in her thirties. Her colleague Lillian Booth was somewhat younger, full-bosomed and more attractive. I felt my chances with the plain-looking Madge were better than with the better-looking Lillian. Madge had got us tickets for a play written by her brother, which was having a good run in a West End theatre. I made a few passes at her and one night even tiptoed to her room and, despite her protests, kissed her. I had written to her from India. She had responded to my letters.

When I returned to Knolly's Road, I was given a larger room on the first floor at a slightly higher rent. As boarding houses went, I was better off than most Indian students. The biggest advantage was that I was in an entirely English and Scots milieu. In the evenings we sat together in the sitting room exchanging gossip, ate our dinner together and often stepped out for an after-dinner stroll on Streatham Common. Although it took me almost an hour by bus and train to get to college, I found the change worthwhile. Also in the vicinity lived an English student in my class named Dennis Wisdom. His father was the headmaster of the local school. Dennis often invited me to his home for a meal. I became a member of the Wisdom family. I later kept in touch with the Wisdoms and attended Dennis' wedding when I was posted in India House. Dennis became a solicitor. He prospered, bought a Rolls Royce and a large house beside the Thames. His young sister Cynthia also kept in touch with me and sent her children to stay with us in Delhi.

Indians abroad tend to stick together. They join Indian clubs, regularly visit mosques, temples and gurdwaras and eat Indian food at home or in Indian restaurants. Very rarely do they mix with the English on the same terms as they do with their own countrymen. This kind of island-ghetto existence feeds on stereotypes — the English are very reserved; they do not invite outsiders to their homes because they regard their homes as their castles; English women are frigid, etc. I discovered that none of this was true. In the years that followed, I made closer friends with English men and women than I did with Indians. I lived in dozens of English homes and shared their family problems. And I discovered to my delight that nothing was further from the truth than the canard that English women are frigid.

I stayed in the Whaley household for over a year. The two nurses moved out to digs of their own — two bed-sitters with their own kitchenettes. Lillian had sensed that I was more attracted to her than to Madge. The day before she left, I had told her of a very good continental film showing in a small cinema in Hampstead. 'Why don't you take me along?' she asked. We met as arranged at an underground station and proceeded to the cinema. When the lights went out, she took my hand in hers. After the picture was over, we went to the pub for a drink and a sandwich and then for a stroll on Hampstead Heath. As we passed Keats' cottage, I recited the opening verse of *Ode to a Nightingale* to her.

She was impressed and rewarded me with a kiss on my hand. We walked arm in arm to Kenwood and found a secluded spot to get to know each other better. It was exhilarating for me to be so close to a pretty girl only slightly older than I and smelling of lavender and starch. For the next year or two I saw a lot of Lillian. We went out for walks to Hyde Park, Kew Gardens, etc. We went to see pictures and to restaurants. She took me to see *The Swan Lake*. It was the first ballet I had seen. I could make no sense out of it. She often asked me to her room, where we kissed the hours away late into the night. I never got beyond what I had with Roma Biswas! I still did not have the nerve to take liberties like fondling breasts and more, but I am sure that she expected me to. And she did not realize that I was still a virgin (though not technically) and would have been grateful if she had taught me a thing or two about sex. Slowly, we drifted apart — without any rancour but with a sense of disappointment. I don't know what became of her.

Someone told me that Satinder Singh, who had been in my class at Modern School, was somewhere in London to study medicine. I was eager to meet him as I had no other Indian friend in England. But I did not know where to find him. One day I was on my way to college by the underground, and as the train doors opened, in walked Satinder. What was more, he had been admitted to the medical faculty of King's College. For the next couple of years we were together most of the time. He was good at games and a good sport when it came to women. He was often short of money and usually borrowed it from me. We ate our lunches together in the college cafeteria and played table tennis in the common room.

An incident in which we were involved took place in the college common room. A well dressed, middle-aged Englishman introduced himself as a member of the British Foreign

Service due for a posting in India. We introduced him to other
Indian students. Suddenly there was a rash of thefts — most of
the victims being Indians. One afternoon I was playing table
tennis and had left my coat on the ledge where Satinder and
this Englishmen were sitting. When I finished and put on my
coat I discovered that my wallet was missing. I thought
Satinder had played a practical joke on me, but he denied
having taken it. My suspicion then turned on the Englishman. I
tried to find out more about him. I did not have to wait long. A
few days later a detective from Scotland Yard came to our
college to check on those who had lost money. He told me that
the fellow had been arrested. He had a long record of thieving
and picking pockets. Amongst his other victims was an
eighteen-year-old English girl whose yearly scholarship money
had been taken from her handbag the day she cashed her
cheque. I was amongst the many students asked to appear
before the Bow Street Magistrate to tender evidence if
required. That was my first experience of British justice. We
sat in the gallery listening to other cases being disposed of. I
was amazed to see that almost all the accused pleaded guilty
and received sentences of fines or imprisonment. Then came
the turn of our 'foreign service' imposter. He was in handcuffs.
With him was his wife, a smartly dressed, attractive woman in
her early thirties. The fellow pleaded not guilty. On the
magistrate's asking him if he wished to cross-examine any of his
accusers, he pointed to me. I was asked to come forward and
take the oath to tell the truth. I narrated the incident in the
common room. He did not ask me any questions. The
magistrate roundly ticked him off for being a disgrace to society
and robbing poor students. In view of his record, he sentenced
him to four years in jail. It took less than ten minutes to dispose
of the case.

Satinder was a lot bolder with women than I. Every Saturday, after our game of tennis or hockey, he was able to pick
up a girl to take home. His prowess amazed me because he
was a man of few words and could hardly converse with
anyone on any topic. I found that out for myself when we
were holidaying in Paris. We were in a pension close to the

Pantheon. Amongst the other lodgers there was a tall, slender, full-bosomed and broad-hipped Afro-American girl, Marie Stokes. She was doing a course in French Literature in the institute where I was attending classes in elementary French. I had many more opportunities of being with her than Satinder had. Although assured that my advances would not be repelled, I was unable to make any. Satinder warned me: 'If you don't fuck the Marie woman in the next three days, I'll fuck her for you.' I knew he meant what he said and pleaded for more time.

Meanwhile, in order to help me get over my nervousness he introduced me to French bordellos. He got a copy of what was known as *The Pink Book*, which had a list of Parisian whorehouses with their addresses. Most of them were in the area of Gare St Lazare. We went to one. We were welcomed by the Madame and escorted to a large drawing room with mirrors for walls. She told us what it would cost; *pourboire* (tips) were extra. She clapped her hands. A dozen girls trooped in, all stark naked. While they twirled their pubic hair as if they were moustaches, champagne was ordered for them. We paid for the champagne and the services to be rendered. We pointed to the girls we wanted and were taken by them to their separate rooms. The one I had washed her privates in a bidet and ordered me to do likewise. She asked me if I would like to come in her mouth. '*Non!*' I replied firmly. As in the past, the act was over within a few seconds. I had to wait for Satinder for almost half an hour before he emerged from his tryst looking very pleased with himself, with his girl smilingly asking him to come again. He called me a *chootia* (cunt-born) and again threatened to take Marie off my hands.

I staved off Satinder by pretending that I had at last succeeded in seducing Marie. I had only got to kissing her thick painted lips. She construed this as the beginning of a love affair to be consummated later. It never was. A few days later she left for the States. We continued to correspond with each other. More than thirty years later she came to see me at Rochester, where I had a teaching assignment. She had put on an enormous amount of weight: the tall, slender girl I had met in

Paris was a mountain of flesh. I took her to my apartment. She had travelled by bus through the night to come to Rochester. While she was having a shower, she told me of her two marriages and of the lovers she had had. She came out of the shower rubbing her enormous torso and behind and continued talking to me. I fondled her breasts and kissed her. 'Honey, you don't want to bed me now: you didn't do so in Paris when I was really beddable.' I gave up the feeble attempt. Later she taunted me: 'You didn't push me too hard or I would have happily given in.'

I saw more of Marie in her house in Detroit where she gave a large party for my wife and me. Her blind mother asked me to sit in her lap. 'Marie has told me so much about you; now I want to see you with my hands.' She ran her fingers over my turban, beard and face as if reading Braille. 'Now I know exactly what you look like,' she said. Marie also visited our home in Delhi. My children, who were told by my wife that Papa's girlfriend of college days was coming for dinner, eagerly awaited her arrival. She brought them gifts. They could not believe that Marie could ever have had any boyfriends. Marie became the subject of one of my short stories, 'Black Jasmine'. It was more fantasy than fact.

I was back in the Whaley's pension in south London. One evening there was a terrible row between Armstrong and the launderette lady. They never had liked each other. Armstrong was very drunk and abusive towards her. All of us were drawn into the quarrel on the side of the lady. Even though Miss Whaley was Armstrong's mistress she was constrained to order him to leave. He swore that he would depart the next morning but cut Miss Whaley out of his will. 'Not a penny of my property will go to you,' he warned.

The next morning Armstrong was repentant. He apologized to all the inmates save the launderette lady. Miss Whaley was more than eager to forgive him and let him stay. The Dunsmuirs, who were on specially cheap rates, also decided to stay on. The others, being on the side of the launderette lady, decided to find accommodation elsewhere.

The only accommodation I could find immediately was a pension run for Indian students by a widow and her son on Worseley Road, between Hampstead and Belsize Park. It was a wretched little place with four other Indian students, two Sindhis, a Bengali Muslim and a handsome young fellow from the Kumaon hills. We only met at breakfast and dinner. The sole advantage of the place was its proximity to Hampstead Heath, which I got to know, as they say, like the back of my hand.

I was not happy to be in entirely Indian company. That was not what I had come to England for. In the few months that I was in this pension, two events took place: one had a decisive effect on my future, the other was a trivial incident which later I converted into a short story.

First the trivial. The young man from Kumaon, I think his name was Shah, did not care to mix with us. After a few weeks he thawed towards me and began to open up. He had an English girlfriend — 'from a very decent, upper class family', he assured me many times. 'Not like the cheap waitresses and nurses most Indian men go out with. Very reserved, very dignified,' he said. After a few days I asked him how far he had got with her. 'I have told you, she's not that kind of girl,' he replied somewhat irritated. 'She will never allow anyone to take liberties with her unless she really loves him.' Some days later he admitted that she had kissed him when he left and was probably in love with him. He was very pleased with the progress he was making. 'When will you do it?' I asked him. He didn't like my using such language. But that was evidently very much on his mind. One Sunday, he wore his best dark suit and liberally doused himself with cologne. He told me that the girl's parents were out for the weekend and he would be alone with her. I wished him luck.

He was back within an hour. I went to his room. He was lying on his bed looking very woebegone. I asked him what had happened. Had she refused to let him do it? '*Kucch na poochho Sardarji* [don't ask me anything] *hamara to dil toot gaya* [my heart is broken].' The story as it unfolded was that, far from being unwilling, the girl had promptly taken Shah to her bedroom and undressed herself. She ordered Shah to do likewise. He dutifully divested himself of his clothes. They embraced. She took his uncircumcised penis lovingly in her hands and remarked, 'I see you are not a Muslim'. All the ardour drained out of the devout Hindu Brahmin from the Kumaon hills. He went limp. I used this incident in my story 'The Great Difference'.

The other thing that happened was the visit of the Maliks to England. They had brought their second son, Shubchintan, who was very slow in his studies, to join an agricultural college in Kent. They also wanted to explore the possibility of finding a match for their daughter, Kaval. They were orthodox Sikhs; their future son-in-law had to be a Sikh. One Tarlok Singh had got into the I.C.S. that year. If they could get him nothing would be better. Failing him, they meant to look for other suitable Sikh boys studying in British universities. I was one of them. The families were known to each other, but the Maliks knew very little about me as a person. They rang me up. I invited them to tea in my digs. They arrived a little before time and were shown to my room. Mrs Malik took a good look around. She sat on my bed and lifted the pillow. She found a *gutka* (a Sikh's daily prayerbook) under it. She made up her mind. If it could not be Tarlok Singh, I was the second best available. Being a senior engineer, Mr Malik was reluctant to give his daughter to the son of a building contractor who often sought his favours. But his wife's opinion always mattered more to him than his own. Besides, my father was by then a leading contractor, with a large chunk of real estate in the heart of New Delhi. Finally it was the small prayerbook under the pillow which proved to be my trump card.

Later that summer I ran into them again. I was holidaying at Windermere in the Lake District; they were in a fancy hotel at the lake's northern end at Bow Ness. One morning I rowed up to Bow Ness to have breakfast with them. They were impressed by my physical prowess. Mr Malik spoke to the lady who ran the hotel and I was offered a very reasonable rate should I spend the rest of my vacation there. The next day I shifted from my pension in Windermere to this hotel with a bar, ballroom and garden overlooking the lake. I hired a rowboat for a month and spent most of the time rowing, fishing for perch or walking in the woods in the surrounding hills. This was Wordsworth's country. I spent more time reading his poems than on my law books.

I thought I had got over my phobia of ghosts. One moonlit night when I was out walking in the woods I came across a small monument with a marble tablet. I was able to read the inscription. It marked the spot where some people had been struck by lightning and killed. I became nervous and felt the presence of the dead around me. I made my way back to the hotel, constantly looking behind to make sure that I was not being followed.

Back in London, I did not return to Hampstead. While playing hockey I had made friends with a tall, handsome, golden-haired boy named Richard Reiss, who was studying engineering. He invited me to spend a Sunday with his family in Welwyn Garden City. I fell in love with the Reiss family. The father, Captain Reiss, had spent some time in India and was one of the founders of Garden City. Mrs Reiss was very much like Whistler's portrait of his mother — tall, grey-haired and dignified. She was a Quaker and a pacifist. There were Richard's sisters, all stunningly good-looking, fair and golden-haired like their brother. Their home was on top of a rise overlooking a golf course. On one side stretched a woodland of bracken, oak and cedar, and wild rhododendrons in full bloom. Why, I asked myself, did I have to live in London and not in this blissfully beautiful woodland township?

Mrs Reiss found me an ideal lodging. Professor F.S. Marvin, then in his late seventies, lived in a lovely double-storeyed cottage with a sizeable garden. He had an Anglo-Indian woman, Mrs Cremona, and her twenty-year-old daughter Doris to look after him. He had a spare room and was happy to have me as a boarder. His two sons lived away. I moved bag and baggage to Welwyn Garden City. It was the happiest period of my five-year stay in England.

I made many English friends. For one, there were people with whom I travelled every day to London and back. I joined the Delcott Tennis Club, and being reasonably good at the game played for it against other local clubs. Nearer Christmas, I found myself in a group of carol singers who practised singing with flute accompaniment on the morning journey to King's Cross. Amongst them was a young, dark-haired girl, Barbara Purdom, who was training to be a ballet dancer. Her father was a writer of sorts; her brother, a film actor. They were Roman Catholics. For reasons beyond my comprehension, Barbara took a fancy to me and in her juvenile enthusiasm determined to marry me. She often invited me over to her house to watch her practice her steps; she slipped love letters in my pocket in the train where she made it a point to sit next to me. I was more embarrassed than flattered by her attentions.

Among other friends I made was Jack Peel and his very pretty Estonian wife, who worked as a waitress in a cafe where I often dropped in for coffee on Sunday mornings. Jack was a born linguist, as fluent in German and Russian as he was in his native English. He was also an accomplished pianist and gave concerts in the village hall. He played tennis for a rival club. Sikhs were no strangers to him, for he had earlier befriended one Gurdial Singh who had walked away with his girlfriend. Through his command of foreign languages, Jack rose to be a senior executive in Lever Brothers and was put in charge of its East European division. He also acted as an interpreter for Winston Churchill in his meetings with Stalin at Yalta. When Jack's Estonian wife died, he married an equally attractive German girl, Erika, who bore him a son, Nicky. Through Jack I made many other friends in Welwyn, including the Ortons who lived in a small village, Weston, and the Behrmans, a German Jew turned a Christian English gentleman. I never lost contact with the Reisses or the Peels. Richard's daughter married a Haryanvi Jat, Randhir Singh, who settled in the United States. When he came to see me, I treated him like a son-in-law. Jack and I continued to play squash at lunch time when I was posted in the Indian High Commission in London. He and his wife have spent a few days with us in Delhi and whenever I'm in London we get together for a meal.

Apart from Paris, I didn't get to see much of Europe. While I was a student, I had spent a summer on the Cote d'Azur. An opportunity to visit Germany came shortly before the Berlin Olympics. The Germans were eager to see Indian-style hockey before they took on the Indian Olympic side. They invited a Joint English Universities Indian Hockey team to participate in a tournament at Weisbaden. Two students from Kings, both Sikhs, Basant Singh from Kenya and I, were included to give the side an authentic Indian look. Both of us were indifferent players.

In Germany I had my first exposure to anti-semitism. Around the playground were benches for spectators. A few of them were painted yellow with the word 'Juden' written on them. I understood what it meant. And while watching the preliminary trials I decided to sit on them rather than on the other benches. One of my hosts told me that the benches were meant for Jews. I replied that I knew, but meant to sit on them as I was a communist (which was not true) and anti-fascist (which I was). They were very upset. Instead of ordering me back to England, as the Captain of our side wanted to, they tried to get round me. I became the most sought after member of the side. I was invited to receptions only meant for Aryans. At one of them I met a huge, over six-feet-tall blonde, a full-bosomed German girl, the very prototype of an Aryan maiden of Hitler's dreams. Through an interpreter I told her that I had never seen as handsome a woman as her in my life. I am not sure how my compliment was conveyed to her in German, but later that evening she came to my room in the hotel and told me in broken English that, since I had liked her so much, she was there to give me a good time. I might have accepted her offer but for one sentence she used: 'Why do you like Jews so much?' That put me off because, in fact, I had liked the few Jewish people I knew at King's more than others. There was Bronowski, who had changed his name to

Baron. He played table tennis for England and ended up as Chief Justice in some African country. There was Lewinsohn, who helped me prepare for my exams. He became a prosperous solicitor. And there was a Miss Jaffe, the brightest girl in our class. She had a nervous breakdown while taking her final exam and was unable to do all the papers. Nevertheless, the examiners gave her a first division. I go out of my way to befriend Jews.

The Four selected German teams did not have much trouble beating our quickly assembled rag-tag side of Indian college boys. But they did not learn much technique from us. When it came to playing against our Olympic Eleven the German side collapsed like a pack of Jokers.

When I returned to Welwyn, I found that quite a few men and women I had known in Delhi had arrived in England. First and foremost there was Kaval Malik who had come to do a course in the Montessori system of teaching. She had blossomed into a ravishing beauty, and she knew it. She often mentioned that her vital statistics were exactly those of a succession of girls crowned Miss Universe. Pratap Lal, with whom I had exchanged turbans at school to symbolize a fraternal relationship, came to do law and journalism. The two were in the same pension run by the Bell family in Ealing. E.N. Mangat Rai, who got into the I.C.S., came to do his probation at Keble College, Oxford; and Amarjeet Singh, who had been admitted to some college in Cambridge, came to do his tripos.

Both Pratap and Amarjeet were very keen on Kaval. Amarjeet, being a Sikh and already having a sister married to Kaval's eldest brother, rated his chances high. Pratap had the advantage of seeing more of her. Mangat Rai was then indifferent and even somewhat hostile to her. I saw quite a bit of these people. Once Mangat Rai, Richard Reiss and I went cycling through Oxford and the Cotswolds. Another time Pratap Lal and I cycled to Tintern Abbey and Wales. At Tintern, much to my chagrin and Pratap's delight, the lodge keeper took me to be his father. However, his seven-year-old daughter had seen through my beard and pronounced us to be of the same age. Once Amarjeet came to stay with me in

Welwyn. He made a great hit with Professor Marvin because he could play a few bars of Chopin on the piano. One afternoon while strolling in the woods he was accosted by an elderly lady who asked him questions he could not answer. 'I am not the Singh you know,' he told her. 'I am a friend of his staying with him.' The lady apologized, 'I knew you looked somewhat different,' she said. An hour later when Amarjeet was waiting to catch his train to Cambridge, the same lady came to him and said, 'Mr Singh, you know I mistook a friend of yours for you.'

My chance to win over Kaval Malik came the following Christmas. I had spent the previous Christmas at a Quaker Hostel in Seer Green Halt not far from Beaconsfield, Milton's cottage where the poet had written *Paradise Lost*, and Stoke Poges Churchyard where Grey had composed his famous *Elegy*. I asked her what her plans were for Christmas. She had none. And the Bells were planning to take a holiday and close their establishment for a few days. I suggested she come along with me to the Quaker Hostel. It was a quiet place largely frequented by elderly widows. I told her of the Friends Meeting House, the Mayflower barn in which we could play badminton and table tennis, the graveyard where the Penn Brothers were buried and the woods surrounding the place.

The hostel was run by a widow, Mrs Cuthbertson. I told her what fun I had had the year before. She replied that she would have to seek her parents' permission before she said yes. She wrote to them. I was pleasantly surprised to hear they agreed to let her go with me. So a few days before Christmas we took a slow train to Seer Green Halt in Buckinghamshire. An old lady who plied the only taxi from the station to the village dropped us at the Quaker Hostel.

I laid siege to Kaval Malik's heart. During the long walks we took to visit Milton's cottage and Stoke Poges churchyard I tried to impress her with my knowledge of English poetry. I did not know much Milton but had refreshed my memory of the *Elegy*. When we got there I recited the first verse; she did not know it and was suitably impressed when I told her it had been composed where we stood. 'And listen to this,' I continued:

> Full many a gem of purest ray serene,
> Dark, unfathomed caves of ocean bear,
> Full many a flower is born to blush unseen,
> And waste its sweetness in the desert air.

I could sense that I had made my mark. None of her other friends had courted her in verse. Although she shrank back if I tried to touch her, her defences began to crumble. While we were at the Quaker Hostel she received several long letters from Pratap Lal. They were full of snide remarks about me and how unpleasant it must be for her to be in the company of a hairy Sikh. He was a gifted writer and a cartoonist. She showed me his letters. I had further confirmation that he was out of the running.

On the way back to London I proposed to her. She accepted my proposal, subject to her parents approval. I wrote to my father telling him of what had transpired and asked him to call on the Maliks. He did. They expressed consent. We announced our engagement. Pratap Lal accepted it in good grace and we remained good friends. Many years later we stayed with him in Bangalore where he was General Manager of Hindustan Aeronautics and saw a lot of him when he became Air Chief Marshal, and Chief of the Indian Air Force. He died in London in 1978. Amarjeet, who had crossed my path many times and never liked me made the acid comment: 'His father's bank balance won.'

Another young man who had given his heart to Kaval Malik was Bharat Ram, scion of one of India's richest families. He was by then married and the father of a son. However, he kept in touch with her for many years till he realized that he could not put me out of the scene. Bharat's family, including his father Sir Shri Ram, came for a holiday to Europe. A few days later Kaval accompanied them to a spa in Germany. I betook myself to the French Alps for a skiing holiday.

Having won her over I was beset with doubts as to whether I had done the right thing. The one person who kept telling me that I had made a mistake was Mangat Rai. He had a poor opinion of Kaval's mental capabilities and did not even rate her looks very high.

Our correspondence began to drag. She found my enthusiasm for skiing and the snows very tiresome. In one picture postcard she sent me from Nuremberg she wrote of a great rally she had witnessed and of 'a new German leader, somebody called Adolf Hitler'. This was at a time when everyone in Europe was talking of nothing else except Hitler and the menace of Nazism. Evidently she didn't read newspapers or books, besides those prescribed in her curriculum. By the time she left for India with the Shri Ram family our ardour for each other had cooled considerably. Besides, I had begun to have doubts about my own future.

For the heck of it, I decided to have a go at the I.C.S. examination. I had only one chance; I knew that my academic record was loaded against me. I did the best I could. I believed my top scoring subject would be International Law. I skipped one paper because I thought I would fare badly in it. Came the *viva voce*. I went to it as badly dressed as I always was, in an ill-fitting dark suit, a red tie and a blue turban. The first question the panel of three members asked me was why I wanted to get into the I.C.S. I replied candidly that I knew I had little chance of making it, but since it was regarded as a test of intelligence I thought I would have a go at it. They laughed. Other Indian candidates had replied to the same question by saying they wanted to serve the people, serve the country, etc. Next they asked me whether while studying law, I had ever visited the courts in England and seen how justice was administered. I told them of my having appeared as a witness before the Bow Street Magistrate and of my surprise at how speedily the case had been disposed of, the number of accused who had pleaded guilty and the severe sentences passed for petty thefts. And how hard English Barristers must find it to make a living. They had another hearty laugh.

The results were announced a month later. I had missed the I.C.S. by one place. Contrary to my expectations, the examiner had given me low marks in International Law. If he had given me another eleven, or if I had scored the same in the paper I did not take, I would have made it. And that for the single reason that I was the only candidate, Indian or English, who was given full marks in the *viva voce*: 300 out of 300. I was also recommended for nomination as a member of a minority community. They took a Muslim, a Christian or a Sikh by rotation every three years. Mohan Singh, who was then a Member of the Secretary of State's Advisory Council for India, rang me up to congratulate me and sent a telegram of congratulations to my father. For a week I rode on cloud nine, decided not to bother with my law exams and dreamt of another year in England doing my probation in Oxford or Cambridge. And to then return home triumphantly as a member of 'God's own service'. Unfortunately for me, a Sikh had been nominated a year earlier and a Christian a year before that. The nomination thus went to a Muslim. I was desolate. Come to think of it, I might have ended my career as a Secretary to the Government instead of struggling for years with law, journalism and writing books.

While on my skiing holiday, I heard that I had done poorly in my L.L.B. examinations. I had just managed to pass but would have to take one paper again. I had scraped through my bar examination and rejoined college to take a Masters degree in Law. My tutor, Dr Potter, told me bluntly that I was not up to it. After six months of struggling with the L.L.M. course I gave up the battle and decided to return home. I would have had to spend another six months to get my Barrister's certificate but a letter prompted by Kaval's father and from Sir Maurice Gwyer, the retired Chief Justice of India and then Vice-Chancellor of Delhi University, helped me to get the licence *in absentia*.

My days with Professor Marvin came to an abrupt end entirely because of me. We had got on very well with each other. He let me drive his car. I helped him in keeping his garden tidy, mowed and swept his lawn and chopped firewood for the winter months. One afternoon an English girl dropped in to see me. She was impressed that I was boarding with as distinguished a man as Marvin, who had written many books. 'Come and meet him,' I said, taking her by the hand. We burst into Marvin's study. He was deep in his thoughts facing his typewriter and visibly upset at being disturbed. I cheerfully introduced the girl and started telling him who she was. He went pale with anger and exploded, 'Don't you see I'm busy? Get out both of you!' I was badly shaken by his outburst. I took the girl home through the woods. I couldn't forgive Marvin for his rudeness. For the next few days I avoided talking to him. This time he was upset and had to explain why he had lost his temper. I had no forgiveness in me. I moved out to a boarding house in Welwyn Garden. Then at Peel's suggestion I went to live with his friends Maurice and Brenda Orton in Weston village some miles away from Letchworth Garden City. Since I had finished with college and was only working on one paper for the Bar finals I had plenty of time on my hands. I found the End Cottage very convenient. The Ortons worked in London. They left in the morning and returned late in the evening in time for supper. I had their cottage all to myself.

The Ortons were an odd couple, of a kind I had never met before. He was a tall, blond, powerfully built man from a working class family with very little education. He was able to conceal his lack of education by adopting an upper-class accent. She was a petite, dark-haired, sophisticated Jewish girl who had been to university. They had met at a party where Maurice had read some of his poems and created the impression of being a working-class poet of the future. They had got talking over drinks that followed the poetry reading session. She had gushed with admiration. He simply took her by the hand to the host's bedroom and proceeded to fuck her. Brenda had never experienced such down-to-earth copulation, devoid of any preliminaries. A few weeks later they were married.

It did not take long for Brenda to find out that Maurice was a boor, prone to violence and wanted a new woman every few days. He could not hold any job for long and blamed the bourgeois society in which he lived for not recognizing his genius. When out of a job he took it out on Brenda. When I moved into their cottage he had set his sights on a nineteen-year-old village girl called Fiona. He insisted on Brenda inviting her home. When he went to drop her back, he tried to take liberties with her. Her mother saw them and told Brenda about it. Another time he picked on an Indian girl and invited her to spend the weekend with them at Weston. He tried to molest her. She was thoroughly frightened and refused to leave my side till she left. There were days when he got into a cussed mood and refused to let Brenda leave for her office. He abused her — 'bitch! whore!' and threatened to beat her if she stepped out of the cottage. Brenda was reduced to tears but was too scared to disobey him. One weekend he came to Paris with me and insisted I find him a woman to sleep with. 'Go and find one for yourself,' I told him. 'I don't want any whore, I want one of your girl friends. They'll never forget me after they've had this,' he said opening his fly buttons and yanking his penis. It was the biggest penis I had ever seen — almost the size of a donkey's. We returned to Weston with him grumbling about having wasted his time and money. I felt very sorry for Brenda but could do very little to comfort her. Despite Maurice, I spent a happy two months in the End Cottage, going on long walks in the morning and riding in the afternoons. But I was finally happy to get away from the Ortons. Later, I heard from Jack Peel that Maurice joined the Air Force and was killed in an air crash in the early months of World War II. A very relieved Brenda took a second husband and was editing a women's journal.

I returned home somewhat shamefacedly. Gossip had gone round that my engagement was at breaking point. I had taken five years to pass exams others had done in three. When my father's friends came to congratulate him on the return of his son and asked him, *'Kaka kee pass kar key aya hai?'* — What has your son passed? he would reply, *'Hor tay pata nahin time bahut pass kar kay aya hai'* — I don't really know what he has passed except that he has passed a lot of time. When told that her grand-daughter was to marry a Barrister Kaval's grandmother remarked, *'Hai! hai! itt putto tay Balister nikalda hai'* — You pull up a brick and you'll find a Barrister under it.

The one person who was genuinely glad to see me back at home was my grandmother. She celebrated my homecoming by getting her cronies together and, with the slapping of a drum, sang village ballads about the return of warriors. The strain proved too much for her. The next morning she went down with a mild fever. It did not deter her from having her early morning bath, spinning her charkha all day while muttering the 'Psalm of Peace' and feeding the sparrows in the afternoon. They came by the hundreds to pick up the morsels of stale chappattis she tore into tiny bits to fling at them. The fever got worse. But she refused to give up her daily routine of prayer, spinning and feeding sparrows. One morning she was unable to get up. Doctors were summoned. She knew her end was near. She sent for the family accountant and asked him to take down what she wished to be done with the little cash and jewellery she owned. An hour later, with her two sons and grandchildren around her sickbed, she bade us farewell and passed away.

Her body was laid out on the floor of the verandah where she used to spend most of the day spinning and feeding sparrows. They flocked there as they used to every afternoon. My mother threw them bread-crumbs. Either because of the coming and going of mourners, or the wailing and the *keertan* organized before her body was taken to be cremated, the crumbs remained unpicked. My grandmother became the subject of a profile I wrote many years later when I was posted in Ottawa and published in *The Canadian Forum* under the title 'Portrait of a Lady'. It has remained my most popular story.

The most awkward was my meeting with Kaval. The silence between us had been construed as a break up of our past commitments — rejection of the other by both. We talked about it for over an hour, felt that if we called off the engagement it would bring a bad name on our families and, since there was no real reason to break up, we decided to go ahead with our plans to get married. I was for delaying it by a few months till I had found a place in Lahore where I intended to set up legal practice. My father had forestalled the problem and rented a two-bedroom corner flat in a newly constructed building on the main highway of the city, The Mall, facing the High Court.

The three months between my return home and my marriage I spent in the chambers of Kirpa Narain, who handled my father's legal business and was one of Delhi's leading lawyers. I took little interest in the briefs he asked me to prepare. I spent more time in Sessions Courts listening to murder cases than those concerning disputes over property. The evenings I spent with Kaval — doing the rounds of Delhi, going to the pictures with the Bharat Rams or for a swim in their pool.

Our marriage was an elaborate affair. Kaval's father was the first Indian Chief Engineer of the C.P.W.D. and this was his only daughter's wedding. My father was by then the leading building contractor and the largest single owner of real estate in the capital. He had been giving presents to other people's children for many years. It was his turn to receive them through his second son.

It was a traditional Sikh wedding, with a brass band leading the procession and me, draped in a bridegroom's veil of jasmine flowers, riding sword in hand on a white horse. The Maliks lived on 1 Tughlak Road, which was a bare furlong down the road from my father's house, 1A Janpath. We went through the ritual of being received by the bride's relations and my being put through a lot of banter and practical jokes by her cousins, followed by a feast. I spent the night in the Malik home. Early next morning, under a vast canopy we sat in front of the Granth Sahib, she demurely covering her face behind a veil; I in a cream coloured sherwani and chooridars with a gilded kirpan in my hand. The *Anand Karaj* (ceremony of bliss) was a solemn affair with ragis singing wedding hymnals. I couldn't resist the temptation of slipping my hand under her *dupatta*, in which she was covered, and tweaking her feet. We went round the Granth Sahib four times, I in front, she following me holding one end of a scarf which I had in my hands. We took our marriage vows — to remain faithful to each other and look upon others as our brothers and sisters. This was on the morning of 30 October, 1939.

The same evening my father arranged cocktails and a dance party on the spacious lawn in front of his house. Over 1000 people responded. Scotch, champagne, wines and brandy flowed; ballroom dancing on a specially laid out wooden floor went on till the early hours. Among the guests were Mr M.A. Jinnah who lived across the road and occasionally dropped in to inspect my father's rose garden. We were allowed to retire at midnight to consummate our marriage. I was later told that one of the drunken guests had run his car over a telegraph peon on his way to deliver a congratulatory telegram. The news was suppressed.

The wedding night was something every bridal couple looks forward to. I did my best to follow the traditional pattern. It was then that I discovered that my bride was a virgin. We had never talked of sex till then nor had she allowed my hands to go exploring beneath her waist. She pleaded with me to be patient. I gave in.

The next evening we left for Mount Abu for our honeymoon. It had been my choice for no other reason than that the entrance of Welwyn Garden City railway station displayed a large poster depicting a marble temple with the legend, 'Visit India: Dilwara temples at Mount Abu'. My English friends asked me if I had seen the place. I admitted I had not but would do so as soon as I returned home. We had to break journey at Ajmer where we were guests of Uttam Singh, an executive engineer working under my father-in-law and his remarkably young and pretty Hungarian-Jewish wife, Maidy. No one could understand why she had married a grey-bearded Sikh older than her father. She had come to India with her mother, who matched Uttam Singh in age more than her daughter did. Maidy proved to be a devoted and faithful wife. It was only after her husband died that she consorted with John Martin, Headmaster of Doon School, and married him. A couple of years after Martin's death Maidy was murdered in her cottage in Dehra Dun. We spent the night at the Uttam Singh's. I could not make any progress with my bride.

The next morning we drove up to Mount Abu. A spacious

bungalow of the C.P.W.D. overlooking the Nakki Lake had been reserved for us. Cook, bearer, ayah and gardener were at our disposal for a week. Also membership of the club and freedom to savour whatever it had in its cellars. We drank up all its stock of English cider. There was also a rowing boat to explore the Nakki. We spent the morning chasing a couple of otters till we drove them out of the lakes to the hills. The English Resident of the Rajputana States threw a banquet for us where the local Sahib gentry and their ladies were present. Our stock in Mount Abu went up. It was the first time that we had tasted Scotch and joined in drinking a champagne toast proposed to us. We returned to our bungalow somewhat light in our heads and feeling on top of the world.

The night was made for loving. A full moon shone on the Nakki and across our beds laid out in the airy verandah of the first floor. The gardener had strewn jasmine and rose petals on our pillows. This time nothing would hold back my ardour and she was mutely ready for what was to come. A little she protested before saying yes; I hurt her a little. A little she bled but our union was at last consummated.

We returned to Delhi still hungering for each other's bodies when I was ordered by my father to go to Mian Channu where Uncle Ujjal Singh was reported to be in poor health. I did as I was told and was away for an agonizingly long week. He was convalescing from his illness and permitted me to return to Delhi.

The honeymoon was over. I had now to set up home and a law practice in Lahore — both entirely dependent on my father's bounty. He gave me a brand new Ford in which to drive up to Lahore with my newly acquired wife, a flat to live in, and a chamber on Fane Road to receive my clients. My father-in-law furnished our flat. My father's closest friend, Basakha Singh, gave me all the law books I needed as a wedding present. Now it was for me to make a go of the legal profession. Or make a flop of it.

5 Lahore, Partition and Independence

HAVING SPENT TWO carefree years in Government College, I was no stranger to Lahore. But coming there to earn my living was a different matter. I had everything laid on for me! A well furnished flat and office, and membership of the two leading clubs — the Cosmopolitan, meant for the Indian élite, and the more exclusive Gymkhana, which was largely an English preserve with no more than a dozen wogs drawn from Oxbridge. My father and father-in-law's status (both were knighted by the British) opened the doors of judges and ministers to me. Given Kaval's youth and beauty, we soon became a much sought-after and photographed couple in Lahore. The only thing missing was the legal clientele. I spent a couple of hours in the morning in my office poring over law books. Then I went to the Bar room to pick up some gossip. I went to the court rooms to hear important cases being argued, spent an hour or so in the coffee house for more gossip and returned home for lunch. For the first few months not a single litigant crossed my threshold. For a while I worked as a junior to Kirpa Narain who had shifted from Delhi to Lahore. One day he collapsed while arguing a case and died before a doctor could be summoned. Such deaths were not uncommon among lawyers. I shifted over as a junior to Jai Gopal Sethi who had the largest criminal practice in the Punjab. He occasionally got his clients to throw a few crumbs at me, as a junior's fees. I was told that I should acquire a good munshi. Munshis were (and are) quite an institution in the Indian legal profession. Where there are no solicitors, as in the Punjab, they do the soliciting — talking to clients, sorting out their papers, fixing the fee, extracting it with their *munshiana* of ten per cent. In my time in Lahore, munshis did a lot more. They went to railway stations and bus stands as hotel agents do, spotted litigants and persuaded them to take on their employer as their advocate. All manner of persuasion was used: their master's wife was the judge's mistress, or vice-versa; he was the ablest 'England-returned Barrister' and played tennis and bridge with the sahibs, and drank and danced with their *mems*. The first clerk I hired was a sharp little fellow from Himachal. He persuaded me to let him go on a tour of Punjab's districts to do some propaganda for my cause. He was away for a month, presented me his travel bills and assured me that many leading lawyers of the district courts had promised to send their appellate work to me. None came. My second clerk was a Shia Muslim. He got me a brief as a junior to a leading lawyer from Lucknow in a case involving two branches of rich Shia zamindars in Bahraich over their property in Lahore. I got a small fee but lost the friendship of the Lahore head of the family. We also lost the case. Thereafter, having nothing to do, I let my munshi hire a maulvi who taught me the Quran for an hour every morning. Some time later the munshi left me on the pretext that taking a salary from a non-Muslim who questioned the existence of God was *haraam* — unlawful.

In sheer desperation, I hired the most expensive munshi in Lahore. Udham Singh was a strapping six-foot Sikh Jat who was a renowned tout. I paid him Rs 10,000 as an advance — a sum unheard of — to secure his services. He was familiar with the villages in Lahore district. Whenever there was a murder in a Sikh village — and there were at least four or five every month — he went to condole with the bereaved family as well as call on the family whose members had been named as accused. He managed to get a brief from one side or the other. Instead of a tenth due to him as *munshiana* he took a third of my fee. However, criminal cases started coming my way. I won some, lost others. I discovered that hiring renowned lawyers at high fees did not really make much difference in a criminal case. If a magistrate or judge was friendly towards me, I got bail for my clients, and often a lighter sentence. There was an Anglo-Indian lawyer who knew hardly any law but managed to get cases through his touts because he was a sahib. Also a

Parsee, who wore a monocle, hummed and hawed his way through his briefs in a fake upper-class English accent and managed to make a reasonable living. There was a Muslim lawyer who gained notoriety for never preparing his briefs and throwing his clients at the mercy of the court. 'Who knows the law better than your honour? Who am I to tell you the real facts of the case? Your honour will no doubt grasp them better than I and do justice to my client!' He did better than most lawyers who burnt midnight oil poring over their briefs and wrangling with judges.

It was a hard, back-breaking, soulless profession. I took on undefended cases in sessions courts for a fee of Rs 16 per day; I appeared free of charge in cases against communists; I took on part-time teaching at the Law College; I was put on the panel of defence lawyers at the High Court and then on the panel of the Advocate-General. I hardly ever made more than a thousand rupees a month. My father continued to subsidize us. He bought us a larger apartment with property which brought us some rent; then a large house on Lawrence Road facing Lahore's biggest park, Lawrence Gardens (later renamed Bagh-e-Jinnah).

Perhaps it was my failure to make it big in the legal profession that soured me. I asked myself, 'Is there anything creative in practising law? Don't I owe more to the one life I have than making money out of other peoples' quarrels? A common prostitute renders more service to society than a lawyer. If anything, the comparison is unfair to the whore. She at least serves a social need and gives her clients pleasure for their money; a lawyer doesn't even do that.' I have no doubt that, had I stuck to the law, I would have made it to the Bench and perhaps even to the Supreme Court. Those with less practice and lesser legal acumen were elevated to the Bench; a couple even ended up as judges of the Supreme Court. I never regretted chucking up the law; my only regret was that I wasted five years studying it and another seven trying to make a living out of it.

My view of the legal profession and those who live by it has not changed. In a party of lawyers there is little talk besides their experiences in court and the rude behaviour of judges. Their only other interest is politics and quite a few switch over to it. That partly explains the amorality of Indian politics and the total absence of statesmen in the Indian scene. As for witty repartee, I heard of only one in my seven years at the Lahore High Court. A senior lawyer was finding it very difficult to persuade an English judge to accept his arguments. Every time he put a new one for consideration, the judge snapped back 'nonsense!' In sheer exasperation the lawyer remarked, 'This morning nothing but nonsense seems to come out of your Lordship's mouth!'

Sex has always been a subject of consuming interest to the legal profession and very much on the minds of younger lawyers of my generation. One fellow used to give parties on Sunday afternoons where he got prostitutes from Tibbi to entertain his guests. He kept himself well informed of the *navan maal* — new goods — that had arrived in the whore-market. A newcomer married to a Cockney regaled us with stories of the frenzy with which the English lass made love and showed us scars on his body where she had bitten him or dug in her nails. At one of these orgies there was a competition to find out who had the hardest stand. A *Concise Oxford Dictionary* was tied on a string with a loop to see which penis could hold it up without bending. They were overgrown children with minds of juvenile delinquents. The poet Akbar Ilahabadi summed them up neatly:

> *Paida hua vakeel, to Iblees nay kahaa:*
> *'Allah nay mujhey Sahib-e-awlaad kar diyaa.'*
> (The day a lawyer was born, Satan exulted:
> 'Allah has blessed me with progeny of my own.')

Having not much to keep me in the law courts, I began to read books on literature which I should have read in my years in college: anthologies of English poetry, Shakespeare's plays and sonnets; Tolstoy, Oscar Wilde, Aldous Huxley, Hindu philosophy by Radhakrishnan, etc. I also began to review books for *The Tribune* (I had to tell my friends that the K.S. at the end of the column was me) and wrote a short eulogistic booklet on

Stalin for the Friends of the Soviet Union, of which I was a founder member in Lahore. On vacation in the Shimla hills I did little besides reading in the mornings and taking long walks in the afternoons. Every afternoon I walked six miles from Mashobra to the Mall alongside my wife who was on a bicycle. We had tea at Wenger's or Davico's, watched the pageant of English officials, Indian Ministers and their over-dressed wives strolling by. And then six miles back to Mashobra. Once, Sir Charles Carson, Finance Minister of the Maharaja of Gwalior, spent a couple of days with us. He told me that he had walked to the Tatapani hot-water sulphur springs on the banks of the Sutlej 5,000 feet below Simla and back in a day, making it 44 miles in all. The following week-end I did the same. I bathed in the scalding sulphur water, drank a bottle of beer cooled in the icy, fast-running Sutlej and was back home by ten pm.

My sister's husband, Jaspal Singh, as tough a Sikh Jat as I had met, took a bet that he could outwalk me. We set out on a full-moon night on the Hindustan-Tibet road. He had two of his nephews with him — both in their early twenties — and two Kashmiri porters to carry our provisions. After fifteen miles, the two boys and the porters refused to go any further. We left them at a dak bungalow and proceeded towards our destination, Narkanda. Later that night we stopped at another dak bungalow in a fir forest to refresh ourselves; Jaspal drank milk by the gallon; I had tea laced with brandy. It was eerie in the moonlit stillness. We were talking very loudly when out of the seemingly untenanted bungalow came a loud yell, 'Bugger off!' We did, and arrived at Narkanda early in the morning. We took whatever the chowkidar could give us: ghee parathas and over-sweetened tea. We started on our return journey. We kept pace all day and late into the evening. My feet began to bleed. At a dak bungalow about ten miles short of Mashobra I stopped to bandage them with rags provided by the chowkidar. Jaspal decided to go ahead to claim victory. I followed a hundred yards behind him. He got to Mashobra at about midnight, told the family that I had given up on the way and went triumphantly to bed. On reaching Mashobra soon after him I went straight to my room. He was boasting about his feat at the breakfast table when I joined him. Technically he had won. We did 72 miles more or less non-stop, and both of us spent the next few days nursing our sore feet. 'If you had studied law books for 72 hours instead of walking 72 miles you would have been a wiser man,' was the only comment my father made.

I was not allowed to undertake any more long walks. But a fortnight later, when my father was away in Delhi and I had to return to Lahore on some business, I decided to walk down to Kalka which was 65 miles downhill most of the way. I left Mashobra while it was still dark, reached Solan (25 miles away) by the afternoon and was having tea at the rest house when my father suddenly turned up. It occurred to him that I did not have a car waiting for me. 'Where is your taxi?' he asked. I had to admit that I had walked down to Solan. He lost his temper and ordered his chauffeur to get a taxi for Kalka and saw me ride away in it. Great pity! The one thing I looked forward to after the marathon walk to Kalka was a shower at the railway station followed by a bottle of chilled beer and a sumptuous meal.

I have cherished memories of the summer months I spent in my parent's beautiful house, 'Sunderban', in Mashobra. It occupied an entire hill, and provided a spectacular view of snow-clad mountains to the north and broad valleys on the other side. My mother had a large cement platform raised which overlooked the road running from Shimla to the Mashobra bazar, Gables Hotel, through the estate of the Raja of Faridkot to a nine-hole golf course at Naldera. We spent most of our mornings and afternoons on this platform sunning ourselves or in the shade of a holly-oak which stood alongside it. The bird life in Mashobra was fantastic: barbets cried all day long, flocks of scarlet minivets flew among the cherry trees, sibias nested in a creeper growing over an elm tree, and fly catchers, including the most beautiful silver-white paradise fly-catcher, with its two ribbons of tail trailing behind it, were not an uncommon sight. Lammergeyers and Himalayan eagles floated in the air. In the early mornings and late evenings blackbirds perched on our roof and burst into song. All through moonlit nights nightjars called to each other. A family of flying squirrels had their nest in our eaves; we often saw them float down from tree to tree and hop about on the tennis court.

Sundays were special. We woke to the peal of bells from St Swithin's Church at the entrance of the Mashobra bazar. It had been built by an English leather merchant from Kanpur and named after the patron saint of cobblers. It was exactly like a village chapel in England with a lichgate, stained-glass windows and a high altar. English folk staying at Gables and Wild Flower Hall on the crest of the hill trooped in to church in their Sunday best for the morning service. After having prayed they strolled about the bazar exuding the fragrance of lavender and French perfumes.

My father was an Anglophile and loved entertaining white people. Once he got the list of residents and sent invitations to dinner to the Europeans staying at Wild Flower Hall and Gables. They came in their dozens, it was war time and nothing very exciting happened in their hotels. We hung Chinese lanterns all the way from the entrance gate up to our house. We had a Goan band to play dance music. The sahibs introduced themselves and their *mems*, drank our Scotch and wines, ate our curried meal, danced and departed. I asked my father what he got out of blowing up thousands of rupees entertaining strangers. 'The English never forget people who extend hospitality to them,' he replied. He was right. A few days later when he was going down to Delhi by rail car an English officer came up to him and introduced himself as one who had been at his party. They got talking. My father landed a lucrative contract to supply provisions to the army.

The Raja of Faridkot was also very fond of entertaining the whites. Every autumn he arranged bull-fights in an open arena. Farmers from distant villages brought their champion bulls. Foreigners and important Indians sat on sofas watching bulls tangle with each other. After the show, the Raja entertained his guests at a banquet with his private band playing. Since we often had English friends staying with us, we were invited frequently. The Raja could be as generous as he could be mean.

He served champagne to everyone, but when it came to whisky his bearers served Indian brands to Indians and Scotch only to the whites. I discovered this one evening when we took Evan Charlton, editor of *The Statesman*, and his wife Joy with us to one of his parties. When I complained to Evan about the quality of the whisky he snorted, 'You're a suspicious bugger! My whisky is okay.' We exchanged glasses. He wrinkled his nose when he tasted mine. The Raja could also be very uncouth. Whenever my father invited him, he would drink himself silly and stay on after the other guests had left. He made passes at my nieces, then in their teens, and at other young women present. My poor parents who usually retired at 9 pm were kept up till midnight.

More than anything else I loved going for long walks. When not bound for Shimla, I explored other mountain roads. There was a solitary, shaded path which ran through a pine and fir forest to an Italian monastery, San Demiano. Another went steeply uphill from Mashobra to a small orchard called Danes Folly, towards Wild Flower Hall. From the top of the hill you could see the Shali peak rising above 10,000 feet, and a broad stream dividing the two mountain ranges. During the rainy season, the valley was often covered over by mists. Mysteriously, the mists would lift and the sun break out, to light the rain-washed emerald green hillsides and set the stream that ran between them sparkling in the light.

Once a year in the autumn there was a fair in the village of Sipi, a mile or so below the Mashobra bazar. Villagers brought their nubile daughters and young sons here to arrange marriages for them. It was rumoured that pretty girls — Himachali girls can be fair, petite, almond-eyed and wanton — were put up for sale to the highest bidder. I saw many pretty girls but never one being taken away by an outsider.

Not having much to do in Lahore, a nice home and a lovely-looking (though by now somewhat over-assertive) wife, I had no dearth of visitors. Foremost among them was Mangat

Rai, who was posted at Lahore. Being in the I.C.S., he was much sought after by Christian families with marriageable daughters. He often invited friends to his home and read pieces he had written. One which received encores was about a hen which laid eggs in a drain. It was always heard with open-mouthed admiration by an ever-increasing circle of lady admirers. After a few months, he began dropping in on us on his way back from office. He hauled his bicycle up the stairs and often stayed on for drinks and dinner. Whatever reservations he once had about my wife had vanished; it was evident to me that he was getting quite enamoured of her. To leave me in no doubt, he wrote me a letter confessing that he was in love with her and sought my permission to continue visiting us. I passed his letter on to my wife. She was highly flattered. I treated it as a joke and wrote back assuring him that he would be as welcome as before. I had reason to regret my magnanimity. Mangat Rai had enormously persuasive powers to bring people round to his way of thinking.

Those days my wife spent her mornings painting in a studio run by Bhabesh Sanyal. Mangat Rai began dropping in at the studio and persuaded her that painting was a futile pastime. She gave up painting. She was a keen tennis player and spent every evening playing tennis at the cosmopolitan Club; he persuaded her that cycling was more fun, so she abandoned tennis and went cycling with him. She was also very punctilious about religious ritual, opening the Granth Sahib every morning and reading a hymn or two. In the evening she wrapped up the holy book for the night. He convinced her of the futility of such ritual. She began to miss out on her daily routine of prayer. He had become a hard drinker; my wife took to drinking hard. He was very open about everything he did. He told my wife that one evening when seeing off his sister at the railway station he had run into a young Christian girl known to us. She had no transport. He offered to ride her back on his cycle. She sat on the front bar. The physical contact roused them. He invited her to his apartment. She accepted his invitation. They spent the night in the same bed. He admitted he felt a little guilty because he loved my wife and not the girl he had bedded.

Instead of feeling let down, my wife admired his candour and was more drawn to him. Inevitably their association came to be much talked about.

Amongst others who became regular visitors to my home were Justice Gopal Das Khosla, also of the I.C.S., and his wife Shakuntala. He was taken by my wife; I with his. So we were level. There was a Canadian couple — Wilfred Cantwell-Smith, who was working on a doctoral thesis on Indian Islam, and his wife Muriel, who was studying medicine at the Lahore Medical College. There was P.N. Kirpal, lecturer in history at Dayal Singh College. He was enamoured of Mangat Rai's elder sister Priobala and hoped to marry her. He was destined to stay in our lives for the rest of our days. There were others, like Nawabzada Mahmood Ali Khan and his Sikh wife Satnam; Wilburn and Usha Lal, who were distantly related to Mangat Rai; Inder Mohan Varma, a lecturer in English at Government College; Bishen Narain and his wife Shanti, both friends of the Khoslas. Others came and went. Occasionally when in Lahore, there was Arthur Lall's younger brother, John, also in the I.C.S. John was a bit of a playboy with an incredible haw haw British accent. He was given to making wisecracks at my expense. 'Kaval,' he said to her one day, 'if you have a sister let her marry your bearded husband and you marry me.' I was the target of the witticisms of both the Lall brothers. With John I settled scores when he brought his fiancee, Hope, a dark, pleasantly plump girl to introduce her to us. The next day he dropped in and asked me what I thought of her. 'She will be a perpetual exercise in faith and charity,' I told him. He made no wisecracks thereafter. My day of reckoning with Arthur had to wait for some years.

Two people whom I met in these years in Lahore deserve mention. One was the painter Amrita Shergil. Her fame had preceded her before she took up residence in a block of flats across the road from ours. She had recently married her Hungarian cousin, Victor Egan, a doctor of medicine who wanted to set up practice in Lahore. Amrita was said to be very beautiful and very promiscuous. Pandit Nehru was supposed to have succumbed to her charms; stories of her sexual appetite were narrated with much slavering of mouths. She had visited Lahore earlier and stayed at Falettis Hotel to find a suitable apartment. She was said to have given appointments to her lovers, three to four every day with intervals of a couple of hours in between. They came, did their job and were dismissed as soon as it was over. My friend of Government College days, the diminutive Iqbal Singh who was then a producer in All India Radio, was said to be her last visitor of the evening. He had the limited privilege of ministering to her needs while she slept. I didn't know how much truth there was to gossip of her being a nymphomaniac, but I was eager to get to know her. I did not have to wait very long.

It was summer. My wife and six-month-old son had gone up to Kasauli to stay with her parents. One afternoon when I came home for lunch I found a tankard of beer and a lady's handbag on a table, and a heavy aroma of French perfume in my sitting room. I tiptoed to the kitchen to ask my cook who it was. 'I don't know,' he replied, 'a memsahib in a sari. She asked for you. I told her you would be back for lunch. She looked round the flat and helped herself to the beer from the fridge. She is in the bathroom.'

I had no doubt it could only be Amrita Shergil. And so it was. She came into the sitting room and introduced herself. She told me of the flat she had rented across the road and wanted advice about carpenters, plumbers, tailors and the like. I told her whatever I knew about such people. I tried to size her up. I couldn't look her in the face too long because she had that bold, brazen kind of look which makes timid men like me turn their gaze downwards. She was short and sallow complexioned (being half Sikh, half Hungarian). Her hair was parted in the middle and tightly bound at the back. She had a bulbous nose with black heads showing. She had thick lips with a faint shadow of a moustache. I told her I had heard a lot about her paintings and pointed to some water colours on the wall which my wife had done. 'She is just learning to paint,' I said by way of explanation. 'That's obvious,' she snorted. Politeness was not one of her virtues; she believed in speaking her mind, however rude or unkind it be.

A few weeks later I had another sample of her rudeness. I had picked up my wife and son from Kasauli and taken them up to Mashobra. Amrita was staying with her friends the Chaman Lals, who had rented a house a little above my father's. I invited them for lunch. We were having beer and gin-slings on the open platform under the shade of the holly-oak. My son was in a playpen learning to stand on his feet. Everyone was paying him compliments: he was a very pretty little child with curly hair, large questioning eyes and dimpled cheeks. 'What an ugly little boy!' remarked Amrita. Others protested their embarrassment. My wife froze. Amrita continued to drink her beer without concern. Later, when she heard what my wife had to say about her manners and that she had described her as a bloody bitch, Amrita told her informant, 'I will teach that woman a lesson. I'll seduce her husband.'

The day of seduction never came. When we returned to Lahore, my wife declared our home out of bounds for Amrita. Some months later common friends told us that Amrita was not well. One night a cousin of hers came over to spend the night with us because Amrita was too ill to have guests. He told us that she was delirious and kept mumbling calls at bridge — she was an avid bridge player. Next morning we heard she was dead. She was barely thirty-one.

I went over to Egan's apartment. Amrita's old, bearded father Umrao Singh was in a daze and her mother hysterical. They had just arrived from Summer Hill in Shimla and could not believe that their young, talented daughter was gone for ever. That afternoon a dozen men and women followed her hearse to the cremation ground where her husband lit the funeral pyre. When we returned to Egan's apartment, the police were waiting for him. England had declared war on Hungary as an ally of Nazi Germany. Egan had become an enemy national. He was lucky to have been taken into police custody.

It took some time for Amrita's mother to get the details of her daughter's illness and death. She held her nephew and son-in-law responsible. She bombarded ministers, officials, and friends (including myself) with letters accusing him of murder. Murder, I am certain, it was not. Carelessness, I am equally certain, it was. My version of her death came from Dr Raghubir Singh, then a leading physician of Lahore. He was summoned to Amrita's bedside at midnight when she was beyond hope of recovery. He believed that she had become pregnant and been aborted by her husband. The operation had gone wrong. She had bled profusely and developed peritonitis. Her husband wanted Dr Raghubir Singh to give her a transfusion and offered his own blood for it. Dr Raghubir Singh refused to do so without finding out their blood groupings. While the two doctors were arguing with each other, Amrita slipped out of life.

Many people like the art critic Karl Khandalawala, Iqbal Singh and her nephew, the painter Vivan Sundaram, have written books on Amrita. Badruddin Tyebji has given a vivid account of how he was seduced by her (she simply took off her clothes and lay herself naked on the carpet by the fire place). Vivan admits to her having many lovers. According to him her real passion in life was another woman.

Amongst the guests who stayed in my apartment while my wife and son were away for the summer was the communist Danial Latifi. He had been in and out of jail and the food they gave him at the Party headquarters did not agree with him. Being at the time close to the Party, I invited him to spend some weeks with me to recoup his health. Danial was a compulsive talker. His flat, monotone voice had a soporific quality. One evening two of my friends dropped in. Both were very drunk. Danial used their polite queries to deliver a long monologue on dialectical materialism and the class struggle. I went out to take some fresh air. When I returned half an hour later, Danial was still holding forth. Both my friends were fast asleep.

Through Danial I received two other visitors in turn. The first was Sripad Dange, then on the run from the police. He had to pretend to be my servant. He spent most of his time reading my books. When anyone came to see me he disappeared into the kitchen. Another was Ajoy Ghosh, also then underground. He was a dour, uncommunicative man. His mistress and later his wife, Litto, dropped in every day and spent many hours with him when I was at the High Court. Many years later in England I asked my friend Everett of the C.I.D. if he had known of these men having stayed with me. He said he had. It had been decided not to arrest them but only keep watch on my apartment and note down the names of people who came to visit my communist guests.

A person who dominated my life in my Lahore days was Manzur Qadir. He was a couple of years older than I, had done his Bar in England and practised in the district courts at Lyallpur (now Faridabad). He had picked up a considerable clientele and enjoyed the reputation of being an upright man of uncommon ability. His father, Sir Abdul Qadir, had been a judge of the Lahore High Court and a litterateur: as editor of *Makhzan* he was the first to publish the poems of Allama Iqbal whose friendship he enjoyed. Manzur married Asghari, the daughter of Mian Sir Fazl-i-Hussain. She was a great beauty. The Russian painter, Svetoslav Roerich, used her as a model for his portraits of the Madonna. At that time, Asghari considered Manzur below her status and felt she had done him a great favour. He was a short, balding, beady-eyed man who wore thick glasses. He was evidently very much in love with his wife and patiently suffered her tantrums. It did not take long for Manzur and me to get acquainted and become friends. Fortunately our respective wives, both equally prickly characters, also hit it off. We began to eat in each other's homes every other evening. My wife shared Manzur's enthusiasm for the cinema: they saw at least one picture together every week. Also his passion for mangoes. Between them they would demolish a dozen at one sitting with gusto.

Manzur was by any standards the most unusual character I had met. He was without doubt the ablest up-and-coming lawyer in the Punjab. He and his uncle, Mohammed Saleem, the famous tennis player who represented India in the Davis

Cup for fifteen years, spent hours arguing points of law after they had done a day's work in the High Court. Both men observed the highest standards of rectitude, a comparatively rare trait amongst lawyers in particular. They took their fees by cheque, or, when paid in cash, gave receipts for the full amount to their clients. They often paid more income-tax than was due from them and had some of it refunded. Manzur was the only person I met in my life who never told a lie and took great pains to avoid hurting people. In due course, he became a kind of litmus paper with which his friends tested their own integrity. When in doubt over a course of action we would ask ourselves, 'Will Manzur approve of this?' Like me, he was an agnostic.

What Manzur and I shared was a love for literature. In his case it was entirely Urdu poetry, to which he re-opened my eyes. He knew the works of many poets by rote. He also tried his hand at writing it, but without much success. He was best at composing bawdy verse which he recited with great verve to his circle of male friends. He was extremely proper when women were around. We spent many vacations together — sometimes at Patiala, where my father-in-law Sir Teja Singh Malik was a minister; at other times in Delhi or Mashobra with my parents. Our friendship became the talk of the town, as instances of such close friendships between Sikhs and Muslims or between Hindus and Muslims were rare.

What proved to be a turning point in my career was Mangat Rai's desire to score over others of our circle as a man of letters. He suggested that, instead of him alone reading his pieces to an admiring audience, everyone should read something he or she had written. Our first meeting thereafter was in his home — a portion of a house he had rented on Warris Road. The theme suggested by him was 'I believe'. We were to write down our beliefs on the values of life. About ten short papers were read. I put down my reasons for disbelief in God, religion, patriotism, friendship, love, marriage, death and theories of a life hereafter. There was nothing very original in what I wrote, and I wrote just as it came to me. My main achievement was that I emerged as a rival to the hitherto unrivalled Mangat Rai. To be fair to him, he was generous in his praise. The next day I received a note of appreciation from Wilfred and Muriel Cantwell Smith. It was my first fan mail and did a lot to boost my morale.

The literary circle became a weekly feature. We met in different homes by rotation. A lot of liquor (mostly Indian brew) was consumed as poems, short stories and essays were read and faithfully applauded by everyone. The two who contributed most were Justice G.D. Khosla and myself. Khosla was more anxious to establish himself as a writer than as a jurist. I had much less to do than any of the others. I used my visits to Sikh villages from where my clients came as backgrounds for my stories. I became the focal point of our meetings. Gradually I realized that scoring high marks in examinations as others in our circle had alone (Mangat Rai scored the highest in his essay in the I.C.S.) had little bearing on the ability to narrate a story which compelled attention. It was an inborn gift — some had it, others did not. Mangat Rai's contributions as well as his attendance at our meetings began to dwindle.

Mangat Rai had begun to cast around for a wife. The first to attract him was a very handsome girl, Lajwanti Rallia Ram, who belonged to a nationalist Christian family. She was as fair as a Kashmiri Brahmin, large-eyed, tall and slender. She got the top position in her M.A. English exam (her father happened to be Registrar of the University). I don't recall how they met, but since Mangat Rai was the most sought-after bachelor in the Christian community, the Rallia Rams could not have had much trouble discovering him and getting their daughter to know him. The two often met in my apartment when we were away at the Club. They announced their engagement, and the date for their wedding day was fixed. Wedding cards were printed and sent out. Lajwanti had her household linen embossed with the initials L.M.R. A few days before the marriage was to take place in a local church, Mangat Rai called it off. Lajwanti was heartbroken. Almost on the rebound she married Mohammad Yunus, a handsome Pathan who was active in the freedom movement (and later one of Prime Minister Indira Gandhi's closest henchmen). The marriage proved disastrous for both.

Mangat Rai resumed coming over to see us almost every day. I did not resent his visits as my wife had become extremely possessive, jealous and demanding of attention. I could not blame her feeling insecure as I had become an outrageous flirt and made passes at women. Her preoccupation with Mangat Rai gave me some relief.

A year or so later, Mangat Rai met another young Christian girl, Champa. She had also topped in the M.A. English exam when her father, S.P. Singha, was Registrar of the University. Champa was dusky, animated and uninhibited. Mangat Rai was attracted to her because of her vivacity. They got engaged. Champa took no chances with a prolonged engagement and the two were married in church. Though invited, we did not attend the wedding. Champa made a few half-hearted attempts to befriend us, but when we did not respond, she decided to drop us.

As I had foreseen, the marriage proved to be a *mésalliance*. Mangat Rai resumed calling on us, and when we were away, wrote long letters to my wife. However, his marriage went on the rocks in a more bizarre way than anyone had anticipated. One summer we were in Shimla at the same time. The Mangat Rais were staying with his sister, Sheila, and her husband Arthur Lall in a house near Lakkar Bazar. We were, as usual, in my father's house in Mashobra. We cycled down to Shimla every afternoon and spent the evenings strolling up and down the Mall with them. It was evident that Champa and Arthur were hitting it off very well. Plans were made for a week's trekking into the interior. A party was formed and porters hired. On the last day Mangat Rai backed out. So did his sister Sheila. Arthur and Champa had a week together in the Himalayan wilderness, spending their nights in deserted dak bungalows. They returned from the trek convinced that they were made for each other. Mangat Rai readily agreed to divorce his wife; Sheila a little reluctantly conceded Arthur's wish to be free of her. It did not turn out that way. When the Singhas heard of it, they came down with a heavy hand on their daughter. Champa asked her husband to forgive her. He did so as readily as he had agreed to divorce her. But for all practical purposes the marriage was at an end.

My Lahore days were coming to a close. Almost from the day I had come to live there, war had been raging in Europe and the Far East. I had strong anti-Fascist views and was convinced that Hitler, Mussolini, their European allies, and the Japanese had to be defeated before India could become really free. Most Indians exulted in the victories of the Axis powers, more out of spite for their English rulers than love for Nazis and Fascists. I wasn't quite sure of Japanese intentions after Subhash Chandra Bose took over command of the Indian National Army. He was too strong a man to become a puppet in anyone's hands, but even about him and his I.N.A. I had serious doubts. My communist illusions were blown sky-high when Stalin made his pact with Hitler, and only partly restored when they went to war against each other. I did not approve of Gandhi's 'Quit India' Movement. I supported the Muslim demand for a separate state in areas where they were in a majority, believing that India would continue to remain one country with two autonomous Muslim majority states at either end.

Not many Indians believed that the English would willingly relinquish their Empire in India. They regarded the Cripps and Cabinet Missions as eyewash. They did not know the English. The young British officers who did their war service in India were a new breed. They refused to join exclusively white clubs, went out of their way to befriend Indians, expressed regret over what some of the English rulers had done in India and sympathized with the Congress-led freedom movement. Unconnected with them, however, one event re-assured me that independence was round the corner. It took place in the summer of 1946.

I happened to be with my parents in Mashobra. I had to return to Lahore and took the evening rail-car to Kalka. There was only one other Indian beside me in it, the rest were British officers in uniform or English civilians. After a brief halt at Barog for dinner we proceeded on our downhill journey. It was a beautiful full-moon night. At a bend near Dharampur, a wheel of the car came off the rails. The driver told us to wait till he got to the next station to order a relief car to be sent up from Kalka. We sat among the pines on a hillside bathed in moonlight. The English were understandably nervous as some months earlier a rail-car had been ambushed by robbers who had shot six English passengers and then run away without taking anything. It was suspected to be the handiwork of Indian terrorists.

Somebody switched on the radio of the derailed car and tuned into the B.B.C Overseas Service. Election results were being announced. The Labour Party had won a landslide victory and Clement Attlee named Prime Minister of England. The English passengers heard the news in stony silence. The other Indian, whom I did not know, and I leapt up and embraced each other. We knew that with the socialists in power in England independence for India was round the corner.

Despite our friendship with the Manzur Qadirs I had no illusions about the general Muslim-Hindu/Sikh divide. Even in the High Court Bar Association and Library, Muslim lawyers occupied different corners of the large lounge and library from Hindus and Sikhs. There was a certain amount of superficial mixing at weddings and funerals, but this was only to keep up appearances. After the Muslim League resolution demanding Pakistan, the cleavage became wide and continued to grow wider. The demand for Pakistan assumed the proportions of an avalanche, gathering force as it went along. Every other afternoon huge processions of Muslims marched down the Mall chanting in unison:

Pakistan ka naaraa kya?
La illaha Lillillah

(What is the slogan of Pakistan?
There is but one God, He is Allah.)

A case in which I appeared as Manzur's junior provided an instance of how deep the poison had spread. It concerned a Sikh widow of considerable wealth and beauty named Sardarni Prem Prakash Kaur. She had been married to the only son of a wealthy contractor of Ludhiana. Her husband was a debauch. He contracted syphilis and died without consummating his marriage. His entire estate came to the young widow. Once, when holidaying in Shimla, she happened to be having tea at Davico's. A young Muslim strolling on the Mall saw her sitting alone by the window. Their eyes met and her smile assured him that he would not be unwelcome. He joined her for tea. They became lovers. The young man was handsome but the good-for-nothing son of a barber. He began to live off Prem Prakash Kaur. They had two sons. Then Prem Prakash Kaur tired of her uncouth lover. Her cousin, Gurnam Singh, as handsome as he was cultured, a Barrister with a large practice in Lyallpur (he was a close friend of Manzur Qadir), decided to rescue Prem Prakash from the clutches of the barber's son. Prem Prakash moved in with Gurnam. Her Muslim lover took her to court over the custody of the two boys. He claimed she had converted to Islam, married him by Islamic rites, that their boys were circumcised and given Muslim names. Besides marriage and the custody of their children, there were criminal cases of trespass and forcible seizure of property. As these cases moved from the lower courts to the appellate, the pattern became clear; if the presiding officer was Muslim, they went in favour of the barber's son; if Hindu or Sikh, they went in favour of the Sikh widow. I entered the scene when the case of marriage and custody came up for hearing before Donald Falshaw I.C.S., then a District and Sessions Judge in Lahore. I was engaged to give the case a non-communal flavour and as one known to be friendly with Donald and his wife Joan.

We were presenting the case of conversion and marriage: an affidavit by a maulvi who had presided over both events with the original of the Nikahnama — contract of marriage — were duly entered as exhibits one and two. Then Manzur (or perhaps it was one of the other panel of Muslim lawyers) presented a third exhibit — a packet in a ribbon, and put it on Falshaw's table. 'And this your honour, is conclusive proof that Prem Prakash Kaur renounced Sikhism and embraced Islam.'

'What is it?' demanded Falshaw.

'Your Lordship may open it and examine its contents.'

Falshaw opened the packet very gingerly, then flung back his hands as if he had received an electric shock. 'What kind of evidence is this?' he roared with his face as red as a tomato.

'This your honour, is the lady's pubic hair. She shaved it the day she married my client and presented it to him. Sikhs, as your honour must know, never cut their hair.'

'Take it away,' roared Falshaw, 'throw it in the garbage can. I'm not accepting this kind of trash.'

But for the partition of India in August 1947 the case might still be going on. Prem Prakash Kaur and all her property were in East Punjab, which came to India. The barber's son was left in Pakistan. Gurnam Singh migrated to East Punjab, became its Chief Minister, and resumed his liaison with Prem Prakash. After he lost his majority in the Punjab Assembly, he was appointed Indian High Commissioner to Australia. A week after presenting his credentials at Canberra, he returned home to take his mistress and his belongings to Australia. His plane crashed and there were no survivors.

The atmosphere in the Punjab had become so charged with hate that it only needed a spark to set it ablaze. The prolonged Hindu-Muslim riots in Calcutta led to massacres of Muslims in Bihar, followed by massacres of Hindus in Noakhali in East Bengal. Then Muslims of the North-West Frontier Province raided scattered Sikh and Hindu villages and slew as many as they could lay their hands on. Others fled their homes to safety in Lahore, Amritsar and East Punjab.

While the killings of Hindus and Sikhs were going on in the

North-West Frontier Province, I happened to go to Abbotabad to appear as defence counsel in a murder case involving two branches of a Hindu family. The case was finished in one day. The next morning, instead of driving down to Taxila to catch my train, I decided to walk the distance of about ten miles. It was balmy weather. The road was absolutely deserted. I saw no signs of life in the villages through which I passed. Men and women peered out of their doorways to see me stride along. It was eerie. A couple of miles short of Taxila a lorry-load of Sikh soldiers pulled up beside me. A young Captain spoke harshly to me, 'Sardarji are you out of your senses? They've killed every Sikh in these villages and you are out as if on an evening stroll. Get in.' I obeyed and was dropped off at Taxila station.

Except for the Station Master and a couple of ticket collectors the railway station at Taxila was also deserted. I saw the train I was to board come along and stop at the outer signal, I heard some shouting but could not make out what it was about. When the train pulled up on the platform, I got into a first-class compartment. I was the only passenger and bolted the door from inside. There was no sign of life at any of the stations through which the train passed. When I got off at Lahore, there was no one on the platform apart from Manzur Qadir who had come to fetch me. He told me that communal riots had broken out in Lahore. The next morning I learnt from the papers that the train by which I had travelled had been held up at the signal near Taxila station and all the Sikh passengers in it dragged out and murdered.

Some days later it was my turn to pick up Manzur Qadir. He had gone to do a case at Gujranwala. On his way back, when his train stopped at Badami Bagh it was attacked by a Muslim mob and its Sikh passengers hauled out and hacked to death. He had seen the massacre with his own eyes. He looked pale and was still unsteady on his legs.

The last time I left Lahore before being forced to quit was to defend three men charged with robbery and murder in the court of the Sessions Judge at Gujranwala. Two of the accused had been members of the I.N.A. and I was engaged by an organization set up to defend them. This was not a political crime but a case of homicide. The men had boarded the night train from Lahore to Rawalpindi and forced their way into a first-class coupé occupied by two young English army nurses. The girls put up resistance; one of them bit the man who tried to pull her down from the upper berth. The other fought back with her hands. The men threw her out of the fast-running train. When the train stopped at Gujranwala, the three robbers disappeared in the darkness. The surviving girl ran up the platform screaming hysterically. Railway police came on the scene and found the body of the other English girl lying along the track. The survivor was taken to Gujranwala hospital and treated for shock before she was taken back to England. The three accused were arrested the next day. They were Sikhs. After the train robbery they had woken up a barber at night and had him cut off their long hair and beards to escape detection.

The surviving English girl was flown back to India after some months, when the prosecution was ready to present its case. The girl was asked to identify her assailants at an identification parade. The police recorded that she had done so correctly and felt they had a water-tight case based on the testimony of the barber, the recovery of stolen goods from the accused, including the victim's handbag with a compact, her lipstick, comb and other items of a lady's make-up. When I arrived in the Sessions Court it was evident that the Sessions Judge, a Muslim, had made up his mind to hang the three men. I pinned my hopes on the honesty of the English girl. I did not bother to cross-examine the barber at any length, nor the police over the recoveries made from the accused: village barbers could be made to say whatever the police wanted them to say; and planting incriminating articles on innocent people was a common practice. I concentrated entirely on the English girl. She was still in a state of shock and broke down many times while narrating the incidents of the fateful train journey. As I stood up to cross-examine her, the judge said to me very curtly: 'Be brief! She has been through a lot. I will not allow you to harass her.'

I protested that I had to do my duty, or be allowed to withdraw from the case. He relented and allowed me to pro-ceed. I asked the girl whether she could tell the difference between one Sikh and another if they happened to be of roughly the same age. She admitted that she would find it very difficult. How then could she be sure that these were the three men who had robbed them, which one she had bitten, and which one had thrown her companion out of the train? She admitted that she could not be sure, yet these men had been arrested by the police and she had been asked to identify them. I asked if she knew that the accused, who had had themselves shaved, were forced by the police to regrow their beards before she was asked to identify them. No, she admitted, she was not aware of that.

The identification parade had been a very shoddy affair. Of the twelve men lined up before the English girl, only three were bearded Sikhs; she had pointed them out. She readily admitted that if all of them had been bearded and turbanned she would have found it impossible to spot the guilty. She also admitted that a police officer had offered to help her identify the accused, but that she had refused to accept his offer. I asked her to look at the three accused in handcuffs in the dock and to point out the one she had bitten, and the two who had thrown her companion out of the compartment. She refused to look at the accused men. The prosecution counsel and the Judge tried to shout me down. I stood my ground and insisted that my question be put on record before the Judge decided to rule it out. The question was recorded. The Judge had second thoughts about ruling it out and very gently asked the witness if she would care to answer it. The girl broke down crying, 'No, no, no. I don't want to look at these bloody villains. Please let me go!' At my insistence, her response was recorded and the girl helped out of the court by two British soldiers.

I made my defence speech to a very irate Judge. He looked as if he would have liked to hang me along with the three accused. I left for Lahore and, a few days later, for Kasauli. I learnt subsequently that the Sessions Judge had acquitted all the three accused for lack of convincing evidence. I had little

doubt in my mind that the three men I had got off scot free
were guilty of robbery and murder. This is the sort of thing that
nauseates me about the legal profession: it has very little to do
with justice.

Suddenly riots broke out in Lahore. They were sparked off
by the Sikh leader Master Tara Singh making a melodramatic
gesture outside the Punjab Legislative Assembly building.
Inside the Chamber, the Premier, Sir Khizr Hayat Tiwana, had
succumbed to pressure from the Muslim League and resigned.
It was now clear that Punjabi Muslims had also opted for
Pakistan. As soon as the session was over, Master Tara Singh
drew his kirpan out of its sheath and yelled *'Pakistan Murdabad'*
— Death to Pakistan. It was like hurling a lighted matchstick
in a room full of inflammable gas. Communal riots broke out all
over the province. Muslims had the upper hand in the killings.
They were in the majority, better organized and more
motivated than the Hindus or Sikhs. The Punjab police was
largely Muslim and shamelessly partisan. The only organized
group to offer resistance to Muslim gangs was the R.S.S., but all
it could do was explode a few bombs which killed perhaps one
or two people. Then it disappeared from the scene. The urban
Sikhs were a pathetic lot: they boasted of their martial prowess
while having none, and waved long kirpans that they had never
wielded before.

One day a Bihari working at a gas station from which I bought
petrol was knifed to death in broad daylight by two Muslim
boys aged eleven and twelve. Unsuspecting Sikhs riding
bicycles were toppled over by ropes stretched across roads and
suddenly raised from either side. And stabbed. Our nights were
disturbed by sudden outbursts of the cries of *'Allah-o-Akbar'*
from one side and *'Sat Sri Akal'* or *'Har Har Mahadev'* from the
other. The Muslims were more confident — they came close to
Hindu and Sikh localities and shouted *'Hoshiyaar! Shikar ka hai
intezaar!'* — Beware, we await our quarry.

Whatever little resistance Hindus and Sikhs put up against
Muslim goondas collapsed one hot afternoon in June 1947.
There were no sounds of gunfire or the yelling of slogans: only

black clouds of smoke billowing out of the city. The entirely Hindu locality of Shahalmi had been set on fire. Hindus and Sikhs began to leave Lahore, with whatever they could carry. A few days later, they were forced out without being allowed to carry anything. Their homes and belongings were taken over by their Muslim neighbours.

I did not know how long we would be able to stay on in Lahore. We had sent our two children to their maternal grandparents in Kasauli. My next-door neighbours on either side proclaimed their religious identities on their walls: a large cross on the one side to indicate they were Christians; on the other in big Urdu lettering *Parsee ka Makaan* — this is a Parsee home. Close by lived Justice Teja Singh. He had often exhorted me and other Sikhs to stick it out. One morning early in August when I drove to his house I found it padlocked. The chowkidar told me that his master had left for Delhi. It was my college friend of London days, C.H. Everett, then head of the C.I.D., who advised me to leave Lahore for a few days till the situation returned to normal. 'Leave your home and things in the care of some Muslim friend,' he advised. Manzur was at the time doing some case in Shimla. I rang him up and we arranged to meet at Dharampur on the Kalka-Shimla road near where the road to Kasauli branches off. The following night my wife, I and our Hindu cook were escorted to the railway station by a posse of Baluch policemen provided by Everett. We left our young Sikh servant, Dalip Singh, in charge of our house till the Qadirs moved in to look after it.

We arrived next morning at Kalka without any untoward incident. I had sent my car ahead to meet us there. We drove up to Dharampur. A few minutes later, Manzur arrived by taxi from Shimla. He told me that some Kashmiri Muslim labourers had been stabbed in Shimla and Muslims were pulling out of the Himachal hill resorts. I handed him the keys of our house. We embraced each other, and we promised to get back as soon as things were more settled.

We spent some days at Kasauli. By then the mass exodus of Hindus and Sikhs from Pakistan and Muslims from East Punjab had begun. There were gory tales of attacks on trains and road convoys in which thousands were massacred in cold blood. Sikhs, who had taken a terrible beating in West Punjab, were out seeking bloody revenge on innocent Muslims in East Punjab and mopping up one Muslim village after another. I decided to run the gauntlet and get to Delhi. I had to make up my mind about what to do. I left my wife and children at Kasauli and took a motor mechanic with me in the event of the car giving trouble. Some miles beyond Kalka I discovered that the gas stations along the road were closed. I returned to Kalka to fill up the tank and take a spare can of petrol. On the way I found our Lahore servant Dalip Singh walking along the road. He told me that Muslim mobs had come to our house in Lahore. The Qadirs and their servants had hidden him on the roof for several days and Manzur had removed my name-plate from the gate and put up his own in its place. However, word had leaked out that a Sikh was being given shelter and goondas wanted to search the house. Manzur was able to get the police in time to prevent them breaking in. That night he put Dalip Singh in the boot of his car and drove him to what was to become the new Indo-Pak border. He gave him money and instructed him to board a train going from Amritsar to Kalka. That is how he came to be there. Not having heard of Kasauli, the fellow had taken the road to Delhi hoping to catch a bus somewhere on the way.

I put Dalip Singh in the car, took enough petrol to get us to Delhi and proceeded on my way. There was not a soul on the road, no sign of life in any of the towns or villages along the Grand Trunk Road. It was only after I had passed Karnal, some sixty miles short of Delhi, that I saw a jeep coming towards me. I pulled up. So did the jeep, about a hundred yards from me. I took out my pistol and waited. After an agonizing five minutes of staring at the jeep, I noticed that its occupants were Sikhs. Two men stepped out on the road with rifles in their hands. I felt reassured and drove up to the jeep. I asked them if it was safe to proceed to Delhi. 'Quite safe,' they assured me. 'We have cleansed the villages along the road of all the swine.' They used the word *sooar* (pig) for Muslims. It churned my stomach.

This was no place to argue with them. I reached Delhi a few days before India was to be declared independent.

I had my father's home to go to. Hundreds of thousands of others, who like me had fled the area earmarked for Pakistan, had nowhere to go. Some were housed in refugee camps; others occupied old monuments, railway station platforms, verandahs outside shops and offices, or made their homes on pavements. The magnitude of the tragedy that had taken place was temporarily drowned in the euphoria of the Independence to come. It was like a person who feels no hurt when his arm or leg is suddenly cut off: the pain comes after some time.

On the night of 14 August, I joined the stream of humanity moving towards Parliament House. With me was my wife's cousin, Harji Malik. We managed to get to Parliament by 11 pm. The throng was immense, disciplined and full of enthusiasm. Periodically it burst into cries of *'Mahatma Gandhi ki Jai'* and *'Inquilab Zindabad'*. A minute before the midnight hour a hush of silence spread over the crowd. The voice of Sucheta Kripalani singing *Vande Mataram* came over the loudspeakers. It was followed by Pandit Nehru making his memorable speech: 'Long years ago we made a tryst with destiny . . . Now comes the time to redeem that pledge. . . . ' And so on. As the speech ended, the crowd burst into cheers and yelled slogans. We embraced strangers and congratulated each other for having gained our freedom. We did not get home till after 2 am.

I was up early in order to get to the Red Fort to see the Union Jack come down and the Indian tricolour go up. Once again the whole route was crowded with people going on foot. Lord and Lady Mountbatten drove up in their six-horsed Viceregal carriage. Many British officers were picked up and carried by the crowd on their shoulders. Almost overnight the much hated English had become the Indian's most loved foreigners.

I stood about fifty yards away from the ramparts of the Red Fort and heard the buglers sound the last post as Lord Mountbatten lowered the Union Jack. The band played the National Anthem as Pandit Nehru hoisted the Indian tricolour and the cannon roared to salute the new President of the Republic. I heard all, but saw very little because tears of joy blurred my vision. And my heart was full of pride. That was all very well, but what was I to do now to make my living? We could not go back to Lahore in the aftermath of the hatred accompanying Independence and Partition.

6 With Menon in London, with Malik in Canada

THE MOST IMPORTANT thing that happened to me with the partition of India was that I was able to get out of the legal profession. I swore never to go back to it. Some temptations to continue were thrown my way. Mr Jinnah sent word to my father that he should persuade me to stay on in Lahore. The indication was clear; he wanted to consider me as a Judge of the High Court. Evidently he had neither wished nor foreseen that in the Pakistan he had brought into being there would be no place for non-Muslims. A similar assurance was given to me by my friend Justice Khosla who had become the second in seniority at the Punjab High Court reconstituted in Shimla. I was no worse than any of the Hindu or Sikh lawyers who had come over and he would see my name accepted. But such was my revulsion against everything about the law that I refused to succumb to these temptations.

What was I to do? There were lots of jobs going. India had opened many embassies and people were needed to man them. Asghari Qadir's brother, Azim Husain, who had opted to stay on in India, was then Deputy Secretary in the Ministry of Information and Broadcasting under the Deputy Prime Minister, Sardar Vallabhbhai Patel. He said he could fix me up as Information Officer in the Public Relations Department of India House in London. It was not much of a job except that it would get me back to England. I was to have a short briefing from Sardar Patel; the appointment would then have to be ratified by the Union Public Service Commission.

My briefing was quite an event. I was asked to present myself at Sardar Patel's house (later the residence of the Italian Ambassador on Motilal Nehru Marg). When I got there I was shown into the private secretary's room beside the entrance and told that I would have to wait some time as the Minister was expecting an important visitor.

A few minutes later an enormous Rolls Royce flying the flag of the Maharaja of Indore pulled up. An officer clad in a naval white uniform opened the door of the car to let out His Highness. They were received by the Minister's secretary and escorted to the drawing room. From where I sat, I could see what was going on. Sardar Patel walked in with the usual scowl on his face and gestured to the Maharaja who had stood up to sit down. He did not shake hands with his visitor. The Maharaja began to talk rapidly in his Oxbridge English. Sardar Patel kept his gaze fixed on his own chappals. It had been rumoured that the Maharaja had been persuading other princes to join the Nawab of Bhopal and resist the Indian Government's plan to take over their states and pension them off with privy purses. As Minister of Home Affairs, Sardar Patel was entrusted with the task of getting them to sign Instruments of Accession. I could not hear what the Maharaja of Indore was saying, but it was evident that he was denying everything he had been accused of doing surreptitiously. Sardar Patel let him run out of breath without once looking up or interrupting him. When the Maharaja finished, Patel simply stood up and said in a voice loud and clear enough to reach my ears, 'You are a damned liar!' And walked away. A very crestfallen Maharaja, followed by his handsome A.D.C., hurriedly made it to the Rolls Royce. Sardar Patel's secretary came to tell me that the Minister was too upset to see me. I was to proceed to London and get my briefing from Sudhir Ghosh, the Public Relations Officer who would be my immediate boss.

A few days later I took a KLM flight to London. In those days air travel was a leisurely affair. We had berths to sleep on and were awakened with hot cups of tea or coffee an hour before we landed at Cairo. We were driven to a small rest-house and given rooms to relax in, take a shower and have breakfast. We were given another hour to stroll in the garden before reboarding the aircraft for London.

I was to stay with Arthur and Sheila Lall in their three-storeyed apartment in Knightsbridge till my family arrived and we found a place of our own. The arrangement suited me admirably. After a brisk walk across Hyde Park I could take a bus or the underground to India House in Aldwych. I did not have to worry about house-keeping as the Lalls had brought their cook (they called him *maalee* — gardener). The Lalls were well-stocked with duty-free liquor.

Arthur was very taken up with Krishna Menon. He assured me that Krishna Menon was the finest brain he had ever met and compared favourably with Stalin (who was not known to have a particularly fine brain). I had briefly met Krishna Menon in my college days and had not detected any signs of genius in him. He was a sour-tempered barrister without briefs and spent his energies building up his India League and paying court to Pandit Nehru whenever he was in England. His appointment as High Commissioner was badly received in India and the Indian community in England as gross favouritism. After hearing Arthur, I thought I had perhaps been wrong in my estimate of Menon, or that he had matured into a better man.

The next morning I reported for work at India House. I introduced myself to Sudhir Ghosh. He didn't seem very pleased to see me. Beneath the glass slab of his working table were a number of photographs and originals of letters exchanged between Gandhi and Sir Stafford Cripps, Gandhi and Prime Minister Attlee, all praising Sudhir Ghosh. It was also evident that Sudhir was having trouble with Krishna Menon and was not on good terms with Indian journalists. He showed me to the tiny cubicle I was to occupy and introduced me to an English girl, Pamela Cullen, who was to be my assistant. He did not tell me what I was to do. 'You can ask Menon when you meet him,' he said. He studiously avoided calling him High Commissioner or even adding Mister to his name.

I had no idea what Public Relations meant nor what I was to do to promote them. Not having been briefed or charged with a specific task I decided that perhaps the best I could do was produce booklets on India — its people, resources, flora, fauna, etc. Politics was far from my mind. Despite having been forced out of Lahore, I remained emotionally involved with Pakistan. On the bone of contention, Kashmir, over which the two countries had gone to war, I felt that Pakistan had a stronger case than India.

For the first four days of my arrival in London, I reported for work at India House every morning. I signed the Visitors' Book and reminded Sudhir Ghosh to introduce me to the High Commissioner. He didn't think it was urgent. I asked Lall. He said it was not for him but Sudhir to do so. However, he told Menon that I had been wanting to call on him. On the fifth day, Sudhir Ghosh took me up to Menon's room. I had a broad grin on my face when I greeted Krishna Menon and extended my right hand. He brushed it aside with his claw-like fingers. Instead of a smile of welcome he had an angry frown on his face. I cheerfully reminded him that I had once travelled with him and Rajni Patel to Paris. He ignored my self-introduction and barked, 'Sardar, haven't they taught you any manners in India? You have been here four days and haven't had the courtesy to call on me. I am the High Commissioner, you know!' My smile froze. I protested I had done my best — signed the Visitors' Book, and asked both Sudhir and Arthur Lall to get me an appointment. Sudhir interrupted to say that it was his fault. 'I'll send for you later,' said Menon, dismissing me. 'I want to speak to Mr Ghosh.'

I returned to my cubicle very shaken up. No one had spoken to me the way Menon had done and without any reason whatsoever. I was determined not to put up with it. I swore to myself that the next time Menon said anything harshly to me, I would hit back, put in my letter of resignation and tell him to stuff it up his dirty bottom. I was out of sorts all afternoon. Instead of doing any work, I took a long stroll along the Thames embankment till my temper came down a little. In the evening there was a tea party in the main reception room. I went to it, took a cup of tea and sat down in a corner. Menon breezed in. I pretended not to have seen him. He came up to me and put his arm round my shoulders: 'Sorry for ticking you off this morning,' he said. 'I hope you had the sense to realize it was not meant for you.' I stood up somewhat flabbergasted at the change of tone. 'I was a little taken aback,' I replied.

'If you don't have that much common sense, you'll never do as an information officer,' he assured me. He patted me on my back and went to shake other hands. I was utterly deflated. The fellow obviously meant to be friendly; it was Sudhir Ghosh he was gunning for. Menon had a convoluted mind.

It did not take me long to get a hang of India House politics. Krishna Menon had his coterie of faithfuls. On top of the list was Arthur Lall, his Trade Commissioner. He had scant respect for the Deputy High Commissioner, R.S. Mani, also of the I.C.S. and his number two man. Mani was a flabby man with a flabbier Belgian wife. He did his best to ingratiate himself with Menon and suffered being treated like a doormat. He remained a doormat. Menon was also allergic towards men in uniform and treated his military, naval and air attaches with unconcealed contempt. His *bete noire* was Sudhir Ghosh who was determined to run the Public Relations Department as an independent establishment of his own. He regarded himself as Gandhi's personal envoy to well-meaning Britons who had sided with the freedom movement. Most of them were Quakers. He entrusted them with official missions without consulting Menon. 'Let Menon do his job and let him leave me alone to do mine,' he often told me as he gloated over the photographs and letters on his table. 'I have spent many years with Gandhiji. I have no hatred in my heart against anyone,' he assured me over and over again. Then he resumed his tirade against Menon. Menon's closest favourites, besides Arthur Lall, were junior members of his staff. Some, like his personal Secretary, Captain Srinivasan of the Indian Navy, he savaged till they proved their loyalties to him. Menon had an eye for good-looking women. He treated the husbands of good-looking women as friends. If he sensed tension between the couple, he became specially considerate towards them: Menon had great understanding for misunderstood wives. Sheila Lall and my wife (after the family joined me) fell in that category. Arthur and I became his number one and number two favourites. Topping us was young Kamla Jaspal who had joined his clerical pool. She was a Sikh, light-skinned with curly black hair and a charming squint in one eye. She came to office dressed as if she were going to a cocktail party. She wore bright coloured chiffon saris, with blouses which left most of her middle, including her belly button, exposed. She wore bracelets of silver, gold and glass which covered most of her forearms and jingle-jangled whenever she brushed her untidy locks from across her face, which was often. Being scantily clad, she often caught colds and had a running nose. She dropped the names of English poets, and she danced a few steps of Bharat Natyam badly; she also wrote bad prose and poetry. She was loud and aggressive in asserting herself. But she worshipped Krishna Menon as if he were an incarnation of Lord Vishnu. Like a good Hindu wife she never referred to him by his name or as High Commissioner but as H.E. — His Excellency. To Krishna Menon, who had been away from India for several decades, Kamla Jaspal represented modern Indian womanhood. He responded to her adoration with flowers and favours, including the use of his Rolls Royce to take her home. He was tiring of his ageing English mistress, Bridgette, who looked after the India League, and was on the look out for a replacement. For a while Kamla courted Bridgette and soon discovered that she could oust her. In India House everyone knew that in order to get on with Krishna Menon one had to get on with Kamla Jaspal. During my first posting in London I cultivated both Bridgette and Kamla.

Menon had reason to trust me more than Sudhir Ghosh and decided to use me as an instrument to get rid of him. He did not have to wait long for the opportunity to do so.

I first discovered how bad things were when I chanced to see a confidential letter Menon had written to Pandit Nehru. He described Ghosh as a 'Patelite'. Evidently, Nehru's relations with his Deputy Prime Minister (Sardar Patel) were strained. He also argued that foreign publicity should be under the Foreign Minister (Nehru) and not under the Home and Information Minister (Patel). Before Panditji could respond to his letter the incident of the missing chit occurred which proved Sudhir Ghosh's undoing.

One morning Menon sent a note to Sudhir Ghosh on a scrap of paper in his own hand, asking him to send me up to see him as soon as I reached the office. Sudhir took no notice of it till a couple of hours later, when Kamla Jaspal came down to check whether or not I had arrived. I went to Ghosh's office to find out what it was about. 'Oh yes, Menon wants to see you without me,' he said reading the chit. He crumpled it up and threw it into his waste-paper basket. When I went to see Menon he asked me why it had taken me two hours to come up. I told him I knew nothing about it till Kamla told me and I had gone to Sudhir's room. Sudhir was summoned. He blankly denied having received any message from him. I left them going for each other, returned to Ghosh's room and pulled out the crumpled chit from his waste-paper basket. Through Kamla Jaspal I had the chit handed over to Menon. I do not know how the Gandhian Sudhir got out of the blatant lie he had told. The next day he left for India; Menon followed him a few days later.

While they were away, I received telegraphic orders transferring me to Canada. P.L. Bhandari, whom I had known as a junior reporter with *The Civil and Military Gazette* of Lahore and who regarded himself as an expert in public relations, was named Sudhir's successor.

A few days later Menon and Ghosh returned to London. Ghosh made only one appearance in India House to take away his pictures and testimonials from his table. His parting kick was to host a large luncheon party at the Savoy Hotel for his English friends. He did not bother to invite me or any other colleagues. In that one party he blew up the entire year's entertainment allowance of the Public Relations Department.

I was still in London when Mahatma Gandhi was assassinated in Delhi on 30 January 1948. I had taken leave to pack up my belongings to proceed to Canada. We were invited to lunch by Sir Malcolm Darling, the retired commissioner of Income Tax who lived in a basement flat near Victoria station. As we came out into the cold, windy, sunny day after lunch I noted scribbled in hand on a placard by a newspaper stall the message: 'Gandhi assassinated'. I did not believe it could be our Bapu. Who would kill a saintly man who had harmed no one? I asked the stall holder. He had tears in his eyes as he handed me a copy of *The Evening Standard*. 'Yes mite, some bloody villain's got 'im,' he said. Tears also welled up in my eyes; I was only able to read the headlines. Instead of going to the shipping office to confirm our passage we made our way to India House to be with our own people. Oil lamps had been lit at the base of Gandhi's portrait. The smell of aromatic incense pervaded the place. Men and women sat on the floor chanting Gandhi's favourite hymns: *Vaishnav jan to tainey kaheeye jo peed paraie jaaney ray* — Know him only as a man of God who feels the suffering of others. And *Ram Dhun: Ishwar Allah teyrey naam, sab ko sammati day Bhagwan* — Ishwar and Allah are but names of the same God, may his blessings be on all of us. We sat there for an hour. In my pocket were theatre tickets I had bought a month earlier to see Mae West in *Diamond Lil*. I was torn with conflict in my mind. Was it right to see the world's greatest sex symbol while Bapu lay dead in Delhi? Ultimately, we decided to go to the theatre. I did not have any shame or sense of guilt when I saw the bosomy woman come out with her punch line, 'Come up and see me sometime.' I would have happily responded to her invitation. From the brochure I discovered Mae West was the same age as my mother.

By the time my order of transfer to Canada came my son had been admitted to Sherrard's Park School and we had paid the term's fees. He was at last beginning to pick up some English. Among the earliest words in his vocabulary was the English word for *akhbaar*. 'It's called a piper,' he gravely informed me. 'Not piper but paper,' I corrected him, 'piper is cockney.' He was adamant. 'But I heard an English boy outside the railway station shouting "Piper! Piper!"' On another occasion when he accompanied me on an evening stroll through Brocket Park, he asked me who lived in the large mansion, 'That's the home of Lord Brocket,' I told him. He was puzzled. 'Is he one of their gurus?' he asked. 'No, what makes you think he's an English guru?'

'They call their guru Lord. At school, they teach us about Lord Jesus,' he replied.

Lord Brocket was a brewer.

I was not altogether unhappy with the transfer. But my wife had strong reservations about it. I would have to work under H.S. Malik who was her uncle twice over, being her father's younger brother and married to her mother's younger sister. The H.S. Maliks were snobs. He was very conscious of being in the I.C.S. and having served as Prime Minister of Patiala. His wife was equally status-conscious and was known in the family as 'the Duchess'. For the Maliks, culture meant being well-dressed, knowing European table manners and having a familiarity with exotic drinks like Old Fashioned, Mint Julep and Manhattan. In the evenings when they met for their pre-dinner drinks they would mention the names of relations and friends and take turns to tear them apart. They made up for slandering them by praising each other. They were a very close-knit, happy family. Both Malik and his 'Duchess' had often ticked off my wife for being sloppily clad. They regarded me as an uncouth son of a parvenu building contractor. The one time I had stayed with them in Shimla when he was Prime Minister of Patiala I had to slink out from the back of their house to avoid sentries posted in front saluting me. The atmosphere in the family was so choked with formality that I often wanted to fart to clear the air.

We took the *Queen Elizabeth* to New York. What luxury! I spent most of the day playing squash. I let the pro relax and took on the passengers — sometimes a dozen a day. I should have spent my time more profitably reading about Canada. All I knew about the country was based on my reading of Hiawatha. I expected to meet a lot of Red Indians with eagles' feathers on their heads. I knew Ottawa was the capital and that there were some Sikhs settled in the west coast. That was the sum total of my information on the country. I was not even aware of the existence of its biggest city, Montreal.

We spent a day in New York and took the night train to Ottawa. In New York we were booked at the Waldorf Astoria.

The few hours we spent in the hotel (four of the family and two servants) blew up my month's salary.

Harji Malik was at the station to receive us. We had been booked in the Chateau Laurier, the most expensive hotel in the city. I discovered that a week's stay in the hotel would cost me another two months' salary. No one was unduly concerned with my plight. I was known to have a rich father.

We were to dine with the Maliks. We got a very cool reception. He was as reluctant to have me as his number two as my wife was to have her husband at her uncle's beck and call. The 'Duchess' was as condescending as ever. The only two who seemed pleased at the turn of events were Harji and myself. She, because she had begun to like me; I because it was a new venture. I knew Malik was more interested in golf (he was a very good player) and mixing with titled nobility than the drudgery of office routine. I expected to run the mission we had newly opened.

The first crisis came a few days after our arrival. We had a Memorial meeting for Gandhiji in the Chateau Laurier. In the absence of a band or recorded music, I played the National Anthem on the piano. Malik made a speech of welcome quoting, as he usually did, Tagore's 'Where the mind is without fear'. Prime Minister Mackenzie King, who was no great orator, replied. Two memorable tributes were paid to Bapu: one by the British High Commissioner, Sir Alexander Clutterbuck, and the other by Leonard Brockington, Canada's leading jurist. More moving orations I have yet to hear.

The Indian High Commission was across the road from the hotel. One morning when it was snowing heavily I stood by the traffic signal awaiting the lights to change so that I could cross over. There was snow over my turban and beard. I must have looked quite a sight. A tall American, evidently a visitor, came and stood by me. He looked me up and down before speaking to me. 'Do you speak English?' he asked me. I nodded. He continued: 'Sir, by your deportment and demeanour, you appear to be a foreigner.'

I admitted that I was. 'May I ask where you are from?'

'I am Indian,' I replied.

He appeared disappointed. 'Are you from a reservation?' he asked. At the time, I did not know what a reservation was. 'No,' I replied, 'I am staying in the Chateau Laurier.'

Another amusing encounter took place a few days later after we had found lodgings of our own. This was with a Sikh gentleman. I saw him standing by the traffic lights across the road. He looked resplendent in his gold brocade turban tied in the style that the Bedi descendants of Guru Nanak have made their own. He wore a black sherwani, white chooridars, and gold embroidered Punjabi slippers. In the depth of winter's snow he looked splendidly out of place. I went across and greeted him, *'Sat Sri Akal.'* He graciously responded and asked me what I was doing in Ottawa. I told him. I asked him what had brought him there and if he did not feel cold in the dress he wore. He told me he was on business and would return in a few days to his wife and children whom he missed very much. As for his outfit, he told me that when abroad Indians should wear their national costumes, 'or how would foreigners get to know our distinct culture and style of living?' I was right in guessing he was a Bedi. I invited him over to dinner. In the evening I fetched him from his hotel. He was in the same attire.

He was a little put out seeing my wife join me at drinks. 'It is not in our tradition for women to drink,' he told her. He learnt that we also went out dancing. He delivered another sermon against adopting European ways. He said he was not enamoured of the West and was eager to return home to his family.

Some months later, I happened to be in Toronto to meet the editors of local papers. I entertained them at a small, select restaurant and returned to my hotel late at night, somewhat high on drink. Nearly a dozen lifts stood on the ground floor with pretty girls in page boys' uniforms to operate them. One of them gave me a friendly smile and greeted me with *'Sat Sri Akal'*. I promptly entered her elevator. As the doors closed I asked her, 'Have you been to my country?' She gave me a saucy look and replied, 'No, but I've known your countrymen. Which floor?' I looked at the number on my room key and replied, 'Eleven.' 'What a coincidence,' she remarked, 'my friend was also on floor eleven. Such a handsome gentleman! His turban was much nicer than yours. All gold and silver. He invited me to spend the weekend with him at Muskoka. We had a wonderful time!' She sighed happily recalling the weekend. Who else could it have been but Mr Bedi who was so eager to get back to his wife and children? I turned the episode into a short story.

Nothing in Canada looked anything like the vision Hiawatha had created in my mind. I never saw any high-cheeked, swarthy men wearing feathers as their headgear. The only one resembling a Red Indian Brave was a white man outside a travel agency advertising tours to Canadian cities. The closest I came to meeting a Red Indian was in Montreal. Walking out of Hotel Ritz Carlton, I saw a brown, high-cheeked man coming down the road on the other side. He smiled at me. I crossed the road to meet him. 'I could see you are an Indian,' I said as we shook hands. He nodded. 'Where are you from?' I asked him. 'I'm from Madras,' he replied.

If Indians like me knew little about Canada, most Canadians knew even less about India. At that time, the situation in Hyderabad was making the news. One morning I received a call from a Canadian arms dealer. Since the High Commissioner was away playing golf in Havana, I was holding the fort for him. 'Is that the new Indian High Commission?' asked the voice at the other end of the line. 'It is,' I replied, 'what can I do for you?'

'It's like this,' he explained. 'In the past whenever we received orders for arms from any of the princely states of India, we informed the British representative in Ottawa before complying with them. We will be extending the same courtesy to you. We have an order for the immediate supply of a hundred thousand 303 rifles from the Nizam of Hyderabad. Payment has already been made in cash. We take it you have no objection to our doing so.'

I sent a telegram informing my government and rang up my boss to return immediately to Ottawa. He was upset with me for interrupting his game and said there was no urgency about the deal. The next day Indian troops marched into Hyderabad.

India got a very bad press. Canadian papers took their Indian news from the wire services or American correspondents posted in Delhi. I persuaded the High Commissioner to hold a press conference to give the Canadian media our point of view.

Over two dozen press and radio men and women responded. The High Commissioner gave a short backgrounder on independent India's policy of integrating the princely states in the new democratic set up. Hyderabad, he said, was an island in Indian territory and could not on any account be allowed to declare itself an independent kingdom. Any questions?

'Where is Hyderabad?' asked one.

I spread a map of India on a board, and ran my index finger round its borders. 'But your High Commissioner has been saying it is an island,' remarked a bright young lady reporter. We decided it wasn't worth trying to brief them and adjourned to Scotch and canapes. There was hardly anything about the High Commissioner's press conference in the next morning's papers. They had more important items of news. Barbara Ann Scott was returning home to Ottawa after winning the world ice-skating title. Her pictures from infancy to being crowned Queen of the Skating Rink hogged the news.

The year in Canada proved to be a turning point in my career. I cultivated a lot of Canadian writers and poets. After reading their works, I invited them over to my home. Amongst them were the poets Irene Page and Abe Klein, the editors of the *Canadian Forum* and *Saturday Night*. My stories were published in these journals. A story I wrote in Montreal of my school days in Delhi was published by *Harpers* of New York. Since my relations with the Maliks had turned cooler, I toyed with the idea of quitting service and taking to writing as a full-time career. 'Nothing venture, nothing gain,' I kept reminding myself. I was in my mid-thirties; if I did not take the plunge now, I might never take it.

Canada not only gave me visions of becoming a writer, but also quickened my interest in nature. When I reached Ottawa it was mid-winter and everything was covered under a mantle of snow. Even parts of the swift-running Ottawa river were frozen hard, with people skating over it. By March the first signs of thaw began to appear. A three-feet wide swathe running from the Parliament House building to the main roads was ablaze with tulips. I discovered that a hot-water pipe ran under it. As the snow melted, tulips sprouted all over the garden. I had spent many weekends skiing at the Gatineau Hills and marvelling at the bare trees with cylindrical tubes of ice covering their branches, tinkling like chandeliers when gusts of wind blew over. They were now covered with tiny leaf. I accompanied the High Commissioner and his family to the West Coast. At Vancouver it rained three days and three nights non-stop. On the fourth day I took a stroll in Stanley Park. The wet paths were strewn with snakes. It was at Victoria, where we went by boat the next day, that I saw nature at its gorgeous best. Empress Park alongside the hotel was ablaze with flowers. Peacocks and quails scampered along dew-washed emerald-green lawns glittering in the sunlight. I walked across the park to the edge of a cliff overlooking a deserted beach. The snow-covered peaks of mountains on the mainland were reflected in the deep blue waters of the ocean. I stood transfixed by the scene around me. As if to complete the mystic experience, I saw a young couple come to the beach, look around to make sure there was no one watching and divest themselves of their clothes. They frolicked about on the sand, ran into the sea, found it too cold and came out to warm themselves in the sun. They embraced and started to make love. I watched them taking turns being on top, quicken their pace and collapse in a blissful heap. It was a perfect end to a perfect morning.

Our return journey was made by train. We left Vancouver in the morning, passed through the Rockies, through dense pine and fir forests, past sparkling streams and lakes with moose and elk grazing by their banks. We broke journey at Banff and Lake Louise, then at Calgary, Kingston and Alberta. That summer I took my family to Algonquin Park. We spent our time rowing over the lake chasing loons and fishing for perch. I also took the family to see the Niagara Falls. While I gaped, awestruck at the massive cascade of water, my wife was not so impressed. 'What's so great about it?' she asked. 'We have the same kind at Okhla.' I made another trip to Toronto and spent the days driving round the Thousand Islands and Muskoka. Never have I seen a country as beautiful as Canada.

In the summer Lord and Lady Mountbatten came to inaugurate the Canadian Trade Fair in Toronto. He had sent word that their Lordships would like to have the staff of the Indian High Commission to provide the escort. We were flattered and only discovered the reason at the function. There was Lord Louis Mountbatten in a sharkskin silver-white naval uniform ablaze with medals and gold epaulettes, with his regal-looking lady beside him. And then behind him stood Sikhs in turbans and beards, black sherwanis and white chooridars. It was a perfect tableau representing the British Empire at the height of its glory. If the audience of thousands had any doubts about its authenticity, Lord Louis set them at rest in his speech in which he repeated many times, 'My cousin the queen; my nephew Prince so-and-so.' And of course the great affection he had received from the Prime Minister and the peoples of India as the last Viceroy and Governor-General of the country.

Returning to Ottawa was somewhat of an anti-climax. Although I still enjoyed playing tennis for the Rideau Club, walking along the Ottawa river, watching islands of logs floating downstream, entertaining and being entertained by Canadian friends, our relations with the Maliks had got so bad that we were barely on speaking terms. Fortunately for us, events in India helped release us of each other. The foreign publicity department was taken over by the Foreign Ministry. Menon was now able to have his way. He asked for my transfer back to London to replace P.L. Bhandari, whom he could not stand. I got my orders some time in October when the maple trees were burning a fiery red. I decided to leave my family in Ottawa till my son, Rahul, finished his term at Rockcliffe Public School. Once more, I took the *Queen Elizabeth* and spent my days on the ship playing squash. Malik was on the same boat; we had to share the same table. His parting gift was to involve me in a game of poker of which I knew nothing. At the end of the game he informed me that I owed a hundred pounds.

Menon was glad to have me back. I was a mere Information Officer. Within a few days of my taking over from Bhandari, he had me promoted to Press Attache and P.R.O. with the rank of First Secretary. He had also managed to get Kamala Jaspal's sister's husband, Jamal Kidwai, to be my number two. Before leaving Canada I had ordered crates of duty-free Scotch to be forwarded to me along with my new Pontiac. Both proved valuable assets in post-War England.

Once again I moved into the Lalls' flat behind Harrod's in Knightsbridge. This time they had an attractive English girl, Cedra Osborne, living in as a housekeeper. She did no housekeeping but was good company when drinks were served. Relations between Arthur and Sheila were nearing breaking point. Arthur, who continued having liaisons with other women, could not stomach his wife responding to anyone. Frequent visitors to the Lalls' apartment included three married men eligible for extra-marital affairs. There was the tall, handsome B.K. Nehru, a cousin of the Prime Minister and visiting London on some important diplomatic assignment; the dapperly-dressed Ashok Chanda, who had taken over as Deputy High Commissioner in India House; and Biju Patnaik (later Union Cabinet Minister and Chief Minister of Orissa), a strapping six-footer who flew his own plane from India to London. When my family joined me we spent a few weeks in an upper-floor apartment rented from the Lalls. Many dramatic scenes took place there. Drawn into our circle was their neighbour Elsa Woodman, wife of the naval attaché in the American embassy. She was a generous hostess and game when her husband was away.

The first of these scenes took place when Arthur Lall was away in India. Biju Patnaik, who was a frequent visitor, had sensed the tension that prevailed between Arthur and Sheila, and between my wife and me. One evening when I was late in office, he casually offered to fly either Sheila or my wife for a weekend in Paris. My wife was in no position to accept his offer; Sheila did so readily. She came back radiantly happy. Sheila never believed in keeping secrets. A few days later, Arthur returned from India. We went to fetch him from the airport. On the way back Sheila told him of her weekend with Biju. He was inconsolable, and drank himself silly that evening. Well after midnight Sheila came up and knocked at our door. In a matter-of-fact, flat voice, she asked, 'K. Singh, do you by any chance have a revolver? Arthur wants to blow his brains out.' She sounded as placid as if she was asking for a sleeping pill.

Arthur continued to nag her day and night till Sheila was flattened out with exhaustion. Just at that time Som Nath Maira, who had been my student at Law College, Lahore and was then studying in Oxford, dropped in. He was a tall, handsome fellow with ingratiating manners. We were having tea. The atmosphere was funereal. He tried to cheer us up. 'What's the matter?' he asked. 'Everyone's looking very *gussa gussa*.' He went across to Sheila, touched her under her chin and pleaded, 'Sheilaji, please smile!' The gesture triggered off one of Arthur's mad rages. He sprang on Maira like an angry tiger, *Haramzada* (bastard)! *Bhainchode* (sister-fucker)! How dare you take liberties with my wife!' Though short, Arthur was powerfully built. But Som Maira was almost a foot taller, twenty years younger and much stronger. At first he thought Arthur meant to indulge in a friendly wrestling bout. As soon as he sensed that Arthur meant to beat him up, he turned the tables and pinned Arthur down on the floor. We watched them fight it out without trying to separate them. Sheila kept murmuring in her gentle voice, 'Arthur, behave yourself!' Arthur realized he couldn't get the better of Som and left the room in a huff, abusing him and warning him never again to cross his threshold.

For the first few weeks after my return to London I was

given a room on the first floor bearing a copper name-plate, 'Countess Mountbatten of Burma'. Next to Nehru, it was the Mountbattens that Menon relied on to keep him where he was. He had apparently spoken to Lady Edwina about the desirability of her taking an interest in Indian affairs. A room was set apart for her whenever she wanted to use it. She did not enter it even once. Nevertheless, I was warned that I would have to clear out if necessary on the shortest notice. For some days it was quite amusing: I would hear a gentle knock on the door and, as I shouted, 'Come in,' the door would quietly be opened by someone hoping to see the regal ex-Vicereine enthroned on her chair. Instead they saw a Sikh grinning from ear to ear. 'You bugger! What the fucking hell are you doing in Lady Mountbatten's room?' my friends would explode.

Lady Edwina never entered the room allotted to her but Lord Louis paid an unscheduled visit. He had accepted an invitation to a reception at India House. His secretary had given him the wrong time and he had arrived half an hour before he was expected. Lord Mountbatten was not accustomed to being the first to come to any party; he much preferred to make his appearance after the other guests had arrived. He was thus out of sorts on this occasion. I asked him to wait a few minutes in the room reserved for his wife and had the great Lord all to myself for half an hour. He was not eager to waste his precious time talking to a nondescript minion of the government. I did my best to keep the coversation going by asking him about his days in India. 'On afterthought, don't you think the partition of India was a mistake?' I asked him. 'Thousands upon thousands of innocent lives were lost because of the hasty way it was brought about.' Lord Mountbatten knew what I was driving at and replied, 'I don't care what people say about me today; I will be judged at the bar of history.'

There were lighter moments in my life in India House. One was when Her Highness the Rani of Mandi died of cancer. She was a great beauty of her times and had been living in London after separating from her husband. The evening papers announcing her death carried photographs of her in younger days. The next morning when I was in my office my Secretary told me that an English gentleman wished to see me on urgent business. I asked him to be shown in. He was a tall man in a black top hat, black coat and striped trousers. He had a parcel in his hand. He introduced himself: 'I am Mr Kenyon of Messrs Kenyon and Kenyon Undertakers. No doubt you have heard of us!' I had often passed by their funeral parlours in different parts of the city and replied that I was aware of the firm.

'No doubt you heard of H.H. the Rani of Mandi?' he asked. I replied that I had read of it in the evening papers.

'Very sad, wasn't it?' he sighed.

'Very sad, indeed,' I replied. 'She was a great beauty.'

'Sir,' he continued, 'Her Highness left a will asking for her body to be draped in her favourite saree for her cremation.' He undid the parcel and unfolded a gorgeous orange-coloured sari with a broad gold border. 'We have a lot of experience dressing gentlemen and ladies who have passed on but we've never handled an Indian lady. I wanted to know how a saree is draped round the body. So I thought I'd personally come to your embassy to get the know-how.'

I had a God-sent opportunity to see a naked Maharani even though dead — but I threw away the golden chance because of my compulsive desire to say something witty. 'I am sorry Mr Kenyon,' I replied, 'I have some experience of taking sarees off but have never tied one on any woman.'

Mr Kenyon left hurriedly with his parcel and went up to see Krishna Menon. He complained to him of the light way I had treated his request. After he had been briefed by Kamla Jaspal, Menon sent for me. 'Sardar, will nothing cure you of your habit of appearing clever?' he asked. Afterwards, he told everyone he met about my conversation with the undertaker.

Then there was Pandit Nehru's first visit to England as Prime

Minister to attend the Commonwealth Prime Minister's Conference. We had decided to bring out a weekly tabloid, *India News*, to mark the occasion. Jamal Kidwai and I had been to the press many times to finalize the layout, select type faces and provide the news we were to carry in our first issue. The front page was to be devoted entirely to Panditji's visit and the importance of the Commonwealth Conference. We sent material for the first page a couple of days ahead of his arrival to the printers. The banner headline read 'Pandit Nehru in London'. When the proofs came for correction the letter P had been substituted by B — 'Bandit Nehru in London'. Was this some kind of joke? I rang up the manager of the press and ticked him off roundly. He was profuse in his apologies. His typesetter had never heard of the word Pandit and thought we meant Bandit. The second set of proofs had the word right. The evening before the great man's arrival another setter was on the job and likewise ignorant of the existence of the word 'pandit'. Once again 'pandit' was changed to 'bandit'. We had to scrap the whole issue and sent a member of the staff to see that the word was printed right.

Senior members of the staff were ordered to be present at Heathrow airport to receive the Prime Minister. It was a cold winter night when the plane touched down. 'What are all of you doing here at this unearthly hour?' he demanded, obviously expecting us to be present and pleased to note that we were discharging our duties. Menon asked me to introduce myself to the P.M. and ask him if he desired me to do anything. I did so only to be snubbed. 'What would I want of you at this hour? Go home and get some sleep.'

The next morning when I reached the office I saw a note from Menon lying on my table asking me to see him immediately. I took a quick glance at the headlines of the papers to see if anything had gone wrong. *The Daily Herald* carried a large photograph of Nehru with Lady Mountbatten in her négligé opening the door for him. The caption read 'Lady Mountbatten's Midnight Visitor'. It also informed its readers that Lord Mountbatten was not in London. Our P.M.'s liaison with Lady Edwina had assumed scandalous proportions. *The*

Herald's photographer had taken the chance of catching them, if not in *flagrante delicto*, at least in preparation for it. He had got his scoop. When I went up to see Menon he barked at me, 'Have you seen *The Herald?* The Prime Minister is furious with you.'

'I had nothing to do with it,' I pleaded. 'How was I to know that instead of going to his hotel Panditji would go to the Mountbatten's home?'

'Anyway, he is very angry. You better keep out of his way for a day or two.'

I did not have to do much dodging as Nehru got involved in the Conference. The only function we had organized for him was a meeting with the international press and a luncheon with editors of the top English papers in his hotel suite. Details of both were given to his secretary, M.O. Matthai. The press conference drew a large crowd, including Pakistani journalists. Their main interest was Kashmir: the Western press was generally inclined towards the Pakistani point of view. People were eager to hear what the Prime Minister of India had to say in his defence.

The conference was scheduled for 10.30 am. Till 10.45 there was no sign of Panditji. I rang up Matthai to tell him that the press people were getting restive. Fifteen minutes later the Prime Minister arrived looking very agitated. Menon and I escorted him to the dais. 'What's all this? Why didn't anyone tell me I had to meet the press?' he hissed loudly enough for the microphones to carry his voice to every corner of the room. Then he switched on his beaming smile for cameramen and asked, 'Yes gentlemen, what can I do for you?'

The Pakistani pressmen sprang to their feet and asked him to explain India's position on Kashmir. He did so very lucidly. It was evident that he had prepared himself but wanted to create the impression that he was speaking extempore. The conference was a great success. Afterwards, when I tried to show him his printed programme mentioning the conference, he brushed me aside. He had made his point at my expense.

Matthai also warned me that no photographs of the Prime

Minister were to be issued to the press without first being cleared by the Prime Minister. He was a vain man who did not want to be caught picking his nose or yawning.

The luncheon for the editors was an unmitigated disaster. The menu had been prepared by Kamla Jaspal and provided for clear vegetable soup for Menon, followed by relays of cups of tea. The editors of *The Times, Telegraph, Manchester Guardian, Observer* and *New Statesman and Nation* were present. We started with sherry before we sat down at table. Soup and the first course with chilled white wine were then served; Panditji had no food or drink fads and quite enjoyed dry sherry and wine. He lit his cigarette to indicate that informal dialogue could begin. He asked why the conservative press was generally hostile to India. The editors answered in turns protesting that it was not so, but that they were constrained to carry dispatches sent to them by their correspondents in India whom they trusted to be impartial. If there were any factual errors they would be willing to carry any corrections sent by India House. Everyone turned to Menon. His head was sunk low over his chest and he was nodding sleepily. Panditji whispered angrily to me, 'Can't you see your High Commissioner is unwell? You must not expose him to outsiders like this.' Then Panditji himself lost interest. When an editor asked him a question, he stared vacantly into space. The question hung in the air without getting an answer. I tried my best to fill in the gaps of silence. Before the dessert was served, Panditji was also nodding with his head sunk on his chest. The editors left without waiting for coffee to be served.

There was more in store for me. After the Commonwealth Prime Ministers' Conference was over, Panditji had a couple of days free to indulge in his favourite hobbies, buying books and seeing Lady Mountbatten. An afternoon was reserved for book buying. Menon deputed me to escort the Prime Minister and sign for any books he bought. He also instructed me to tell the P.M. what a good job he was doing as High Commissioner and that there was no truth in adverse reports Indian journalists had been sending to their papers. I picked Nehru up from his hotel and asked, 'Sir, what sort of books would you like to see?' He snapped back, 'Books to read, what else!' I tried to explain that several book stores specialized on different topics — rare books, the Orient, religion, philosophy, travel, etc. He brushed aside my query and ordered the chauffeur to drive to a well-known bookstore on Oxford Street. We arrived at our destination. He was recognized and the sales assistants fawned on him. He browsed over a few titles. When one of the assistants asked him if there was anything special he was looking for, he replied, 'Bernard Shaw.' Shaw had died a few weeks earlier and there was a revival of interest in his books. The works of Shaw were put together and I signed for them on behalf of India House. Some people came to ask Nehru for his autograph, and he happily signed for them. I bought a book of poems and had him inscribe it for me. The shopping expedition was over. On the way back to the hotel I asked Nehru if he got much time to read books. 'Of course not,' he snapped.

Two evenings before Nehru was due to leave he invited Lady Mountbatten to a quiet dinner for two at a Greek restaurant in Soho. The restaurant owner recognized them and rang up the press to get publicity for his joint. The next morning's papers carried photographs of the two sitting close to each other. I knew I was in trouble again. I arrived at the office to find a note from Menon on my table saying that the Prime Minister wished to see me immediately. I rushed to Claridges Hotel and reported myself to Matthai. 'Go in,' he said mechanically. 'Have you any idea what he wants to see me about?' I asked nervously. 'None! He'll tell you.'

I gently knocked on the Prime Minister's door and went in. He was busy going through some files. 'Yes?' he asked raising his head.

'Sir, you sent for me.'

'I sent for you? Who are you?'

'Sir, I am your P.R.O. in London.'

He looked me up and down and said, 'You have strange notions of publicity!'

Soon after Nehru departed I was summoned to New Delhi to have my appointment confirmed by the U.P.S.C. So were all the others who, like me, had been picked up and sent to different countries. I assumed it would be a rubber-stamp interview: we had been in service for about two years and not likely to be discarded unless found totally wanting. I was wrong. Of the dozen or more interviewed, the majority were rejected. I was amongst the luckier ones and told to return to my post. This visit was counted as home leave.

On my way back from the interview, which took place in Metcalf House, I happened to pass through Subzi Mandi. The street was blocked by what seemed to be some kind of fracas taking place ahead. I asked the driver to stop and went out to find out what it was. 'We've caught a couple of Muslim swine trying to take a cow for slaughter,' one of the crowd informed me. I pushed my way through the mob and came to the centre of the scene. There were a cow and three men — two Muslims and a Sikh — surrounded by men armed with steel rods and long knives. My arrival, clad in suit and tie, deterred them. 'What's going on?' I demanded angrily. 'These two fellows are butchers; this Sikh sold the cow to them,' I was informed. All three men were shaking with fear. The Muslims had been stripped naked and seen to be circumcised. They were to be battered and stabbed to death. The Sikh was to be beaten up and taught a lesson. I put my arms in front of the butchers and shouted back, 'No one is going to touch these men! I have seen enough of this during partition. It has to stop.'

The crowd turned nasty towards me. 'Do you understand that these men were going to butcher this cow? What kind of a Sikh are you?' I held my ground. 'I will not let you touch them. If anyone does, I'll have him arrested. I am a government official.' They were not impressed. But no one was willing to make the first move. I thought of a way out. 'Let's take them to the police station and see what we can do.' The crowd let me do what I wanted. I led the cow, and put my arms around the two butchers; the bloodthirsty mob followed in trams clanking madly at us to clear the way. We arrived at the Subzi Mandi police station. I introduced myself to the Inspector in charge, a

Punjabi Hindu, and pleaded with him to take the butchers in custody. The Sikh had meanwhile slipped away into the crowd. 'They have committed no crime, why should I arrest them?' he demanded. 'To save their lives,' I pleaded. He was adamant. I threatened him with my status as an official. He could not care less. 'I don't care who you are or what the crowd will do to these fellows. They deserve what is coming to them.'

I resumed my march with the cow and the butchers through the crowded bazar to Tees Hazari where there was a veterinary hospital. By the time I got there, the crowd had thinned. The vet was a white-bearded Sikh. I pleaded with him to take the cow in custody and to arrest the two men on the charge of cruelty to animals. He was adamant. 'I see no injury on the cow. And if they want to kill these snakes I am not going to stop them,' he said walking away. I turned to address the few would-be killers who remained. 'Look, I will release the cow here and now and take these fellows to some place where I can teach them the lesson they deserve.' They agreed, they had had enough, their tempers had cooled. I let the cow loose. It ran across the open ground with its tail raised, kicking its hind legs in the sheer joy of being released from human bondage. I ordered the two butchers to get into my car. 'Where do you live?' I asked them.

'Daryaganj.'

'Don't you fellows realize how dangerous it is in these times to slaughter kine?'

'Janab, we had nothing to eat for two days. We pooled our resources to buy this cow. Now we are ruined.'

I dropped them at Daryaganj. They did not go to their homes. I saw them turn back to go and look for the cow they had bought.

I am not a brave man. I was amazed at the audacity I had shown in the face of danger. I asked the chauffeur to take me to Gurdwara Sisganj in Chandni Chowk. By now I had given up visiting places of worship. Sisganj marked the site of the execution of the ninth Guru, Tegh Bahadur. According to legend, he had laid down his life to protect Hindus from persecution. It was the best place to go to for one who in his small way had saved the lives of two Muslims. At Sisganj I offered obeisance at the Guru's shrine, which is in an underground cell where the trunk of the banyan tree under which he was beheaded is preserved. I thanked the Guru for giving a coward like me the courage to uphold what I thought was a Sikh's duty. I broke down; tears of gratitude welled up in my eyes. When I left, my legs shook. I had come close to being murdered.

At home I narrated the incident with great pride. Far from being applauded I was called *'bewakoof'* — a fool — and *'gadha'* — a donkey — by my father's friend Sohan Singh of Rawalpindi who was staying with him. My mother was angry that I had put my life in jeopardy. My father kept silent. I knew I had the approval of the one man who mattered more to me than anyone else.

After a few days in Delhi I returned to London to resume work. My stock of duty free Scotch from Canada came in very handy in Scotch-deprived, thirsty post-War England. I kept an open house in the Lalls' apartment every Wednesday. Some I invited — others just came assured of a welcome. Menon made it a point to drop in because most of my guests were journalists.

At one such party our chief guest was Professor C.M. Joad who had earned fame and notoriety because of his books, his appearances on radio and stories of his womanizing. In one of his appearances in a series 'Any Questions?' he had brought the house down when answering the question, 'How many guns' salute is fired when a lady Vicereine has a male child?' The only one in the panel who raised his hand to answer the question was Joad. 'I don't know how many guns are fired,' he replied in his squeaky voice, 'but I know that the A.D.C. is fired.' Joad was a grubby, ill-dressed little man with a small goatee. He was known to proposition women with the simple formula, 'Wouldn't you like to be bedded by a celebrity?' Apparently it worked very well. However, he had recently been caught travelling by train without a ticket and fined. This made the front pages of all the papers. Joad accepted our invitation; he had heard that I invited well-known authors and poets. Unknown to me, Menon did not like Joad. And unfortunately for me Menon and Joad arrived at the same time. Menon briskly walked up the stairs (he always ran up the stairs) saying loudly enough for Joad to hear, 'If I had known you had invited that fellow, I would never have come to your party.' He stopped on the landing for me to go ahead and introduce him to my guests. Instead, I went down to help Joad take off his overcoat. As we proceeded up the stairs, Joad asked me at the top of his voice, 'Isn't that fellow Menon?'

'Yes sir,' I replied.

'What is he doing here? I thought your party was for writers, poets and other educated people.'

The two avoided each other. Joad settled down to his Scotch and was soon surrounded by female admirers. Menon had his cup of tea with only Arthur Lall as his audience.

Menon was a complex character, the most unpredictable and prickly I have ever met. I had first met him on the London-Paris train when he and Rajni Patel were on their way to attend some conference. At Dover, he and Rajni jumped the queue of passengers awaiting immigration clearance. When the immigration officer told them to go back to the line, Menon accused him of racial prejudice. The fellow let them through. Menon had a chip on his shoulder about being a black and picked up quarrels on imaginary racial insults. For a time he had worked as a waiter at Shafi's and Ramaswamy's restaurants to pay for his studies at the Bar. He never picked up any practice but got to know socialist politicians and was on the panel of editors of the Pelican series of books. Till he became High Commissioner he was always very hard-up and eager to accept any hospitality extended to him. He was slim, middle-sized and dark, with sharp features and bright, shining eyes. He had a broad forehead, his curly black hair greying at the temples, a large nose and high cheekbones. Women found him handsome. He was very tense, his face was never at rest and twitched with animation. He was always very well-dressed in suits made by a well-known firm of tailors. He could not bear others being badly dressed. Once he cancelled his morning appointments, took me to his tailor, chose the material and had me measured for two suits. I thought he meant to gift them to me and thanked him profusely. They were not gifts; I had to shell out several hundred pounds, but they were the best suits I had and lasted me over twenty years. Menon was not generous with his money, except when it came to his lady friends and with children. Even with them, it was seldom more than bouquets of roses for one, cheap plastic toys for the other.

Menon lived frugally in a room alongside his office. He ate very little but filled himself with cups of sugared tea and salted biscuits. However, he did not mind blowing up large sums of money buying a Rolls Royce for the High Commissioner (himself) and a fleet of Austin Princesses for the use of Indian visitors and India House officials. With his limited requirements he had no need to accumulate wealth. Nevertheless, he did so. He didn't spend a penny of his salary but set up many sub-organizations of his India League and got money from rich Indians and his English friends as donations to his organizations; in return, he gave the latter contracts for the supply of arms to India. He had no scruples in business matters. He was also a congenital liar and regarded truth as good enough for the simple-minded and lying as the best exercise for the mind.

Menon's first reaction to any proposal put to him was to reject it. Those who got to know him better learnt to put their proposals in the negative and invariably got his approval by his rejecting them. He built up a reputation of being a workaholic. He kept long hours which he wasted on trivia, like checking the menus of the canteen and the consumption of petrol by the office cars. He forced me to sleep in the office on many nights. There was never enough work to justify imposing this discomfort on me. He knew that I was very keen on games and looked forward to Saturday afternoons, when I played tennis or hockey. Without fail, he would ring me up before lunch on Saturdays and ask me to attend some meeting he was holding in the afternoon. He had a strong streak of sadism.

Menon's bad temper and discourtesy had to be experienced to be believed. As with many men, he was at his worst in the mornings before his gastric juices started flowing. I saw him hurling a file in the face of Jagannath Khosla and yell, 'Have you any brains in your head? Get out!' Then he put his head between his hands to cool off and asked me, 'I shouldn't have spoken to him like that. Should I have?' I conceded he had been a little rough with a senior officer. He summoned Khosla back and apologized. Khosla replied, 'Sir, it is a privilege to be ticked off by you.' One morning when Menon failed to get a long-distance call, he screamed at the operator. The plucky English girl shouted back, 'Don't you dare talk to me like that! I am quitting. You can keep your bloody job.' Menon ran down the stairs, put his arms around the angry girl and apologized. Once I brought David Astor, the owner-proprietor of the *Observer*, and his aide William Clarke to meet him. He called the English a race of brigands. On the way down in the elevator David remarked to me, 'You must have quite a job doing public relations for Menon!' His deputy, Ashok Chanda, knowing Menon's predilection for denying anything he said if he later found it embarrassing, insisted that he put all his orders in writing. He often breezed into my office and triumphantly announced, '*Hum shala ko phaeel mein aisa mara! bhooleyga nahin*' — I gave the fellow whose sister I fuck such a hiding in the file, he'll never forget it. Sir Dhiren Mitra, our legal adviser, never lost his cool. He continued placidly puffing his pipe and dismissed Menon with '*pagul hai*' — he is mad.

Those who silently suffered Menon's tantrums were handsomely rewarded. Of them the most dramatic was the instance of Brigadier Harnarain Singh and his wife Rani. Menon took an instant dislike to the Brigadier. The latter described himself as the Chief of Moron, a small zamindari near Phillaur in the Punjab. Menon always addressed him as the chief of the morons. The Brigadier did not know what the English word meant and would protest in his nasal whine, 'Sir, who cares for such titles these days!' His wife Rani also liked to be treated as an aristocrat. She was the daughter of Sardar Sohan Singh, a wealthy landowner of Rawalpindi. Her name Rani confirmed her aristocratic assumptions. Menon got to know that she had been spreading scandal about his affair with Kamla Jaspal. He summoned her to the office, roundly ticked her off and called her a bitch. A very tearful Rani craved forgiveness. Thereafter, the couple assiduously courted Kamla Jaspal and became one of Menon's favourites. Another two senior officers who were treated like scum but accepted their treatment without protest were Captain Srinivasan and the First Secretary, D.N. Chatterjee. Srinivasan, a married man with children, impregnated his attractive English stenographer. It was after Menon had extracted many pounds of flesh off the hapless naval Captain that he allowed him to divorce his Indian wife, marry the vastly pregnant English girl — and retain his job. Chatterjee had divorced his Bengali wife (one of Lord Sinha's progeny) and wanted to marry a Belgian heiress. By the rules of the Foreign Service he was required to submit his resignation before his application could be considered. Chatterjee had to suffer months of humiliation before Menon forwarded his application with the recommendation that it be accepted. Chatterjee retired as an Ambassador.

Merit did not matter very much to Menon; unquestioned loyalty did. He persuaded the Prime Minister to constitute a panel to interview applicants living in England for the Foreign Service. He got Harold Laski appointed Chairman with him and another to constitute it. The panel selected P.N. Haksar (the only one who merited selection), Jagan Nath Khosla, Kamla Jaspal and Rukmini Menon (a clerk and the sister of a junior officer in the military attaché's department). Later he also managed to get Keki Darashah and Prithi Singh, who had an English wife, in the subordinate Foreign Service. He held out similar promises to me; he would have me elected to Parliament and perhaps made a minister in the government. But my days as a Menon favourite were fast drawing to a close.

Menon was never rude to me. For many months I enjoyed

special favours and my colleagues who wanted things done by him used me as their via media. I travelled with him to distant towns in England where he was invited to speak. Kamla Jaspal briefed me on his personal requirements. Amongst items I had to carry were bottles of lemonade: he drank a glass for his nightcap.

Though his English was heavily Malayali-accented he was a witty speaker. He was full of acid wit and sarcasm against the English and people who could not retaliate. At his first meeting with senior army, navy and air force officers training in England, he addressed them as 'Macaulay's children'. He did not enjoy other speakers scoring over him and could be quite childish in the ways in which he got the better of them. Once, speaking at the convention of Master Cutlers at Leeds, he was at his acid best and extracted much laughter from his audience: the English enjoy laughing at themselves. Unfortunately for Menon, the chief host who rose to propose the vote of thanks turned out to be a better orator than Menon. His jokes and anecdotes got even louder applause. I saw Menon beckon a waiter and ask for another cup of tea. As the speaker was building up to a climax, Menon raised his cup with a shaking hand. Just as the speaker was about to deliver his punch line, Menon dropped the cup from his hand and spilt tea all over the table. The punch line remained undelivered and the banquet came to an abrupt end.

My most memorable venture with Menon was the visit to Dublin where we were to open an embassy — Ireland's first full diplomatic mission. Menon decided to take his defence attaches and their wives with him. I was included in the party and asked to bring my wife along. Our party was received at Dublin airport with a guard of honour. We were put up in Dublin's swankiest hotel. The next morning Menon was to present his credentials to the Irish President. My phone rang early morning. It was a very sick sounding Menon asking me to come to his room at once. I found him groaning in bed. 'I am very sick,' he moaned, 'cancel all the day's engagements.' I was aghast. 'Sir, they must have made a lot of preparations. Let me get the hotel doctor and see what he has to say.'

'Can't you see, I am a sick man?' he growled. I got the hotel doctor. He could not diagnose anything wrong with Menon except that he might be suffering from exhaustion. Menon was inconsolable. 'Get the Chief of Protocol on the line.' While I was trying to get the right number, we heard the stamp of marching feet come to a halt beneath our window. 'What is that?' asked Menon. I looked out. 'Soldiers drawing up. I expect they are to escort you to the Presidential Palace.' Menon began to feel better. He went to the bathroom to shave and brush his teeth. When he came out we heard the sounds of a military band down the road and coming to a halt outside the hotel. Menon had a quick look from his window. He got into a black sherwani and chooridars and told me, 'Sardar, go and get dressed. We don't have much time.'

Menon was now in great form. We were taken in a convoy led by a band and a troop of soldiers. Curious Dubliners lined the roads and Menon waved to them. The credentials were presented and accepted. President Douglas invited Menon to his home for a cup of tea in the afternoon and Menon asked my wife and me to accompany him. We were led to a book-lined study with a peat fire smouldering in the grate. The President made polite enquiries about India. Menon launched into a long harangue about India's mineral and hydro-electric resources, its industries and agricultural potential. The President heard it in silence. At the end of his long monologue, Menon asked the President how Ireland was faring. 'Nothing much worth the talking,' drawled the President. 'We don't have much to export except invisible items like poets, novelists, and dramatists.'

That evening we held a reception for the Irish President, Prime Minister and leaders of the Irish opposition. Amongst those who turned up was Eamon De Valera. Following the reception, we were guests at a concert of European classical music. As we were being shown to our box, an announcement came over the loudspeaker that Ireland's first foreign Ambassador had arrived. The audience rose to applaud him. A beam of light searched the crowded hall to pick up Menon. Instead of him, it focused on me — with my turban and beard, I looked more authentically Indian than any other in our party. I tried to dodge the beam by going to the back row, but the beam pursued me. Menon enjoyed my discomfiture and kept pushing me to the front. No one was able to acknowledge the applause of the audience.

India House would have got on my nerves earlier, but for some breaks I got. Twice during my posting my parents came to spend the summer with us. I took them with my family to the Isle of Wight. We had the hotel almost to ourselves because of some scare about an epidemic. The band played music we asked for; my son, Rahul, and daughter, Mala, went up on the stage and sang with the band. My mother's happiest moments were at the amusement arcade, where she put many six-pennies in the slot of the 'laughing sailor'. As he exploded with bellyfuls of laughter, she went into hysterical fits of giggling till tears streamed down her face. Back in London, Madame Tussaud's was a must. I also managed to get them invitations to tea at Buckingham Palace. For my father, this was always the highlight of his visit to England. He met retired Viceroys, governors, and commissioners he had known. My father had heard much praise of English theatre and wanted me to take them to a play. By then he had become hard of hearing, and my mother understood no English. I took them to the Windmill Theatre known for its topless girl dancers and risque jokes. My mother took a bagful of grapes to eat during the performance. She kept crackling her paper bag and annoying people sitting around us. And oblivious of the storyteller's attempts to build up his story to a climax, she spat the pips of grapes into the bag with a loud '*thoo*'. After seeing half the show, I decided to take them home. 'You come to see these *besharam* (shameless) naked girls every week?' she asked me by way of thanks.

On their next visit, I took them to Branksome Tower Hotel in Bournemouth. This was much more to my father's taste, who liked upperclass joints where people dressed for dinner and ordered French wines with their meals.

Nothing specific happened to sour my relations with Menon. Of the two women he was close to, we became more friendly with Bridgette, who was very distressed by Menon's infatuation with Kamla Jaspal. She regarded Kamla as a designing seductress who had brought Menon a bad name. I had made the mistake of telling this to Menon. He snubbed me and told me to mind my own business. Then some comment on Kashmir appeared in the *Manchester Guardian*. Menon and Haksar drafted the reply; it was sent to me for my signature as the press attaché. I could have drafted a similar reply — and perhaps have phrased it better — but I was not even consulted. The correspondence continued in the paper. In all, I signed three letters I had not written. I felt slighted and let my hurt be known to everyone in the office. Then, instead of talking to me directly, Menon began to convey his orders through Kamla Jaspal. I told her not to bring messages to me as I was always available to the High Commissioner on the phone. Menon accused me of being rude to Kamla. His infatuation at the time was at its peak.

My relations with my wife had also worsened. Almost every evening we had a quarrel. If she was unhappy with me, I was unhappy with her. The only chance of escape was to send the family back to India.

At that time my first collection of short stories, *The Mark of Vishnu and Other Stories*, largely based on my days as a lawyer in Lahore, was published by Saturn Press. It did not sell very well but got excellent reviews in the literary journals. Although I was saddled with two hundred unsold copies I felt the venture had been successful as quite a few of the stories were reproduced in *The Illustrated Weekly of India* by its Irish editor, Sean Mandy. I had other books brewing inside me — some translations from the Sikh scriptures, a short history of the Sikhs and a novel based on the partition of India. I had enough money laid aside to last me six months in England. I told my wife of my decision to resign from service and try my hand at writing as a career — alone in England. She made no comment.

I booked the family and our servants on a P & O boat to Bombay. Govind (*All About H. Hatter*) Desani found me a basement flat in Highgate close to one end of Hampstead Heath. I shifted my personal belongings and books to this apartment and saw the family off at Tillbury. I had to give the government three months' notice of resignation; three months leave was due to me, so the next morning I put in my application for leave and quit office without waiting to find out whether or not it was approved. I took myself off for a long weekend to Branksome Towers Hotel where I had earlier taken my parents and family for a holiday. It was a very painful stay. I missed my children running around the lobby and the garden. I knew I had taken a leap in the dark, not knowing where I would land. I had thrown up a reasonably good job which would inevitably have ended in getting me an ambassadorship to some country. I had no basis for thinking I could make a living out of writing. When my money ran out I would again be living on my father's bounty. I also kept reminding myself that I had only one life to live; what I was doing in the office would be done as well by my successors. They too would be invited to Buckingham Palace once a year, be addressed as 'Your Excellency', swill duty-free liquor and retire into oblivion. I might prove a flop as a writer, but the gamble was worth taking. It was too late to look back now.

I settled into my Highgate flat and got down to work. I realized that in the highly competitive world of writing one had to specialize on some subject to make a mark. I decided my best bet was Sikh religion and history. No Sikh had published anything on the subject in England or the United States: all the so-called Sikh specialists were English. I had been brought up in a Sikh household and knew many prayers by rote without knowing their meanings. My vocabulary of the *Sant Bhasha* in which most of the Granth was written was very inadequate. I acquired a Punjabi-English dictionary, earlier translations done by Trump and Macauliffe, and got down to translating in verse Guru Nanak's morning prayer *Japji*. When finished, I showed it to my friend Guy Wint who was freelancing for both the *Observer* and *Manchester Guardian* as well as teaching in St Anthony College, Oxford. He not only made some suggestions to make it read better but also persuaded Probsthain to publish it.

I went on to write a short history of the Sikhs entirely based on published works but brought up to date. I added my own prophecy that, if the pace at which young Sikhs were beginning to give up emblems of the Khalsa faith (unshorn hair and beards) continued, the Khalsa form of Sikhism would disappear by the turn of the century and the Sikhs, like the Jains and Buddhists, would relapse into the mainstream of Hinduism. It was readily accepted by Messrs Allen & Unwin. It was not a profound book and had some historical errors and printers' devils as well. However, being the first book on the subject after many decades, it was widely reviewed in the British press. It also created quite a storm in orthodox Sikh circles in India. Who was I to say Sikhs would disappear when the last Sikh Guru had prophesied that most of the world would within a foreseeable future embrace Sikhism?

I now felt a little more confident of myself as a writer. I made new friends who boosted my morale. Amongst them was an American, Stella Alexander, the divorced wife of a British diplomat who cultivated people who mattered and threw parties based on champagne supplied by me to introduce me to people she knew. Amongst them were Edmund Leach (later Rector of Kings College, Cambridge and knighted) and his wife Celia, a painter and novelist. They invited me to share their cottage in Hertfordshire. I began to spend my weekends with them and became a great favourite of their two children, Louisa and Alexander. In their home I also met Elizabeth Bott, a young Canadian girl studying sociology at the London School of Economics. Though somewhat of a blue-stocking, she wore thick glasses and carried a mop of untidy hair, I was much taken up with her. She was highly intelligent, and she read my stories and the manuscript on Sikh history. I began to rely on her judgement more than anyone else's. She was a connoisseur of good food, wines and classical European music. She introduced me to psychiatry. I had read Freud and Jung, and she gave me books by Melanie Klein. They opened new horizons for me.

The Leaches and Elizabeth Bott saw me through months of despair and uncertainty.

The time had come to bid a final farewell to India House. Jamal Kidwai had taken my place. When I went to bid him goodbye he told me that Menon wanted to give a farewell reception for me. I told him flatly that I wanted no reception and did not wish to see Menon. He pleaded with me and said he would give the reception and Menon would come only for a few moments. I knew Menon would do nothing of the sort, but agreed to come to Kidwai's party. Reluctantly, I also went to see Menon. He was courteous and said that despite our misunderstanding he regarded me as a friend. 'You don't have any friends,' I told him bluntly as I left. As I had anticipated, Menon did not turn up at the farewell reception. Kidwai apologized on his behalf to say that Menon was unwell and confined to bed. But I saw him briskly go down the steps and get into his Rolls Royce: lying was Menon's second nature and came as easily to him as discourtesy.

Why Menon got where he did under the patronage of Pandit Nehru remains, and probably will remain, unexplained. Panditji had him elected to Parliament and sent to the United Nations to lead the Indian delegation. His marathon thirteen-hour speech on Kashmir won India a unanimous vote against it. He was then made Defence Minister against the wishes of almost all the members of the Cabinet. He wrecked army discipline by promoting favourites over the heads of senior officers. He was vindictive against those who stood up to him. More than anyone else he was responsible for the humiliating defeat of our army at the hands of the Chinese in 1962. Pandit Nehru stuck by him to the last.

The last time I spoke to Menon was on the telephone. I happened to be in London working at the India Office Library. I was sharing a flat with Sheila Lall. We had a common telephone. Every night she was out with one of her many lovers. The telephone rang, but when I picked it up and said 'hello' it went dead. I complained to Sheila. 'That must be Krishna,' she told me. 'He wants me to be his mistress — no strings attached.' The next time the telephone rang, instead of saying the customary 'hello' I spat out with venom 'You bloody bastard, I know who you are. Stop ringing up at this hour or you will hear worse.' There were no calls after that.

Menon is the subject of a couple of biographies and a road is named after him. I think in my long years I got to know him better than his biographers or any of the leftists who acclaim him as a great son of India. General Shiv Varma summed him up aptly when he said, 'Menon was a bachelor, the same as his father.'

7   Purging the Past and Return to India

FOUR YEARS OF tension and heavy drinking took a toll on my body. There was tension in the office and at home. As one suffering from migraine takes aspirin for relief, I sought relief through liqueur: sherry before lunch, wines with lunch, liqueur with coffee. Every other evening there was a cocktail party. Every dinner was preceded by Scotch, accompanied with wines and cognac or Drambuie to round it off. I slept badly and woke up at odd hours between 3–5 am to nurse my hangovers and brood over my wretchedness. By the time I quit India House and sent my family home, I was a dyspeptic wreck. I consulted a doctor. He gave me a thorough check-up before he pronounced the verdict: 'Nothing wrong with you. I suggest you take a break from your daily routine of work and drink and get out into the country. What you need is naturopathy, not medicine.' He suggested the name of a nature-cure clinic in Champneys (Hertfordshire) run by an Austrian named Dr Leaf.

I wrote to Dr Leaf asking him if I could spend a few days in his establishment. I received a catalogue listing rates charged for examination, treatment, board and lodging. It seemed expensive but I decided to give it a try. I drove to Champneys. It was summer. Everything looked green and sunwashed. Champneys was an old mansion standing in the midst of extensive lawns with ancient oaks, beeches and chestnuts which were then in bloom. What must have been stables and servants quarters had been converted into rows of cubicles for patients.

I was shown to a tiny wooden cubicle furnished with nothing more than a bed, a table and a wicker chair. There was only one

lavatory for twelve inmates. And no bathroom. It took me a day
to understand why both were unnecessary.

Dr Leaf received me in his office. After hearing what I had to
say he asked me to tell him in precise detail what I ate and
drank every day. He made a note of all the items of my
breakfast, elevenses, lunch, afternoon tea, cocktail snacks and
dinner. He told me to see him next morning. At dinner time I
joined other inmates in the cafeteria. They consisted of an
assortment of people: film stars, chorus girls, businessmen,
shopkeepers, civil servants and lawyers. Among them was a
tailor from Leeds, who kept pulling his trouser out in front to
show how his paunch had disappeared and how much weight he
had lost. I was not surprised, as there was nothing to eat besides
salads and yogurt. Men and women on my table ravenously ate
the one orange provided, and sipped glasses of warm water.
They seemed very happy with the treatment and the strict
discipline imposed on them. No one was allowed to leave
Champneys till the treatment was over. Locals who saw them
strolling half-naked on the lawns or basking in the sun eyed
them suspiciously and sniggered as they put their index finger
on one side of their heads to indicate mental disorder. They
described us as Champneys Chimps or Leaf's Loonies.

The next morning when I presented myself in Dr Leaf's
clinic, he had on his table a glass bowl full of what looked like
somebody's vomit. 'This Mr Singh is what you put inside your
belly every day — eggs, bacon, toasts, coffee, cakes, biscuits,
steaks, vegetables, Scotch, wine and liqueurs. I put them in
this bowl last evening after you told me of your daily intake.
Now look at it!' I saw bubbles come up in the mess. 'Just smell
it,' he ordered. I bent over the bowl and drew back abruptly.
'Precisely!' he continued. 'What do you expect if you dump so
much garbage in your belly every day? The first thing we have
to do is to cleanse you inside out. Then I will prescribe your
diet and massage.' He scribbled something on a piece of paper
and handed me over to a man in a medical white coat.

I was taken to the treatment room. 'I have to give you a
Colonic Irrigation,' said the man, holding something which
looked like a large penis attached to a cord. He smeared it with

vaseline. He ordered me to strip and lie down on my belly on a table covered with a rubber sheet. Then he proceeded to insert the penis in my anus. The pain was excruciating; I wondered what catamites got out of buggery. He managed to get the entire thing in my rectum and let a jet of warm water flood into my bowels. A suction pump extracted the contents. More warm water was pumped in and sucked out. The irrigation lasted almost a quarter of an hour till there was nothing left inside me.

I took a hot shower. I was ordered to rub myself with salt dissolved in large buckets. It was thick as mud and I felt I was scrubbing myself with sand. The salt rub was followed by an oil massage and another hot shower to rinse oil off my body. I was told to have the lunch prescribed for me at the cafeteria and spend the afternoon in the sun. The lunch consisted of a single orange; the drink was a glass of warm water spiked with honey. I returned to my cubicle feeling clean and famished. After the Colonic Irrigation I understood why no one needed a loo. I tried to read, but hunger made it difficult to concentrate. I went out into the garden. It was strewn with coffins without lids in which men and women lay stark naked, exposing themselves to the sun. I lay down in one with my shorts on: I couldn't embarrass myself in front of naked women.

The first four days were difficult, with just one orange at lunch, one for dinner and gallons of tepid water. I felt a humming in my ears. I was assured that was normal. The craving for food and the humming would soon disappear. I thought of nothing but food. In the dining room the only talk was of good restaurants, juicy steaks, ice-creams dripping with chocolate sauce. There was no talk of women. There were lots of nice looking girls around but it was food everyone wanted, not sex. On the fifth day I played tennis with people who had been on the two-oranges-a-day diet for a fortnight. The tailor from Leeds became quite a friend. He had been there for three weeks. He showed me his photograph before he came; it was of a fat man with an enormous paunch. 'Now look!' he said pulling his trousers in front for the umpteenth time. 'All gone!' he said beaming with pleasure. He introduced me to the lady friend he had picked up at Champneys. She too had been there for three weeks. Her blonde hair looked more golden, her waist and hips were shaped like an hour-glass. 'It's surprising what real hunger can do to you! Takes them poisons out of the system, and see the result!' she said with a happy smile. They told me of arthritics whose limbs had unlocked; of people with ear, nose and throat problems who could hear better, see better and had their sinuses cleared.

The denouement came the day before the tailor and his lady friend were to be discharged. They decided to celebrate it by going on a binge. Being a jovial man, the tailor had become a great favourite with the staff. Contrary to clinic rules they let him and his friend go out of the premises. The couple went pub-crawling. On their empty stomachs the liquor hit them hard. When it came to closing time he bought a bottle of Scotch from an off-licence store and came back to Champneys. Both were roaring drunk. They spent the night together. They were still high next morning, shouting obscenities to the world as they went round arm in arm. The staff did its best to pump the liquor out of their systems. Neither Colonic Irrigations nor salt rubs, neither cold showers nor hot black coffee had any effect. When Dr Leaf heard of it he was furious. He ordered the tailor and his friend to be expelled immediately and fined the staff who had let them out. The couple were beyond caring. 'It was worth it,' said the tailor jovially as he shook hands with me. 'The best of the three-week treatment was the way we treated ourselves last night. Wasn't it, sweetheart?' he said turning to his friend. 'Sure it was,' she replied drowsily. 'Never enjoyed myself more in my life.' I learnt later that the tailor's friend was a prostitute from London.

After three weeks of living on two oranges and gallons of warm water spiked with honey, I felt thoroughly cleansed and lighter. I had to break my fast with a carton of yoghurt. It took me quite some time to eat a few spoonfuls without getting out of breath. Dr Leaf instructed me on what I should avoid in my diet. Shun fried foods and lessen the intake of liquor. I left Champneys feeling much better except that the ordeal seemed to have impaired my vision. The first thing I did on my return to London was to visit an optician. He examined my eyes and the glasses I wore. 'You need to change your glasses,' he told me. 'By some miracle your eyesight has improved.' I was very pleased with myself. Being described as a chimp or a loony didn't matter.

After returning to London, I got down to serious work. I finished my *Short History of the Sikhs* and then decided to start working on a novel. The theme I had in mind was the partition of India and the horrible massacres that accompanied it. I wasn't sure how I should go about it. I considered several plots and thought of many characters. I was obsessed with the idea that every individual had the trinity of Hindu gods in him: Brahma (the Creator), Vishnu (the Preserver) and Shiva (the Destroyer). But in every person one or the other aspect of the trinity predominated. Perhaps the Brahma aspect could be best portrayed by a peasant farmer; Vishnu by an upholder of the law like a magistrate; and Shiva, through a communist who wanted to destroy evil to build a better world. I took my notebook with me and decided to work on a draft in the peace of the Italian lakes. I first drove to Bellagio, but found it too full of noisy tourists. By chance I discovered a much smaller lake higher up in the mountains called Lago Elio on the Italian-Swiss border. It had only one pension with a couple of rooms. I shifted to Elio and hired a boat for a month to have my exercise (there were not many walks around) by rowing and swimming. I spent most of the day working on the novel. After an early dinner, I rowed the boat to the other end of the lake where there was no habitation, stripped myself and plunged into the lake. The summer evenings were long and warm; the night came on well after 10 pm. From my window I could see the lights of villages on the Swiss side. For many days the only excitement in the little village was the *Tour de France* cycle race. A handful of villagers came in every evening to drink and listen to the progress of the race over the radio. One evening I saw the entire northern sky on the Swiss side explode with fireworks: a Swiss had won the cycle race.

It was extremely still and hot one night. After having rowed for some time, I decided to cool myself in the waters of the Elio. I took my boat in the middle of the lake, divested myself of all my clothes (I did not have swimming trunks) and jumped in. The boat began to drift northwards. I swam after it. All of a sudden I heard the roar of a motor boat coming towards me. Its powerful headlights were beamed on me. I tried to get back into my boat. But the more I tried to clamber in, the more it tilted and slipped out of my grasp. I was caught by the headlights of the patrol boat. I had apparently drifted too close to the Swiss border and the Italian customs wanted to know what I was doing there. They couldn't believe what they saw — a dark man with long hair falling about his shoulders with his beard dripping with water. What kind of human monster had the Elio thrown up? I caught some of the expressions of disbelief — *Deos Meos* ('My God'), *'Cara Mea!'* ('My dear'). Mercifully, one of the patrol had heard about me from his little daughter. They towed my boat back to the pension with me hanging on to its rear. I got out of the water, wrapped my turban round my head and put on my clothes. I thanked them in my best Italian and bade them goodnight.

After a reasonably productive month in Lago Elio, I was back in London to catch my boat for Bombay and home. I was back in India in 1950. No one was impressed by the fact that I had a couple of books published in England. No one in the family wanted to read the reviews I had brought with me. All they wanted to know was how much I had earned in royalties. It was very little. Behind my back my friends and relations made fun of me. 'He could not pass his examinations but has begun to write books,' they said. I was described as a *nikhattoo* — a shirker, who does not earn his living. One day Sir Shri Ram, whose home I often visited because of my wife's schooldays' friendship with his son Bharat and Bharat's wife Sheila, asked me, 'Do you do any *kaam-vaam* (work or something), or do you live on your father's earnings — *baap kee kamaee ka khaata hai?*' These remarks stung me because they were true. My wife and children were living with my parents; my only income was from stray articles I wrote for local papers or by giving talks on All India Radio. It seldom amounted to Rs 1000 per month. My son's fees at the Doon School were paid by my wife from the money her father had given her. She sought the advice of Mangat Rai and Bharat Ram more than mine. My morale was at its lowest.

I decided to get out of Delhi. My father had an ice-cream factory at Bhopal with a house on the lakeside he had rented for the manager. It was lying empty. I got a servant who would cook for me and took the train to Bhopal. I had to suffer yet another put-down on the way. In my compartment were three Sindhi gentlemen. They were engaged in talking business and took no notice of me. At a wayside station we ordered tea for ourselves. One of the three opened a very fancy tin of biscuits and offered one to me. I shook my head to say no and thanked them. Then one of them reprimanded me: 'The Seth himself offers you his products and you say no. What kind of a man are you?'

I realized that this man was Seth Mangha Ram, the leading producer of biscuits in India. We got talking. He told me of his humble beginnings as a street-hawker in Sukkhur (Sindh) and how he had built up his biscuit business. God had been good to him, he said. He was now a multi-millionaire. I asked him about his family. He told me about his sons. He was happy they had passed their matriculation examinations and were in business with him.

'Why haven't you sent them abroad for higher education?' I asked him.

'What for?' he retorted. 'They know how to make biscuits. They don't have to go abroad to learn anything.'

I persisted in badgering him about opening new horizons for his progeny. He felt needled and turned on me.

'You were educated abroad?' I admitted I was. 'How long did you spend in *vilayat*?' he asked.

'About five years,' I replied.

'How much are you drawing as your salary?' he asked. I mentioned the figure of my last salary. Seth Mangha Ram made a quick calculation and snorted.

'*Tumhaarey baap ka to sood bhee nahin nikla*' — your father has not even realized a reasonable interest on his investment.

The house, Aashiana, was a sparsely furnished double-storeyed building. I occupied a room on the upper floor. The balcony gave a splendid view of the lake and flocks of sarus cranes which sported in the shallows. In between working on my novel, I watched their courtship dances through my field glasses. The only other distraction were women servants from the Nawab's palace, who came in mid-morning to bathe. There were usually five or six of them draped from head to foot in their burqas. There were no houses in the vicinity and the road that led to the palace was some distance from the place where they divested themselves of their clothes. Even Aashiana was beyond the range of human vision. My powerful field glasses brought them almost within arm's reach. It was a lovely spectacle! Once freed of their garments the women splashed about, throwing water at each other, soaping themselves, ducking under water and then drying themselves in the sun.

In the afternoons I took long walks in the woods or went to the railway station to acquaint myself with the way trains were directed to different platforms and the duties of the staff. A railway station was the central part of my novel.

While I was in Bhopal, Rawle Knox of the London *Observer* and his wife Helen came to spend a weekend with me. He had been granted an interview by the Nawab. After sending off his piece to the paper, I took them to see the Buddhist stupas at Sanchi. One night we accompanied a party of shikaris into the jungle in the hope of seeing a tiger. We sat up in an old shooting tower beside a pond, drinking till the early hours. We never got to see a tiger. The shikaris were angry with us because our ceaseless talking had kept animals away from the pond. They vented their frustration on a couple of sambhars which were dazzled by the glare of their car's headlights.

By the end of the month, I had finished the draft of my novel. I named it *Mano Majra* after the village in which I had located it. Back in Delhi, Tatty Bell, the American wife of Walter Bell of the British High Commission, offered to type it out for me. After she had finished the job she told me bluntly,

'It's no good! Nobody is going to publish it.' I was downcast and wanted to tear it up. I am glad I did not. Instead, I sent it to the Grove Press as an entry for the best work of fiction from India. I sent it under the name of my friend I.M. Verma because one of the judges was Krishna Menon. It won the first prize of a thousand dollars and a contract to have it published. The novel was published as *Train to Pakistan* in Britain. The first person to whom I broke the news was Tatty Bell. She rewarded me with a kiss and a cocktail party. She was very kissable and a generous hostess.

I felt I should take on a job. Posts of Producers of Programmes for A.I.R.'s External Services had been advertised. I applied for the one in English; Prakash Shastri, whom I had known in my Lahore days as the founder of Alliance Française and who had a pretty French wife, applied for the French. Both of us were selected. My immediate boss was Professor Daruwala, who had taught me English at Government College. The head of the department was Miss Mehra Masani — as handsome and efficient a woman as any I have ever met. One of our colleagues was Nirad C. Chaudhuri. Within a few days I discovered I had very little work to do. My programme, which went on the air after midnight, consisted of news (read by a news reader), concerts of classical music (selected by a music expert) and short features of no more than ten minutes — also usually written and recorded by an outsider. I finished whatever was expected of me in fifteen minutes. The rest of the day in office was spent gossiping with friends — Nirad Babu after he had written his piece, or Krishen Shungloo who had as little to do as I but kept up the pretence of being heavily overworked. There was also a bevy of pretty girls — Kanta Gupta, a Muslim steno typist in the French division and others. I invited them to my room to while away the hours. What was even more dispiriting was that our transmissions were so feeble that very few people were able to pick them up. We discovered that one night when Prakash Shastri, who was both producer and news reader, didn't show up till half an hour after his programme went on the air. The engineer in-charge of transmission was at his wits end. In sheer desperation he switched on his transmitters and announced: 'This is the French Service of All India Radio. I'm sorry our producer has not arrived and I cannot speak French. So here is some music.' There were no complaints from our French listeners. Shastri was fired from his job.

After two years with All India Radio and very little to show for it, I became desperately anxious to get on to something more worthwhile. My break came with the visit to India of Dr Luther Evans, Director General of UNESCO. I was asked to interview him for the Domestic Services. The interview went well and Evans was impressed. I invited him home for dinner. He was even more impressed with my father's style of living (his being a Knight was a great help) and his hospitality. I wrote to my friend Prem Kirpal who was then Deputy Director of the Cultural Affairs Department in UNESCO to follow up my prospects of joining him. A month later I got an offer to join the Department of Mass Communications to look after the press, film and radio. I accepted it with alacrity. In my notice of resignation to A.I.R. I wrote that I had very little work to do and suggested that the post be scrapped. Much to the chagrin of my friend Krishen Shungloo, who was hoping to take over from me, the post was abolished.

8 Parisian Interlude

I WAS NOT a stranger to Paris and knew something of what
UNESCO did. I had visited Paris many times during my
student days in London and done a three-month course in
spoken French at the Institut du Pantheon close to the
Luxembourg gardens. When P.R.O. in London, Prem Kirpal, as
Secretary to the Indian delegation led by Dr Radhakrishnan,
managed to have my name included as its press officer for a
UNESCO conference in Florence. I took my wife along. We
drove all the way across France and the Alps into Tuscany. I had
practically nothing to do except listen to long-winded orations
on 'culture knowing no frontiers' and 'the need to sow the
seeds of peace in the minds of men'. I saw a good deal of Dr
Radhakrishnan. His opening speech was a *tour de force* of oratory
and won him a standing ovation. Many delegates wanted to
meet him. He received them lying on his bed, where he spent
most of his time reading and writing. Among other visitors was
the film actress Myrna Loy. She became very coy when he
asked her to sit by him while he reclined on his pillow. He put
her at ease by taking her hand, and asking her how many
husbands she had had. It was known that she intended to marry
the leader of the American delegation, Dr Sargeant. Amongst
others I befriended was Carol Laise, who was attached to the
American delegation. She was later posted to India, married
Ambassador Bunker and in her own right became Ambassador
to Nepal.

The three weeks in Florence gave me the opportunity to
visit art galleries, see the Leaning Tower at Pisa, the Palio at
Sienna and some of the Italian lakes. The visit to the Garda still
haunts my dreams. We had driven all afternoon through
sweltering heat looking for a hotel in which we could eat and
spend the night. We hit the Garda — mile after mile of water
shimmering under a hot sun. We came to a narrow causeway

running through the lake. The signboard read San Simione. We decided to try to find a place there. It was a fishing village on a rocky island with a few small hotels. We checked into one. After a wash I decided to take a look at the island. I went up a dusty road which ended in a cemetery with lots of pine trees. I lay down on a bed of pine-needles and watched the blue sky slowly turning dark. I heard the voices of singing fishermen wafting across the water as they returned homewards. I dozed off. I don't know how long I had slept among the dead when I was woken by a nightingale in full-throated song on a branch above my head. A full moon had come up, cutting a swathe of quicksilver across the lake. I lay entranced by the bird's song in the moonlit night — Keats must have heard something similar when he went into ecstasy. Loathe to break the spell, I lay where I was. I watched the moon rise higher and higher in the clear night sky. The nightingale became aware of my presence and flew away. The spell was broken.

Two years later, Kirpal again managed to have my name included in the Indian delegation led by Maulana Azad for a conference in Paris. The Maulana assumed that I had come to Paris to have a good time and did not assign any work to me. Every time I asked him if there was anything I could do, he would answer '*Sardar Sahaib, maza kariye*' — enjoy yourself. The one time I was asked by a senior delegate to get his approval of a particular proposal, I had to disturb him at his hotel in the evening. He was very curt. His evenings were sacred as he enjoyed his Scotch by himself. He wanted his drinking habits to remain unknown in order to preserve his image of the *Imam-ul-Hind* — the think-tank of Muslim India. In the delegation there was also Professor Habib, a charming academic, who was somewhat confused about India's attitude to the admission of Communist China. When it came to voting, he cast India's vote against India's proposal. It had to be rectified.

How seriously could one take UNESCO? I had always been allergic towards people who spouted culture. 'You have to come out with new ideas,' Kirpal told me. He never spelt out what kind of ideas they had to be. However, Paris was a pleasant city to live in for some time. I had happy memories of it and regretted I had never been able to make friends with any Frenchmen or women. The only ones willing to take the hand of friendship I extended were émigrés — white Russians or Americans who had settled there, or Jews who felt insecure in the anti-Semitic atmosphere that often became evident. Despite their high-falutin talk of culture and *poesie* the French were the most money-minded nation I had come across. Wherever you went — to a restaurant, cinema or park to hire a row boat — after paying the money prescribed a hand was invariably stretched out for a *pourboire* (tip). And despite all the bowing, hand-kissing and courtly speech, they could be incredibly discourteous. What a fine place France could be if there were no Frenchmen living in it!

However, there I was in Paris again in the summer of 1954 with a five-year contract in my pocket. We were received at the station by the Secretary of the Ambassador. The Ambassador happened to be none other than my wife's uncle, H.S. Malik, transferred from Canada to France. Temporary accommodation had been found for me near UNESCO, then housed in what had been Hotel Majestic, headquarters of the German Secret Police (Gestapo) during World War II. The first evening we dined with the Maliks. They were cool towards us, as we were towards them. I resolved to have as little to do with them during my stay in France as I could.

The next morning I signed myself in at UNESCO and called on my immediate boss, an American called Schneider and his number two, a French Jew who had changed his name from Philippe Wolfe to Philippe Desjardins when he joined the French Underground. Both spoke English and French with equal fluency. I sensed that Schneider was not on good terms with Luther Evans who was looking for a replacement for him. Schneider had reservations about my appointment. Desjardins was eager to become one of the deputy directors of the department and felt that Evans had inducted me into the organization to make me the other deputy director. He assiduously cultivated my friendship and helped me find temporary accommodation for six months in a pleasant, secluded, one bed-room flat in Cité Negrier, a cul-de-sac branching off a busy street close to the Eiffel Tower. It was owned by the Chinese wife of a French diplomat.

A couple of weeks after we had settled in and I had my son admitted to the American International School, Evans asked me to arrange a meeting for him with editors of British newspapers in London. I proceeded to London and, with the help of Richard Powell of the English Commission for UNESCO, persuaded a few of my editor friends to come to lunch to hear Evans' plans for UNESCO. The English were sceptical about UNESCO and regarded Britain's contribution as a waste of money. Our guests were courteous enough to evince interest in what Evans had to say. Unfortunately, Evans, like many Americans, had a very loud, booming voice. It carried to the ends of the large hall which was unusually crowded at lunch-time. While Evans was expounding his vision of the UNESCO of the future at the top of his voice, an American lady came up behind him and tapped him on his shoulder. Evans stopped his oration and turned round. 'I want to tell you that you have a very loud voice,' she said very curtly. 'At the other end of the hall, I could hear every word of what you were saying and I wasn't one bit interested in what you had to say.' Evans was crushed.

Back in Paris, Evans informed me that I was to be one of the staff to attend a conference in Montevideo, Uruguay and that I should familiarize myself with the budget proposals for the Department of Mass Communications to be able to answer questions put by delegates. It was obvious he wanted me to prove my mettle and see if I would be able to cope with the job of the deputy director of the department. I knew nothing about budgeting and my aversion to anything that had to do with accounting made it difficult for me to grasp what the proposals meant. However, I boarded the chartered flight across the Atlantic to Recife in Brazil. It was a long overnight journey made by propeller aircraft. After another short break for refuelling at Rio de Janeiro, we arrived in Montevideo on a soft summer afternoon.

Montevideans had never seen a Sikh before. They stared at

me with disbelief. Our hosts had arranged seats for us to watch a football match between two top Uruguayan teams. When I arrived there everyone turned to gape at me. The game was stopped for a few minutes till they were convinced that I was just another human being. My photographs were splashed on the front pages of the next morning's papers. However, if Uruguayans knew nothing about India, there were important Indians who did not know of the existence of Uruguay. One proof of this was a letter I received from Surjit Singh Majithia, then Deputy Minister for Defence. I had written to him asking him to speak to Dr Humayun Kabir, Secretary of the Education Ministry, to support my proposal to include translations of the sacred hymns of the Sikhs as part of its programme to publicize literatures of different nations. Majithia's reply came on an envelope addressed to me at 'UNESCO, Palacio Nacional, Montevideo, Uruguay, France.' When my Spanish secretary saw it she was upset. 'Your people don't even know there is a country called Uruguay?' she asked. 'You shouldn't worry,' I assured her. 'This comes from our Ministry of Defence. If they do not know you exist, they can't go to war against you.'

A most interesting experience took place on my third day in the city. I was standing in the foyer of my hotel when a short, wizened, old man with only one eye, approached me and greeted me with 'Sat Sri Akal, Signor!' I answered his greeting and asked him in Punjabi if he was a Sikh. 'Si, Signor,' he replied in Spanish. To prove it he took out an old, battered British passport and pointed to the photograph in it: it was of a young Sikh in his early twenties with only one eye. He pointed to his chest and said in rustic Punjabi, *Naon* (name) Chanchal *Seonh* (Singh). *Pay* (*peo*, or father) Sohan Seon; *Maoo* (mother) Gurdeep Kaur; *pind* (village) something or the other in district Lahore. Then he began to count *ikk, do, tinn, chaar* up to ten. Beyond these words he could neither speak nor understand what I said in Punjabi or English. I asked my Spanish secretary to help me out. It was an incredible story. Chanchal Singh had left Punjab as a young lad intending to settle in Canada. At that time he spoke no language other than Punjabi. The Canadian authorities refused to permit him to stay. He escaped to the

United States. He met the same fate there and was ordered to leave the country in a few days. He hitch-hiked his way southward through Mexico and Brazil. No country would have him till he reached Uruguay and got a job as a farm labourer. He married a Spanish labourer's daughter and had a large family by her. They were given both Sikh and Spanish names: Dilbagh Don Pedro Singh, Santi Carmelita Singh, and so on. Chanchal Singh, who spoke only Punjabi till he was twenty, could now not understand a word of it — fifty years had completely wiped it out of his memory.

I have found that it takes much less than fifty years to erase the memory of a language if one is not exposed to it orally or visually. A Punjabi Muslim businessman (I think his name was Anwar), invited me to dine with him and his Spanish wife. Both spoke English fluently. When she was busy in the kitchen I spoke to my host in Punjabi. He had difficulty in comprehending what I was saying. 'Words sound familiar but I can't recollect what they mean,' he said by way of explanation. 'I have been in Uruguay for twelve years, my work is entirely in Spanish or English. All these years I have not spoken Hindustani or Punjabi to anyone nor kept in touch with them through books or magazines. Now I can neither speak nor understand a word of what you are saying.' In twelve years the tablet of his memory had been wiped clean of his mother tongue.

The Montevideo conference got very little publicity in the international press. Uruguay was not on the world map and UNESCO was regarded as a big bore. M. Shareef, Secretary of the Pakistani delegation, claimed my special attention for not having opposed my induction to UNESCO. In return he wanted me to provide him women he could bed and was very disappointed with me when I was unable to do so. Then he asked me to arrange a press conference for him. I had it announced in the local papers and circulated to all delegates. No one turned up. Shareef made his speech to me. I had it transmitted to Pakistan where all the papers carried it.

The leader of the Pakistani delegation was Education Minister Ishtiaq Hussain Qureshi, who had been a teacher in

St Stephen's College, Delhi during the two years I was there. An amusing incident took place at a small formal luncheon where many heads of delegations were present. Mr Qureshi was sitting alongside me; facing us was the leader of the Australian delegation. Qureshi looked somewhat glum because that morning he had received information that he had been dismissed. (Shareef had told me about it.) The Australian facing us picked up Qureshi's card and introduced himself. 'Mr Minister, my name is so and so: I am with the Australian Ministry of Education.' They shook hands. To keep the conversation going, the Australian said very cheerfully, 'The one difference between you Mr Minister and a civil servant like me, is that I know when I get back to Canberra I have my job waiting for me. A minister can never be sure how long he will last.' I had to kick the Australian under the table to tell him to stop. He simply turned on me and said angrily. 'Why the hell are you kicking me?' I had to confess what I knew, and replied, 'Because you are talking to a minister who has lost his job this morning.'

I did not live up to Luther Evans' expectations and refused to appear before the budget committee. He couldn't now make me deputy of the department. He announced the elevation of Malcolm Adiseshiah, a defrocked Tamilian Christian priest as his Second Assistant Director General on par with the Frenchman, René Maheu who he did not much care for. My only achievement at Montevideo was to have my proposals to include translations of selections from the Sikh scriptures accepted.

I did not get to see much of Uruguay. My Spanish secretary took me to her father's ranch where I saw gauchos ride bareback and lasso a heifer. They slit its throat, then its belly to empty out its entrails. The carcass with its head and skin intact was put on a tripod made of steel bars with a smouldering fire underneath. Then boys and girls danced and sang till the heifer had been roasted. With their cowboy knives they cut huge slices from its body and ate them on paper plates. Flagons of homemade Vino Rosso were poured into their tumblers. The meat, with all its juices intact, was delicious. So was the wine. I also took a bus ride across the Rio Negro and did some bird watching in Montevideo. Two South American birds which remain in my mind are the Orneiro, which builds a two-chambered nest very much like our weaver bird, the Baya. And the Tijerata, the scissor bird, which has two long tails that criss-cross like a pair of scissors.

A month later I was back in Paris. And very depressed for having proved a flop at Montevideo. Schneider was retired. Evans got a Norwegian, Tor Gjesdal from U.N. Public Relations, to take his place. Gjesdal brought his own deputies from New York. I was left virtually without any staff to administer except my loyal secretary, Yvonne Le Roughetel. Gjesdal didn't much care for me, and whenever he called a staff meeting he would say with a deep sigh, 'Mr Singh, I really don't know what to do with you! Perhaps you can write a book on UNESCO?' There were days when I drowned my despair in drink. In the evenings I would put on Indian records I had brought with me. Lata Mangeshkar singing *'Jogee mat ja; paoon padoon mein teyrey'* — Yogi don't leave me I beseech you — proved too much and I would go out in the garden to shed some tears. The gloom partly lifted when I got a telegram from Barney Rosset of Grove Press that my novel *Mano Majra* (now better known as *Train to Pakistan*) had been adjudged the best work of fiction for the year (1954). I bullied Prem Kirpal into throwing a party and have Luther Evans present the cheque to me in the presence of Sir Ramaswamy Mudaliar who was then visiting Paris. The award gave me enough money to buy a Mercedes Benz.

The UNESCO project for translations of selections from the Sikh scriptures had been steered by me through the National Commission and UNESCO almost single-handed. I was sent to Delhi to arrange for the selection of passages and pick a panel of translators. It gave me an experience of what Sikh scholars could be like. I called on Hukam Singh, then Speaker of the Lok Sabha. He suggested I get one Dr Tarlochan Singh from Ludhiana to be convenor and coordinator. I suspect Hukam Singh did not know much about this man except that he professed to be a Doctor of Divinity (nobody knew from where) and was very hard up. Hukam Singh rang up Tarlochan Singh, who arrived in Delhi the next day. He was a long-bearded Granthi-type with a strong dislike of others in the field, particularly Dr Gopal Singh Dardi. We decided on a panel of four translators: he stubbornly refused to have Dardi's name included. Another panel of scholars were asked to select passages. Dr Radhakrishnan agreed to write the preface. When Dardi heard that he had not been included in the panel he wrote to me protesting and beseeching me to include his name as a UNESCO nominee. I wrote back saying that I had nothing to do with the selection but had sensed that both Tarlochan Singh and Kapur Singh, who had been a close friend of Dardi at one time, had strong reservations against him. Dardi turned nasty. Being a congenital name-dropper, he threatened to take up the matter with Prime Minister Nehru. I wrote back equally rudely telling him to do his worst. Things were never the same between us till the last year of his life.

Kapur Singh was another prickly character. He claimed to have a doctorate in philosophy from Oxford. He got into the I.C.S. through nomination as a Sikh. After a few years in service he was dismissed for corruption. He never forgave the Indian Government for the insult. He joined the Akali party, was elected to the Lok Sabha and was the principal author of the Anandpur Sahib Resolution, describing the Sikhs as a nation apart from other Indians and demanding 'self-determined status' for them. He had a very exaggerated opinion of his learning and regarded other Akalis as brainless rustics. He also had an explosive temper.

The selected passages were translated and sent to me. They made poor reading. Instead of sending them back to the translators who had been handsomely paid, I persuaded UNESCO to let me hire an English poet to polish them up. I engaged the services of Gordon Fraser, a minor poet suggested by my friend Guy Wint and spent a fortnight with him in London to make sure he did not take too many liberties with the original. The translation with an erudite introduction by Dr Radhakrishnan was published by Messrs Allen & Unwin under the title *Selected Sacred Writings of the Sikhs.*

A postscript to the publication was Tarlochan Singh turning nasty towards me. Messrs Allen & Unwin advertised the book with my name on the top of the panel of translators as they had published me earlier and I was better known in England than the others. They had not consulted anyone about it. Tarlochan Singh went to Krishna Kripalani, Secretary of the Sahitya Akademi, and wrote to Dr Radhakrishnan accusing me of having manoeuvred to get my name on top of the list. I protested my innocence. They did not believe me. I got Allen & Unwin to write to them saying that I had nothing whatsoever to do with it, and that at my request had now put my name at the bottom of the list of translators. Only Kripalani apologized to me. I decided to have nothing more to do with Radhakrishnan or Tarlochan Singh.

When my lease for the Cité Negrier apartment was over, Yvonne Le Roughetel found us a pleasant little bungalow in a suburb called Bourg La Reine near Parc de Sceaux. We shifted to our new abode. We got a very pretty English girl, Mary, to cook and run our home. My son, much to his disgust, had to be transferred from the American International School to Lycee La Canal and my daughter put in a French convent as a day boarder. At the time both were very unhappy with me. Neither could speak French and had trouble following their teachers. Mala resented being described as a *negre* (black) and, despite my assurances that *negres* were nice people, remained inconsolable. Later in life, both grudgingly admitted that but for my forcing them into French schools they would never have learnt to speak the language.

Our new home was on a road named Rue du Colonel Candelot alongside a railway track. I woke to the swishing sound of the first train applying its hydraulic breaks to come to a halt at Bourg La Reine ('Bugger the Queen' to my English friends) station. My early morning dream was usually of drowning in a waterfall. I caught the 9 am train which dropped me at Etoile. The first call was at the cafeteria to have a hot croissant with butter and a piping hot cup of coffee. Then I went to my room to scribble my draft on UNESCO, dictate a few letters to Yvonne and await my wife who came at noon to join me for lunch. Then with Kirpal we went out looking for restaurants which provided good fare at reasonable prices. One thing about Paris was that almost every restaurant served delicious food. If the weather was inclement we could lunch in the UNESCO cafeteria or restaurant. Wine was *de rigeur*. By the time I returned to my room my head was fuzzy with drink. An English stenographer, who was totally blind, would make our afternoon tea. Then it was time to return home before the rush-hour traffic started. It began to dawn on me that, while living in Paris was pleasant enough, I was doing very little to justify my existence. That did not deter me from taking the family for walks in Parc de Sceaux and feeding the swans. We made it a point to get out of Paris over weekends. Kirpal was always with us. He was seen with my wife and children more than I was. Unescans living in the neighbourhood asked me if I spent the weekends with the Kirpals.

We also had occasional visitors from India. The first was my youngest brother Daljit. He had one look at pretty Mary and decided to seduce her. She got scared of his advances and sought my wife's protection. My wife stayed in Mary's bedroom till my brother tired of waiting to get at her and fell asleep. Then we had the Bharat Rams. Sheila came from Moscow where she had gone with a delegation of Indian women. She had been allowed to take her personal jewellery — I believe worth over Rs 12 lakhs — to exhibit. Her jewellery attracted the Russian women more than the Indian dancers and singers had. We had very little room in the house, but she refused to stay in a hotel. Her husband, who was in England, was to join her in Paris before long. Sheila left for India and Bharat stayed on a few days longer. Before leaving he asked me if he could take my wife out for lunch and to suggest the name of a good place to eat at. On a slip of paper I wrote out Tour d'Argent, the most expensive restaurant in Paris, and assured him that every cab driver knew it. I told my wife, 'It's your only chance to eat there.' They went to the restaurant, Bharat had a look at the menu and the prices. 'There is nothing here for a vegetarian,' he said. He found a cheaper place where he could get his daal-bhaat. It takes more than business acumen to become a billionaire. You also have to know how to conserve what you have inherited.

Talking of conserving one's earnings, I met the best living example in Baldoon Dhingra. I had known him in Lahore when he joined Government College as a lecturer. He was a dapper little fellow full of enthusiasm and literary ambitions. In Lahore, he published an essay which he had sent as an entry to some university competition. The printed edition gave the impression that it had won the prize. It had not. On Partition, he came to Paris and learnt to speak French fluently. He and his wife Kamla laid siege to Dr Radhakrishnan and had him persuade the Director General of UNESCO to give him a job. He was given a lowly one temporarily in the Mass Communication Department. His wife supplemented his income by lecturing in different parts of Europe. They had a tiny one-room apartment. When their two daughters came for vacations from school in England they slept in their parents' car parked in the street below. They had also devised a plan to get their meals free of charge. At UNESCO House there was always a reception or two going on in the evenings. Kamla would come wandering in and ask the hosts if they had seen her husband anywhere. They hadn't, but would she have a drink before resuming her search? Then Baldoon would come around looking for his wife and be persuaded to stay for a drink. Kamla would breathe into his ear, 'I have not cooked anything at home. You better eat whatever you want here.' They made a meal of the canapes and cocktail sausages. They trained their daughters well. One or the other would turn up at lunch time to seek advice from Baldoon's colleagues and be persuaded to have lunch with him. It took me some time to realize that I was feeding the girls at least once a week. Kirpal and other Indians were looking after them on other days. The Dhingras' greatest achievement was the way they organized their elder daughter's marriage. They found out when Dr Radhakrishnan was to visit

Paris and wrote to him asking him to bless their child on the occasion. Armed with his letter agreeing to give the benediction, they approached the Indian ambassador with whom Dr Radhakrishnan was to stay to permit them to have the marriage ceremony performed in his residence, as they could not arrange for a *havan* elsewhere. He readily agreed. And also agreed to hold the wedding reception. Kamla had made Signor Montessori (Madame Montessori's son) her *dharam bhai* — brother in faith. She told him that it was customary for a mother's brother to provide gold bangles at his niece's wedding. He had gold bangles made for the girl. The Dhingras were generous with their invitations. They invited just about everyone they knew in Paris and London. The cards mentioned that the Vice-President of India would grace the occasion and bless the bridal couple. Everyone accepted. Everyone came armed with an expensive gift. All that the Dhingras paid for was the printing of the cards and postage. The Dhingras ingenuity inspired me to write the short story 'Mr Kanjoos the Great Miracle'.

Kamla often came to have a meal with us. After my family had returned to India, she invited me to dine with her provided I brought the ingredients for the food which she would cook for me. I never dined with her. Nobody quite knew what Baldoon Dhingra did in UNESCO. Whenever anyone went to his room, he was found vacantly staring at a blank wall. They hoped one day he would come out with some world-shattering thought. The Director General's patience began to run out. Under Radhakrishnan's pressure he was given two extensions of six months each. Then fired. Before I left Paris, Kamla tried to persuade me to take some items she had bought for her house in Delhi as my personal baggage. They consisted of a bath tub and marble tiles for her bathroom. I refused. Baldoon stayed on in Paris, took on an English mistress and sired a son through her. Kamla was very angry. With their savings she had built property in Delhi. Now there was a bastard to lay claim to it. A few months later, Baldoon died in Paris of acute anemia.

There were half a dozen Indians besides Adiseshiah, Kirpal

and myself in UNESCO. There was Dr Naidu, a scientist who had a European wife and a pretty daughter, Leela. Once she came to see me in my office in her school uniform and smudges of ink on her face. She was hardly fifteen. I could see she was going to make a ravishing beauty. She did. She caught the eye of Tikki Oberoi, son of the leading hotelier of India. They made a disastrous marriage. She gave him twin daughters before she deserted them to join the film industry in Bombay. She then married Dom Moraes.

There was also a young South Indian couple. He was a budget officer and very competent at his job. The two were desperately anxious to have children. But much as he tried, his wife failed to conceive. He began to cast around. Every weekend he had some important business to attend to in Geneva. He would leave Paris on Friday evenings and return on Monday in time to get to office. One Monday morning he had just time to take a quick shave, change into fresh clothes and dash off to office. His wife thought she would iron his suit. While she was doing so she chanced upon a little packet in the inside pocket. Its contents made no sense to her because they had had no occasion to use such things, but it looked very suspicious to her. She went to an American lady neighbour to ask her what it was. When told, she was understandably very upset and determined to haul her husband over the coals. Her friend persuaded her not to do so. 'I'll fix him for you once and for all,' she assured her. The lady bought a bottle of Ellerman's embrocation, which is meant to relax horse's muscles but is strong enough to inflame the human skin. She smeared the insides of the pocket's contents with the embrocation and put it back in the husband's coat pocket. He wore the suit on his next weekend visit to Geneva. It was his last visit there.

There were other incidents in UNESCO that have stayed in my mind. One was to do with the problems of rats. Hotel Majestic had underground tunnels which led to the extensive sewage canals that ran beneath the length and breadth of the city. They were infested with monstrous-sized sewer rats. They found their way to the food stores of UNESCO's restaurants and cafeterias and caused heavy losses. UNESCO's night guards were given flashlights and pistols to shoot the rats. They were unable to cope with them and some were bitten. Luther Evans was appraised of the problem. Being a man of common sense, he suggested that UNESCO buy a few cats and let them cope with the menace. The cats had a wonderful time, killing and eating the rats. By the time the rats disappeared, the cats had multiplied and become like savage little tigers. In the absence of rats, they began to break into UNESCO's food stores and cause heavier losses than before. Once more Luther Evans came to the rescue. The services of cat catchers were acquired. Over a weekend, they rounded up over eighty cats, put them in sacks and loaded them in their trucks to be drowned in the Seine at some spot far from Paris. When they got to their destination, the cat-catchers were overcome with remorse. Drown eighty innocent cats? Why not let them loose to fend for themselves? That is exactly what they did. The cat-catchers returned to UNESCO House and collected their fee. In the next few days, one after another, the cats found their way back to the Hotel Majestic. The episode was the subject of my story 'Rats and Cats in the House of Culture'.

As one would expect in an organization where people, besides stenos-typists and menial staff, had so little to do and much spare time on their hands to keep up the pretence of being overworked, there was more than the usual quota of crackpots. One instance will suffice. There was a young Czech girl, whose name I forget, who was a keen table-tennis player. Before going home in the evening she spent an hour or more vigorously bashing a celluloid ball. My son, who sometimes came with his mother to get a ride home, often played with her. She was a shy, reticent girl whom everyone liked. She lived alone and had no boyfriends. One morning she did not show up or send word to explain why she had not come. One of her friends went to the girl's apartment to see if all was well. She was known to have some kind of heart ailment and frequently went for a check-up. When the woman got to the apartment, she found the door ajar and the girl lying crumpled near her telephone. She was removed to hospital where the doctor pronounced her dead. Her women friends in UNESCO refused to accept the doctor's verdict and swore that the girl was under a spell. And what she really needed was somebody who knew the secret mantra which would bring her out of her trance. Who could know more about mantras than the dark man who wore a turban and beard and was also known to be the girl's friend?

A delegation of three women came to see me. Had I heard of what had happened to the Czech girl? I replied I had and was very sorry to hear that one so young and likeable had gone so early in life. 'But Mr Singh, surely you don't believe she is dead!' they remonstrated. 'She is under an evil spell. We wondered if you knew the right mantra to get her out of it.' I was stupefied. I tried to argue with them. 'The doctor would know whether she is in a trance or dead,' I protested. 'What do doctors know about such things?' they maintained. 'If you know the mantra we will take you to her and you will see for yourself that she is not dead; just in deep sleep.' I pleaded ignorance: though I was an oriental I had no esoteric knowledge. 'Ask Dhingra or Prem Kirpal or one of the other Indians or Pakistanis,' I suggested. I don't know whether or not they had any success with them but the next day the head of Personnel, a dry-as-bones Englishman, William Farr, asked me to come to his room. Several women, including those who had been to see me, were sitting in his waiting room. I went in. Bill Farr held his head between his hands and asked, 'If there is anything you can do to the poor Czech girl, we will be very obliged. You see she is to be buried this evening. We don't want to bury her alive.' I was even more pained with the cold-blooded Englishman's request. 'Bill, are you mad? You listen to all those crazy women and expect me to revive the dead! What kind of loony-bin is this anyhow?'

That shook the man a little. 'I know it sounds odd, but since these ladies insist that you know the right mantra, I thought there was no harm in asking you to try.'

I was not keen to write a book on UNESCO; I knew I would not stay there very long. I had a five-year contract: only the contracts of duds were not renewed. I hadn't yet been relegated to that category. And five years were too long to be doing little besides enjoying good food and wine and visiting chateaux on the Loire. I would have to make the break soon. I found a lovely little pub in a village called St Jean au Bois (St John's Wood), deep in a forest near Compiègne where the armistice was signed between the French and the Germans to end World War I. It was barely forty minutes drive from Bourg La Reine, but appeared a million miles away from habitation. The woods were so dark and deep that walking alone even in broad daylight gave me an eerie feeling. The food was wholesome. The wine potable. A few wood-cutters, farmers and caretakers of the Chateau came to have their evening drink at the pub. We exchanged greetings. They left me alone. They had heard what I was there for: the French have an exaggerated respect for an *ecrivain*. It was a good place to be alone with one's thoughts and put them on paper. I began to work on my second novel, *I Shall Not Hear the Nightingale*.

A pleasant interlude in my otherwise unexciting tenure with UNESCO was to cover UNESCO's Executive Board Meeting in Madrid. I very much wanted to visit Spain: my earlier attempt to go there as a member of the International Brigade when the Spanish Civil War broke out had got no further than putting my name down on a form while in London. (The only people who were able to lay their hands on it were the C.I.A. I was branded as a communist sympathizer, had endless trouble getting American visas and remained on their alert list till the 1970's). Kirpal and I decided to go by car. My secretary, Yvonne Le Rougetel, decided to take a free ride with us. I had to do all the driving as Kirpal was a notoriously indifferent driver. We drove at a leisurely pace covering a couple of hundred miles a day and stopped overnight in small hotels. I anticipated trouble at the Spanish frontier, but since we carried diplomatic passports we were let through without fuss. As soon as we entered Spain I noticed the difference in the landscape and the standards of living in the two countries. Every Spanish town we passed through looked run down and swarmed with people, mostly children. The fare in restaurants was limited, the wines (except sherry) second rate. However, hotels in Madrid were like other good hotels in Europe.

Kirpal had some work with the Executive Board; I had nothing to do. I spent my time profitably visiting galleries and museums. I tried to persuade Kirpal to come to the Prado with me. 'I've seen the Louvre; it has the best of every artist of the world. I don't want to waste my time in Madrid,' he asserted. After my second visit to the Prado, I told Kirpal that the Prado had a better collection than the Louvre (which was not true) and that when he returned to Paris his colleagues were sure to ask him whether he had been to it. What kind of head of the Cultural Department was he if he did not even know the names of great masters? He felt I had a point. The next day he went up and down the corridors of the Prado and 'did' the famous art gallery in fifteen minutes flat. When questioned by his colleagues in Paris he praised the Prado collection as perhaps richer than even the Louvre. They were dismayed by his remark: 'Dr Kirpal, how can you say such a thing? The Louvre is three times as large as the Prado and, as art collections go, much the richest in the world.' Later Kirpal remonstrated, 'K. Singh you are always misleading me.' I had to admit that it was the only way of getting him to visit the gallery.

One evening while we were having tea in the crowded reception hall of our hotel, Kirpal decided to ring up Elizabeth Adiseshiah and invite her for dinner. He went to the residents' telephone attached to a wall and rang up. When he got her on the line he yelled at the top of his voice, 'Lizbeth, this is Kirpal. How are you?' Everyone in the hall stopped talking, all eyes turned on him. He continued, 'Lizbeth, what are you doing for dinner? Come over to our hotel and eat with us. Malcolm is going to some formal banquet.' He came back triumphantly to the table and announced, 'Elizabeth will join us for dinner.' I replied, 'I know: so does everyone else in the hall. Why do you have to yell whenever you use the phone?' He looked abashed. 'Her hotel is five miles away from here,' he answered.

It reminded me of Winston Churchill's comment on a cabinet colleague, Mr Brown, who during the war occupied the neighbouring cabin. One day he was talking very loudly over the phone. Churchill asked his Secretary to go over and tell Mr Brown not to talk at the top of his voice. The Secretary returned to inform Churchill, 'Sir, the Minister is talking to Scotland.' Replied Churchill very acidly, 'I am sure he is but tell him to use the phone.'

I am ashamed to admit that among the things I enjoyed most in Spain were bullfights. On my first visit to see a bullfight, I was accompanied by a very frail English woman, Mrs Powell, and a big, muscular Frenchwoman on UNESCO's staff. The most attractive spectacle in any bullfight is the opening when banderilleros, matadors, picadors and toreadors in their broad black hats and red tunics enter the arena on horseback, salute the judges and seek permission to start. The fight starts when an enormous black bull is let in. The sudden change from its dark cage to the sunlit arena and the thunderous applause bewilders it and it looks around to see what it is all about. It sees a man on horseback at the other end of the arena; its bewilderment turns to rage and it charges towards the horse and rider. The cavalier (banderillero) gallops towards the oncoming bull. It seems horse and bull will meet in a dreadful collision. A split second before they meet the horse swerves a few inches and the rider drops two spiked shafts into the bull's neck. It is a breathtaking spectacle. What follows is very crude. Picadors armed with long lances goad the bleeding bull; the bull charges into the horses and probably breaks their ribs. The horse's vocal cords are severed before it enters the fight so that its whinnying in pain cannot be heard. The finale is again a display of great finesse. A matador armed with a red cape and a curved sabre approaches the now tired and bloodied bull. Each time the bull charges at the red cape, the matador deftly steps aside. The macabre death dance continues till the bull is utterly exhausted. Its head droops and its tongue hangs out. Then, standing on his toes barely a foot away from the bull's horns, the matador aims his sabre at a spot between the bull's head and neck. The crowd roars *aura* ('now'). He pushes the sabre in as if it was a dart aimed at a dart board. If correctly aimed the sabre goes in like a knife into a pat of butter. The bull slumps to the ground — dead.

In the first fight, the sight of so much blood made me sick and brought vomit to my throat. The tough-looking

Frenchwoman burst into tears and walked out saying she could not stand such wickedness any more. The frail Mrs Powell was very excited and cheered every move. After my initial revulsion, I began to enjoy the fights that followed, and felt guilty that I was enjoying this cruel sport. The session ended with the judges awarding prizes to the matadors. A good performance was rewarded with the ears of the bull he had slain. If the performance was exceptional, the judges gave him the bull's tail for keeps. The brochure in English explaining the technicalities of bullfighting solemnly stated that, if the judges were very pleased with the matador's skill, they could award him the arse of the bull. However cruel and gory the sport, it had this redeeming feature: the slain bull's meat was put up for sale outside the stadium. If I were a bull I would rather die fighting an uneven battle than be slaughtered in an abattoir.

Altogether different was Flamenco dancing. In London I had seen the great Antonio on the stage. It was so much easier to understand and enjoy than Russian ballet. Perhaps it was its Moorish origin and likeness to Kathak, that gave me a rapport with it. The singing that accompanied Flamenco also sounded familiar.

Back in Paris, I knew my days in UNESCO and Paris were drawing to a close. The moment of truth came when Tor Gjesdal's secretary came to give me the report that he (Gjesdal) had made on me. Rules required that I read it and put down any comments I wished to make. 'I am not interested in Gjesdal's opinion of me,' I told his secretary and refused to open the envelope. The secretary insisted that I read and sign it. I tore up the envelope and threw it into the wastepaper basket. When the secretary went back empty-handed and told Gjesdal what I had done, he sent for me. I could see he was shaken. 'You should have at least read what I had written; you had no right to assume that it was an adverse report,' he said. 'Mr Gjesdal, I am not interested in knowing your opinion about me. I have decided to quit because there is nothing for me to do here.'

I sent in the required three months' notice to Gjesdal to be forwarded to the Director General. Luther Evans had by now got over his admiration for Gjesdal and the cronies he had brought with him from New York. He summoned Gjesdal and told him that he held him responsible for my deciding to quit. Gjesdal tried to make up with me. He asked me to attend a meeting of the United Nations Associations being held in Geneva to answer any questions delegates may ask about the activities of UNESCO. The meeting was about the most pointless I have ever attended. Delegates largely consisted of American and European dowagers in large hats who had the good of the world in their hearts. The first three days they discussed other U.N. organizations like UNICEF, WHO and ILO. No one seemed to be interested in UNESCO. I spent my hours solving *The Times* crossword puzzle. In order not to be disturbed, I switched my earphone to Spanish, which I did not understand. One afternoon while deep in my crossword, I heard the Spanish word for UNESCO pronounced *Unethko*. I quickly switched on the English, only to hear the Chairman announce that they were fortunate in having Mr Singh of UNESCO amongst them and that he would now invite me to answer all the questions put by delegates on that organization. I hadn't heard any of them and did not have the presence of mind to ask them to repeat what they had said. Sweat poured down my forehead as for one seemingly endless minute of silence the delegates looked at me and I looked at them. The Chairman must have concluded that I was some kind of nut. 'Mr Singh has nothing to say, so we can pass on to the next item on the agenda,' he announced.

I returned to Paris and reported to Gjesdal that no one had asked any questions on UNESCO. A few days later he got a report from the Chairman that questions on UNESCO had remained unanswered.

The last sop Gjesdal threw my way was to send me to Denmark and Sweden to meet people interested in UNESCO activities. I spent a couple of days in Copenhagen, called on some editors and spent the evenings at the Tivoli gardens, famous for their bars and hookers. No one evinced much interest in UNESCO. It was the same in Stockholm. There, besides a family of busty blondes who entertained me in their home, I saw for the first time miles of beach where no one had a strip of clothing on their persons. It was not a particularly edifying sight: old men, women and the obese are best seen with their clothes on.

My next port of call was the university town of Malmo. I arrived there by train in the early hours of the morning. I found the hotel where I had been booked. Through the plate glass window, I could see the hotel guard fast asleep on the sofa. I rang the bell and slapped the door many times without succeeding in rousing him. I dumped my suitcase at the door and decided to take a look at the town. I trudged through the cold, deserted streets for over an hour before people started coming out of their homes. I was famished and looked for a cafe where I could have a cup of hot coffee and a croissant. Reaching a building with a brightly lit basement which had a cafeteria, I joined the queue outside. To hide my embarrassment at being stared at, I held my newspaper in front of me as I shuffled along. When I got to the counter and looked around, I found myself to be the only man in the hall. It was a girls' school and what I had joined were students queuing up for their breakfast. I looked very foolish but kept a straight face. I took a mug of coffee and a bun. There was no cash counter where I could pay. I held out a palm full of Swedish coins to the waitress who had served me. She smiled and said in English, 'School, free.' I gulped down my bun and coffee and fled to my hotel. There were no takers for UNESCO in Malmo either, and I returned to Paris.

I sent my family home and decided to spend the leave due to me working on my novel. I have never believed in goodbyes and farewell parties. The only one in UNESCO who knew I was leaving was Paulette Matthews, a sixty-year-old widow of Anglo-French parentage who had a cottage in the village of Faviers, close to a small town, Houdan, between Paris and Versailles. She offered me the use of the cottage where her ninety-year-old mother lived in the care of a German *au pair* girl. Her only other employee was a club footed gardener, Jacques, who came in for the day to tend her flowers and fruit trees. There was a small cottage in the garden rented by a bank clerk who worked in Houdan. He had a one-year-old girl; his wife was expecting her second in a few months. Besides them, there was a little dog, Junta. So one evening I walked out of Hotel Majestic as I had on other evenings over the past two years, but instead of driving to Bugger the Queen (Bourg la Reine) I drove to Paulette Mat-thews' cottage in Faviers.

It did not take me long to settle down to work. I made my own breakfast and sat in the shade of a massive pear tree loaded with fruit, working on my novel. Paulette's aged mother was a late riser and had the *au pair* girl, Marianne, to sponge and feed her in her room; I rarely saw them. Marianne was busy all day, sweeping the floors, dusting the furniture and helping the gardener. I could see that the gardener had a crush on the German girl and resented my presence in the house. The bank clerk left early and came home very late. His wife was having trouble with her second pregnancy and couldn't look after her one-year-old daughter. The child turned to me. She spent most of her time with me in the garden and slept in my lap when she was tired. I took her out in her pram, with Junta running ahead of us through fields with standing corn flecked with poppies, and skylarks trilling away in the blue heavens. Paulette returned home late in the evenings in time for drinks and dinner. Only on weekends was she there all the time. On Sundays I drove her and Marianne to church — both were Catholics — and brought them back. Occasionally, Marianne and I went out in the early hours to pick mushrooms. I also took her to Chartres cathedral and Versailles.

During these months my only contact with UNESCO was Prem Kirpal. Once a week I went to his one-bedroom apartment. We went out for dinner with his then lady friend, Raymonde Sokolovsky, a petite French-Jewish girl who was into spiritualism, Ouspensky and Gurdjieff. Some evenings she invited us to her apartment, played the piano and gave us dinner. Prem often made passes at her, she responded and hoped that he would some day propose marriage to her or take her to bed. Kirpal was in the habit of making passes and withdrawing when visions of the bed or a wedding ring loomed. In her frustration, Raymonde turned to me for solace.

The two or three months' stay at Faviers were quite fruitful. I was able to finish the first draft of my second novel and gained the friendship of Raymonde and Marianne. Raymonde came to stay with us in Delhi during a UNESCO conference: Marianne kept in touch through letters. I stayed with her and her husband and daughters in Wuppertal whenever I happened to be in Germany. Our friendship continued even after she divorced her husband. It was later, when she got involved with some Hindu cult, shaved off her hair and took to wearing saffron that communication between us snapped. I had succeeded in talking her out of rigid Catholicism and church-going; I failed to wean her off her newly-found enthusiasm for some obscure ashram near Hardwar. She stayed with us in Delhi on her first visit. I tried my best to understand what she was getting out of bathing in the Ganga, worshipping gods whose names she did not know and singing bhajans she did not understand. The bank manager's wife, daughter and son came to see me with Paulette on one of my visits to Paris. The one-year-old child I had known had grown into a pretty fifteen-year-old schoolgirl. A few years later she sent me her wedding photographs.

I sold my Mercedes Benz (at a loss) and came to Paris to catch the night train to London. I had not told anyone of my date of departure. But at the station to bid me farewell there were three ladies from UNESCO with whom I had had very little to do when they were working with me.

I returned home to Delhi. Once again I was without a job and with very little money in my pocket or in my bank account. All I had on the credit side was a collection of short stories which brought me some good notices but no money, a short and unsatisfactory *Short History of the Sikhs* which was condemned by orthodox Sikhs, and a novel which brought me money which I had spent. And the manuscript of a second novel which had yet to be accepted by a publisher.

Among those who greeted me at home was a one-month old Alsatian pup presented by a friend of my father's to my daughter, Mala. To start with, he resented me as an intruder in his tight little human family consisting of my wife and our two children. He slept in the same upstairs bedroom in my father's house and used the roof of the porch as his lavatory. Till then he had no name. I decided to name him Simba after the marmalade cat we had abandoned in Paris. As with most Alsatians, Simba was a one-person dog. He belonged to my daughter, my wife fed him, took him to the vet for his shots and for any ailment he had, but he adopted me as his master. He was as human a dog as I have ever known and shared our joys as he did our sorrows. By the time we moved into our own ground-floor apartment in Sujan Singh Park, he had got over his frisky puppiness and grown into a powerful full-sized German Shepherd. He still shared our bedroom, where he had his own cot. And for his sake more than ours we had an airconditioner put in the room. Often at night he would sniff into my ears and ask me to make room for him. I did. He would heave himself on to the bed with a deep sigh of gratitude, and take over more than half of my bed for the rest of the night.

We would talk to him. If we pretended to cry, he would sniff soothingly in our ears and join us wailing: *booo, ooo ooo*. If he was naughty, we'd order him to the corner. He stayed there with his head down in penitence till we said, 'Okay, now you can come back.'

Simba developed a special relationship with Mala's ayah, the seventy-five-year-old Mayee. 'Vey Shambia!' she would greet him as she opened the door to let Simba out in the garden. She waited for him to do his business in the garden before going to the neighbouring gurdwara to say her prayers. He knew he was not allowed inside the gurdwara and sat outside guarding her slippers. Just as the morning prayer was about to end, he would take one of her slippers in his mouth, trot home and hide it under a bed. Mayee would follow him pleading, 'Vey Shambia! Where have you hidden my slipper?' He followed her from room to room wagging his tail till she found the missing slipper.

Simba was always impatient for his evening walk. He would put his head in my lap and look appealingly at me: 'Isn't it time?' his eyes asked. 'Not yet,' I would reply. Then he would bring his leash and put it at my feet. 'Now?' I would tell him not to be so impatient. Next he brought my walking stick and dropped it on the book I was reading. 'Surely now!' There was no escape. He whined and trembled with excitement as we left. As he jumped on to the rear seat of the car his whining became louder. He liked to put his head out of the window and bark challenges to every dog, cow or bull we passed on the road. He had to be let off at the entrance of the Lodhi gardens. He raced the car, stopping briefly to defecate, and resumed the race to the parking lot. At that time there used to be some hares in the park. He would sniff them out of the hedges and then go in hot pursuit, yelping as he tried to catch up with them. They were too fast and dodgy for him. But he became quite adept at hunting squirrels. He learnt that they ran to the nearest tree and went round its bole to evade pursuit. He would steal up to the tree and then go for them. In the open ground they had no escape. However much I reprimanded him and even beat him, he could not resist killing harmless squirrels.

On Saturday evenings he could sense from the picnic basket being packed that the next day would be devoted largely to him. Long before dawn he would start whimpering with excitement and wake everyone up. It was difficult to control him in the car. When we got to the open countryside near Suraj Kund, or Tilpat, we had to let him out to prevent him jumping out of the car. He would chase herds of cows and scatter them over the fields. Once he nearly got his face bashed in by the rear kick of a cow. And once he almost killed a goat.

Three to four hours in the open countryside chasing hares, deer or peafowl made him happily tired. It was a drowsy, sleepy Simba we brought back from our Sunday morning picnics. He was not so impatient now for his evening walk.

He was, again, restless for his after-dinner stroll round Khan Market, where we went to get paan. He would stop by the ice-cream man and plead with us to buy him one. He was passionately fond of ice-cream. He was also very possessive. Once somebody had two lovely pups for sale under a tree in the market. He resented our paying attention to them. Whenever we stopped by the tree he would savagely bite its bole. Everyone in and around Sujan Singh Park knew Simba. We came to be known by the children of the locality as Simba's parents.

Simba was also feared. Once when going out with my wife and daughter in the Lodhi gardens, a cyclist slapped my daughter on her back and sped on. My wife screamed, 'Simba get him!' Simba chased the man, knocked him off his bicycle and stood over him baring his fangs. The poor fellow folded the palms of his hands and pleaded forgiveness. Another time, as I was stepping out of my flat after dinner, I heard a girl shout for help. Two young lads were trying to molest her. I ran towards her with Simba following on my heels. The boys tried to run away. I ordered Simba to get them. He ran and brought one fellow down on the ground. He was a big fellow and much stronger than I. But with Simba at my side, I had no hesitation in slapping the man many times across his face and roundly abusing him, calling him a goonda and a budmaash. He asked to be forgiven and swore he would never make passes at women again.

We always took Simba with us to Mashobra or Kasauli. He was happiest in the mountains. I often put him on the leash to make him pull us up steep inclines. He liked Kasauli more than Shimla because of its herds of rhesus monkeys and langoors. He waged unceasing warfare against them, and against hill crows which flocked round when he was having his afternoon meal.

Most dogs have a sixth sense. Our Simba had seventh and eighth senses as well. I will mention only one episode to prove it. My wife and I had to go abroad for a couple of months. Our children were in boarding schools. We decided to give our servants leave and lock up our flat. Simba was to be housed with

Prem Kirpal: the two were on very friendly terms, as Prem was always with us on our Sunday outings and a regular visitor to our home. He happily agreed to take Simba. Being a senior government official, he had a bungalow on Canning Lane with a large garden. Simba had been there many times and sensed that we meant to leave him there. He did not seem to mind very much.

My wife returned to Delhi a few days before me. She went to Canning Lane to fetch Simba. He greeted her joyfully but refused to get into her car. Prem was very pleased over his success in winning Simba's affections. My wife reluctantly gave in. 'If he is happy with you, he can stay here,' she said. Apparently they mentioned the date I was due to return, and Simba heard them. The evening before I returned to Delhi, Simba walked all the way from Canning Lane to Sujan Singh Park and scratched at the door with his paws to announce his arrival. He knew I was coming next morning. Prem was more dejected at Simba leaving him than he would have been had I stolen his mistress.

Simba aged gracefully. The hair about his mouth turned white. He developed cataracts in his eyes. Sometimes he got feverish: there were times when my wife spent whole nights with his head on her lap, stroking his head. He was then well over thirteen years old. When I got a three-month teaching assignment at Swarthmore College, we had to leave him in the care of his real mistress, my daughter Mala. She had to take him to the vet almost every day. He didn't get any better. His legs began to give in. She sent us a cable 'Return immediately, Simba seriously ill.' The next day, we received another cable from Mala: 'Simba passed away peacefully.'

Apparently, the vet advised Mala that Simba was in pain, his legs were paralysed and he couldn't last much longer. With her permission he gave him a lethal dose of something which put him to sleep. If I had to talk of my close friendships, Simba would be amongst the top in my list. We never kept another dog. One can't replace friends.

9   Discovery of India

WHILE I WAS at UNESCO, Tarlok Singh of the Planning Commission sounded me on the possibility of my becoming Editor of *Yojana*, which they proposed to launch to publicize the Five-Year Plans. To start with, it was to be a weekly journal in English and Hindi, and later in other regional languages. It would give me the opportunity to travel around India, see community development programmes, visit dams, factories, rural clinics, stay in small towns and villages. The salary was not very much but the prospect of getting to know my country was very tempting. My father had given me a ground-floor flat in Sujan Singh Park and a car. The flat was furnished with carpets and furniture which my wife had brought in her dowry. The only items I owned were my books and some old prints I had bought in London. I did not need more and didn't want to be described as a *nikhattoo* again. I decided to accept the offer.

I had two offices, one in the Publications Division in the Old Secretariat near Metcalf House and close to the western bank of the Jumna, the other in the Planning Commission's office in New Delhi. This had the great advantage of my being able to pretend that I was in the other office when I was in neither. I had to drive six miles along the outer Ring Road past Kotla Feroze Shah with its Ashoka Pillar, Gandhi's Samadhi, the old walls of Mughal Delhi, Zeenat Masjid, the Red Fort and Nigambodh Ghat. Every morning I got a refresher course in the history of Delhi. On my way back I often stopped for a while at Nigambodh Ghat and watched the dead being put on funeral pyres and set alight. The exercise did me a world of good and purged me of a lot of pettiness. I felt lighter.

The Director of the Publications Division was a Mysorean by the name of U.S. Mohan Rao. To start with, he was uneasy with me. Technically he was my boss, but I drew a higher salary than his. He was a swadeshi product with his manners and speech deeply embedded in his native Udipi, a town famous for its south Indian cuisine. He had not seen anything of the world besides Mysore, Bombay and Delhi and was not sure how he would deal with a man who had been educated in England, written some books and spent a good part of his life in foreign lands. He took me to my office to introduce me to the staff specially chosen to bring out *Yojana*. The Hindi edition was to be edited by Manmath Nath Gupta, a Bengali who had been in jail as a terrorist. Right from the beginning he wanted to make the Hindi edition independent of the English; I resisted his attempts to do so. My own staff consisted of two Mysoreans, Srinivasachar and a young photographer, T.S. Nagarajan and a Delhi-born girl, Sheila Dhar. There were many others in the English and Hindi editions whose names now elude me.

As advised by Tarlok Singh, I first went on a Bharat Darshan tour, taking Nagarajan with me. In a month we covered almost the entire length and breadth of the country. I made extensive notes on whatever I saw and the people I met. Nagarajan shot hundreds of rolls of film in black and white. We returned to Delhi with plenty of material to launch *Yojana*.

I had very little experience of running a journal. *India News*, which I had edited for India House in London, consisted entirely of material sent from Delhi by the Ministry of External Affairs. Jamal Kidwai did most of the work. I simply okayed it for the printer. It was different with *Yojana*. I was expected to do much of the writing or get others to write for me. We made several trial mock-ups and chose the appropriate type-faces. I spent several nights at *The Times of India* press in Daryaganj, reading and correcting galleys. I was very excited over editing a truly Indian journal.

I had a champagne party to launch *Yojana*. This was unheard of in a country committed to prohibition. Editors who came (Indian journalists are generous with other peoples' liquor) wrote caustic comments on the launching and the first issue. Their reactions hurt me because *Yojana* was my child and I expected favourable comment on its appearance and contents.

I had more disappointments in store. I went round newspaper
stalls. Most of them hadn't heard of *Yojana*. There was a lot of
backchat against me at the Publications Division. This
much-fancied editor they had brought from London or Paris
had proved a total flop! The man in charge of distribution, a
nasty little Punjabi, went around telling everyone that he had
huge stocks of unsold copies in his godowns and would have to
get rid of them as waste to ragpickers. I discovered that
thousands of copies meant to be posted to distant parts of India
were still in the office godown a week after the first issue had
been printed. It was deliberate sabotage. I stormed in to
Mohan Rao's office which was always crowded with his cronies
and visitors, and threatened to resign. I had the letter of
resignation with me, pointing out the Publications Division's
negligence in marketing the journal. My quitting a month after
I had joined would have adversely affected Mohan Rao's career.
He was a naive but well-meaning chap. He calmed me down.
'Heavens will not fall [his *takia kalaam* — a pillow word which
he used all the time] if copies of *Yojana* have not been sent out
in time. I will look into it at once,' he assured me. I was
determined not to give in. 'That Punjabi fellow in charge of
distribution has to go. Or I go,' I told him firmly. 'Anyone who
gloats over selling *Yojana* as *raddi* is not going to touch it.'

Mohan Rao was not happy with the man and utilized my
threat to get rid of him. He was suspended from service. Like a
good Hindu, instead of explaining why he had not done his job,
he tried to appease his gods by doing *godaan* — giving a cow in
charity. Neither the cow nor his gods came to his rescue. He
was fired.

Yojana proved to be a non-starter: all government
publications are non-starters. People suspect them to be
propaganda; they take statistics put out by government with
doses of salt. Anyhow, who wants to read about trees planted at
Vana Mahotsav, the number of compost pits dug and megawatts
of electricity produced? I also had to publish uninspiring
speeches delivered by ministers. The columns I wrote were
smothered under government garbage.

A comic example of official fiddling with statistics was an all-India competition to encourage villagers to dig compost pits. Cash prizes were offered for every village, groups of ten villages, the district and the State. Village-level officers made up figures of compost pits, district officers doubled them; State-level officers doubled them again. When added up, the total under compost pits amounted to more than the area of the State. If the number of trees claimed by government media to have been planted at *Vana Mahotsavs* was correct, the whole of India would by now be a vast jungle.

There were also tensions within the Planning Commission. The head (Vice-Chairman) was the kindly and able Sir V.T. Krishnamachari. Most of the burden rested on the shoulders of Tarlok Singh who worked round the clock and was a great one for writing learned reports. It was commonly said that India was run by three legislative bodies, the Lok Sabha, the Rajya Sabha and the Tarlok Sabha (Planning Commission). The Finance Minister, the acerbic-tongued T.T. Krishnamachari, had an unkindly dig at Tarlok Singh. He said that for all the paper wasted by the Planning Commission, India could have floated another ship. Unknown to me, the placid-looking Tarlok Singh also had his dislikes. One of them was the highly emotional and volatile S.K. Dey, the father of the Community Development Programme. I heard him speak at a seminar in Mussoorie where he delivered an impassioned harangue on the need to change the dietary habits of Indians. Indians had millions of stray, half-starved cattle and many more millions of half-starved humans: his solution was that Hindus take to eating beef. I was astounded at his audacity. And gave his speech wide publicity in *Yojana*. The day after the issue appeared Tarlok Singh rang me up and expressed his acute displeasure at seeing so much space wasted on so worthless a windbag.

I realized *Yojana* was getting me nowhere because it was not getting anywhere. Copies were mailed to Community Development offices and government departments all over the country. I got no feedback because few officials bothered to read it. News agents refused to take it; the few who did on a sale-or-return basis usually returned copies sent to them. My only consolation was the devotion with which my colleagues worked for me. Sheila Dhar became a close friend. She was a warm, large-hearted woman of ample proportions and a malicious wit. She was an excellent mimic: I find mimicry of other people's accents and mannerisms irresistible. She was also a very good singer of classical Hindustani music and was well into being rated among the masters. I did not have an ear for classical music but occasionally accompanied her to her lessons from her ustaad, Pran Nath. Sitting on the floor has always been a pain in the arse, but I sat for hours listening to Sheila's rich, husky voice rendering various ragas. Nagarajan saw me as his father-figure and became like a member of my family. When he married Meenakshi and brought her over to introduce her to us, like a dutiful daughter-in-law she prostrated herself on the carpet to touch my feet. I didn't know how to respond to the gesture, except by helping her to stand up and kissing her on both cheeks — a liberty Tamilian fathers-in-law do not take with their sons wives.

After a while I also got to like Mohan Rao. Although his method of running his department was chaotic, he was anxious to keep everyone happy. He did not assume any airs and, unlike many others in the office, was utterly honest in money matters. I often joined him for lunch in his room and shared the contents of our tiffin boxes, and went for post-prandial strolls on the Ridge. What I enjoyed most was his south Indian accent. One morning while I was having coffee with him his telephone rang. He picked it up and quickly put his hand on the mouthpiece to tell me who was at the other end of the line — 'It is yum yum yameer, yumpee [M.M. Amir, Member of Parliament]. He wants to discuss something private with me.'

Along with editing *Yojana*, I took assignments that came my way. One was from UNICEF to write a booklet on its work in Afghanistan. They wanted to send the photographer P.N. Sharma with me. I offered to cut down costs by taking pictures myself. I had seen the latest model of a Zeiss Ikon camera with Bharat Ram. It had a built-in exposure meter and focusing device. All one had to do was aim the camera and click: it was foolproof. I asked Bharat to lend it to me for a few days. The UNICEF director agreed to try me out. I was to shoot an entire roll on the first day and fly it back to Delhi. If the quality of the pictures was passable, I could take all the pictures myself and be paid for them. I got to Kabul; I clicked away and put the roll on the plane to Delhi. The following day P.N. Sharma arrived in Kabul. He told me that the entire roll sent by me was blank. I had forgotten to take off the lens cap. There is no such thing as a foolproof camera.

I wish I had done better as a photographer. Having failed miserably, I had to share a room with Sharma in Kabul Hotel, the only one in the city at the time. He was a good photographer and a great boaster of his prowess with women. Bald and beady-eyed though he was, he had no problem seducing pretty girls and, if he was to be believed, knocking them to multiple orgasms. He was an orthodox Brahmin who wouldn't eat anything which remotely smelt of meat. Unfortunately for him, and more fortunately for me, the only cooking medium Afghans used was a *raughan* made of lamb fat. So for Sharma even rice pilaf was out. All he could eat was fresh fruit — juicy watermelons, luscious Kandhari grapes and pomegranates. They were no doubt very good for his health but proved devastatingly wind-producing on an empty stomach. By the time we returned to our respective beds Sharma was like a jet plane. He produced a series of the most resounding farts I have ever heard. When I protested, he gave me a long lecture on the varieties of farts listed in ancient Sanskrit texts. The ones he was letting off, he assured me, were *uttam padvi* — of the highest order and entirely free of odour.

The next day we called at the venereal diseases clinic run by UNICEF under an Indian doctor, Paranjpe of Bombay. A year earlier a European expert sent out by UNICEF to investigate the prevalence of diseases in Afghanistan had reported that syphilis and gonorrhoea were rampant. He had apparently not stepped out of his hotel nor consulted Afghan doctors, but based his conjectures on his reading of Afghan history: Afghanistan was the route of innumerable invasions from Central Asia to India, and invading armies were notorious for spreading venereal disease. As a matter of fact, there was very little of it. Prostitution was forbidden. Some women were known to hang around mosques in their burqas and solicit outcoming worshippers. When spotted they were put in jail.

I only saw two cases come to the clinic — one middle-aged woman, the other a young man in his twenties. The woman was the wife of a truck driver who plied his vehicle between Kabul and Peshawar. She had more than half a dozen children when she was stricken by an itch in her genitals. She thought that it was due to the excessive demands made by her husband. The woman did not hesitate to take off her burqa and her salwar in front of the male doctor, the Afghan nurse and the two of us. The doctor examined her in our presence and told her she had syphilis. And that she would be treated only after she brought her husband to the clinic. She was told that her husband had probably picked it up at some brothel in Peshawar and passed it on to her. The woman was furious; she was not interested in being cured of her itch as much as she itched to get at her husband's throat. He had been telling her how much he missed her when he was away.

I saw the young Afghan sauntering up and down the street when I came to the clinic. He wanted to make sure that no one recognized him as he entered. He ran up the stairs, presented himself to the doctor and explained his mysterious ailment. 'Take off your salwar,' ordered Dr Paranjpe. He hesitated. 'In front of all these people? And the woman!' he said, pointing to the nurse. 'Yes,' replied Paranjpe, 'they are doctors.' The poor fellow went pink with embarrassment. Ultimately he pulled up his long shirt and covered up his face before he undid the cord of his salwar. Paranjpe examined the tell-tale sore on his limp penis. 'You have syphilis,' he told the young man. 'I will only treat you if you bring the woman with whom you copulated to the clinic.' The young man swore that he had not been near a woman, not even a prostitute. The doctor refused to treat him. Ultimately he stammered, 'I must have got it from a boy. I buggered one a few days ago.' It was a lie; Paranjpe told him so and ordered him out. In Afghanistan sodomy was socially more acceptable than sex with a strange woman.

More prevalent than venereal disease were malaria, typhoid, typhus and tuberculosis. We were to travel across the country to Kunduz and Mazhar-i-Sharif on the river Oxus, close to the Soviet border. The Minister of Health ordered the director of Health Services, a very sour-tempered Dr Hakimi (who later became Health Minister) to escort us. With us were two European doctors, a Finnish woman of uncertain age who spoke Pushto and Farsee, and a Swede. We set out one morning in a brand new station wagon. The countryside was an amazing study in contrasts: barren mountains suddenly gave way to lush green valleys growing rice and fruit. There were lots of streams with crystal clear water. *Chaikhanas* along the route at which we stopped to eat were usually located along running streams, their courtyards covered over with grape vines. The Afghans were very friendly. The only thing which irritated me was the way they addressed me. To them I was *Lala* (tradesman or moneylender), as most Afghan Sikhs were.

The rest houses, where we liked to stop for the night, presented a problem. There were never enough rooms for everyone to have one to themselves. The Finnish lady doctor asked me if I minded her sharing one with me. I agreed as that would save me from Sharma's flatulent explosions. However, it presented another kind of problem. I had never shared a room with a woman of beddable age. Would she expect me to go over to her? I lost sleep thinking about it. The next morning there was Sharma to taunt me, *'Laaley! mem dee phuddee layee ke nahin'* — did you fuck the white woman's cunt? When I admitted that I had not, he called me a *phuddoo* — cunt. The same happened the next two nights and at Mazhar-i-Sharif. On our way back we stopped at Bamiyan to see the remains of Buddhist caves very much like those at Ajanta, with two massive Buddha monoliths hewn out of solid rock. It was very warm. The lady doctor asked me if I would like to accompany her to bathe in the broad stream that ran through the valley. I agreed. We found a secluded spot. I kept my underwear on; she stripped herself naked and frolicked about in the stream. She was only a little older than me but well preserved. If she meant to convey some kind of message I did not catch it. We went back to the rest house and joined our party. That evening she told me, 'If you don't mind Mr Singh, this time I will share my room with the Swedish doctor.' So she did for the next three nights. Sharma was not far wrong in describing me as a *phuddoo*.

At the end of a three-week sojourn in the country, I wrote a booklet entitled *From Aryana to Afghanistan* which was published by UNICEF. For my pains the Afghan Government gave me a palmful of lapis lazuli. According to the rules, I had to seek my government's permission to accept the gift. I called on the Secretary of the concerned Ministry and asked him how to go about it. He looked at the stones and told me: 'If you hand them over to the government, you'll never see them again. I suggest you put them in your pocket and forget about the Sarkar.' I did.

The other assignment came from the Government of India. At that time millions of Hindus, Buddhists and Christians were fleeing from East Pakistan into West Bengal. The government was eager to publicize this mass exodus in the English-knowing world. One morning I was rung up by H.M. Patel, Secretary of the Ministry of Finance, and asked to see Finance Minister T.T. Krishnamachari. The next day I dutifully presented myself in H.M. Patel's room and asked him what the Minister wanted of me. 'He'll tell you himself,' replied Patel as he led me to his boss's spacious room. 'I want some author who is known in England and America to do a booklet on refugees coming out of East Pakistan. It has to be done at once. We thought of three names, Mrs Jhabvala, Nirad Chaudhuri and yourself — in that order.'

'Sir, Mrs Jhabvala is vastly pregnant and she doesn't speak Bengali. Neither do I. Your best bet is Nirad Chaudhuri. He was born in East Bengal and is better known in the English-speaking world than either Ruth or I.'

'Can you sound him out? He can ask for whatever he likes. Money is no problem.'

'Sir, Dr Keskar [Minister of Information and Broadcasting] has put a ban on Nirad writing for any government organization,' I told him.

'Who is Keskar?' scoffed the Finance Minister. 'You tell Chaudhuri that the ban has been lifted. He can ask for any sum he likes.'

I was delighted. Nirad was passing through very lean times. He had a wife and two sons to support. Also an adopted boy and a young, ravenous Alsatian dog to feed. Nirad did not have a telephone. I sent my chaprasi with a note to his home on Nicholson Road, asking him to see me as soon as he could as I had good news for him.

Nirad came to my office next morning. I told him what had transpired between the Finance Minister and myself. 'The ban is over; your money troubles are also over,' I told him.

He looked me straight in the eye and asked, 'So the Government of India has decided to raise its ban on me?'

'Yes,' I replied enthusiastically.

'But Nirad Chaudhuri has not decided to raise his ban on the Government of India,' he replied and strode out of my office leaving me flabbergasted. He was that kind of man: poverty did not make him compromise with his self-respect.

I had to undertake the task myself. Armed with an interpreter and a photographer I visited dozens of refugee camps and talked to scores of men and women who had left their homes and lands in East Pakistan to survive on a miserable dole of one rupee per day per family in India. There were no cases of physical violence, but quite a few of Hindu girls being taken away, converted to Islam and given in marriage to Muslims. Just about everyone I questioned on why he or she had left Pakistan, answered with one word, *bhoy* — fear. I also saw something of the reluctance Bengalis have to better their lot. The men spent their days gossiping with each other or sat by ponds holding rod and line in the hope of catching fish to supplement their ration of rice and dal. Amongst them was a young man in his twenties who had been to college and spoke English. I found him sitting on a stool looking vacantly into space. Inside the tent was his bosomy, attractive wife scrubbing utensils and surrounded by four or five little children. 'You speak English?' I asked the young man. He looked up without getting up from his stool and nodded. 'How long have you been in this camp?' I asked. He thought for a moment and replied, 'Two months! Three months!' I asked him in exasperation, 'Did you try to look for a job in Calcutta? You are an educated man.'

With complete nonchalance he replied, 'I did. I found nothing suitable for my temperament.'

What a contrast it was with Punjab's ten million Hindu and Sikh refugees who came from Pakistan in 1947! You saw young girls plying tongas, old men who had known better days pedalling bicycle rickshaws. Rarely did you see a Punjabi stretch out his hands to beg for alms.

The booklet I wrote was entitled *Not Wanted in Pakistan*. It was published in the name of a private publishing house so that it would appear that it was the work of an independent author and publisher. The day after it was released someone rang me up and asked who had commissioned me to do the writing. Without as much as asking him who he was, I told him. It was someone from the Pakistan High Commission. The following day I got a very acerbic note from the Pakistan High Commissioner, Arshad Hussain. In Shakespearian English he wrote, 'Alas! Alack! Even you who claim to be such a friend of Pakistan should write such calumny against my government.' It was no use my protesting that I had seen with my own eyes hundreds of thousands of refugees who had fled his country because they felt threatened.

I had been with *Yojana* well over a year when I received an offer from J.C. Jain, Managing Director of Bennett Coleman, to take over the editorship of *The Illustrated Weekly of India* from its retiring Irish editor, C.R. Mandy. I went to Bombay, met Mandy and discussed the terms of employment. I returned to Delhi to consult my wife and Tarlok Singh. My wife was adamant. Bombay, she insisted, was a very unhealthy place to live in and she would not expose her family to the hazards of a hot-damp climate which produced all kinds of diseases. Tarlok Singh scoffed at the *Weekly*. 'Who takes it seriously?' he asked.

'It's just a picture magazine with photographs of newly-married couples and strip cartoons. With *Yojana* you are doing something for your country.' I was not impressed with my wife's reasoning — millions of people lived happily in Bombay, I told her. Nor with Tarlok Singh's sermon on patriotism. I would have taken the job but for meeting a project scout of the Rockefeller Foundation who happened to be in Delhi. He came over to see me and told me he had read my little book, *The Sikhs*, and had been quite impressed. 'Wouldn't you like to do something more definitive on the subject than that small book based on secondary sources?' I jumped at the idea. I told him that I would have to give up my job and do a lot of travelling. 'We'll look after all that,' he assured me. 'You make out the project and what it will cost and I will see that the Foundation accepts it.'

I got down to making out the project. It would take me three years to do the research in Delhi, London (India House Library), see original documents on the Ghadr Movement in Canada and the United States, and meet people in Japan, Singapore and Burma to collect material on the I.N.A. He forwarded my proposal to New York, recommending its acceptance. I invited him to dinner. To impress him I also asked Carol Laise, then First Secretary at the American Embassy, to meet him. The dinner was a disaster. Carol was in the habit of wearing very little during the summer months and stretching her legs wide when she sat, baring her thighs and more. The Rockefeller chap was scandalized. Next morning he called on Carol Laise to express strong disapproval of her baring herself so shamelessly before natives. Carol ordered him out of her room and rang me up to tell me what had happened. I told the Rockefeller projects scout that he had no business to talk to a close friend in the way he had. He told me to mind my own business. The project was approved, but the fellow did his best to put in as many spokes in my wheel as he could.

I had to find an institution to sponsor the project. I thought the most convenient would be Delhi University. I called on the Vice-Chancellor, Dr V.K.R.V. Rao, a man who, like many other south Indian Brahmins, had an enormous opinion of himself. I was surprised at his reaction. 'Mr Singh, I am not going to allow you to use my University as an instrument of your convenience.'

I was appalled by his discourtesy. My next choice was the Aligarh Muslim University. I thought it would be a good gesture to have a Muslim institution sponsor a project on Sikh religion and history, and so do my little bit to kill the false notion that Sikhs and Muslims were traditional enemies. The Vice-Chancellor, Colonel B.M. Zaidi, invited me to Aligarh to discuss the matter with teachers in his history department. I came up against yet another hurdle in the person of Dr Nurul Hassan (later a Vice-Chancellor and Governor of West Bengal). Nurul Hassan's reputation as a historian was so much hot air. He had produced very little published material based on historical research and resented others who had done so. 'You can't do any real research on so vast a subject in three years,' he said quite firmly. His colleague, Professor Rashid Khan, who had once taught history at Khalsa school in Sargodha, demurred. 'The Americans are paying the money; he thinks he can do the research and writing. All we have to do is to lend the name of Aligarh Muslim University,' he pleaded. The Vice-Chancellor overruled Nurul Hassan and issued a formal letter to the Rockefeller Foundation agreeing to sponsor the project.

I wrote to J.C. Jain turning down the editorship of *The Illustrated Weekly* and put in my resignation as editor of *Yojana*. I hired a Granthi to take me through the Granth Sahib, and asked my Urdu teacher of Modern School days, Moulvi Shafiuddin Nayyar, then with the Jamia Millia Islamia, to teach me Persian so that I could read records of the Sikh Durbar which were in that language. So at the end of two years I was out of one job and into yet another.

10 Sikh Religion and History

I HAVE MENTIONED earlier that when I decided to make writing a career I realized my only chance of getting noticed in the highly competitive world of creative writing was to specialize in one subject and convey the impression that I knew it better than anyone else. My choice was my own community. I had been brought up in an orthodox Sikh family, knew the prescribed five daily prayers by rote and was familiar with Khalsa traditions. Though by the time I made the decision I had been disillusioned by all religions including my own, I had a strong sense of belonging to the Sikh community and was emotionally involved in its vicissitudes. My first short history of the Sikhs was admittedly a second-rate work, but my translation of the morning prayer *Japji* had given me a sense of fulfilment and hope that I could do better. Then came the UNESCO project for the translation of selections of the Sikh scriptures, with which I have already described my association.

The Rockefeller grant that I now received provided for a research assistant and a steno-typist. About the latter I had no second thoughts. I wrote to Yvonne Le Rougetel. This woman, though of very modest means, never bothered about money; she readily accepted the pittance I offered and flew over to Delhi at her own expense. I was uncertain about the research assistant. Captain Bhag Singh, Editor of *The Sikh Review* of Calcutta, suggested that I give Tarlochan Singh, who had squabbled with me over the *Selections*, another chance as he was in dire financial straits and could do with a steady income for some years. Reluctantly I agreed to give him another try and asked him over to Delhi to see me. I was to rue my decision.

Tarlochan Singh was invited for dinner. Carol Laise, then a Senior Counsellor in the American Embassy, happened to drop in. I was due to leave for Oxford in a few days to deliver a series of lectures on the Sikh religion under the auspices of the Spalding Foundation. I told Tarlochan Singh of what I could offer him — I would only require assistance to check the accuracy of my translations of scriptural texts and appending diacritical marks on the transliterations. I also told him of the invitation to speak at Oxford. He listened in silence and got the addresses of the Rockefeller and Spalding Foundations from me. A few days later when I delivered my first lecture in Oxford (the audience was no more than six), I started off by saying that my interpretation of Sikhism was not accepted by many Sikh scholars. At the end of the lecture, the Secretary of the Foundation told me 'I am glad you started the way you did. Take a look at this!' He handed me a telegram received from India. It said precisely what I had said — that my views on Sikhism were not acceptable to Sikh scholars and therefore I should not be allowed to speak on the subject. Signed Tarlochan Singh. I ignored the telegram and went on to deliver my second lecture the next day. Some time later, the Rockefeller Foundation sent me a photostat copy of a letter they had received. It said that the Foundation should reconsider its decision of giving me the grant which had obviously been influenced by my close friendship with a senior officer in the American Embassy called Carol Laise (he hadn't got the surname right), and that the signatory of the letter had already compiled data on Sikh religion and history and should receive the grant for further research and publication. Signed Tarlochan Singh.

Neither the Spalding Foundation nor Rockefeller took any notice of these communications. People like Tarlochan Singh are not uncommon in India. Behind the camouflage of flowing grey beards and spouting shlokas they store malice and envy. Tarlochan Singh died in 1993 in dire poverty.

The most fulfilling thing I have done in my life was working on Sikh religion and history. This was the only time I went through the Granth Sahib with pencil in hand, marking words I did not understand. I made my own selections and translated them as I thought best, trying to retain the music of the original. I used the language of the Old Testament as my model. I spent several months in London working in the India Office Library. During this time, apart from collecting material for the volumes I was planning to write, I also finished the draft of a biography of Maharajah Ranjit Singh (later published by Allen & Unwin, Blackie's and Orient Longman), as well as a book on the ten years of anarchy that followed the Maharajah's death, the Anglo-Sikh wars and annexation of the Punjab. This was also published by Orient Longman.

The stay in London gave my wife and me opportunities to renew old friendships. Eleanor Sinclair and Susan Hicklin had found us a small flat on Upper Berkeley Street. From the battered state of the sofa and frequent calls by the police it appeared that the previous tenant had been a prostitute. The Manzur Qadirs happened to be in London to have their second son, Asghar, medically treated. We spent most of our evenings together. It was during this stay that Manzur and I once went to spend an hour in a newsreel cinema (in those days there were many such in London). One of the shorts was of a parade in Peking on the birth anniversary of Dr Sun Yat Sen. I made some comment about how great a man he was. 'Who was he?' asked Manzur who read nothing besides law books and Urdu poetry. 'Don't tell me you've never heard of Dr Sun Yat Sen,' I said to him. He got irritated and snorted '*Koee hoga sala Bengali doctor*' — must have been some kind of Bengali doctor. At dinner that evening in his home, I told his daughter Shireen about her father's remark. 'Oh really, Daddy! How can you have said such a thing about one of Asia's greatest leaders!' Poor Manzur was squashed. 'For God's sake don't go about spreading this story,' he pleaded with me. When he was appointed Foreign Minister of Pakistan by Field Marshal Ayub Khan I sent him a telegram 'Congratulations from Dr Sun Yat Sen, the famous Bengali doctor.'

Among the people I befriended at the India Office Library was Professor Robert Crane who also had some kind of grant from an American university to research on the Indian freedom movement. He used to arrive at the library with three assistants. They spent an hour in an ante-room smoking and drawing up lists of the documents and books they wished to consult. The lists were handed over to the librarian. Crane and his assistants then went down to the cafeteria to have coffee. An hour later they returned to the library to make sure that what they wanted had been located. They were given the books and documents which they passed on to the photostat section to be copied. Then they adjourned for lunch, where I often joined them. 'Don't mind my saying so, Dr Singh, but you are wasting a lot of time reading all the old stuff here. You should simply have them photocopied and take them home to read at leisure,' he advised me. What he said made sense but, being an old fashioned plodder, I couldn't change my ways. I had occasion to meet Crane years later when I was at Princeton and he at Duke. We also taught a summer holiday course at the University of Hawaii, and his family spent a few days with us at Kasauli. Dr Crane's modern methods of research did not bear any fruit.

After my wife returned to India, Guy Wint often came to spend the night in my flat when he was in London. He slept in my bed, I slept on the battered sofa. One evening when I expected him and had dinner ready, he failed to show up. I didn't hear from him the next day, nor the day after. Then his wife Freda rang up from Oxford to tell me why. On the train from Oxford to London, Guy had a stroke. He sensed that something was going wrong with him. He gave his visiting card to a fellow-passenger. The man promptly informed the guard, who sent a message to Marylebone station. An ambulance van was waiting for him. He was taken unconscious to a hospital. The doctor informed Freda who then rang me up. Guy was saved, but suffered partial paralysis. Even when at his fittest he was never very articulate; but now when he came round, his speech was slurred and he had a slight limp.

Having done all I had to in London, I proceeded to Canada and the United States to collect material on the Ghadr Party. I spent a fortnight at Vancouver looking at the gurdwara records. Some old Sikhs who had been there at the time of the *Kamagata Maru* episode were most helpful. They handed over leaflets and pictures they had hoarded for almost half a century. I was amazed to find that several of them, who had spent the best part of their lives in Canada, had not bothered to learn English. 'We don't need to know English to do odd jobs like mowing lawns, clipping hedges and shovelling snow in front of houses in winter. Five or six words like "Odd job man, madam! Sure! Thanks and Okay" are enough,' they assured me. Old files of the *Vancouver Sun* yielded a harvest of day-to-day happenings when the *Kamagata Maru* was held up in the Burrard inlet, the intra-Sikh violence that followed its departure with killings in the gurdwara, the murder in court of police inspector Hopkins, and the trial and the execution of Bhai Mewa Singh for the murder.

From Vancouver I proceeded to San Francisco to hunt records of the earliest meetings of what later became the Communist Party of India. I stayed in the campus of Berkeley University. Two lady professors, Miss Fisher and Margaret Bondurant, who headed the department of Indian Studies, gave me local contacts and loaned me theses written on the Indian (largely Sikh) migration to Canada and the United States, on the discrimination practiced against them and records of the prolonged trial of the German Consul, Franz Bopp, who had encouraged and financed Indian immigrants to organize rebellion against British rule. I collected plenty of untapped material on the beginnings of anti-British feeling among the hitherto loyal Sikh community.

From San Francisco I proceeded to Tokyo to explore material on the Indian National Army organized by Rash Bihari Bose, 'General' Mohan Singh and, later, by Subhash Chandra Bose. I arrived there on New Year's eve and stayed at the International Centre. I couldn't concentrate on my reading and writing as the next room was occupied by a middle-aged but well-preserved American professor and his very young English mistress. The partition wall was very thin; I could hear every word they said to each other, the sounds of their kissing, the creaking of their bed and their noisy exclamations as they made love. I envied the professor's vitality; in the ten days I stayed at the Centre I could hear them first thing in the morning, at siesta time and the last thing at night.

I had written to the Japanese Ministry of Defence about

what I was looking for. I was asked to present myself at the office. It was a bizarre interview. I was escorted by a soldier to a cold, sparsely furnished room. Seated on the table were three Japanese officers in uniform, looking exactly alike. They stood up and bowed to me. I bowed to them and sat down. One spoke through an interpreter and asked about my business. I explained at length that I was a Rockefeller Scholar looking for material on the I.N.A. From the few guttural questions that followed, I could sense they wanted to make sure that I was not an agent of the C.I.A., or of Indian intelligence. At the end of an hour of interrogation they told me they had no records of the I.N.A. except a booklet, which they placed before me. It was in Japanese. I told them I could not read Japanese. They did not react. I asked them if they could put me in touch with Japanese officers who had contacts with either Mohan Singh, Narinjan Singh Gill or Subhash Chandra Bose. Most of all, I would like to see Major Fujiwara who was the liaison officer with the I.N.A. While my request was being translated I leafed through the book and saw some pictures of Indian officers with Major Fujiwara seated in the centre. I saw a faint smile light up on the face of one of my interrogators. Facing me was no other than Major Fujiwara himself. He spoke English fluently and had learnt a little Hindustani as well. I never got to know why they put me through the charade. My request to interview the Major was turned down abruptly with two words spoken in English: 'Not allowed.' The pointless interview was over. All I got was the booklet in Japanese.

However, I was able to visit the home of Rash Bihari Bose, where his Japanese widow, daughter and her husband were living. They had very little to tell me because Bose was away from home most of the time. His daughter had scarcely seen him till the last year of his life. I asked her where her father had died. Without a trace of emotion on her face she pointed to the wooden floor at her feet and replied, 'Here.'

Having drawn a blank in Tokyo I proceeded to Hong Kong. There was a beautiful gurdwara along a hillside overlooking the sea. The building had been donated by a Parsee; Sindhi Sikhs and the Khalsa had amicably divided hours of worship between them. The morning *kirtan* sung by a man and wife team was most pleasing to the ear. In my speech to thank them for the *saropa* they gave me I complemented them for running the gurdwara so harmoniously. Later, the president of the committee told me that things were not so smooth as they seemed and that every year when they had elections they had to send for the police to maintain order. He also gave me a booklet on the Sikh religion. The text was in Mandarin and English and allegedly written by a local Sikh, to be distributed among the Chinese. In my hotel room I discovered that the English text had been entirely taken from my book *The Sikhs Today* published by Orient Longman. I told the president that this was blatant plagiarism. He admitted that he too was surprised when a man who worked in the post office gave him the manuscript. He promised to ask for an explanation from the alleged author. That evening the man came to see me and made a clean breast of what he had done. 'I thought you had died long ago. How was I to know you would turn up in Hong Kong and see this book? I am not going to let you return to India without having dinner with my family. Only then will I believe that you have forgiven me.' I had a very pleasant dinner with his family. Generally the Hong Kong visit was useful as I met several Indian businessmen who had helped Mohan Singh and Subhash Chandra Bose.

An encounter I had with another fellow Sikh in Hong Kong remains in my memory. I was walking down a street with my camera strapped to my shoulder. A white-bearded Sikh sat with a muzzle loader guarding a Chinese jewellery store. As he saw me come along he began to shake his head. 'Sardarji *deson aaye ho?*' — have you come from the country? I nodded. He shook his head more vigorously. 'You have cut our noses — *nak vaddha ditta*. You have let these Chinese bugger your arses — *Cheenian tun bund marva layee.*' (This was soon after the Indo-China war of 1962.) 'My Chinese wife now taunts me all the time. *Kukkar khaan jogey ho* — you can only eat tandoori chicken. You cannot fight. There were we in the Shanghai police; we would grab six Chinese by their pigtails and haul them to police stations. Now we cannot look them in the eye.' I couldn't but agree that the Chinese had knocked the hell out of us.

I also visited Singapore, and saw the jail and the hospital attached to it. Outside the hospital I noticed a little shrine tended by a Tamilian. A marble plaque bore a legend in Gurmukhi: *Samadhi Karnnee Wala Baba* — the shrine of the wish-bestowing holy man. People who came to the hospital for treatment made offerings here for good luck. The self-appointed Tamilian caretaker lived on the offerings. When I asked him about the Baba, he knew nothing; he had inherited the post from his father who had told him that it marked the site of the cremation of a famous Sikh who had died in the jail over a hundred years ago. I made a quick calculation and came to the conclusion that perhaps this was the place where Bhai Maharaj Singh was cremated. This man had continued to fight the British after the Sikh Kingdom had been annexed in 1849. After his capture, he was sent to Singapore. I could not think of another eminent Sikh who could have died there over a hundred years ago. I was foolish enough to put my wild conjecture in a Sikh journal. The Sikh community of Singapore, already split into many factions (they had nine gurdwaras based on caste and regional differences), found yet another issue on which to quarrel. The orthodox quoted the writings of Guru Gobind Singh forbidding the worship of shrines and graves. Others maintained that this was obviously a hallowed spot, as the writing on the marble plaque indicated. My article weighed the scales in favour of the shrine worshippers. They went ahead and raised a gurdwara around it. Such are the hazards of superficial research. I was responsible for yet another gurdwara. Once before I had hazarded a guess that a derelict monument close to Akbar's tomb at Sikandra near Agra was the place where the ninth Guru, Tegh Bahadur, might have stayed before coming to Delhi where he was executed in 1675. Promptly the Agra Sikh community raised a gurdwara on the site.

I proceeded to Rangoon. Once again I met several Indian businessmen who had collaborated with the I.N.A. I made detailed note of their doings and impressions of the I.N.A.'s performance on the field of battle. I came to the conclusion that, like the Ghadr party, the I.N.A. provided gunpowder to Indian nationalist propaganda but had little concrete to show in the way of achievements. After almost a year of encircling the globe I was back in Delhi. The real work of putting everything down on paper had yet to begin.

I envy people who say they enjoy writing: I have always found it a pain in the arse. If I had waited for inspiration, I could not have written anything. I had to impose severe discipline on myself. It was during these years that I got into the habit of rising early — between 4 and 5 am, making myself a mug of ginseng and getting down to going over my notes and organizing the material. My father had given me his beautiful teak-panelled study, with an exotic Persian carpet and a fireplace. Yvonne sat in a room in the nearby annexe with my cousin Kulbir (to the last day Yvonne pronounced his name as Culbur), who worked as my father's secretary. I had sworn not to get up from my chair till I filled the blank sheets of paper on my table. More often than not, what I wrote was unreadably bad. I had it typed, and then rewrote it. At times I rewrote every line five or six times till it read smoothly. I took a coffee break. Mid-morning coffee had become an institution in my parents' home. My mother presided over the function and poured coffee, cream and sugar for everyone. Many visitors dropped in to join us.

On Sundays and holidays Krishen Shungloo and his wife, Sarojini (Bitto), would join my wife and me to have coffee in one of the restaurants in Connaught Place. I looked forward to being with the Shungloos. Krishen was very well read and had published a collection of his poems in Lahore. He was forever planning to write a novel. Once or twice he took two months leave from All India Radio to start working on it. He would then be in a high state of tension. He would buy himself a new notebook and a stack of pencils. He insisted on discussing the novel with me before getting down to writing it. The four of us met often at Volga restaurant. His face flushed with excitement as he lit one cigarette after another, he would ask me, 'K. Singh, what do you think of this as a title for a novel: *The Woman with Golden Breasts*?' I had to concede it sounded provocative and would be a highly saleable title. 'But what will it be about?' I would ask. He would relax and sit back. 'That I have yet to decide. First things first. The title of a book is always the first thing anyone reads.' Shungloo never got beyond writing titles in bold letters with his name under it. The woman with the golden breasts never exposed them to human gaze. It was from Shungloo that I learnt that writers who think of the titles of books before they embark on writing them seldom get very far.

I liked Shungloo from the day I first met him in Lahore. He had just returned from Oxford. He was a tall, elegantly dressed man with impeccable manners. He didn't seem to be doing anything besides reading books and writing poetry. He lived in a joint family and apparently did not need to earn his livelihood. Things changed after Partition when the family lost its property in Lahore. He had to look for a job and got one with All India Radio. He married another Kashmiri, Sarojini (Bitto) Sapru. She took a job as a teacher in a nursery school. They continued to live with his parents. We resumed our friendship in Delhi. We saw more of each other than anyone else. We took our dinners to each others' homes so that we could drink, gossip and eat together. He was bone-lazy. To the best of my recollection the only programme he wrote and produced during his tenure with A.I.R. was 'Drum', based on the different percussion instruments used in Indian music. He gloated over this for a long time.

Once Shungloo commissioned me to co-produce a programme on Kashmir. We travelled together by train and bus. We had to share a room for the night at a wayside dak bungalow. I couldn't get much sleep because of his loud snoring. I had never heard such stylish snoring before. Interspersed with grating nasal emissions were words in English: 'Oh, no no! — oh yes! yes! by all means', etc. At the end of our week-long visit we agreed to share equally the programmes we were to write and produce. It ended up by my having to write all of them. I had got used to Shungloo's lethargy and inability to do serious work.

What kept me to a schedule of writing was a vague fear that I might never get it done in time. The fear of early mortality haunts most writers. With me there was the additional fear that, after I had written, I may not find a publisher. The second fear was dissipated sooner than the first. A young American couple had befriended us in Delhi. Jack Curran, a tall, handsome man and a product of Princeton, had done a thesis on the R.S.S. and was Second Secretary with the U.S. Embassy. His wife Cathy who looked like a film-star, was an heiress of the Proctor and Gamble family. Jack had maintained his contact with Princeton and apparently told some members of the faculty of my research project. As I was putting finishing touches to the first volume of my *History of the Sikhs*, I got a letter from Princeton University Press informing me that they would be interested in considering my work. I sent them Volume I. It was accepted. It boosted my morale and I got down to working on the second volume with greater confidence. My three-year grant was coming to an end. I needed one more year to finish the project and requested the Rockefeller Foundation to extend the grant by another year. My request was summarily turned down — no doubt by the very man who had initiated it and then fallen out with me. I had to work another year on my own to finish the second volume. I had unexpected resistance from Yvonne Le Rougetel. She would not part with the bound manuscript; she hugged it to herself as if it was her baby. We had an unpleasant showdown before I was able to extract it from her and forward it to Princeton.

I acknowledged my debt to my parents by dedicating both the volumes to them. I expressed my gratitude to Yvonne Le Rougetel who spent four years working with me in Delhi on a salary that an Indian typist would have spurned. And to Aligarh Muslim University which had agreed to sponsor it. At the end of Volume II I appended two words in Latin: *Opus Exegii* — my life's work is done. To write on Sikh religion and history was my life's ambition. Having done that I felt like one living on borrowed time, at peace with myself and the world. It did not bother me if I wrote nothing else.

The publication of my two volumes by two prestigious

university publishing houses, Princeton and Oxford, opened the gates of the groves of academe to me. The boy who could not pass his school and college examinations became a professor, and without having done a doctorate came to be addressed as Doctor Singh. The first to invite me was the University of Rochester. I got there in winter with the entire countryside under a blanket of snow. I spent a fortnight at the Holiday Inn, which was well beyond the grant given to me. I lived on the bread and butter and coffee available in the room. Then I was given a single bedroom meant for visiting lecturers in a students' hostel block. I had no courses to teach but a few lectures were arranged for me in different institutions. I spent most of the time exploring the industrial city which was the centre of the Kodak and Xerox factories. It was an ugly, nondescript town of long straight streets with tumble-down houses, gas stations and eating joints for truck drivers. The only two pleasant spots were Highland Park which had yet to come into its own and an enormous cemetery where forefathers of the town slept — amongst them the notorious gangster, Buffalo Bill Cody. About the only pleasant place for shopping and recreation was an enormous shopping plaza with a rotating, chiming clock which showed the time in different parts of the world in its central hall. I spent many afternoons there looking at the time in Delhi.

The one memorable experience of Rochester was the visit one Sunday of my Black friend of student days in Paris, Hazel Marie Stokes. My Parisian memories of her were of a tall, slender woman of very amiable proportions with a mop of stubbornly curly hair on her head and thick kissable lips. We had kept in touch through letters and Christmas cards. She had become a school teacher, married and divorced two husbands but borne no children. She lived with her blind mother in Detroit. She took a Greybound bus and travelled through the night to get to Rochester. I was at the bus station to receive her. I wondered what she would look like after thirty years. She stepped out of the bus, a massive hulk of brown flesh. She embraced me with great warmth and exclaimed, 'Honey! you've gone fat and old.'

I complimented her: 'Marie you haven't changed one bit. I had no difficulty in recognizing you.'

She guffawed with laughter. 'Liar! I know I've put on a little weight.'

We took a cab to my apartment. She had slept very little and was tired and hungry. 'I'll take a quick shower, change and then you can take me out for breakfast,' she said. She went to the bathroom but kept the door open to keep talking to me. If I said something she didn't catch she came out soaping herself and asked, 'Honey, what did you say?' I wasn't sure what was on her mind. After her bath she came out stark naked to towel herself and continued telling me of her husbands, her mother and her work. I got up from my chair, kissed her and led her to my bed. 'Honey, you don't want to bed me,' she said. 'So let's just talk of old times. Okay?' I was relieved. I certainly did not want to bed her but felt that perhaps she would expect one to do so and feel let down if I did not try. She got into a purple dress — her taste in loud, garish clothes had not changed. I took her to the shopping plaza which was open on Sundays. She had a breakfast of eggs, bacon, waffles and coffee. 'Big woman needs big breakfast,' she announced cheerfully. 'Now I must look for some new dresses; I love shopping.' We walked round the shops. She examined new shoes and dresses. Nothing would fit her. She asked if there were special stores catering for oversized men and women. There were. She spent the rest of the morning trying on different dresses in cubicles and coming out to get my approval. 'Don't you think this looks nice on me?' She bought new dresses, new shoes, artificial jewellery and whatever else caught her fancy. In her now sexless life she needed to overeat and go on spending sprees. At lunch she tucked into a massive steak with a blob of butter on it, onion rings and potatoes stuffed with sour cream. She followed this up with ice-cream topped with hot chocolate sauce. By the time the lunch was over, it was late afternoon and time for her to return to Detroit. I saw her off at the bus station and gave her a warm farewell kiss. She had filled my day with much cheer and chatter. When I returned to my apartment it looked desolate and depressingly silent.

The next invitation came from Princeton University. I was to teach a course on Comparative Religions for three months, from January till April. I decided to settle in before my wife joined me a month later. I flew to New York, spent a couple of days with Professor Hazard and his wife Susan. I had befriended him during a week's visit to Warsaw and heard him speak on Soviet Law, which he taught in Columbia University. I could not believe that anyone could handle a subject as dull as Soviet Law with so much clarity and wit. He had given me precise instructions about how to get to his house in Manhattan and what the cab fare would be. That visit taught me how foolish stereotype notions of people can be. It is generally believed that cab drivers the world over are crooks. New York cab drivers have a worse reputation than others. From the time I got into my cab at Kennedy airport I kept my eye on the meter. The cabbie was an Italian and a compulsive talker. He noticed my looking wide-eyed at the buildings we passed. 'Foist toime in Noo Yok?' he asked me. 'Almost the first time,' I replied. 'I spent half a day here on my way to Canada,' I replied. 'Great city this Noo Yok,' he went on and began pointing to different buildings. I began to suspect he was taking me for a ride. I kept a hawk's eye on the meter as it ticked away. 'Why don't you stop for a while in my home — it's on our way, meet the missas and have a cup of tea or sumpen?' I felt he was a smartie but I wouldn't let him get away with it with me. 'No thanks,' I replied firmly. 'My host will be waiting for me at his doorstep. I rang him up from the airport to tell him I had arrived.' He didn't mind my snub and went on chatting merrily. 'Best country in the world to live in,' he continued. 'See, I am Italian, but I like it much better here: good money, good people.' When we arrived at Professor Hazard's doorstep, he slammed down the meter to show a series of zeros. I had seen the figure; it was exactly what Hazard had told me. 'How much?' I asked him. 'Nothing,' he replied. 'It's your foist day in my country. Have a nice stay.' And drove off. I felt thoroughly ashamed of myself.

The Hazards had a large three-storeyed house facing the Ramakrishna Mission, with Harlem on one side and Central Park on the other. The top floor was occupied by a Polish student who helped with the housework for his keep. They were evidently very well off. I was told to treat their home as my own whenever I happened to be in New York.

The next evening I took the train to Princeton. It was bitterly cold. I took a cab to the address of the apartment given to me for my stay. The letter giving me instructions had two keys in it. The cab dropped me and two suitcases on a deserted street with bright lights showing through windows. The path from the road to my doorway had three feet of snow on it. I lugged my two cases through the snow. By the time I got to the door my shoes and socks were soggy wet and my fingers stiff with cold. I fumbled with the keys: every country has its own kind of locks and keys and it takes some time to get used to them. Ultimately, I got the door to unlock. Then I felt the walls for the light switches: different countries have different kinds of switches: in India you press them down; in the States you push them up. I tried to press one down further before I pushed it up and was dazzled by the flood of light. On the table in the hallway was a placard reading 'Welcome to Princeton.' Indeed! I said to myself, as I quickly hauled in my cases and divested myself of my wet shoes and socks. It was Saturday and I had not seen any cafes on the way from the station. Where would I have dinner? I looked in the sitting-room. The table had been laid for dinner with a loaf of bread, bread-knife beside it. There was also a bottle of Scotch. I opened the fridge. It was stacked with eggs, milk, wine, bottles of soda, honey and jam and chocolates. On the rack were tins of soup and vegetables. I went up the stairs to the bedroom. The bed was made for me to slip into. The bathroom had rolls of toilet paper, cakes of soap and a bottle of cologne. To this day I do not know who had done this for me, nor was I able to pay for the goodies.

I was attached to the department of philosophy and religion. In the past it had had eminent scholars, like Professor Hitti teaching Islam. At that time, Walter Kauffman who, besides his own books, had translated several German classics, was head of the department of philosophy. He had made quite a name for himself with his *Faith of a Non-Believing Jew*, his translation of German poetry and books on philosophy. Dr Phillip Ashby was the head of the department of religion. Amongst his colleagues was a distinguished scholar of Judaism, Professor Diamons. He was away on a Sabbatical. I was given his room for the three months I was to be in Princeton. The two departments shared the same building but little else besides the lounge, where they would help themselves to hot coffee and biscuits. Philosophers looked down on teachers of religion as priests; teachers of religion disdained philosophers as snobs who had nothing to be snobbish about. And both philosophers and teachers of religion were looked down upon by members of other faculties, particularly the economists who had a brand new, white multi-storeyed building designed by a Japanese architect across the road. The most famous name still fresh in the minds of Princetonians was that of Albert Einstein whose home in the Institute of Advanced Studies had become a temple of worship. There were only two other Indians in the faculty at the time, both mathematicians, Dr Harish Chandra and Dr Bhanu Murthy. There were no Indian students. Princeton was an entirely male institution. However, in my class of sixteen students two women were allowed to sit in.

The macho image Princeton tried to cultivate had its lighter moments. Students were allowed to entertain women in their hostels over the week-ends. Coming from well-to-do families, most of them also had their own cars, which caused congestion on the campus. The police wanted the University to ban students bringing cars. President Goheen (later Ambassador to India) gave students the option of either keeping their cars or being able to entertain their lady friends over weekends. Being healthy young gentlemen, the students opted for the girls. Regulations required the ladies to leave men's hostels before midnight. However, one winter night a fire broke out in one of the hostels at 3 am. The fire brigade had to use their long ladders to rescue students living in the upper storeys. Amongst those whose lives they saved were a number of ladies in different stages of undress.

One should not get away with the notion that life in an American university campus is all fun and games. Many a night when I returned from New York by bus I saw the whole campus, including the libraries, ablaze with lights till well after midnight. Students were at work. My own experience of teaching taught me to take my lectures seriously. Every book I recommended for reading was read by the time I delivered the next lecture. I found it difficult to keep pace with the students and often failed to answer the searching questions they put to me. At the end of the term they were good enough to give me an ovation, but inside me I knew that I had not come up to the mark.

It did not take me long to make friends. The Heffelfingers had written to their relation Lucia Ballantyne, who was married to a handsome professor teaching at Trenton. She had inherited some of the Heffelfinger wealth and lived in considerable style in a large three-storeyed house with a cook and a maid-servant — rare commodities in the United States. She was also a do-gooder and invited young convicts — mostly blacks — for weekends when they were allowed out of jail. She asked me over as soon as she found out where I was staying. She also invited a most attractive blonde, Georgine Hall, a divorcee with two attractive children — a girl aged fifteen and a boy aged twelve. Georgine appeared frequently on TV and was recognized wherever she went. We hit it off at once. She took me over from Lucia and often invited me to dine with her and her children. She also took me for long drives in the countryside. People were surprised to see us together so often. By then I had also become better known, as several articles written by me had appeared in *The New York Times*. Even faculty members began to take me more seriously than I deserved. I went up in Georgine's estimation as a celebrity. I thoroughly enjoyed her attention. One evening she rang me up and asked me to come immediately to Princeton hospital where her daughter had been admitted with cuts and bruises sustained in a car accident. The girl was bleeding profusely and screaming with pain; Georgine was trying desperately to contact the girl's father to inform him. The girl did not want to see him: she pleaded with the doctor to let me be with her in the operating theatre while she was being cleaned up and stitched. The doctor could not make out where a dark man with a turban and beard fitted in the set up. He let me stay by her. The girl clutched my hand as the nurse removed her clothes and she was laid on the table. She was a beautiful girl with a smooth skin. I kept reminding myself that I was a friend of her mother and should therefore look upon her as a father would towards his child. The girl was put under sedation and was soon fast asleep. As I came out of the theatre I had a brief meeting with the girl's father. I assured him and Georgine that all was well and they could return to their respective homes to sleep.

Amongst others who extended their friendship to me was the philosopher Walter Kauffman. He often invited me to his home, where he entertained celebrities, mainly Jewish. After my wife joined me, the circle of our friends got much wider. Winter gave way to spring, the snow to green pastures and bursts of magnolias. Anyone who has not seen magnolias bloom in the United States has missed one of the most beautiful sights in the world. When I was not away delivering lectures at other universities (they earned me more money than my salary), we went out with some family or the other. Amongst the celebrities living in our neighbourhood was Louis Fischer, who wrote a biography of Mahatma Gandhi. He did not have any teaching assignment in the university, but invariably had his lunches in the university cafeteria. We often walked back together. At a drug store I once picked up a carton of ice-cream; both my wife and I were ice-cream addicts, but we used to buy the cheapest variety available. Louis Fisher took to buying the most expensive and handed it over to me for my wife. 'She has a most interesting face,' he would tell me by way of an excuse. 'I love ice-cream but being diabetic I am forbidden it. I enjoy giving it to people I like.'

An incident in Princeton had an amusing outcome. One

summer day I was basking in the sun on a wooden bench in my back garden. A tiny splinter of wood got into my thumb. I did not take any notice of it till it turned septic. Phil Ashby noticed the swelling on my hand and without giving me time to think took me to the university clinic. The doctor decided to send me to hospital for surgery. I was put in the hands of two black university policemen and driven to the surgery.

While awaiting my turn I heard the surgeon talk to my policemen: 'Who have you got with you? Is he a convict or charged with a crime?' The policemen lowered their voices and I could not hear what they said in reply. I was ushered into the surgery. The doctor asked me what I did and what had happened. His tone changed. He began to address me as Doctor or Professor. 'It's a simple felon,' he told me. 'I'll take it out but you'll have to spend a couple of days in the university hospital.' The felon was cut out, my hand bandaged and I was handed back to the black policemen. 'I'd sure like to see more of you Dr Singh. My wife would be happy to meet you,' said the doctor.

I had to spend two days and nights in the hospital. I was kept under sedation, which was unnecessary because I felt no pain. People, including Mrs Goheen, wife of the President, brought me chocolates and flowers — which were welcome. In America they make a lot of fuss over little things.

Some time in April every year there is a grand auction of lecturers and professors in a New York Hotel. Academics who are not happy where they are, or think they deserve better, are there in large numbers. So are Deans of Studies from different universities. They meet over drinks, lunches and dinners. Deans on the look-out for replacements or involved in setting up new departments examine the *curriculum vitae* of those available and make offers. There is a lot of haggling over terms of employment. It is truly like a slave-market, where not looks but the number of books or learned papers published by applicants are at a premium. Robert Crane suggested that I come there, if not for a job, then to meet other Indologists, orientalists, and experts in other disciplines.

I was not interested in a university job in the United States:

though the money was good, it did not give me a sense of fulfilment. While I was at this gathering, the Dean of Studies at the University of Hawaii, a Japanese Nisei, offered me a six-week course of teaching summer classes in Indian religions and contemporary Indian history. It meant staying on in Princeton or another place for a month before proceeding to Hawaii. The Dean promised compensation for that, air-fare for my wife and me to Hawaii and onwards to India. After consulting my wife, I decided to accept the offer. It would give me enough money to pay for the air passage of my daughter Mala, who was then studying at New Hall, Cambridge (England); she could then spend her summer vacation with us in Hawaii. I also got a letter from Mrs Ellen Wattumul, the American wife of a wealthy Sindhi merchant, that she would let me have one of her furnished apartments on the beach at a very low rent. After staying with American friends in New York, Philadelphia, Chicago, Washington and spending a couple of days with Marie Stokes and her mother, as well as making more dollars lecturing at Winconsin, Duke and Rochester, we flew over to Hawaii. A few days later Mala joined us. She was in a terrible mood. She had not done well in her studies and hated Cambridge. She held me responsible for her poor performance because I had dragged her along with me from Delhi to London to Ottawa to Paris and back to Delhi without letting her settle down anywhere. She said I had sent her to Cambridge simply to impress my friends that I had a daughter there. Since she was unhappy it made me unhappy. I was glad to be away most of the day at the university and joined the family only in the evenings.

I had largish classes to teach in Hawaii. Most of them were not serious students but keen to add a little something academic to surfing, sea and sun-bathing. Quite a few were young women who worked in department stores, cafes and restaurants. In my class on Indian religions, which Mala attended gratis, there were two nuns as well.

I had a pleasant little room at the university. It belonged to an Indian scholar, Sharma, whose wife's photograph sat on my working table. She must have been quite a stunner. While I put away Sharma's books in a shelf, I let his wife's photograph stay where it was. Hawaii gave me more time to polish up the lectures on religion that I had delivered at Princeton. I also read up histories of the Communist Party of India, the Freedom Movement and India's performance after Independence. There was plenty of time to indulge in good food. Once a week, members of the faculty, including Robert Crane, would go to Chinese restaurants. While our Chinese specialists ordered the meal, a bucket of ice cubes and a bottle of Rye whiskey was put on our table. By the time the meal was over we were full of Chop Suey and American whiskey. What sort of teaching my fellow professors did in the afternoons could be anyone's guess. After two or three such lunches, I cried off and preferred walking over to the East-West Centre to eat in the cafeteria. The atmosphere in the Centre was very lackadaisical. Most of the fellows there were not distinguished scholars and, being insecure, regarded visiting lecturers with suspicion and hostility. They could not believe that I was not interested in taking up a job at the Centre.

I had my own problems with my students. None of them had the slightest knowledge of India, its history or religion. I had to make my lectures very elementary and fill them in with as many anecdotes as I could unearth. Particularly upsetting were two Nisei Japanese girls who would start nodding with sleep as soon as I started speaking. It became a challenge keeping them awake. I failed in this task. I wreaked vengeance on the girls by failing both of them in the mid-term papers. When they came to see me in my office I told them off roundly. 'How would you feel if, while you are talking to a person, he or she fell asleep? It is most off-putting.' They apologized and explained that they worked in a night club till it closed at 3 am. They hardly had three hours of sleep before coming to my lecture. They dropped out of the course.

While I spent my mornings on the campus, my wife and daughter spent them in shopping plazas. When I returned, I went bathing in the sea for an hour. Besides its lovely beaches, Honolulu is a great place for a voyeur. Everyone is scantily clad, and all the doors and windows there are kept wide open to let in the sea-breeze. Just about every high-rise apartment you train your field glasses on yields a harvest of men and women in the nude. When my wife and daughter were not there, I spent many pleasant hours thanking the Creator for creating beautiful people.

Hawaii has much else to offer. The sweetest and juiciest fresh honey-dew melons, pineapples, avocado pears and, above all, macadamia nuts are grown on these islands. Apart from them, we were introduced to wild rice grown in swamps and garnered by Red Indians. It is a lot more succulent than the finest basmati and is best eaten without adding anything to it. It is also very expensive.

The main island of Hawaii, Hilo, is a short flight from Honolulu and has a live volcano around which the flora and fauna are noticeably different from elsewhere. A couple of Indian women teachers who were preparing Peace Corps students bound for India gave us some Indian *bhojan*. The surprise item came at the end of the meal: they had grown paan creepers in their garden and rolled us *maghai* paans in the wilderness of Hilo.

At the end of my tenure of teaching, I resolved to give myself a treat: I would dine at a night-club where dinners were served by bare-bosomed waitresses. 'Be your age Papa,' said my daughter to me. 'You must be going senile,' said my wife. I stuck to my resolve. In the end they decided to come along with me. The visit to the night-club proved most unrewarding. As soon as we entered, a bare-bosomed waitress came to help me off with my raincoat. 'How nice to see you here professor,' she said to me with a meaningful smile. She was one of my students.

One place to which my wife and daughter did not pursue me was the health club which I frequented regularly for a sauna bath. Among the masseuses was a young, attractive, athletic Black girl. Every time I went there she would say with mischief in her eyes. 'Honey, wouldn't you like me to give you a nice massage?' 'No, I would not,' I would reply. 'Why? Is there something wrong with me?' she would ask very saucily. 'On the contrary, everything is too right with you. That is why I can't trust myself having you fiddle with my body.' She would break into a happy peal of laughter.

Native Hawaiians don't believe in working too much. I saw them sitting on the wooden steps of their porches swilling beer and singing with their banjos all day. They also appeared to have no hang ups about sex. One evening when I emerged from the health club, my wife and daughter came along for an evening stroll on the beach. They walked ahead. I was attracted by an American woman taking out her poodle. As the little dog emptied its bowels, the woman took out toilet paper from her handbag and cleaned its bottom. While I was watching this spectacle a Hawaiian girl, evidently full of beer, came along and said, 'Hello.' She started walking with me and asked me what I was doing in Hawaii. 'Having a good time,' I replied. 'Why don't you settle here?' she asked. 'You could marry me and we'd keep a nice home.' I was startled by her propositioning me in this blatant manner; she did not look like a prostitute. 'How can I marry you? I have a wife and daughter with me. And a son at home. See them walking ahead at the end of the road?' She glanced at the two figures and replied, 'But they've gone ahead; you can leave them and come along with me.' I thanked her for her generous offer, apologized for my being too old for her and quickened my steps.

We were in Hong Kong when we heard of the devaluation of the rupee. My savings in dollars had doubled in their rupee value. We bought all the pens, watches and pearl necklaces we would be allowed to take in by Indian customs.

I was to visit Princeton again a year or so later, this time as one of the three professors to take a group of American students round the world. One of the other professors was a sociologist, Felix Moos, a Nazi turned ultra-patriotic American serving with the C.I.A.; he was accompanied by his Japanese wife, Fusa, and ten-year-old daughter. The second was George Stoney, a film producer from New York, twice divorced and with a mistress; I was the third. We were to spend two months each in Germany, India and Japan. I was to introduce the young men and women to German, Indian and Japanese literature; and prod them into creative writing. Stoney was to introduce them to making films; Moos was to be overall incharge and make arrangements for our stay in Japan. He took little interest in his assignment and left his batch on its own for most of our stay in Germany. I don't recall what Stoney did. But it gave me the rare opportunity to read up modern German classics translated into English from Broctli, Manu, Itesge to Brecht, and Gunter Grass. Our Indian stay was divided equally between Delhi and Hyderabad. The students stayed with families in New Delhi. Moos, who was to arrange our board and lodging in Japan, left us to fend for ourselves. Stoney and I were very fed up with Moos and by the time our assignment was over we were not on talking terms with him.

I had one more teaching assignment in America. This was at Swarthmore College, a Quaker institution about forty miles west of Philadelphia. It was a small college but recognized as a member of the prestigious Ivy League. The calibre of students was as high as I had encountered at Princeton. I had two classes to teach — on Indian religion and contemporary politics. Lecturing was a small part of my job, more time was taken up by seminars, getting students to write on topics chosen by them, and in discussions at my house. It proved very rewarding. One of my female students chose to study Chitpavan Brahmins. Her essay won her a scholarship to Pune. I got her to write an article on the community, the first in a series to be published in *The Illustrated Weekly of India* which set the pace for its upward circulation. After lectures and discussions I wrote up all I had said and heard. This gave me the material I needed for a small booklet, *Introduction to India* (Vision Books), which went into several editions.

In the three months I stayed at Swarthmore the only friends we made were a Dutch-Austrian couple, the Van Ooms. They had two small children. We came to an arrangement mutually suitable to us. Once or twice a week we would dine with them and they would take my wife to the pictures. I stayed back as a baby sitter, put their children to bed, told them stories and was even bullied into singing lullabies till they agreed that sleep was better than hearing me sing. Then I was able to work on my lecture notes.

11 *Bombay,* The Illustrated Weekly of India *(1969–79)* *and the Aftermath*

BOMBAY, YOU WILL be told, is the only city India has, in the sense that the word city is understood in the West. Other Indian metropolises like Calcutta, Madras and Delhi are like oversized villages. It is true that Bombay has many more high-rise buildings than any other Indian city: when you approach it by sea it looks like a miniature New York. It has other things to justify its city status: it is congested, it has traffic jams at all hours of the day, it is highly polluted and many parts of it stink. Arthur Koestler compared his arrival at Santa Cruz airport to having a baby's soiled diaper flung in his face. Bombay discharges the sewage of its ten million or more inhabitants into the sea so close to the shore that a good bit of it is carried back to the land with incoming tides: used condoms can be picked up in the shallows. The stench of human shit prevails over some parts of the seafront. Since it has very few public conveniences, its bazaars smell of stale urine. Twice a year, early in spring and autumn, fish along the coast die in their millions and the acrid smell of rotting fish is overpowering. Bombay has no parks or gardens worth speaking of: only a few small parklets where people go round and round narrow paths like animals in cages. Usually the only place where one can take a walk of sorts is Marine Drive, running from the Chowpatty sands to Nariman Point. This has a dual highway crowded with speeding cars and buses on one side, and massive cement-concrete tripods along the sea walk to prevent it from making further inroads. The tripods are placed at convenient angles which make it easy for the citizens to rest their feet, let down their trousers or pull up their dhotis to defecate. Nevertheless Bombaywallas throng to Marine Drive in their thousands morning and evening to jostle their way through masses of humanity. Old people sit on benches placed *en route* to take in the sea air and gossip. Marine Drive is Bombay's pride and its joy. After sunset, as the street lights are switched on, they gape at it in amazement and call it a Queen's diamond necklace.

However, there are some points in favour of Bombay. It has a heterogeneous mix of races, religions and linguistic groups. They mind their own business and do not bother with their neighbours, nor are they unduly concerned if they are happily married, divorced, having affairs or living in sin. People of diverse ethnic and religious backgrounds get on reasonably well. Till 1982 Bombay did not have many communal riots, but it would be wrong to conclude that the different communities have affection for each other. Every community thinks it is better than the others and behind their backs uses derogatory expressions to describe them. Parsees regard themselves as a cut above everyone else. They are indeed the most prosperous, and have given to Bombay more than other communities. They are conscious of their superiority and look down on the rest as *ghatees* — coastal trash. Others regard Parsees as effete, senile Bawajis, most of whom are highly eccentric and on the verge of lunacy. Since they are very voluble, they are also known as *kagha khaus* — crow eaters. Then we have Gujaratis, largely in trade, commerce and industry. Their language, Gujarati, is more widely spoken than Marathi, the language of the more numerous Maharashtrians. The Gujaratis are generally peace-loving, law-abiding and vegetarian. Behind their backs they are referred to as Gujjus. Bombay has a variety of Muslims who, though they have little to do with each other, get together when there is anti-Muslim violence. Besides the major divisions into Sunni and Shia, there are Ismailis (of two kinds), Bohras (of two kinds), and Memons (Cutchee and Halai). They are lumped together as Mian Bhais. There is also a sizeable community of Christians, both Catholic and Protestant, known to the rest as *Makapaos* — bread eaters (from *pao*, Portuguese for bread). The latest arrivals are Sindhis and Punjabis. Slowly but surely they have captured a sizeable chunk of the city's business and real estate and are consequently eyed with suspicion as grabbers. But Bombay's outsiders outnumber the self-styled insiders who call themselves Sons of the Soil and insist on calling Bombay by its original name *Mumbai,* after its patron goddess Maha Amba. No educated Indian calls it anything other than Bombay.

Bombay is much the richest city of India. More than half of India's income-tax comes from this one city. Bombay is also India's most corrupt city: more than half of the black money in circulation is generated in Bombay. It has more millionaires than the other three metropolitan cities put together. It attracts an endless stream of outsiders who hope to make their fortunes here. It also probably has more prostitutes and call girls than any other city in the world. Bombay's rich live very well: in large air-cooled apartments facing the sea, with rooftop gardens and bathing pools. A Sindhi multi-millionaire has a glass-bottomed pool above his bar-cum-sitting room. Whenever he has parties he hires young girls to bathe in the nude so that his guests can watch them from below while they sip their Scotch. Bombay provides the best food in India: Mughlai, European, Chinese and vegetarian. It has more good, cheap restaurants than any other Indian city. All said and done, Bombay is the most enjoyable city of India — if you can find a place to live in.

I knew all this about Bombay when I was first invited to take over the editorship of *The Illustrated Weekly of India.* At the time I turned down the offer in favour of the Rockefeller grant to write a history of the Sikhs. In the spring of 1969, when I was at Swarthmore I got another letter from J.C. Jain, General Manager of Bennett Coleman & Co., publishers of *The Times of India,* asking me if I would now be interested in taking over *The Illustrated Weekly of India.* I wrote to Jain expressing interest in the job but wanted to know what had happened to Raman, the current Editor. He wrote back to say that, whether or not I accepted his offer, Raman was being sacked. By the time I arrived back in Delhi, Jain himself had been fired, but the offer was still open to me.

After spending a few days with my parents in Delhi, I left by train for Bombay. My wife decided to stay back in Delhi. My son, Rahul, made things easier for me. He was Assistant Editor with *The Times of India*. He decided not to work for the same establishment as his father, and became instead the first Editor of the Indian edition of *The Reader's Digest*. He also gave up his board and lodging arrangement with a young Parsee couple, Firdaus and Amy Jehangir, to me. The same afternoon I moved into the Jehangir's third floor apartment near Churchgate Station and made friends with their one-year-old-son and six-month-old boxer pup, Bella.

The next morning I walked over to *The Times of India* office. I introduced myself to the guards and the lift men. I was escorted to my room on the third floor. It was half an hour before office time. The only member of the staff present was the Assistant Editor, Subroto Bannerjee, who had held the fort since Raman's dismissal. I asked him why Raman had left. 'Not on his own,' he replied. 'He was fired. Editorship had gone to his head. His lunch break would extend to late afternoon. He often came back drunk and threw up. Once while he was trying to sleep it off, his telephone rang. He hurled it down on the floor and smashed it. It had to be put together with araldite.' He showed me the cracks on the phone. 'Then he accepted some invitation to go abroad and left without getting the permission of the management. When he returned, he was handed a notice terminating his services.'

I asked to see the names of my would-be colleagues and what they did. I told Bannerjee that I would send for them in turn after I had examined some past issues of the journal. The issues of the previous twelve months were put on my table. *The Weekly* had a modest circulation of about 80,000, entirely because it had no rivals. Painters, poets, short-story writers and dancers were eager to appear in its pages. When I examined its past copies critically, I found very little that was readable and a deadly sameness in its contents.

Mandy, the much-respected Editor before Raman, was happy to write his weekly column 'Gallimaufry'. No one except he knew what the word meant. It means a hodge-podge of foods — a *khichdee.* That is precisely what *The Weekly* was — a jumble of articles without any central theme. It consisted of the tittle-tattle at cocktail parties given by Parsee dowagers with outlandish names like Lady Nimboo Pawnee, which made Mandy the lion of Bombay's Parsee-dominated social circles. A few pages were devoted to 'They were Married' and consisted of photographs of newly-married couples from different parts of India, all looking very tight-lipped, glum and unhappy. Being a 'Family Magazine' it had some pages devoted to children, including 'Aunty Wendy's column', wherein a succession of Aunty Wendys addressed loving sermons to their nephews and nieces. The rest consisted of syndicated features bought from the United States and strip cartoons ('Superman' was the top favourite). The first and often the only page most readers turned to was 'What The Stars Foretell', a weekly forecast of future events, also bought from a foreign syndicate.

Raman's contribution was to Indianize the journal by injecting massive doses of Indian art, reviews of classical Indian music, with pictures of singers and dancers. He was also into religion — and mostly into himself. In one issue on Satya Sai Baba, whom he worshipped as God incarnate, he had eight pictures of himself, his wife and son paying homage to the godman. With the advent of Raman, *The Weekly* had shown a marginal increase in circulation. But it remained as deadly dull as before and was usually seen in doctors', hair-dressers' and dentists' waiting rooms. If I could not brighten it, I couldn't have made it any duller. I had three clear objectives in my mind: inform, amuse and irritate. I would use it to tell Indians about their own country; I would try to shake them out of their mental lethargy and provoke them into thinking by publishing controversial articles; and, being somewhat of a joker, I would try to amuse them. With that triple formula I felt I could not fail.

I had to contend with long-term contracts made by Subroto Bannerjee with NASA on Space Research and with an Indian author on a strip-cartoon biography of Gandhi. They occupied nearly six pages each and were due to go on for another six months. It had to be a slow process of change. I had a new design made for the cover page, closely resembling the old one, but improving on it. I cut out 'They Were Married' and issued notice to Aunty Wendy that I meant to abolish the children's pages. I met photographers on the staff and wrote to others outside Bombay asking them to send me more explicit and animated photographs on topics of contemporary interest.

Members of my staff came to see me in turn. Subroto Bannerjee I found very personable, but like a good Bengali he was content to let things go on as they were and provide plausible explanations why they couldn't be better. As for the others, it took me some days to tell one from the other, and longer to take their measure.

I had a secretary, meant exclusively for me — Swamy, a Tamilian. Swamy was as kindly a man as he was efficient at his job. But he was a prude. Once when a friend in New York sent me copies of a journal called *Screw* devoted to hard-core pornography Swamy, as was his practice, opened it to lay it on my table. He was shocked by the center spread. It had eight pictures of female genitals under the caption 'Who said all cunts are alike?' There was an amusing epilogue to the incident. I ran into the head of the Bombay Customs and told him that while my copies of *Playboy* were regularly seized for obscenity, a really obscene journal entitled *Screw* escaped their attention. He made enquiries and discovered that the officer concerned had assumed that *Screw* was an engineering magazine.

The last of the staff to be interviewed by me was 'Aunty Wendy.' This happened to be Fatma, wife of Rafiq Zakaria, then a senior minister in the Maharashtra government. She was not on the pay rolls of *The Weekly* but brought in her contribution and proof-read it once a week. She had been told that I meant to abolish 'Aunty Wendy' and came armed with a letter stating that she would not be writing for the journal any more. I read it and tore it up. 'I am dismissing "Aunty Wendy", not you,' I said. 'If you wish to continue your association with *The Weekly* we can think of other things you could do.' She nodded her head. She invited me to her home for dinner to meet her husband and children.

The Zakarias took me by storm. They were a tempestuous family, where shouting at each other was followed by periods of comparative calm. He had an uncontrollable temper: one never knew when he would flare up. She was more contained but determined to get what she wanted by persistent nagging. They entertained a great deal, but only invited people who could further his career. He was brought into politics by Morarji Desai, once Chief Minister of Maharashtra. For years Desai's portrait had the place of honour in the Zakaria sitting room. When Morarji went out of favour, his portrait was removed and replaced by one of Yashwant Rao Chavan, the then Chief Minister of Maharashtra. His wife helped him in achieving his political ambitions. She made his engagements, confirmed them every morning and kept his files in order. Zakaria wanted to distinguish himself from his colleagues by appearing to be a man of letters. Here too his wife helped him collect material and in editing what he wrote. After a book on Indian Islam, he and his wife wrote a fictional biography of Sultana Razia. I had given it an unfavourable review; they thought I had praised it. For reasons known only to him, Zakaria suspected me of being prejudiced against Muslims: my dispensing with 'Aunty Wendy', he thought, was meant to dispense with the part-time services of a Muslim. The boys had been brought up on stereotyped notions about Sikhs, that they hated Muslims and went berserk at noon etc. Fatma's mother, a big, portly woman who was staying with them, had warned them against using taxis driven by Sikhs. She couldn't quite make out what I was doing in their home and to her last day referred to me as *chhapeywala* — the fellow from the printers. Other members of the household consisted of a Goan Man-Friday called Pascal Lobo, a wafer-thin Maharashtrian maid-servant with protruding teeth called Vasanthi and a cook who never exchanged a word with me. I called him 'the assassin' because he looked as if he could put poison in my food. They lived in a large government bungalow guarded by armed policemen and a white pariah dog who had taken residence there. I was able to come to terms with all of them save the cook and the dog. The cook never exchanged a word with me; the dog bared its fangs at me, whenever I came or left.

At my first evening with the Zakarias we took measure of each other. They served me Scotch; Zakaria kept up the pretence that being a member of the Congress party he did not touch liquor. I was told that I wasn't to tell anyone that I was served whiskey in their home. The three boys, Mansoor (from Zakaria's first wife), Arshad and Fareed gaped at me in disbelief. Zakaria began his bulldozing tactics. Why didn't I give his wife a permanent job on the staff? He would speak to the Chairman of the Company, retired Justice K.T. Desai and the General Manager Tarneja, but the initiative had to come from me. I had no idea how good or bad a worker Fatma would prove to be, but I could not resist the pressure put on me. I might try her out as a sub and see how she acquitted herself. But Zakaria dictated the proposal I sent to the management. Fatma Zakaria was to be one of the three Assistant Editors. Zakaria spoke to Desai and Tarneja. The proposal was promptly accepted. Within a few days Fatma was installed as Assistant Editor and quietly assumed the powers of my seniormost aide. No one could see me without being cleared by her; all telephone calls to me were first received by her. Even my social life came to be regulated by her. At least twice a week I had dinner with them; on other days, if I had not been invited out, food was sent to my apartment. She proved to be an extremely possessive woman who could not tolerate my making friends with other women or men she did not approve of. There was, however, a very positive side to her character. Although she did not and could not write, she organized the commissioning and publishing of articles. She was an excellent sub and unsparing in her endeavour to see *The Weekly* come up. Her dedication to her job and to me was complete. Without her I could not have run the journal.

Within a few days my life fell into a routine. I made it a point to get to the office an hour before anyone else. By the time others started coming in, I had cleared my correspondence and edited articles meant for the new issue. I had no dearth of visitors. The cartoonist R.K. Laxman breezed in, ordered coffee and wasted a good part of the morning exchanging gossip. Fatma always came in with him, and at other times whenever she wanted. Laxman, who thought nothing of wasting other people's time, never allowed anyone in his cabin when he was at work. I didn't resent him because he was a good raconteur and undoubtedly a genius; in my opinion the best cartoonist of his times. More considerate was the second cartoonist, Mario Miranda. He went out of his way to work for me and designed the bulb logo in which I have been encaged ever since.

There was the usual quota of do-gooders and people concerned with the country. Without exception, they opened the dialogue with the question *'Yeh desh kahan ja raha hai'* — where is this country going? I usually joined the other editors in the lunch room. I introduced new items like artichokes and avocado pears to the menu and occasionally got important figures from the film world, politics and social life to join us. Most of the afternoons were spent reading proofs. Initially I made it a point to select photographs for *The Weekly* myself and write their captions. Bachi Kanga caught on very fast and I began to leave this task to her. During my first few months I was amongst the last to leave the office. I walked home through the crowded streets, past the Parsee well to Churchgate. I made friends with Bihari Bhaiyyas who sold newspapers and magazines on the pavements, and asked them how *The Illustrated Weekly* was selling. Back in the Jehangirs' flat I was welcomed by Bella — wheezing, slobbering and shaking her behind to make up for her stubby tail. I played with her till her ears suddenly picked up and she tilted her head sideways, to make sure she was hearing right. Of the hundreds of cars that ran by on the road below, she could pick up the sound of her master's engine. She would bark with joy and run to the door cocking her head till the elevator stopped and the door opened to let him out. Thereafter she had no use for me.

In course of time I got to be on greeting terms with people I met on the road, in cafes I frequented, as well as coconut vendors, paanwalas, dogs, beggars and street walkers. I cultivated a taste for fresh coconut juice — there is nothing in the world to match it to freshen the taste in one's mouth — or cleanse the bladder of impurities. Paan became a horrible addiction: I could not do without it after every meal and needed to be chewing something in order to concentrate on my work. I ignored dentists' warnings that I was ruining my teeth and exposing myself to the risk of mouth and throat cancer.

Churchgate, being an upper-middle class locality, did not have many street walkers. If there were any I was slow in recognizing them. One evening while returning home after dinner, a lady standing under a street lamp asked me for the time. The Gangabai Tower clock stared us in the face but I consulted my watch and told her the precise hour. She thanked me in polished Urdu: *'Bahut Shukriya, Sardar Sahib!'* It was only when going up in the lift that it occurred to me that the lady meant to proposition me. Another girl who attracted my attention lived on a pavement near a gas station which also had a couple of paanwalas and a bhelpuri seller on the drive-way leading to the pumps. She was a beggar in her mid-twenties and on friendly terms with the bhelpuriwala who gave her his left-overs. I never saw her solicit anyone, nor as much as look up at strangers. She was mentally unbalanced and had apparently been thrown out by her husband. Much as I tried to draw her in during conversations with the paanwala or the bhelpuri seller, she ignored my presence. I got to see what she looked like after the monsoons broke over Bombay in the second week of June. The outbreak of the monsoon is an experience not to be missed. Weeks before its advent the pavements around Churchgate have people selling umbrellas and gum-boots. It finally comes in cascades flooding the roads with knee-deep water. I was curious to know how the beggar woman coped with the inclement weather. On such days the bhelpuriwallah couldn't have had many buyers, and I thought that perhaps I could buy the evening meal for the girl. When I went to fetch my paan there was no bhelpuriwallah. The girl lay huddled on the steps of a shop barely an inch above the swirling rain water. She obviously had no worldly goods and not even a change of clothes. She haunted my mind through the night.

When I woke the next morning, the Gangabai Tower clock

showed 5 am. It had poured all night and flooded the maidan, making it look like a lake. The rain had now come down to a drizzle, but the sky was overcast. In the greying light of the dawn I saw the figure of a woman draped in a dirty white dhoti in the middle of the maidan. She was sitting on her haunches splashing water between her thighs with a tin can. She was evidently cleaning herself after having defecated somewhere behind the bushes. I got out my field glasses and focused them on her. Having done with her ablutions, she looked around to assure herself that she was not being watched. Then she took off her dhoti and poured muddy rainwater over herself, paying special attention to her breasts and middle. It was the beggar woman. I watched her till she put on the same dirty dhoti round her wet body and sloshed her way back to her pad near Churchgate Station. How was it that no one had spotted this beggar maid in this vice-ridden city? I found the answer a few days later. I had been passing by her pavement lodging every night but not seen her there. Had her husband taken her back? I could not contain my curiosity and, while buying bhel, which I had no intention of eating, asked the vendor as casually as I could what had happened to the woman. His voice choked as he replied: *'Kucch na poocho sardarji'* — don't ask me anything Sardarji, *'bharoohey phusla kay lay gaye'* — pimps inveigled her away. The poor thing probably ended up in some brothel in Kamatipura.

The monsoon brought other experiences. Often I had to take a spare shirt to the office and carry my chappals in my hands when wading through the muddy water. When it poured, the umbrella barely protected my turban from being drenched. There were also other unexpected hazards. One morning, as I approached Flora Fountain I saw a large sewer rat coming towards me pursued by kites and crows dive-bombing on it. I thought it safer to cross to the other side. So did the sewer rat. I was in the middle of the road when it scampered after me and, finding no other shelter from its persecutors, sought refuge between my legs. It tried to claw its way up my trousers. I jumped about in a frenzy trying to shake off the rodent from my leg and waved my umbrella to ward off the kites and crows now hovering over my head. A crowd collected on the pavement to watch the spectacle. I managed to knock off the sewer rat and ran across to safety. Far from eliciting the sympathy of the spectators, one taunted me, *'Arey, Sardarji choohe say dar gaya!'* — look at this big Sikh getting scared of a mouse! I tried to protest that it was not a *chooha* (mouse) but a big sewer-rat. It dawned on me that there was no word in Hindi to distinguish a rat from a mouse. And later, that no Indian language made any distinction between a tiny mouse and a bewhiskered cat-sized rat. Of the rodent species all they knew were mice and bandicoots. Our languages also make no difference between snow and ice — both are *baraf*. They have no word for a seagull — it's just a *jal kauwa* — a water crow, even though there are over a dozen species of seagulls on our coasts.

There were some amusing incidents in the office as well. One afternoon the sculptress, Freda Brilliant, and her husband, Herbert Marshall, dropped in to see me. They were close friends of Krishna Menon: she had done an extremely good head of Menon in bronze. He claimed to be a Russian scholar and had published an English translation of Mayakovsky's poems. I found them too pushing for my liking and had kept my distance from them. They apparently did not sense this. She came in with open arms, pouring out a stream of endearments. 'Darling, darling Khushy! How are you?' I made polite enquiries about what they were doing in India and ordered tea for them. She was negotiating for the sale of her heads of Nehru and Menon with the National Art Gallery and to see if she could get other assignments. They had been to an exhibition of Indian handlooms and bought a brightly coloured shirt full of small, round mirrors. She held it out for me to admire. 'Don't you think it will look nice on me?' I assured her it would. 'Let me put it on for you,' she said. 'Both of you turn your faces to the wall and I will change my shirt.' Her husband and I dutifully turned our faces to the wall. Suddenly Freda shrieked, 'Get out!' Her shriek was followed by a crash of chinaware. We turned round to see what had happened. There was Freda trying to cover her bare bosom with her hands. The bearer who had brought in the tea saw the half-naked memsahib and in panic dropped the tray. The story did the rounds of the office for many days.

A similar incident took place when Peggy Holroyde came to spend an afternoon with me. She had travelled by train from Delhi and had to catch a night flight back to her home in Australia. I picked her up at Bombay Central station, deposited her in my apartment (I was then living in Sentinel House, Colaba) and returned to office. After resting for a time, Peggy went into the bathroom to take a shower. Just then the door bell rang. She took a towel and, while drying herself, opened the door. It was Fatma Zakaria's servant Pascal Lobo with my evening meal in a tiffin box. Pascal was taken aback. Not Peggy. She continued drying herself while Pascal put the tiffin box in my kitchen and beat a hasty retreat. I had much to answer for at the Zakarias' household: How was it that a naked Mrs Holroyde had opened the door expecting me? How well had I known her? etc. There was no point in my protesting that Peggy was that kind of girl — or rather, not that kind of girl.

Then there was the pretty Italian girl, Marcia Graziano, a disciple of Acharya Rajneesh. She was young, petite, with muddy blonde hair and large grey eyes. She tied a saffron-coloured bandanna round her head, wore a shirt and tehmad. She looked most fetching in her Sadhvi's attire; she was serious-minded and rarely smiled, and wanted me to meet her Guru, read his printed sermons and become a disciple. She left a sheaf of booklets with me. On her second or third visit I tried to make a pass at her. 'Marcia, you want to convert me to your faith? I am quite willing. I don't have to meet your Guru and read all the books you bring me. My price is different.' She pretended not to understand what I was driving at. When on her subsequent visits I repeated the offer to convert, she fixed me with her grey eyes and asked: 'You want to sleep with me, don't you? If you like my body you can have it. The body is nothing; it is the mind and the spirit that matter.' The straightforward offer to have cold-blooded sex deflated my lust. I had no doubt that if I had wanted to take her to bed she would have kept her part of the bargain. But she would also have proved to me that the body, bereft of the spirit to enter into a physical relationship, would have amounted to very little. Marcia became a friend. When she returned to Italy we continued writing to each other. On my way to Bellagio she entertained my wife and me to a sumptuous Italian dinner at Rome. When I met her next in Los Angeles she had married a TV film producer and apparently made a happy marriage.

Two characters who came into my life in Bombay would make excellent subjects for novels: Anees Jung and A.G. Noorani. Anees I had met earlier when I was conducting a party of American students round the world. She introduced herself as one who had just returned from the States after taking a degree in literature, had met our son Rahul in Bombay and been asked by him to get in touch with us. This was the way Anees got round people — to my wife any friend of Rahul was a friend of the family. She was invited for lunch. She turned out to be an engaging conversationalist — speaking English without a trace of an American accent and Urdu in the quaint Hyderabadi way which I found very endearing.

Anees was an incorrigible name-dropper. She also happened to know the people whose names she dropped.

She lived in a world of fantasy with delusions of grandeur. She told me about the Hyderabad aristocracy — the Jahs, Dowlahs and Jungs, and of her father, Nawab Hoshiar Jung, who she said had been a minister in the Nizam's government. Actually, he had only been a *musahib* (companion) whose conversation the Nizam enjoyed. I am sure Anees inherited the trait from her father, because she was a more engaging conversationalist than any woman I had met. She told me of the palatial residences they had lived in and the English governesses they had employed. Where the family wealth had disappeared to, I was never told.

Anees re-emerged in my life when I was editing the *Illustrated Weekly*. She had applied for the post of editor of *Youth*

Times, a new monthly magazine that *The Times of India* group were planning to launch from Delhi. The interview board consisted of the Chairman, Justice Desai, Rajni Patel, Ram Tarneja, the manager and I. She had already got round Patel and Tarneja but had not been able to see Desai. Patel and Tarneja suggested that, instead of the panel interviewing the dozen or more candidates, the decision be left to me — my stock in the management was at the time very high. I chose Anees. She set up her office in *The Times of India* building in Delhi. Within a few weeks she had become a great favourite of Ram Tarneja, the man who mattered most. Soon the General Manager rose in her affections: she initially referred to him as Tarneja then as Ram, and finally Tannu. She was in and out of Bombay as often as she wished. She kept up with me but couldn't stand Fatma Zakaria; Fatma could not stand her. Every evening when she was in Bombay, she made it a point to sit in Tarneja's car parked in the porch, so that people leaving the office for their homes could see her in the General Manager's car and get the right message. She mattered. It is odd that, despite Anees' compulsive name-dropping, lion hunting, consorting only with the top people, bitching against most women including my wife, and feeding me on endless stories of her conquests of the high and mighty and then denying them entirely, I not only remained friendly with her but, in my later years, looked forward to being with her more than with most other women.

A.G. Noorani was an entirely different kind of person. He was a lawyer and a journalist. Also the most cantankerous and touchy person I have met. Despite his knowledge of the law he did not have much of a legal practice as he picked up quarrels with his clients, solicitors and judges. He had, however, begun to make a name for himself as a journalist writing on politics, the constitution and corruption in high places. He was meticulous about checking his facts and wrote with remarkable clarity. We became friends. He maintained that he had only two interests in life, *vakalaat aur siyasat* — the law and politics. He had one other interest as well.

Our friendship lasted for a year or two. We met almost every evening to take a stroll on Marine Drive. Back in my flat, he sipped orange juice (he was a strict teetotaller) while I had my quota of Scotch. Then we went out to dine, trying out different restaurants in the neighbourhood. To start with, he was very proper and reserved. He dressed in European clothes, wore a tie, socks and shoes on the warmest of days. He was particular about his looks and constantly brushed his well-oiled hair with his hand and took a long approving look at the mirror before setting out. He fancied himself a latter-day Mohammed Ali Jinnah, with the same cold austerity in his deportment and the same clarity of thinking. He soon thawed under my bawdiness. I was pleasantly surprised by his collection of dirty verse and risque jokes. This was an aspect of his personality which he did not expose to anyone else. Nor his penchant for white women. He could be extremely naive. When two Canadian girls, both film producers, came to see me with letters of introduction we took them out for dinner. After dinner we walked with them to their hotel — Sue Dexter, a six-foot tall girl, and I in front, the smaller and younger girl with Noorani a few steps behind us. After we bade them goodnight I found Noorani in a high state of excitement. 'Yaar, you know what that girl said to me? When I asked her if she was married, she replied, "Yes I am, but I commit adultery." Now what do you make of that, except an open invitation to bed?'

For the next few days Noorani set siege to the girl, rang her up to invite her to his bachelor apartment. Ultimately the girl tired of his persistence, rang me up and asked me to get Noorani off her back. 'Did you tell him you commit adultery?' I asked her.

'Yeah, I did but I did not mean to commit it with him.'

Not deterred by this setback, he picked on a Belgian divorcee I introduced him to. She had a large car and took Noorani for long drives to Juhu beach. However, every time on their way back home, she would run out of gas and proclaim that she had forgotten to bring her purse. Noorani paid for the petrol many times without getting anywhere with the woman. It was the same with a very attractive German secretary at the Consulate. He pursued her till she wearied of him. For a time she took a room in a pension behind my apartment. I tortured Noorani by telling him that I often saw her in the nude going in and out of the bathroom. Ultimately it was a rich Gujarati businessman who made it with the German girl, leaving Noorani in the cold.

I thought Anees Jung and Noorani would make a nice couple. They had heard of each other, read each other's articles but never met. Some kindly person arranged for them to meet in Delhi — with a view to matrimony.

They agreed to talk it over a morning cup of coffee at the Oberoi Hotel. Noorani was very fussy about time. Anees was not so particular. The Oberoi has many restaurants and they had not fixed where their tryst with destiny was to take place. Noorani waited impatiently in a restaurant on one floor, Anees sat calmly in another, looking for a character who might be Noorani. After half an hour Noorani concluded that a woman who could keep him waiting for that long was not worth knowing. At the same time Anees decided she had waited long enough. The two found themselves in the same elevator. Noorani was in a temper and took the chance of giving her a dressing down: 'May you be Miss Jung?' he asked deliberately, mispronouncing her name as 'Joong.'

'Yes, I am Anees Jung,' she replied.

He held up his wrist watch and pointed to the time. 'You were supposed to meet me at 11 am. Now it is well after 11.30.' Anees tried to explain that she had been waiting for him in another restaurant. Noorani's temper did not cool down. The two began to quarrel. What was designed to be the first meeting between lovers ended in an angry exchange of words and gruff farewells without a cup of coffee.

Let me return to *The Weekly*.

I thought it best to do some writing myself so that my colleagues got a clearer idea of what I had in mind. I drastically edited, at times almost rewrote, stories sent by contributors. They were happy to see their names in print and receive remunerations which were higher than those paid by other journals. The first story I wrote myself as editor was on the trial of Raman Raghav. With an iron rod this man had bashed in the skulls of between thirty to forty slum dwellers — men, women and children. He was due to be tried in the court of a Sessions Judge of Bombay. I approached the prosecuting counsel and was able to borrow his files from him. I also got the police to permit me to take photographs of Raghav when he was brought to court. The photographer Jitendra Arya came with me.

When Raghav was taken out of the Black Maria in handcuffs and leg irons I told Arya to be ready with his camera. Raghav was a dark, stocky and powerfully built man in his mid-forties. As soon as he saw the photographer he began to scream and jump about, hurling obscenities at everyone. 'Take him now!' I shouted at Arya. 'Let him calm down,' replied Arya. I realized that Arya would never make a crime photographer and should stick to taking portraits of celebrities and bare-bosomed girls. The picture he finally got was a very tame affair. I sat through the Sessions trial for the three days it lasted. Raghav was more than ready to admit his crimes and repeated confessions he had made to the police and the magistrate who had committed him. He was shown the heavy iron rod which he had used as his weapon. He handled it lovingly as if it had been a close friend. For a moment everyone in the court became nervous. 'Don't be frightened,' he assured us, 'I won't kill any of you.' He was quite nonchalant in his attitude towards the Judge. When the names of the people he had killed were read out to him and he was asked whether he had murdered them, he replied, 'Yes, I did. I killed all of them and you can hang me. I am not afraid of dying.' It was evident that he was a psychopathic case and his defence counsel should have pleaded insanity. When the Sessions Judge passed the sentence of death on him, Raman Raghav showed no emotion. The High Court, which had to confirm the death sentence, had him medically examined and declared insane. He spent many years in chains in a lunatic asylum before he died.

No other newspaper or journal carried the Raman Raghav

trial in as much detail as *The Weekly.* Our circulation began to rise. Next, I featured the ghazal singer Shakila Bano Bhopali. I had heard her sing in Delhi. She was a fair, round-faced woman in her thirties with the sauciness of an upper-class courtesan. She did not have much of a voice but made up for it by a lot of animated banter and risque jokes which she interspersed in her songs. She was low-brow and the top favourite of the hoi-polloi who fancied themselves as connoisseurs of Urdu poetry. She was happy to have herself written about in an English magazine. Arya took many photographs of her in action. I put her picture on the cover and did a lengthy article giving her background and the training she had received from her mother, Jamila Bano. Shakila was delighted; her stock in the ghazal singers' market rose and she was able to double her fees. Many readers protested. What was happening to the respectable family magazine — it was carrying lead articles on murderers and singing girls!

I followed this up with a feature on sleazy cabarets. One photograph was of a scantily-clad couple dancing a tango in such close proximity as to almost suggest that they were copulating. The acting General Manager, Mankekar, summoned me to his room to express his disgust. I told him to pipe down. I continued to run *The Weekly* as I thought best, with every issue carrying at least one picture of a bare-bosomed tribal lass or a white hippie stepping out of the ocean on a Goan beach. I took good care to make the captions as prosaic and informative as I could: with tribal girls there was never any reference to the size of their breasts or buttocks, only the names of the tribes, their numbers, their habitat, etc. With hippies, the captions mentioned the menace of drugs and the resentment of puritans against having their adolescents exposed to temptation. Rival weekly tabloids like *Blitz* and *Current,* which carried similar pictures, seldom did more than mention the girl's vital statistics and in parenthesis ('and this is not her telephone number'), or had some silly doggerel as a caption. I was never charged for obscenity.

What gave *The Weekly* its biggest break was the series we

carried on the different communities of India — Chitpavans, Ayyangars, Iyers, Lingayats, Vokaliggas, Memons, Bohras, Maheshwaris, Kayasths, Jats, Aggarwals — just about every religious, ethnic, caste or sub-caste I had heard of. These articles gave the genesis of the concerned communities, their habitat, with the achievements of their great sons and daughters. Every issue was bought up by members of the community. Our sales shot up. From being at the bottom of the list of Bennett and Coleman's publications, we overtook them one by one, surpassing them by wide margins. I was caddish enough to celebrate each triumph by ordering baskets of sweetmeats and distributing them to everyone in the office. In the board room where the editors were occasionally summoned to meet the directors, there were charts showing the circulations of our magazines. Others had their ups and downs or remained static, but *The Weekly* graph showed an ever-upward trend, rising like a victorious phallus at an obscene angle. I gloated over my circulation. It did not make me popular with my fellow editors. The last magazine we overtook was the Hindi *Dharmayug*, edited by the litterateur, Dr Dharam Vir Bharati. He was quite upset when one of my staff went to his cabin to present him with a laddoo to mark our achievement.

The next spurt in our circulation came with the Indo-Pak war fought over the liberation of Bangladesh. I was commissioned to cover it by *The New York Times*; I used the same articles with many more pictures for *The Illustrated Weekly*. I was fortunate in being able to predict the outbreak of hostilities and their outcome. However, I must admit that it was neither my features on criminals, courtesans, cabaret dancers, communities, film stars or politics which hit the highest mark, but those on cricket prepared almost entirely by Raju Bharatan and illustrated from his private collection. We touched an all-time high circulation of 410,000 copies. We could have sold as many more again, but were constrained to limit circulation as with the advertisement-editorial ratio a higher circulation meant more loss than gain. I had every reason to get puffed up:

within five years *The Weekly* had more than quadrupled its circulation.

After the Bangladesh war was over, I visited Pakistan twice to see how Zulfiqar Ali Bhutto was doing and how a defeated Pakistan was taking the drubbing of its army. On my first visit I met Bhutto in Karachi and again in Islamabad. The second one was more profitable, as I met Begum Para and her children in Karachi, and Bhutto and General Tikka Khan in Islamabad. I do not have much to say about the meeting with Bhutto other than what appeared in *The Weekly,* except that I conveyed a personal message from him to Mrs Gandhi. She disdainfully ignored it saying 'He is an absolute liar.' The meetings with Begum Para and Tikka Khan were quite memorable.

Begum Para, one-time super vamp of the Indian screen had put on a lot of weight after she married Nasir Khan (brother of superstar Yusuf, alias Dilip Kumar) and borne him two beautiful children, a daughter and a son. Her husband died, leaving her very little beside a flat in Bandra and a couple of films. She felt that she had a right to some of the millions that her brother-in-law was making. She also had a considerable inheritance in Pakistan waiting to be claimed by her. I met her through Rukhsana Sultana, her sister's daughter. I saw quite a lot of Begam Para and her children in Bombay. Many Sunday mornings the family joined me at the Gymkhana Club bathing pool to swim and have breakfast. Begum Para often brought up the question of money. If anyone could loan her Rs 40–50,000 she could have her old films re-screened and make a fortune. I didn't take the hint. In sheer desperation she migrated to Pakistan to stake her claim to her inheritance. Two of her brothers were in high places, one a minister in Bhutto's government. It didn't take her long to discover that her relations were not willing to part with anything, and she was on weak ground having earlier opted for India. She earned a little by flogging films she had brought with her and appearing on TV. Her children were unhappy. After the free and easy atmosphere of Bombay, the girl who was rapidly growing into a beautiful young lady, found the puritanical atmosphere of Pakistan very stifling. Begum Para wrote me several letters asking for help in returning to India. I wrote back that I would be coming to Karachi soon and we could talk over the matter.

I arrived in Karachi early in the evening. Begum Para and her children were at the airport to receive me. So was the Chief of Protocol — because I was a guest of the government. We were conducted to the V.I.P. lounge. The children had their fill of cakes and biscuits and were sent home. Begum Para accepted my invitation to dine with me at the hotel where I was to stay the night, before catching the morning flight to Islamabad. The Chief of Protocol dropped us at my hotel. Begum Para came with me to my room. I ordered soda and ice and took out the bottle of Scotch I had brought with me. At the time there was no prohibition in Pakistan. I had heard stories about Begum Para's drink problem. She had to cut down on it because of the price: a bottle of Scotch cost twice as much in Pakistan as it did in India. 'Would you like a drink?' I asked her, not sure whether she was still a drinking woman. 'I'll take a little,' she replied. 'I haven't seen genuine Scotch for ages.'

I poured out two stiff whiskys and handed her one. We resumed talking in Punjabi. I was not halfway through my glass when I saw her's was empty. I poured out another one for her. She tossed it down and I had to refill it before I resumed drinking my own. By the time I had finished my quota of three large whiskys, Begum Para had had nine. The bottle was almost empty. I told her we must eat soon as I had to catch the early morning flight. Reluctantly she got up to accompany me to the dining room.

The dining room was on the first floor. We had to climb up a spiral marble staircase to get to it. The place was crowded. As usual in Pakistan, there were very few women in the room. People recognized Begum Para because of her appearances on TV. They were intrigued to see her in the company of a Sikh.

We were shown to a table for two. We ordered our meal. 'Would you like to have something to drink while waiting for your meal?' asked the waiter. 'Nothing for me,' I replied and looked at Begum Para. 'I'll have another Scotch and soda,' she said. She had another two before soup was served. She began to slur over her words, her eyes took on a glazed look. She wanted to have yet another drink with her meal. I put my foot down firmly.

At long last the meal came to an end. I got up to assist Begum Para with her chair. She stood up, swayed a little and collapsed on the carpet. The waiters came running to help her get on to her feet. I took her arm to help her walk to the stairs. All eyes in the dining room were turned on us. I was doubly careful going down the spiral staircase. I gripped her fat arm and ordered her: 'One step at a time.' We made it to the foyer. I ordered a taxi for her and waited patiently for the ordeal to be over. A taxi drew up in the portico. I gave the driver a hundred-rupee note and told him to take the lady home. He recognized Begum Para and knew where she lived. I opened the rear door of the taxi and went back to help Begum Para. As she stepped forward, she missed her step and once again collapsed on the ground, this time with a loud fart. She sprained her ankle and began to howl with pain. *'Hai Rabba Main Mar Gayee!'* — O God, I've killed myself. A crowd gathered. Being a Muslim country no unrelated male would touch a woman. I did my best to haul her up to her feet. She was far too heavy for me. I pleaded with the car-driver for help. My advance tip came in handy. We got her on her feet and pushed her into the seat. I slammed the door and bid her a hurried farewell. I got through the crowd and made for my room as fast as I could.

A few minutes later there was a knock on my door. I opened it to be confronted by a sub-inspector of police who had a cigarette dangling from his lower lip. He pushed his way in and took a chair. He eyed the nearly empty bottle of Scotch and the debris of sodawater bottles. 'Passport!' he ordered rudely.

I took out my passport and handed it to him. He leafed over its pages. 'Did you report your arrival at a police station?' he asked in an insolent tone.

'I have been exempted from doing so,' I replied.

He took a second look at the visa and found nothing wrong with it.

'What is your business in Karachi?'

'I have no business. I am on my way to Islamabad.'

He continued to leaf through my passport and smoke his cigarette.

'What do you do? Are you in the dry-fruit business?'

'No, I am a journalist.' My patience with the cocky sub-inspector was coming to an end.

'Where will you be staying in Islamabad?'

'With your Prime Minister, Mr Bhutto. I am his guest.'

That was not strictly true but it had an electrifying effect. The policeman quickly stubbed out his cigarette and stood up. 'Are you some kind of minister-shinister?'

'No,' I replied. 'I just happen to know Mr Bhutto personally.'

The fellow gave me a smart salute and marched out.

I was as eager to be the first Indian journalist to interview General Tikka Khan as the General was determined to have nothing to do with any Indian. He was angry that he had been dubbed by the Indian press as the 'Butcher of Bangladesh' and was smarting under the ignominious defeat inflicted by the Indian army on Pakistan. He did not acknowledge my letter asking for an interview. It was my friend Manzur Qadir who interceded on my behalf and persuaded him to talk to me as 'a friend of Pakistan'.

General Tikka Khan received me courteously in his bungalow. He was a short, stocky man with a dour look. He looked more like a bank clerk than a soldier. With him was his orderly, a huge man in a Pathan-style skull cap with a stiffly-starched turban. As I looked around I noticed paraphernalia usual in the homes of army top brass — regimental insignias, trophies and photographs in silver frames. On the mantelpiece and the walls were quotations from the Koran, including one which I was able to decipher. I kept it to myself as I felt it might come in handy in my dialogue with the General.

He was a bitter man. He maintained that stories published in the Indian and the foreign press of mass killings and gang rapes committed by Pakistanis were untrue. 'We are a God-fearing people, my soldiers were a disciplined body of men. They didn't go about shooting innocent Bengalis and molesting their women. It is you Indians who spread these lies and had British newspapers publish these calumnies against us,' he said, looking directly into my eyes.

I made a mild protest. I told him that I had visited Bangladesh soon after the war and heard stories of atrocities committed by Pakistani troops and officers from the mouths of Bangladeshi Muslims. 'They could not all be lies,' I said. 'And I saw the enormous anger against Pakistanis. But for Indian troops to protect them, Pakistani prisoners of war would have been lynched by Bangladeshi mobs.'

'There might have been a few incidents,' he conceded. 'There are some black sheep in every herd. And you know how prone Bengalis are to exaggerating everything!' He quoted an Urdu couplet:

> *Shauq-e-tool-o-peych is zulmat qade mein hai agar*
> *Bengalee ke baat sun aur Bengalan kay baal deykh.*

> (If you like to add length to a story, put a twist in its tail,
> Hear a Bengali talk (endlessly) and gaze upon his woman's long hair.)

I found it very amusing and put it down in my notebook, fodder to tease my Bengali friends with. I went on to ask the General why the Pakistanis had put up such a miserable performance on the field of battle. 'It was not a fair fight,' he replied. 'First you cut off air contact between West and East Pakistan. Then your men infiltrated deep inside East Pakistan, long before we were compelled to declare war. All these stories of the Mukti Bahini were propaganda. The Mukti Bahini were Indian soldiers trained for guerrilla warfare; there were very few Bengalis in it to start with. You armed them, your officers led and directed them. Our troops had to face the enemy in front as well as in their rear.'

The orderly volunteered his opinion: *'Awaam hamarey khilaaf ho gayaa tha'* — the people had turned against us.

The General did not approve of his orderly expressing an

opinion and raised his hands to silence him. I cashed in on it. 'That is exactly what I have been saying. What can an army do if the entire populace of a country rises against it?'

'It was Indian propaganda,' maintained the General. I did not have very much more to ask him. I pointed to the quotation from the Koran on the mantelpiece and, feigning innocence asked, 'What does it mean?'

The General read it out loudly: *'Nasr min Allah Fateh-un qareeb*. It means Allah grants victory to those whose cause is just.'

'General Sahib, Allah in His wisdom granted us victory because our cause was just.'

For the first time during the interview, the General smiled. 'Sardar Sahib, I suspect you knew what the quotation meant.' I admitted I did. And took my leave.

*T*he *Weekly* brought me other rewards. The Editor's Page came to be widely read: it prepared the way for my later career as a freelance columnist. It also opened many doors to me. I was sought after by the Chief Ministers of States and members of the Central Cabinet. (The Railway Minister, Pandit Kamalapati Tripathi, gave me a free pass to travel anywhere in India.) Mrs Gandhi was more than willing to grant me interviews whenever I sought them. My name was suggested by Fatma and Rafiq Zakaria to Rajni Patel, then a great favourite of Mrs Gandhi, for the award of a Padma Bhushan in recognition of my supposed contribution to Journalism and Literature. In 1975 I received the Award from President V.V. Giri.

Success went to my head. I became a name-dropper. It was only my wife and daughter who brought me down a peg or two. But there were many more to inflate my ego. I began to think of *The Illustrated Weekly* as my child, that it would languish the day I left it. Such hubris can be fatal. My day of reckoning was not far off.

There were some redeeming features of my tenure as editor.

I did have positive views on some subjects which I aired with complete freedom. One was the plight of Indian Muslims. I felt they were discriminated against and were under a cloud for supposedly harbouring pro-Pakistani sympathies. Every time there was tension with Pakistan their loyalties became more suspect. They found it difficult to get jobs in the government and almost impossible to get them in privately-owned industry and business houses which are largely controlled by Hindus. They had virtually no forum to ventilate their grievances, except Urdu newspapers which had small circulations restricted to their own community. I made *The Illustrated Weekly* a forum for Indian Muslim opinion. Whenever there was a Hindu-Muslim riot, since most of the loss of life and property was Muslim, I adopted a distinctly pro-Muslim stance. I also felt that friendly relations with Pakistan were a must to instil a sense of security in the minds of Indian Muslims. I did my best to put Pakistan's point of view on issues where Indian and Pakistani stands were at variance. On the hundredth birth anniversary of Mr Jinnah, the founding father of Pakistan and therefore a name hated in India, I produced a special issue paying tributes to him, with his picture on the cover. An order of 10,000 copies was received from Pakistan. It was cancelled when the issue appeared. And entirely because, in a profile written by Jinnah's friend, J.N. Sahni, he recalled his joining Jinnah and his Parsee wife for lunch at the Bombay High Court when Jinnah took a glass of sherry and ate ham sandwiches. Though true, this was not acceptable in Pakistan. Although in the 1971 war over Bangladesh I denounced General Yahya Khan's military regime and General Tikka Khan's genocide of Bengalis, *The Illustrated Weekly* was the only Indian journal to persist in pressuring the government to release the 93,000 Pakistani prisoners of war when it was over. I took a delegation of four members, including Gaganbhai Mehta (once India's ambassador to the U.S.) and the writers Khwaja Ahmed Abbas and Krishan Chandra to call on Mrs Gandhi in an attempt to facilitate the release of POWs. She snubbed Gaganbhai, calling him an American stooge and silenced Abbas and Krishan Chandra. Then she turned on me and said how my writings were embarrassing her. I replied that the object of my exercise was to embarrass her and I was glad it was succeeding. She fixed me with a look of contempt and said, 'Mr Singh, you may regard yourself as a great editor, but let me tell you, you do not know the first thing about politics.' I agreed I knew very little about politics and added, 'Mrs Gandhi, I believe that what is morally wrong can never be politically right. Holding prisoners of war after the war is over is morally wrong.' Mrs Gandhi again turned her large, dark eyes on me and snubbed me. 'Thanks for lecturing me on morality.' And dismissed us. I felt she would never talk to me again. But a few days later, when she was in Bombay staying with the Governor Ali Yavar Jung and his wife Begum Zehra, she sought me out in the large, crowded reception room and chatted away in a most friendly manner. I knew I had driven my point home.

The Weekly carried a large number of articles on Islam, Islamic history and the Indian Muslims' role in the freedom movement. I recruited two Muslims on the staff: the celeb-rated novelist Qurrutulain Hyder (later winner of the Jnanpith Award) and M.J. Akbar who rose to the top in the profession, became editor of *The Telegraph* and member of Parliament. At each of the three Eids in the year we carried a box on the cover page offering good wishes to our Muslim brethren. Once, on Rakhsha Bandhan, I persuaded Lata Mangeshkar to tie a *raakhi* on the wrist of Dilip Kumar (Yusuf Khan). We put the picture on the cover page. I believe I did succeed in making Indian Muslims look upon me as a friend: when I was nominated to be a member of the Rajya Sabha many said, 'We have another Muslim in Parliament.' Others who disliked my views called me an unpaid agent of Pakistan. I treated both views as compliments.

My hour of trial came when in May 1975 Mrs Gandhi imposed an Emergency on the country and arrested, among others, Jayaprakash Narayan whom I admired. I had spent a few days with him and his wife during the famine in Bihar in 1967. However, I felt that his call for a total revolution, which involved gheraos of legislatures to prevent members elected by the people from discharging their duties, as a violation of a basic rule of democracy. I wrote to him saying so. He sent me a long reply defending his position. I published his letter in full. Conditions of anarchy had come to prevail. Every day there was a bandh of some kind; schools and colleges were closed for weeks in the affected parts of the country. Large processions marched through streets, smashing up shop windows and wrecking cars parked on the roads. Mrs Gandhi was driven to despair. Her position became vulnerable when Justice Verma of the Allahabad High Court held her guilty of electoral malpractices and disqualified her from membership of Parliament. She was persuaded by her son Sanjay and advisers like Siddhartha Shankar Ray to suspend the constitution, arrest members of the opposition and muzzle the press.

I was at the time in Mexico and arrived back in Bombay on the morning after the Declaration of Emergency. I was dismayed. I was with members of the *Times of India* Group who resolved not to give in to censorship imposed on us. Amongst those who refused to protest was Sham Lal, editor of *The Times of India*; amongst those who avoided making any commitment either way was Inder Malhotra. That evening my friend Rajni Patel, member of the Board of Directors of *The Times of India* and a confidante of Mrs Gandhi, rang me up and told me bluntly: 'My friend, if you are looking for martyrdom by going to jail, we will be happy to oblige you.' The Chairman of the Board, Justice K.T. Desai, counselled patience: 'Take your time. But if you refuse to publish we have to look for another editor,' he said.

My attitude to the Emergency was ambivalent. I supported the move to clamp down on law-breakers (including Jayaprakash Narayan), but felt that censorship of the press would prove counter-productive as it would deprive editors like me, who supported Mrs Gandhi, of credibility. For three weeks I did not publish *The Weekly*, and when forced to resume publication gave instructions that no photographs of Mrs Gandhi or her ministers were to be used. I was treated gently, as I was regarded by Mrs Gandhi and Sanjay as a friend. I was summoned to Delhi to meet Mrs Gandhi. I protested against censorship imposed on people like me. I had my say. Before leaving I told her, 'My family is sure that if I spoke my mind, you would have me locked up.' She smiled and bade me goodbye. *The Weekly* was treated as a special case. I published articles by critics of the Emergency and pleaded for the release of political prisoners.

My meeting with Mrs Gandhi was meant to be secret. I arrived back in Bombay to find a letter on my table reading, 'How did your meeting with Madam Dictator go? George.' It was from George Fernandes who was then underground. A few days later four senior members of the R.S.S., against whom warrants of arrest had been issued, coolly walked into my office, had coffee with me, and asked me what had transpired at my meeting with the Prime Minister. I got the impression that the R.S.S. was not against the Emergency and would be willing to cooperate with the government if its leaders were set at liberty.

For some weeks every article of *The Weekly* had to be cleared by the censor. They only bothered with politics and there wasn't much of that in my journal. The editor of *Debonair*, the Indian version of *Playboy*, told me that whenever he took his material for clearance, the censor would skip over stories and girlie pictures saying, 'Porn *theek hai*, politics *nahin* — pornography is okay, politics is not.'

The sort of irresponsible arrogance the Emergency created among people in power was illustrated a few days after my return from Delhi. A luncheon in honour of President Fakhruddin Ali Ahmad was hosted by Governor Ali Yavar Jang at Raj Bhavan. The President had read some article critical of the Emergency, and assuming (wrongly) that it was in *The Illustrated Weekly*, asked me in a bantering tone, 'What are you up to? Has no one told you of the Emergency?' I didn't know what he was talking about and protested my ignorance. Nor did S.B. Chavan, Chief Minister of Maharashtra, who was sitting next to the President. Without checking on the facts, he nevertheless ordered action to be taken against *The Weekly*. When I returned to the office I was handed an order requiring every article and illustration to be sent to the censor well ahead of publication. I rang up Mrs Gandhi and got her press advisor Sharda Prasad on the line. Mrs Gandhi was due to leave for

Moscow that evening. Sharda Prasad was able to spot the offending article. It had appeared in *Femina*. The President agreed he had made a *faux pas*, S.B. Chavan was asked to withdraw his order against *The Illustrated Weekly*, and he had to do so within two hours of having issued it.

There were a lot of people who were jailed out of spite by members of the Gandhi family. One was Primila (Kinna) Lewis, the daughter of our close friends Wilburn and Usha Lall. She was married to an Englishman, Charles Lewis, who worked with the Oxford University Press. They had a very young son. Kinna had organized farm labourers in villages around Delhi, and Mrs Gandhi had a farm house in one of these, near the village Chhattarpur. Kinna had tired of being kept in jail and separate from her family. Her sister and mother approached me to use my influence with Mrs Gandhi to have her released. Kinna was willing to tender a written apology. I went to Delhi to see the Lieutenant-Governor, Kishan Chand, a classmate of mine from our days in King's College, London. He promised to take up the matter and assured me he would be able to manage Kinna's release. Mrs Gandhi refused to relent. The poor girl spent the year and half of the Emergency in gaol. Later, she wrote a book about her experience. She portrayed herself as a heroine without admitting that her will-power had crumbled and she was willing to apologize. I believe it was the same with Gayatri Devi, Rajmata of Jaipur and many others. Amongst the wholly innocent who were picked up were Bhim Sain Sachar, ex-Chief Minister of the Punjab, then in his late seventies. One thing Mrs Gandhi did not suffer from was compassion. The Emergency powers turned the heads of many civil servants: they became rude and tyrannical. There were others who, though unhappy, carried out orders issued to them without protesting. My friend Kishan Chand was one of them. After the Emergency was withdrawn and enquiries instituted against the misuse of power, Kishan Chand could not stand the strain. He wrote a short note in Urdu: *Zillat say maut acchi hai* — death is better than disgrace — and jumped into a well.

Being the editor of a popular weekly, I was much sought after by the film industry. I never was, nor am, much of a film-goer. And the little that I had seen of Hindi movies did not generate any respect for actors, directors, producers, music composers or playback singers. Some of my Lahore friends had done well: Balraj Sahni, Uma Kashyap (Kamini Kaushal) and Dev Anand were highly rated actors; B.R. Chopra was among the top producer-directors; Chetan Anand had many flops to his credit. A whole lot of new actors, directors and singers had come up. I saw their photographs in film journals like *Filmfare* and *Stardust*.

My interest in film personalities was quickened by Devyani Chaubal, the younger sister of Nalini who had worked with me briefly in London. I read Devyani's bitchy pieces on the private lives of film stars written in a brand of Hindustani-English (Hinglish) which I enjoyed. Our first meeting at a luncheon party gave us the feeling that we were meant for each other. She was a big woman a couple of inches taller than I and of considerable bulk. She was nevertheless good looking, with dark eye-lashes which curled upwards like scimitars. She had a husky, masculine voice and was a wonderful mimic. She was often in trouble with film stars for what she wrote about them.

Once Devyani did a profile of Dharmendra, then on top of the film world. She portrayed him as a champion stud who could service three or four women every day. Dharmendra had a wife and children. Also a mistress — Hema Malini, who became his second wife and the mother of another two children. Besides these two, Devyani alleged that if the starlets appearing with him were eager for sex, he would willingly oblige. Dharmendra was furious. He waylaid Devyani somewhere near the race course. Devyani tried to run away but her bulk and sari did not help her get very far. I am not sure whether Dharmendra beat her up, but she lodged a complaint of assault and battery against him. The next days' papers reported the episode on their front pages. Despite my affection for Devyani, I wrote in my column that, had I been in his shoes, I would have done exactly what Dharmendra had done to her. The police decided not to take any notice of Devyani's complaint. Dharmendra came to thank me for getting him out' of a police case. When Devyani came to my office she roundly abused me for letting her down, but it did not make any difference to our friendship.

A few months later Devyani was in another scrape, this time with an actor whose stock was fast going down. Apart from his sex-escapades, she cast aspersions on his acting skills. She happened to be at a film party at the Sun-n-Sands hotel in Juhu. Having exchanged gossip with the guests, she was sitting on a parapet overlooking the beach and gazing at the sea. Two sons of the actor, both high on alcohol, spotted her and came on her unawares. 'You bloody bitch, how dare you write nasty things about our father!' they shouted. 'Now take this,' said one pouring the contents of a bottle of beer on Devyani's head. She shouted for help: '*Bachao* — save me.' None of the guests felt honour bound to bachao her: they enjoyed her discomfiture. The lads emptied another bottle of beer on her head and told her in plain words what they would do if she wrote that kind of thing again. With difficulty Devyani extricated herself and lodged a complaint at the police station. Next morning she came to see me in the office to narrate her nightmarish experience. Tears flowed down her cheeks, but I was not sure if she was really upset with the threats held out to her or whether she looked forward to their being fulfilled. 'You know what those fellows said? They said we'll fuck you till you are black and blue; we'll bugger you till your fat arse is sore.' Through her tears she repeated their words accompanied by the gestures they had used, as if relishing the experience.

Devyani took me to Raj Kapoor's private cinema to see the opening shots of *Satyam, Shivam, Sundaram*. I took along members of the Sindhi family who lived above me — Sheila, her daughter Jyoti and their maid servant Fatima, all very eager to meet the great actor. Zeenat Aman was present. I sat between Raj Kapoor and Zeenat. Devyani was in the row behind, with my guests. We saw Zeenat stepping out of a village pond with her wet sari clinging to her body and displaying her very shapely bust. 'I am a bosom man,' said Raj to me with enthusiasm, 'aren't you?' I agreed that shapely bosoms had their points. 'What's your *laal paree* (red fairy) like?' he asked. He was referring to Sheila who was draped in a bright red sari. He assumed she was my mistress.

'I have no idea,' I replied.

'Go on, you so and so!' he insisted. 'She looks all right to me. But one can't really tell what's inside the blouse, can one?'

Once Rafiq Zakaria took me to a musical concert. We arrived a little late. He gave a front-row seat meant for him to me and said, 'You talk to her.' The lady sitting in the next seat gave me a smile. She certainly was an extraordinarily good-looking woman, but I could not place her. When the lights went up I told her that we had not been introduced. 'I am Meena Kumari,' she replied. The name rang a faint bell but failed to enlighten me further. 'What do you do for a living?' I asked her. She did not deign to reply — just lit her cigarette and turned to talk to the person on the other side. Meena Kumari was then the topmost actress on the Hindi screen.

With Nargis Dutt the introduction came through Gulshan Ewing, editor of *Femina*. I had seen her do the star role in *Mother India*. Gulshan told me that Nargis wanted to see me. I was very flattered. The Dutts were not doing very well. She had retired from the films; he had yet to make his mark independently. They had two children at Sanawar School, not far from my cottage in Kasauli. When Nargis arrived in *The Times of India* building everyone recognized her. My stock went up. Very coyly, she asked me if she could stay in my cottage during the Sanawar Founders' week in October. 'Only on one condition,' I told her. She looked a little apprehensive. 'My condition is that thereafter I have your permission to tell everyone that Nargis slept in my bed.' She broke into peals of laughter, 'Done!' she said, extending her hand to me. We were nominated to the Rajya Sabha at the same time and were given seats next to each other. Whenever anyone tried to introduce us, she would say, 'You don't have to introduce us; I have slept in his bed.'

I met Parveen Babi at a party given by Dev Anand. Normally at cocktail parties I took a couple of drinks by myself in a quiet corner and slipped out unnoticed. That evening Parveen came and sat on the carpet near my chair. What beautiful long hair she had! And what bewitching eyes! I laid on flattery as thick as I could. I left the party after midnight and would have stayed longer but for the fact that I had to catch an early morning flight to Delhi. I got very little sleep and arrived at Santa Cruz airport as required an hour before the flight. I went to the bookshop to pick up some magazines. A young lady who looked vaguely familiar smiled at me. I went up to her. 'I am sure we have met before,' I said to her. 'Don't tell me you do not recognize me! Only a few hours earlier you were telling me you had not seen anyone as beautiful as me! I am Parveen Babi.' She forgave me and even did me the honour of coming to dine with us in Delhi.

The closest I got to becoming involved in films myself was a proposal by the Ivory-Merchant duo to take on my novel *Train to Pakistan*. They asked Zafar Hai to direct it. A well-known Urdu writer was commissioned to write the dialogue. He did so after weeks of drinking my Scotch evening after evening to help him get the Punjabi words right. Shashi Kapoor had agreed to finance the film and play the lead male role. I also met Shabana Azmi whom I regarded as the best actress on the Hindi screen and who was to play the heroine. After six months the project was dropped without as much as a word of regret by others for having wasted my time and gallons of Scotch.

Of the many film personalities I met, much the most colourful was the comedian I.S. Johar. I did not have much of an opinion of him as an actor and was initially put off by his crude attempts to gain publicity. As his acting career declined his ploys to keep himself in the news increased. I published a few of his articles in *The Illustrated Weekly*. In the absence of anything more interesting to sell to the media, he announced his engagement to Protima Bedi. Both had been married and had grown up children. Protima had divorced Kabir Bedi and made most of India's journals by having herself photographed streaking nude on the sands of Juhu beach. She had a nice figure. Johar had married Rama through whom he had a son and a daughter. Rama ditched him and, without getting a divorce, married his cousin Harbans in Delhi — hence the name Rama Bans. She returned to Johar in Bombay. She was the only woman I knew who had two living husbands and was cheerful about being polyandrous. She did not live with Johar, but often went to dine with him and once a week she took me with her. Johar was an avid bridge player. From his apartment in Lotus Court, Rama rang him up at the Cricket Club of India (C.C.I.) to tell him of our arrival and to order a Chinese meal from the club. While we awaited his return I played with his very cuddlesome little Peke named Pheeno — the snub nosed. Rama emptied the drawer by his mattress (he slept on the floor) and showed me packets of photographs of scantily-clad young women who wanted Johar to help them get into the films. When he arrived, he took out his best Scotch. He drank very little, Rama was a teetotaller.

Johar was a great storyteller, including of tales connected with his sex life. I could never be sure how much of what he told me of his past was true and how much he made up to hold my interest. I didn't see anything of Johar after I left Bombay. I had never taken him seriously as either an actor or producer of films. I was pleasantly surprised to see the play *Bhutto* written by him and staged in Delhi. It was very well conceived, with repartee worthy of an Oscar Wilde. *Bhutto* was superbly portrayed by Suhel Seth. I wish Johar had seen it. He was by then dead.

I was in Bombay when my father died in Delhi. My relations with my parents were like those that exist in traditional Indian families. Rigid rules of courtesy were observed, but no confidences were exchanged. He did not have any favourite among his four sons. Perhaps I came closest to being one, but I had disappointed him by not being the conventional success he had hoped for. Like most fathers, he had a soft spot for his only daughter whom he loaded with gifts and to whom he left an unencumbered estate bigger than the portions he gave his sons. My mother distinctly favoured her youngest son, Daljit. A bitter quarrel had arisen between my eldest and youngest brother. My mother never liked my eldest brother's wife and blatantly sided with Daljit. I knew nothing about my brothers' falling out over the division of property and dragging each other to court till my father wrote to me and asked me to come over. I was mortified to learn about the trivial issues they were wrangling over. My uncle, Ujjal Singh, had tried to arbitrate between the two and failed. I took over the unpleasant job. While Daljit appeared more amenable to reason on the surface, he broke his solemn promise given in writing to me by taking over a joint society when his eldest brother was away. I confronted him in front of my parents and angrily rebuked him of being a *daghabaaz* — betrayer. He broke down. He swore by his mother — he was always swearing by her — not to do it again. I tore up the proceedings of the meeting in which he had assumed control of the enterprise and succeeded in making a mutually acceptable partition between them.

Relations between my parents underwent a sea change over the years. For years he laid down the law with a heavy hand. As he began to get older and hard of hearing, his dependence on his wife increased. She began to tick him off for making people repeat whatever they had said — *hain? kee kyaah?* — and being clumsy. He dropped food on his tie and coat while eating. He no longer lost his temper but submitted meekly to being put in his place. Whenever I visited him, he asked me to read the papers to him and solicited my opinion on important events. He was never one for exercise: walking up and down his lawn was all he did to keep himself fit. He also observed no dietary rules. He had a large breakfast of cornflakes, eggs, sausages, toast and honey and tea. He had a couple of gins before lunch; for afternoon tea he took slices of cake, biscuits or Indian sweets. He took two to three Scotchs before dinner and often brandy afterwards. Dinner consisted of at least four or five courses: soup, fish, meat, vegetable and pudding. When travelling, he ate whatever was available on railway platforms. On his way to Mashobra by car he sampled the pickles at a dhaba four miles up the road from Kalka and ate *pedas* at Jablee. He never put on weight and remained slim to the last. He was a great one for taking pills — to whip up appetite, to digest what he had eaten. He had several operations — for kidney stones, cataract, piles and hernia. One thing he never missed was his sleep. No sooner did he put his head on the pillow than he was lost to the world. More than anything else, it was sound sleep that sustained him for ninety years.

It was sad to see him age and become frail. I made it a point to come to Delhi every fortnight and spend an hour with him in the mornings and either have my evening Scotch with him or get him over to dine with us. The last time I saw him alive, he looked frailer than ever, and evidently aware that he did not have many days left. When I was taking my leave he asked me when I planned coming to Delhi next. I told him I would be back in a fortnight. 'Fortnight?' he asked. And said no more.

A week later my wife rang me to say he was not well and she was going over to see him. An hour later she rang again to say he was much better and she had had a drink with him. My mother and sister were with him. A few minutes later, she rang a third time to tell me he was dead. This was at 8.30 pm on 18 April 1978.

I was numbed. For a long time I sat still not knowing what to do. Then I rang up the Zakarias and asked Fatma if she could tell Rahul and put us on the early morning flight to Delhi. She never failed me in a crisis. A few minutes later the Zakarias came over to see me. After half an hour I asked them to leave me so that I could get some sleep.

I got no sleep that night. I kept going over events in my father's life. A self-made man, a generous father who I had barely known as a person with human failings. I knew full well that if it had not been for his constant support, I would never have been able to write a single book.

Having once been the biggest builder of New Delhi, his death made the front pages of all the daily papers. There was a large turnout at his cremation at the electric crematorium. And an even larger one filling the entire lawn of Sujan Singh Park at his last obsequial ceremony. I was asked by my brothers to make the final oration. Fortunately I was able to say my piece without breaking down.

Nishaan-e-mard-e-momin ba too goyam?
Choon marg aayad, tabassum bar lab-e-ost.

(You ask me about the signs of a man of faith?
When death comes to him, he has a smile on his lips.)

My father did better than face death with a smile; he had a glass of Scotch in his hand a few minutes before he laid himself on his death bed.

When I was in Bombay I was forced to ask myself the question: how much of a Sikh am I? I had rejected religious belief and ritual. I retained the outward symbols of the Khalsa faith, i.e., wearing my hair and beard unshorn. I had never bothered with the other Ks like the steel bracelet (*kada*), comb (*kangha*), underwear (*kaccha*) or sabre (*kirpan*). Nor did I think that eating or drinking could or should have any bearing on a person's religious beliefs. Contrary to Khalsa tradition, I ate *halaal* (kosher) meat, including the abominated beef. I made no secret of my addiction to Scotch. I had tried out other things forbidden by tradition like smoking (I even tried pot), and taking paan with tobacco. I relinquished these through no revival of religious fervour but because I felt that what I could not do openly was not worth doing.

The publication of my books on Sikh religion and history had made me acceptable to the Sikh community. They did not take my protestations that I was an agnostic seriously. Wherever I went, I was invited to address congregations at gurdwaras and presented with *saropas*: a small, saffron-coloured under-turban and a kirpan. I was grateful for this recognition and came to the conclusion that, as long as I kept up the appearance of a Khalsa, the Khalsa would acknowledge me as one of themselves and give me the applause they felt was due to me. If I abandoned it, they too would abandon me. This nurtured in me a sense of belonging to the Sikh community. I knew from experience that Sikhs who cut off their hair and beard were regarded as outcasts. And no matter how much they prayed in gurdwaras, how heavy the steel *kadas* they wore and aggressively asserted they were Sikhs, the Sikhs did not consider them as one of themselves.

I nurtured this sense of belonging as best as I could. During the tricentenary celebrations of the birth of Guru Gobind Singh, three Sikh scholars were chosen to go abroad to lecture on Sikhism. Since both Kapur Singh and Gopal Singh Dardi had more clout than I, they chose the United States, Canada and Europe; I was left with Germany, France and England. All of us were well provided with funds for our expenses. My meetings in Germany and France drew very small audiences. Whatever I said had to be translated into German and French and made little impact. It was different in England. A mammoth meeting was arranged at the Albert Hall in London. The evening before the scheduled meeting I walked to Albert Hall to see if it had been advertised. I was thrilled to see a huge hoarding with my name on it as the main speaker. Others on the list of six included the Archbishop of Canterbury, and P.N. Haksar, the acting High Commissioner for India. I feared that the hall would be half empty. The next day when I arrived at the venue I saw hundreds of Charabancs lined up in the parking lots. Sikhs from all over England had come to attend the meeting. I took my place on the dais. On the table were glasses of water for the speakers. I took a few sips and then quietly emptied my hip flask full of Scotch into it: I often did that when I was nervous. The Scotch loosened my tongue. When my turn came I spoke of the Punjab countryside with the mustard in flower, the whistle blasts of flour mills, the aroma of burning camel thorn; I told them how privileged I felt for having been chosen to be the bearer of greetings from their Sikh brethren in India to them living in England. Many of my audience, thoroughly homesick, were in tears. I warmed to my theme of Guru Gobind Singh's concept of *Dharam Yudha* — battle for the sake of righteousness. I rounded it off by telling them that, having chosen to live in England, they should now totally identify themselves with their adopted land and say with pride 'I am Sikh; I am British'. My speech was greeted with thunderous cries of *Boley So Nihal, Sat Sri Akal.* I was very proud of my performance and very proud not only of being a Sikh but that Sikhs were proud of me.

Excerpts from my speech had been widely reported in the British and Indian press. When I returned to India I found that I had a couple of hundred pounds left over from the money advanced to me, but nobody asked me for an account. I felt this money did not belong to me but to the Sikh Panth. I returned whatever I had left with me. Neither Kapur Singh nor Dardi bothered to render accounts nor returned anything. When they heard what I had done, they called me a *bewakoof* — an idiot.

In Bombay it was Kehar Singh Gill who claimed me as a member of the community. He raised money to send me to Uganda for Guru Nanak's birth celebrations. I was more eager to see the wildlife in Kenya and Uganda than speak on Sikhism. I flew from Bombay to Nairobi and onwards to Kampala. My host, Chandan Singh, drove me through dense forests and hills to Jinja on the banks of the Nile. Chandan Singh had come out of India as a humble carpenter but made good as a builder. He lived in a spacious bungalow and had a couple of cars. I joined Guru Nanak's birthday procession, which was led by a band of the Ismailia Girls School (all Muslims) and marched through the streets of Jinja to their gurdwara. I spoke in Punjabi. At other meetings arranged for me by local Indians I spoke in English. Chandan Singh, who didn't understand a word of English, was always present. In the evening, when we relaxed with our Scotch, he would tell me naively, '*Khushwant Singhji, samajh tay kucch nahin aaya, par anand bahut aaya*' — I didn't understand a word of what you said but I thoroughly enjoyed myself. Amongst my audience was Sardar Inder Singh, a multi-millionaire with business interests in many African countries. His mansion in Jinja overlooked the point from where the Nile took off from Lake Victoria for its thousand-mile journey through Uganda, the Sudan, and Egypt to the Red Sea. He told me of hippopotami which often raided his garden, and of crocodiles basking in the sun just outside his compound. He sensed my interest in wildlife. 'You must go to Murchison Falls,' he said. 'There is nothing like it in the world.' Murchison Falls were on the border between Uganda and the Sudan, several hundred miles from Jinja; I had neither the time nor the money to go there. Both were taken care of by Sardar Inder Singh. He had his own aircraft, and a young Ismaili pilot who flew him wherever he wanted to go. We flew to Murchison Falls. I have never seen so much wildlife crowded into so small an area: hippopotami, giraffes, crocodiles, antelopes and zebras by the hundreds; and a fantastic variety of birds of all shapes, sizes and colours. We were back in Kampala by the evening. On the last meeting I addressed at the gurdwara in Jinja, the congregation garlanded me with five-pound notes. I don't know how many there were — but at a rough guess there were well over one hundred, making a total of at least £500. I was sorely tempted to accept the gift. But, once again, I felt the money did not belong to me but to the Panth. I took off the garland of notes from around my neck and placed it before the Granth Sahib.

Kehar Singh Gill got round Bombay University to organize a series of lectures on Sikhism. The Vice-Chancellor invited me to deliver them. I did not have to work very hard on them as I had delivered a similar series earlier at Madras University when my uncle, Sardar Ujjal Singh, was Governor of the State. As at Madras and elsewhere, the majority of the audience was Sikh. It was during these lectures that I got a letter from my son Rahul, then on some *Readers Digest* assignment in England, informing me that he had cut off his long hair. He held me responsible for his decision. He had been brought up in an agnostic atmosphere; he had never been taught to pray and had found recitations of the Granth Sahib at Akhand Paths incomprehensible and tedious. He did not understand what long hair and a beard had to do with ethics or religion. And since almost all his friends were English, Hindu or Muslim, he had no particular sense of belonging to the Sikh community. I realized that he was right — but, strangely enough, it wounded me deeply and I wanted to cancel my lectures. I knew it would hurt my wife (even if she had given up praying) and my parents even more. I forwarded the letter to my wife without comment. She wrote to say that she did not want to see her son again. I wrote back to tell her that we had no right to dictate to a grown-up man when we had not bothered to bring him up as an orthodox Sikh. And by cutting him off, she would only be hurting herself. What surprised me even more was my father's reaction. My sister's sons had cut off their hair and had been accepted, though reluctantly. Rahul was his favourite grandson. He had done well in his studies and had played tennis for Cambridge University with his long hair tied in a chignon. In the first draft of his will, my father left his large house on Janpath with three acres of lawn and an annexe to my son. He said nothing but was visibly unhappy. Rahul made a very handsome Sikh in his turban; without it and his beard and moustaches trimmed he looked like a non-descript Maulvi. It took us some years to get accustomed to him in his new shape.

I had had two extensions of my contract with Bennett and Coleman and expected to get a third one. However, conditions in the company and the country had changed radically. After many years under government control, Bennett and Coleman was returned to its proprietors, the Jains. Mrs Gandhi was voted out of power and replaced by Morarji Desai. I was not able to come to terms with either Ashok Jain, who became Chairman of the Company, or Morarji Desai, who became Prime Minister. I continued to support Mrs Gandhi and defend her son, Sanjay. In one issue we had carried a readers' opinion poll on the most popular man in the country. The vote was overwhelmingly in favour of Sanjay Gandhi, a man more hated by the new government than even his mother. Morarji Desai was upset with *The Illustrated Weekly* which remained the most widely-read journal in the country. On writing to him asking for an interview when he came to Bombay, I got a three-line reply telling me to see him at Santa Cruz airport to find out if he would have time to receive me. I went to the airport, muscled my way through his crowd of admirers and greeted him. He looked angrily at me and mumbled, 'So you think Sanjay is the hero of the country!' I protested that it wasn't my opinion but that of the readers. 'What readers?' he snapped. 'It was all rigged.' As he was about to get into his car, I said to him, 'Morarjibhai, I take it you don't want to see me.' He paused a while before replying. 'No, I will see you. You come to my son's apartment at 5 pm.'

When I arrived at Kanti Desai's residence there was another crowd of people in the verandahs and in his father's bedroom. Morarji was sitting on his bed talking to them. He saw me and told his callers to leave. 'I have given him an appointment, I would like to talk to him alone,' he ordered. The crowd left. Morarji asked me to sit by him on his bed. He was a different man from the one I had met that morning at the airport. He accepted my version that a majority of the readers had voted for Sanjay but maintained that the whole thing must have been rigged. (He was right, as later I discovered that a single person had sent hundreds of 'readers' votes in favour of Sanjay.) I switched on my tape-recorder and asked him a whole range of questions about the Emergency, his detention in jail and his plans for India. I asked him specifically whether he intended to re-impose prohibition after it had flopped everywhere it had been tried. He was adamant: prohibition was a directive clause of the constitution, it had succeeded in many parts of the country, particularly in his native Gujarat and he intended to enforce it all over the country. When I had run out of my questions he asked me to switch off the tape-recorder: he wanted to talk to me man to man, or as friends. 'You make fun of my insistence on prohibition and advocating urine therapy. If I persuade you that drinking is bad for you, will you give it up?'

'Morarjibhai, I have been drinking for fifty years and have never been drunk even once in my life. If I persuade you that drinking is not bad for you, will you have a drink?' I asked in reply.

He thought over my suggestion for a while and replied, 'That is a fair offer; if you persuade me that drinking alcohol is not bad for the health, I promise to try it.'

He went on to extol the benefits of urine therapy. He told me innumerable cases of sickness, which had been declared incurable by doctors, responding to fresh urine. 'I have a prescription for curing cancer as well. Give up every kind of food. Just live on fresh grapes and warm water and it will get cancer out of your system.'

He was friendly enough for me to question him on another of his fads. 'Morarjibhai, I have also written about your vow of abstinence from sex.' Before I could proceed further, he cut me short, 'I do not wish to discuss the subject with you.' The interview which had lasted well over an hour was over.

Morarji Desai, despite his fads, was a straight and honest man who rarely told a lie. That did not go for his son, Kanti, on whom he doted. As far as he was concerned, Kanti could do no wrong. A few days later, when Ashok Jain invited me for breakfast at his house in Delhi, I broached the subject of my contract. Quite gently but firmly, he told me that Kanti Desai had strong reservations about my continuing as editor and that my contract would not be renewed. Weeks later, when it got known that my tenure as editor was to end within a few months because of pressure brought by the Desais on the proprietors, Morarji rang me up from Delhi. 'Do you believe me that I did not say a word against you to Ashok Jain?' I replied, 'Morarjibhai, if you say so, I will believe it because I know that you do not tell a lie.' That did not apply to Ashok Jain or Kanti Desai. Ashok Jain denied ever having told me that the Desais had said anything to him about me. When questioned by the Avinashlingam Commission set up by Morarji's government to look into the charges of vindictiveness made against it, Kanti Desai went on record to say that he did not know who I was.

I returned to Bombay to settle my affairs. I had three months to hand over charge to my successor and took three months leave to look for another job or work on my novel *Delhi*. On my own I recommended the name of R.G.K. as my successor. It was summarily rejected. The date of my departure was fixed. I wrote a last sentimental piece of farewell on my editorial page saying that my bulb logo would not be appearing in *The Weekly* any more. Some mischief-maker conveyed to the management that I had written a nasty piece against Bennett and Coleman. A week before I was to relinquish my post, I came to the office as usual an hour before anyone else. At ten o'clock, a senior clerk came in with a letter from the General Manager, Ram Tarneja: 'Sir, I tried to deliver it to you yesterday, but you had gone home. I am sorry to be the courier. I hope you will forgive me,' he said. It was a one-paragraph letter informing me that my services were terminated forthwith and I was to hand over charge to M.V. Kamath with immediate effect. In short, I was fired one week before I was due to retire.

I sent for Fatma Zakaria, gave her the letter and asked her to inform the staff after I had left. I picked up my umbrella and walked out of *The Times of India* building.

Gratuitous discourtesy towards editors had become the hallmark of the Jain family. They had treated their most distinguished editor, Frank Moraes, with the same lack of courtesy. Inder Malhotra and Prem Shankar Jha, both distinguished in their respective fields, were humiliated and forced to quit. Giri Lal Jain who spent his life serving them and edited *The Times of India* with distinction for over nine years was shown the door with less regard than I.

I got to work on the next chapter of my manuscript of *Delhi*. There were Allama Iqbal's lines to inspire me:

Jahaan mein ahle-eemaan soorat-e-khursheed jeetay hain,
Idhar doobey, udhar nikley; udhar doobey, idhar niklay.

In this world men of faith and self-confidence are
    like the sun,
They go down on one side to come up on the other.

I spent the remaining three months working on my novel. Several offers of jobs came my way, including the editorship of the *Free Press Journal*. After toying with them for a while, I turned them down. I had had my fill of Bombay and wanted to return to my family and Delhi. The Zakaria family, Kehar Singh Gill, Harjeet Kohli and some other Sikhs came to see me off at the station. By the time I was an hour's journey away from Bombay, my nine years with *The Illustrated Weekly of India* were out of my mind. The next morning I got off at Nizamuddin railway station to be received by my wife and daughter Mala. I felt reassured that I had been forgiven for having so callously distanced myself from them.

Scenes of Bombay kept haunting me for several months: oddly enough, it was not the people but the monsoon, the sound of dancers' bells practising for *gudi padwa* along Marine Drive, the sheets of rain coming down like a gossamer curtain, the dogs who wagged their tails as I passed them on my way to office. For the first few months after returning to Delhi I went to Bombay as often as I could to keep up my close contact with the Zakarias and other friends. I soon discovered that to Fatma I meant no more than a past memory. She was quick to switch her loyalties and affections to her new boss, Giri Lal Jain, and began to spend as much of her time in his office as she had done in mine, to look after his appointments, invite him over and send food to him. That, I confess, hurt me deeply. It took me a long time to talk myself out of the hurt. I came to the conclusion that there is a disease which may be named bossophilia (love for the boss) which usually afflicts females; it is a professional hazard to which working women are exposed and most succumb to it. A working man usually develops bossophobia and comes to look upon his boss as the hated, un-understanding, unsympathetic joker. A working woman develops an Electra complex and sees her boss as a benign combination of her father, lover or a newly acquired husband. Fatma was an extreme instance of bossophilia. She replaced one worshipful boss as soon as he retired with an equally worship-worthy boss. The experience soured me against Bombay; my visits became less frequent and I made my peace with Delhi which was the city to which I belonged and loved most.

After a few months in Delhi I was offered the editorship of *The National Herald*. My six months with *The National Herald* were very frustrating. I was approached by Yashpal Kapoor, one of Mrs Gandhi's cronies and the repository of much of the money she had collected for use during elections. He offered me the salary I had drawn as editor of *The Illustrated Weekly*. I knew *The National Herald* was in the red. It had not been able to pay subscriptions to PTI and UNI and its circulation was not more than a couple of thousand. I accepted the offer when the paper had stopped being printed because of prolonged strikes. The first thing I did was to address the workers and editorial staff and exhort them to resume work. I told them that I would draw no salary till each one of them had been paid. They got their wages; I got nothing.

But I was indirectly compensated. I met Mrs Gandhi almost every other day. I also saw her advisers like Pranab Mukherjee and daily hangers-on like Sita Ram Kesri and Kalpnath Rai. I was able to see, as the Indian cliché goes, her style of functioning, and something of her family life. I sensed that she wanted to distance herself from Yashpal Kapoor but was unable to do so. Despite my complaining that Kapoor rarely came to office (he was scared of being beaten up by unpaid workers), she would not reprimand him. Every second month or so, when the workers threatened to go on strike again, suitcases full of currency notes would mysteriously appear in the office: the workers' arrears were cleared, and we were able to pay subscriptions due to PTI and UNI and get supplies of newsprint.

I suspected that the man behind this generosity was Charanjit Singh of Campa Cola. The police were anxious to find out how the paper survived. Twice during my tenure the office was raided by them. I knew nothing about these raids till after Yashpal Kapoor, if he was there, and the accountant had been interrogated. The police never entered my room. My only two companions during office hours were the Assistant Editor, Tharyan, and an attractive freelancer, Sunita Budhiraja. Few people dared to come to the *Herald's* office because of police surveillance round the clock. Apart from the episode of finding a packet of obscene photographs of Babu Jagjiwan Ram's son, Suresh Kumar, and his college-going mistress, nothing very exciting happened in my time as editor of *The National Herald*.

I beguiled away the hours in office befriending a couple of rock pigeons who made their nest on the ledge outside my window. I told the sweeper and the chaprasis not to disturb them. In my diary I noted the day the eggs were laid and when they were hatched. I watched the ugly, hairless nestlings grow feathers, extend their beaks wide when begging for food, learning to exercise their wings and then flying away. My six months with *The Herald* were not altogether wasted.

I did not mind working without money, but having no readership was galling. I was approached by Aveek Sarkar of the *Anand Bazar* Group to take over the editorship of *New Delhi*, a fortnightly journal they planned to launch from the capital. After consulting Sanjay, I agreed to take the job. A very elegant little office with wood panelling was got ready for me in the PTI building on Parliament Street. A staff of assistants consisting of Javed Laiq, Chaitanya Kalbagh, Vivek Sen Gupta, Madhu Jain and the photographer Raghu Rai was hired. I persuaded Nandini Mehta to join me. Within a few issues we were able to establish *New Delhi's* reputation as the best-written magazine in the country. However, the circulation remained static at around 35,000! The journal had to be printed in Calcutta, the printing staff were frequently on strike and the fortnightly often became an outdated monthly. I did a few long feature articles for the journal. One was on Shraddha Mata, the Tantric Sadhvi who, according to M.O. Matthai, had borne an illegitimate child to Prime Minister Nehru. I spotted her at the Nigambodh cremation ground. She was a well-preserved, bosomy lady in her sixties. She became quite friendly with me. Every time I went to Jaipur I called on her at Hathroi fort, where she lived in isolation surrounded by her dogs.

I was the only Indian pressman in Islamabad when Zulfiqar Ali Bhutto was hanged in Rawalpindi jail. My friend, M.A. Rahman, who was one of the team of prosecuting lawyers and close to General Zia-ul Haq, had an inkling about the timing of the execution. He persuaded me to come over to be present at 'an historic event' and also fixed an interview with General Zia-ul Haq, the first to be given by him to an Indian. I was able to meet the family of the Nawab of Kasur, believed to have been assassinated by Bhutto's hirelings, and get a detailed account of the last days of Bhutto and his execution at the hands of a Christian, Tara Masih — who then stole his gold watch. *New Delhi* was the only Indian journal to carry what could be described as an eye-witness account of the reactions of Pakistanis on the hanging of their leader. The articles were widely quoted by other papers. In the end, it was the shoddy printing schedule that cooled my enthusiasm for *New Delhi*. Once again, I found myself with a lot of time on my hands.

I got down to translating Allama Iqbal's *Shikwa* and *Jawab-e-Shikwa*. I wrestled with a verse first thing in the morning. I pestered friends like Mujtaba Hussain and the poet Ali Sardar Jafri about the precise meaning of words. And several evenings I had Mujahid Hussain of the Pakistan embassy and his ravishingly beautiful Begum by my fireside to go over what I had translated. The translation was accepted and published by the Oxford University Press. It was released at a function by the Pakistani Ambassador, Abdul Sattar, and extracts from the original were read on the occasion by Yasmeen (Muneer) Shaikh, followed by my reading the relevant translation. Although the publication could not be sold in Pakistan because of stupid laws forbidding the exchange of literature, extracts of my translations were widely reproduced in Pakistani journals and several reprints of the book were quickly sold out in India.

12   With the Gandhis and the Anands

THERE ARE NOT many examples in history where the poisoned relationship between a woman and her daughter-in-law influenced the course of events of a nation. It is possible that in medieval times such strains compelled mother-fixated monarchs to turn their back on their wives, or hen-pecked rulers to abandon their mothers, but India provides a unique example of a modern democracy — the world's largest as Indians never tire of reminding everyone — where a woman was so riled by her widowed daughter-in-law that it coloured her judgements and divided the ruling elite into two camps: those who sided with her and those who sided with her daughter-in-law.

The story is as commonplace as any mother-in-law versus daughter-in-law conflict, and its details too petty to deserve notice except for the fact that the parties involved happened to be the Prime Minister of India on the one side, and on the other the widow of her favourite son who she (the Prime Minister) and many others, including myself, hoped would succeed her as the ruler of India. This made the silly wranglings of two women into matters worthy of comment. And despite the trivia, they became the subjects of absorbing interest to every Indian family where such tensions are endemic.

My narrative is based on a short period of personal acquaintance with the parties concerned, especially Maneka and Sanjay Gandhi. I came to enjoy the friendship of Maneka and her mother—though I suspected that often they tried to sell me stories in the hope of giving them wider publicity. Despite being regarded by Mrs Gandhi as belonging to Maneka's camp and even her principal mentor and therefore an 'enemy' (an expression she used for me to a Sikh delegation), I have tried to be as even-handed as possible.

Let me begin with the *dramatis personae*. First, Mrs Indira Gandhi and her faction. Indira Gandhi was at the time in her mid-sixties. She was as well-preserved and handsome a woman for her age as any that I have known. She had been Prime Minister of India from 1965–77, out of power for two and a half years, and back again in power since 1980. Long years at the helm of affairs of the nation had lent her a certain imperious arrogance and intolerance of criticism. It should be borne in mind that Indira Gandhi had made no great success of her own marriage. Her husband, Feroze Gandhi, was the son of a Parsi liquor vendor of Allahabad. After bearing him two sons, Rajiv and Sanjay, she deserted him to live with her father to act as his housekeeper and hostess. According to M.O. Matthai, Pandit Nehru's personal Secretary for many years, neither father nor daughter was sexually inhibited. The Nehru family had its own share of problems. This is significant, as later Mrs Gandhi maintained that Maneka did not fit into her family or class.

Indira Gandhi dispensed with able and honest advisers if their views were not palatable to her; only a handful who said what she wanted to hear retained her confidence. In domestic affairs, amongst these was Mohammad Yunus. His chief qualification was being abusive towards people who had fallen out of favour with Nehru or Mrs Gandhi. He was nominated to the foreign service, and served as an ambassador. After retiring from service he was given important assignments, such as head of the Trade Fair Authority of India, and then nominated to the Rajya Sabha. Yunus was known to boast that he kept cabinet ministers waiting outside his office and ticked off senior bureaucrats who crossed his path. His son, Adil Shahryar was a childhood friend of Mrs Gandhi's younger son, Sanjay. The two had been involved in several 'pranks', including stealing motor cars. Adil migrated to the United States where he ran foul of the law and was sent to jail. Rajiv Gandhi as Prime Minister obtained pardon for him. Adil died a few years later in Delhi.

Amongst advisers and confidantes on domestic affairs was

Dhirendra Brahmachari, a handsome, semi-literate yoga instructor from Bihar who acquired considerable influence over the household and wealth for himself: he had his own aircraft, imported cars, a herd of Jersey cows, a gun factory, a film studio and other real estate. He had also been cited as a co-respondent in a divorce case. Brahmachari was addressed as Swamiji. There was also R.K. Dhawan, who had been Pandit Nehru's stenographer and after his death joined Indira Gandhi's personal staff. He was an obsequious man with incredible *savoir-faire*. After having worked under Usha Bhagat he gradually replaced her as Mrs Gandhi's chief confidante.

Rajiv, Mrs Gandhi's elder son, grew into a tall and very handsome young man. Having failed to take his degree from Cambridge University, he became a pilot in Indian Airlines. He married an attractive Italian girl, the daughter of a builder from a small town near Turin. They had two children, Rahul and Priyanka. Rajiv and Sanjay never got on. When Sanjay made a mess of his Maruti car project and exposed his mother to charges of manoeuvring to get money for him, Rajiv held him responsible for giving the family a bad name. When Sanjay rose to power, Rajiv retired into a sulk and had as little to do with him as he could. They barely exchanged courtesies when they met for meals in the family dining room. Mrs Gandhi had a poor opinion of Rajiv's intellect. However, after Sanjay's death she successfully built him up as her successor. Rajiv proceeded to get rid of Sanjay's men and replace them with his own. His choice of many advisers included men who had been in the restricted atmosphere of an expensive school with him.

On the other side of the mother-in-law versus daughter-in-law drama was the Anand family. The most important of them was Amteshwar, the youngest daughter of Sir Datar Singh, landowner and cattle breeder from Montgomery (now Sahiwal in Pakistan). His eldest daughter had made an unhappy marriage, and joined the ashram of Anandmayi Ma. There were also two sons — one having worked for some years with Ralli Brothers, gave up the job on his father's death to take over the family estates. He grabbed

Amteshwar's share of the inheritance. The two, who had once been close to each other, were then engaged in bitter litigation. The other son, Channi, had a medical condition and was not normal and had to be kept in Bhopal.

Amteshwar had a modest education. She was sent abroad for higher studies. Before she could complete her course, she was asked to return home and married off to a handsome army officer, Tejinder Singh Anand. The marriage was not a success. Nevertheless, the Anands had three children: Maneka, Viren and Ambika.

How and when did the two women, Indira Gandhi and Amteshwar Anand, come together? I have Maneka's version, corroborated by her mother. Maneka first met Sanjay Gandhi on 14 December 1973 at a cocktail party given by her uncle Major-General Kapur (the husband of Maneka's father's sister, a renowned beauty of her time) to celebrate their son Veenu Kapur's forthcoming marriage. Sanjay, being a school friend of Veenu, was present. It also happened to be Sanjay's birthday. He was in high spirits (not alcoholic, as he never touched liquor). He was the most sought-after bachelor in India: handsome, a son of the Prime Minister, grandson of Jawaharlal and great grandson of Motilal Nehru. He was engaged in trying to make himself into an automobile manufacturer. He was known to have an eye for pretty girls but carefully avoided getting entangled with those he suspected 'fell' for him with designs of becoming members of India's first family. Maneka was then seventeen years old: a lanky, freckled lass, attractive enough to have won a college beauty contest and modelled for a firm of towel manufacturers. She was, and is, highly photogenic.

It would appear that at this first meeting Sanjay was drawn towards Maneka. He spent the evening talking to her. The two agreed to meet the next day — and perhaps regularly. Amteshwar was quick to sense Sanjay's liking for her daughter. Although she said she was alarmed at the prospect of having Sanjay as a son-in-law, I am pretty certain that she saw in this relationship a partial fulfilment of her own life's ambition to become a somebody.

Thereafter, Sanjay and Maneka saw each other every day. Sanjay was not a restaurant- or picture-going young man and was shy of being seen in public where he would be recognized; he preferred to see Maneka either in her home or bring her to his own. Early in 1974 he invited Maneka to a meal. Maneka was understandably nervous of meeting the Prime Minister and, when she did, she did not know what to say. It was Mrs Gandhi who broke the ice. 'Since Sanjay has not introduced us, you better tell me what your name is and what you do,' she said.

Mrs Gandhi had no reason to try and size up Maneka. Sanjay had brought home different girls at different times. She had never on her own introduced her son to anyone she thought would make a suitable daughter-in-law. As with her elder son, she was willing to leave the choice of the proper wife to her son.

Amteshwar Anand claims that she did her best to discourage her daughter from entering into what she felt would be a misalliance, and she sent Maneka away to Bhopal to spend some days with her grandmother, Lady Datar Singh. In July 1974 Maneka returned from Bhopal. On the 29th of the same month a formal engagement ceremony took place in the Prime Minister's house at 1, Safdarjung Road, followed by a lunch where members of both families were present. Mrs Gandhi gave her daughter-in-law-to-be a gold and turquoise set and a Tanchoi saree. A month later on Maneka's birthday (26 August 1974) she gave her an Italian silk sari.

Soon after, Sanjay had to undergo a hernia operation. After attending college in the morning, Maneka spent her afternoons and evenings with her fiancé in the private ward of the All India Institute of Medical Sciences. A few weeks after his discharge from hospital and convalescence, Sanjay and Maneka were married through a civil ceremony (on 23 September 1974) at the house of Mohammad Yunus. Mrs Gandhi was generous in the wedding presents she gave her new daughter-in-law: twenty-one expensive sarees, two sets of gold jewellery, a *lehnga*, and perhaps the most precious of all, a khadi sari made out of yarn spun by her father Jawaharlal Nehru when he was in jail. Mrs Gandhi welcomed Maneka as a traditional Indian mother-in-law would welcome her *bahu:* she did up the bedroom, arranged artifacts on the dressing table and chose bangles Maneka would wear on the night following her wedding.

What followed in the next three years can best be described as a roller-coaster ride for the Gandhis and the Anands. When Sanjay and Maneka married, the two families were on top of the world. Their fortunes dipped as Mrs Gandhi and Sanjay came under attack over the Maruti fiasco. The imposition of Emergency saw them on top again. They went down when both Mrs Gandhi and Sanjay were defeated in the elections, and then prosecuted (persecuted would be the more appropriate word). This nightmare lasted over two years till both mother and son rode back to power. Sanjay's career ended when he crashed to his death. Maneka and her mother were cast out of the Gandhi household; Mrs Gandhi's life ended with her assassination on 31 October 1984. Maneka was able to redeem some of her marital dues by becoming a Member of Parliament and a minister for a short period. Her mother, Amteshwar, went into oblivion.

Before I go into the details of these vicissitudes in their fortunes, I had better explain my own intrusion in the two families' affairs. When I was editing *The Illustrated Weekly of India* and living in Bombay Sanjay was struggling with little success to get his Maruti off the assembly lines. He, and because of him, his mother were getting a very rough time in Parliament and the press. It was alleged that hundreds of acres of prime farmland near Gurgaon and close to the end of the runway of Palam Airport had been made available to the car project at throw-away prices by Bansilal, the wily Chief Minister of Haryana. He said with impeccable rustic logic, *'Bacchra pakar lo to gai upney aap chalee avai gee'* — If you catch the calf, the mother is sure to follow on her own. By providing the land he required, Bansilal had caught Sanjay and got Sanjay's mother in his grip.

I spent three days in Delhi investigating the Maruti project. I found out the prices of land around the Maruti factory from my cousin Ajit Singh who had recently built a factory and a house close by. He had paid the same price as had Sanjay. I visited the Maruti plant. I had expected to see assembly lines like those of General Motors or Ford; all Sanjay had built in two years were a couple of corrugated sheet roof sheds and a foundry. He had a prototype of a Maruti ready for me to try out. It was somewhat noisy but had a good pick-up and held the road well. Sanjay kept egging me on to drive faster. Then he took the wheel and literally flew over ploughed fields and dust tracks. Back in Bombay, I produced a special issue of *The Illustrated Weekly* with Sanjay's picture on the cover. It was entitled 'Sanjay, the man who gets things done.' I refuted charges of land being given to him cheaply and being close to a militarily sensitive area. Sanjay and his mother had reason to be beholden to me. I came to be dubbed as their *chamcha*.

Maruti never came off the assembly line in Sanjay's lifetime. Soon after my defence of the project was published, Mrs Gandhi got into dire political trouble. At one time she contemplated resigning. According to many observers of the political scene, including myself, it was in all probability Sanjay (perhaps terrified of what his traducers would do to him) who persuaded her to hit back — declare an Emergency, lock up all Opposition leaders, suspend democratic rights and muzzle the press. So it came to be: in a countrywide swoop carried out during the night, thousands of political leaders, including Jayaprakash Narayan and Morarji Desai, were taken into custody, and the press placed under censorship. Mrs Gandhi assumed dictatorial powers with Sanjay as her principal adviser.

Later that summer in 1975, I heard my door bell ring one Sunday afternoon, which I reserved for an oil massage followed by a hot bath, washing my long hair and dyeing my greying beard. I was not expecting anyone and had a board on the door reading, 'Please do not ring the bell unless you are expected.' I could be very short with unexpected visitors. I opened the door prepared to roundly tick off anyone intruding on my privacy. There stood two middle-aged women draped in expensive saris, jewellery and exuding the fragrance of expensive French perfume. After a perfunctory apology of 'Sorry to descend on you like this without warning' they introduced themselves. 'I am Amteshwar Anand and this is my friend Indira Dhody.' I was embarrassed: my hair was dripping wet and hanging over my shoulders, my beard was tied up in a beard-band: 'A Sardar's Sundays are devoted to *kesh* (hair) and *darhee* (beard),' I explained. Amtesh smiled and replied, 'Not to worry. I am the daughter of a Sardar and married to one.' I recognized her as Sir Datar Singh's daughter and Maneka's mother. 'I knew your parents and one of your brothers, Channi. But I don't think we have met before,' I said.

'Yes, we have!' she replied. 'I called on you in Paris when you were with UNESCO. I was on my way to the States on a scholarship. We are also distantly related through your aunt Sardarni Ujjal Singh.' She told me about her friend: 'Indira and I are partners in the garment export business.'

Amtesh went on to explain why she had come to see me. Maneka wanted to start a monthly magazine, *Surya*. Sanjay had suggested they seek my advice on how to go about it. I agreed to assist, provided I got permission from my employers.

The next morning I sent a note to the General Manager asking for permission to help *Surya*. It was Emergency time and people knew who was what. The General Manager sent me the necessary permission, adding that I should do my best to make Maneka Gandhi's magazine a success.

I came to Delhi and discussed the project with Maneka, Sanjay and Amtesh. I sensed that Maneka was making too many demands on Sanjay and he wanted to involve her in some activity which would reduce her pressure on him. I was made Consulting Editor of *Surya*. The first half-a-dozen issues of the journal were almost entirely written or rewritten and edited by me. I refused to accept any remuneration: I was no doubt flattered to be on close terms with Mrs Gandhi, Sanjay, Maneka and her mother.

There was no question of *Surya* not being a success. Ads poured in without the asking. After a few issues, the circulation rose to 50,000 copies. I went to Delhi at least once a fortnight, spent my evenings with the Anands and visited Sanjay and Maneka in the Prime Minister's home. Once I happened to be there when Rajiv and Sonia were celebrating one of their children's birthdays. I noticed that the two brothers and their wives occupied different ends of the house and had very little to do with each other. On another occasion I was in Sanjay's room: he gave me an air settee which sank to the floor as I sat on it. He put a cup of tea in my hand and went to see someone. Two enormous donkey-sized dogs, an Irish Wolfhound and another, perhaps a Great Dane, loped in and stood over me drooling into my cup of tea. If I tried to move, they bared their teeth and growled. Fortunately, Mrs Gandhi came in looking for Sanjay, saw the predicament I was in and ordered the dogs out of the room.

What Sanjay did during the Emergency gave him the image of a monster. When he had slums cleared in Delhi it was bruited about that he had run bulldozers over the homes of innocent people; when he launched on the family planning programme, wild stories were circulated of people being pulled out of cinema houses and bus queues and being forcibly sterilized. The Emergency was soon broadcast as being a dark period in Indian history. It cannot be denied that thousands of innocent people suffered arbitrary arrest and imprisonment on orders issued by people who had been put in key positions. In many instances they acted on their own, without the knowledge of Mrs Gandhi or her son.

The most dramatic personality changes took place in the Anand family. The Colonel acquired political and economic clout. But the most striking change of all was in the attitude of Amteshwar Anand. From a nonentity she became the principal lady-in-waiting to the Empress of India, Indira Gandhi. She became haughty beyond belief. However, I could sense a certain apprehension that this honeymoon with unbridled power could not last forever. When I told her of instances of gross injustice, she passed the information on to Sanjay and Mrs Gandhi.

What happened to the Gandhi-Anand households was the

classical instance of hubris getting its just dessert. Mrs Gandhi was fed with stories to prove that the Emergency had raised her popularity to an all-time high and that she could give herself legitimacy by having it endorsed through a general election. Sanjay was shrewder and advised her against taking this risk. Mrs Gandhi had her way. She lifted the Emergency, released all political prisoners and announced a general election for March 1977.

Retribution on a scale undreamt of by her or her supporters followed. Opposition leaders joined hands to form a peoples' Janata Party and swept Mrs Gandhi's Congress into the dustbin. Mrs Gandhi was trounced by a buffoon, Raj Narain; Sanjay by a local gun-toting landowner and muscleman. Naveen Chawla, Ambika Soni and Rukhsana Sultan — all three Sanjay favourites whom people had feared — became objects of ridicule and derision. The greatest blow was reserved for the Anand family — and of them the hardest hit were Amteshwar and her husband. Maneka still had Sanjay and the Gandhi name. Amteshwar was stripped of all importance. The innumerable fair-weather friends she had acquired disappeared into the thin Delhi air.

The prosecution launched by the Janata Government against Mrs Gandhi and her Emergency excesses has been extensively written about; her 'misdeeds' have been recorded in reports compiled by the Shah Commission. Splits in the Gandhi family widened. Rajiv's envy for the sudden eruption of his ne'er-do-well brother now turned into hate. He held Sanjay responsible, perhaps rightly, for the catastrophic fall in the status of the family, from being the most respected to social and political outcasts. Neither he nor his Italian wife Sonia did anything to prop up Mrs Gandhi's shattered morale, and withdrew into their one-family sub-shell. Sanjay had no option but to fight back. In the hour of crisis it was Maneka who showed surprising reserves of strength and guts. Amteshwar also realized that her only chance to ever win back the brief glory that had been hers was in the restoration of her son-in-law and his mother to power.

I stood by the Gandhi family during their days in the dog house. Members of my family were highly critical of me, as were all my friends. There were some lighter moments. On my visits to Delhi I combined working for *Surya* and calling on the Gandhis and the Anands. I had some very embarrassing moments. One morning Maneka brought Sanjay to my apartment. While I was talking to them, in walked my three-year-old-granddaughter, Naina, holding my wife's hand. She acknowledged Maneka's greeting of 'Hi Naina!' with a broad smile. Maneka asked her, 'Say namaskar to Sanjay.' Naina walked up and stared at Sanjay with her face a few inches from his. '*Nahin* — no, *Sanjay bahut bura aadami hai* — Sanjay is a very bad man. *Iskee maan bhi bahut buree aurat hai, logon ko jail mein daltee hai* — his mother is also a very bad woman; she puts people in jail.' I did not know which way to look. Sanjay went pale; Maneka's face flushed with anger: 'They are brainwashing little children,' she said angrily. My wife saved the situation: '*Beta, aisy naheen boltey. Koee kahey teyree maa buree aurat hai to tujhey kaisey legey?*' — Child, you should not say such things. How would you feel if somebody called your mother a bad woman? Naina lost interest in Sanjay and turned to her Naani to ask her what a jail was and whether it was true it had no doors or windows.

I felt sure Sanjay would never come to my home again. He did so that very afternoon. It was winter and I was taking the sun in my patch of lawn at the rear of my apartment. While we were talking, I noticed some urchins gathering on the other side of the hedge and whispering to each other. I feared another anti-Sanjay demonstration. But to my relief, as we stood up the boys shouted: 'Sanjay Gandhi, Zindabad'.

Adversity brought other aspects in the characters of the two families to the fore. Mrs Gandhi soon got over her mood of despair as the Morarji Desai government launched a campaign to harass her, Sanjay and other officials who had played active roles in the Emergency. She was not allowed to retire from the scene. Nor was Sanjay. They were forced to fight back.

Since Sanjay was the main target of the Desai regime,

Mrs Gandhi's maternal instincts were concentrated on protecting him from harm. One of the many charges against Sanjay (and V.C. Shukla, the Information and Broadcasting Minister during the Emergency) was that they destroyed the negative of a film, *Kissa Kursee Ka*, a highly derogatory portrayal of Mrs Gandhi's lust for power. The case was going against the accused and both feared they would be convicted. Sanjay felt that if he could get Nani Palkhiwala to defend him more than half his battle would be won. He knew Nani was my friend and asked me to approach him. Nani, who had defended Mrs Gandhi in her election case, had withdrawn from it when she declared the Emergency. He had also been victimized by Sanjay. However, I persuaded Nani to receive Sanjay and Maneka. He was gracious enough to invite them for breakfast.

The Sanjay-Maneka visit to Bombay was quite an experience. Before I left Delhi for Bombay Mrs Gandhi sent for me and expressed fears of violence being done to her son. I assured her that I would look after him and have him stay with me. The morning the two were to arrive, a mob began to collect in the street below my apartment. I rang up Sanjay and asked him to postpone his visit. He was determined to go ahead. I went to receive the couple at Santa Cruz airport. There was an even bigger crowd there shouting anti-Sanjay slogans. We drove through a howling mob with a carload of security men following a few inches behind our rear fender. Arthur Bunder Road, where I lived, was closed to traffic. Sanjay and Maneka went to the house of a friend; I went to my office and rang them up asking them to shift over in the afternoon when the road was clear. I later learnt that the cordon round my flat was organized by my friend, Soli Sorabji, with the approval of Nani Palkhiwala. They were determined not to let Sanjay and Maneka stay with me since that would expose me to the wrath of the mob. In the evening I went over to pick up Sanjay and Maneka and brought them over to my apartment. The crowd began to collect again. As Sanjay came out on the balcony, people started shouting abuses at him. Sanjay simply looked at them with glazed eyes without uttering a word. Maneka yelled back. I took them indoors and rang up people I had invited to meet the couple, asking them not to come. Nevertheless, Shobha De turned up, saying she had not received my message. She accompanied us to the Taj where I took my guests for dinner. A police car followed hot on our heels. While at dinner, Shobha excused herself — I thought to go to the loo. A few minutes later, photographers arrived on the scene. I apologized to Sanjay and Maneka. They accepted my word that I had nothing to do with it. They spent the night with their friends. The next morning I picked them up and took them to see Nani Palkhiwala. At breakfast Sanjay broached the subject of Nani taking up his case. Nani was courteous but firm. 'I am sorry, I will not appear for you,' he said. And that was that.

That afternoon I took the two for lunch at the Gymkhana club. Once more word went round and, by the time we left, there was a crowd of photographers waiting for us at the gate. It was the same on the way back to the airport. The only act of courtesy Sanjay received was from an airlines official who took his ticket from him, gave him his boarding pass and hustled him out of the crowd into the V.I.P. lounge — and on to the aircraft. I was greatly relieved to see Sanjay return unharmed. I rang up Mrs Gandhi and told her that her son was on his way back.

I was with Sanjay and Maneka when he had to face the Shah Commission. Sanjay was anticipating trouble and took his muscleman with him. The room was packed with anti-Sanjay hoodlums. As soon as he entered bedlam broke loose and it was a free-for-all with flailing arms and chairs flying around. Sanjay's shirt was torn. He fought back with his bare fists. He was a powerful man; I was impressed with the way he defended himself. Maneka had her share of being hustled around. I took shelter behind Kiran Bedi of the police and watched the scene. What little respect the two had for the Commission was displayed by Maneka. She jumped over the railing, plucked Justice Shah's two pens out of the pen holders and gave them to me to keep as mementos.

It was during these days that I was summarily dismissed from the editorship of *The Illustrated Weekly of India* and returned

to Delhi. I took up the editorship of *The National Herald* owned
by the Gandhi family. One afternoon I found a packet on my
table that contained a dozen photographs of Babu Jagjivan
Ram's son Suresh Kumar having sexual intercourse with an
eighteen-year-old college girl. The photographs showed them
in different postures. Maneka got a similar packet in her *Surya*
office. That evening a man claiming to be an emissary of
Jagjivan Ram came to see me. He said that Babuji was willing to
ditch Prime Minister Morarji Desai and cross over to
Mrs Gandhi's side if his son's photographs were not published
in *The National Herald* or *Surya*. I drove over to Mrs Gandhi's
house carrying the packet with me. As I broached the subject,
she asked me to come out in the garden: she suspected her
house was bugged. I asked her if she had seen those highly
obscene pictures of Suresh Kumar and his friend. Yes, she
replied, Maneka had shown them to her. I told her of the offer I
was asked to convey. 'I don't trust that man,' she replied.
'Jagjivan Ram has done more harm to me and my family than
anyone else. You have it conveyed to him that he should come
over to us before I tell Maneka not to use the pictures.'

There was no follow up. Both *Surya* and *The National Herald*
published the entire set with black strips across the genitals of
the two lovers to avoid prosecution for obscenity.

Some months later Colonel Anand's body was found on a
dusty track near their farm not far from Delhi. A loaded pistol
lay by his side. Amtesh and Maneka tried to make it out to be a
case of murder, but a verdict of suicide was returned.

The Colonel had spent his life being unloved and had
decided to call it a day. He was also suicide-prone. It ran in the
family. A year or two later his brother, following a quarrel with
his wife, swallowed poison. His body was found lying in a
shallow bank of the Sukhna lake in Chandigarh. Colonel
Anand's departure went largely unmourned. There was the
usual *bhog* ceremony at which Mrs Gandhi was present.
Thereafter I did not hear anyone speak of him.

In the two-and-a-half years of the Janata regime, during
which Mrs Gandhi was imprisoned twice (once for a night,

another time for six days), her chief morale-boosters were Sanjay and Maneka (with Amteshwar close behind her). For Maneka it was a trying time: attending classes in college, running *Surya*, visiting her husband in jail or accompanying him to the Shah Commission, organizing mass demonstrations and facing hostile crowds. The family had few friends left. I was amongst those few.

For the Gandhis and the Anands the nightmare ended in January 1980 when Mrs Gandhi won back her Prime Ministership by a convincing electoral triumph over the Janata Party. Sanjay (and with him Maneka) were once again on top of the world. And riding on their shoulders was Amteshwar Anand. Her ego-balloon, deflated more than once in recent times was again bursting with self-esteem.

The cloud-nine period was all too brief. On the morning of Monday, 23 June 1980 Sanjay killed himself (and his co-pilot Captain Saxena), crashing his two-seater plane on the southern ridge in Delhi. At the time, Amteshwar and her other daughter, Ambika, were holidaying in England. The news was broken to them by Swraj Paul, a businessman who had ingratiated himself into the Gandhi-Anand family. Amteshwar and Ambika were put on a specially chartered Air India plane to bring them back to Delhi. The plane touched down at Rome airport to pick up Rajiv and Sonia who were staying with Sonia's parents. Other passengers on the aircraft were Sumati Morarji, the owner of a shipping line, and V.C. Shukla. They were on the lower deck of the first class; the others in the first class lounge on the upper deck. Periodically Sumati, V.C. Shukla and Swraj Paul came down to be with the Anands. All three exhorted Amtesh that she should do her best to keep the two families together. And now that Sanjay was gone, they should rally round behind Rajiv.

Sanjay's death came as a profound shock to everyone. I was numbed. In a highly emotional tribute published in the *Evening News* and reproduced next morning in *The Hindustan Times*, I suggested that Sanjay's mantle should naturally fall on the shoulders of his young widow who had stood by him and shared his vision of India. Rajiv had never shown interest in politics and his wife had expressed abhorrence for it. I had to pay dearly for this emotional outburst. One sentence I used to prop up Maneka became like the dead albatross round my neck. I wrote that she was no namby-pamby character as some people thought. 'When roused, she can be like Durga on a tiger.' This was construed as my deifying Maneka. Amongst those who thought that I had mischievously put up Maneka against Rajiv was Indira Gandhi.

If Mrs Gandhi had harboured any resentment against Maneka she had not said or done anything about it as long as Sanjay was alive. There may be some truth in the belief that she both loved and feared her second son. Sanjay was more relaxed in the Anand's home than in his mother's. At the Anands he was fussed over by everyone, including the servants of the household; in his mother's he had a rival in his elder brother. Mrs Gandhi disliked Sanjay's preference for the Anand home to hers. It did not take long after Sanjay's tragic death for the Gandhis to make it known to Maneka that she was a misfit in the Prime Minister's residence. A week after Sanjay's death, Mrs Gandhi suggested to Maneka on her own that she work as her Secretary. A few days later, Dhirendra Brahmachari came to her room to inform her that Mrs Gandhi was too embarrassed to tell her so, but Sonia had put her foot down on the proposal, and had threatened to return to Italy with her family unless Mrs Gandhi withdrew the offer to Maneka. I have little doubt that Sonia was the more favoured daughter-in-law, just as Sanjay was the more favoured son. Now that Sanjay was gone Mrs Gandhi had no choice except to lean on Rajiv, her only remaining child. She had no great affection for Maneka and resented Amteshwar's bossiness. It did not take much for this feeling to turn into unconcealed hostility.

Mrs Gandhi became more and more irritated by Maneka's presence and found fault with everything she did. At a formal banquet given in honour of Mrs Margaret Thatcher, while Rajiv and Sonia were seated at the main table with the chief guest, Maneka was relegated to the table meant for the staff, with Dhawan and Usha Bhagat. Mrs Gandhi told me that Maneka was rude to people, and one day she sent for me and asked me to speak to Maneka to behave better.

I offered to take her on the staff of *The Hindustan Times* and spoke to K.K. Birla about it. He agreed provided Mrs Gandhi sent him a note or spoke to him. She did neither. Maneka was ordered to sever connections with *Surya* because it was 'a rag' (which it had always been with Mrs Gandhi's approval). Maneka, who was passionately fond of animals and had been elected President of The Society for the Protection of Animals, was told to resign. She wrote a personal biography of her husband. After approving of it Mrs Gandhi found serious errors in it a day or so before she was to release it: all printed copies had to be withdrawn and a new version with no more than a couple of sentences altered was issued in its place. Mrs Gandhi made her aversion to Amteshwar known to Maneka: Amteshwar stopped going to No. 1, Safdarjung Road.

Both families were highly superstitious. A few days after Sanjay's death I happened to call on Amteshwar at her house in Jor Bagh. I saw stepping out of the house a priest in dhoti and wooden sandals murmuring Sanskrit shlokas. Following him was a man carrying an earthenware pitcher of water on his head. And following the man was Amteshwar Anand. 'What's all this?' I asked her. She could not conceal a smile as she told me. 'That Mrs Saxena, the widow of the co-pilot killed with Sanjay, rang me up and said that the two boys had come to her in a dream and were complaining that they were very thirsty as it was very hot where they were. I consulted this Panditji and he advised that we set up a *piaao* (drinking-water booth) outside Mrs Gandhi's house. I am going to do that.' A necklace with a half moon and star was gifted to Maneka. Vijay Raje Scindia told her that it was a tantric emblem to make people ill. Maneka, who had been keeping unwell took it off and suddenly started feeling better.

The relationship between Mrs Gandhi and Maneka deteriorated very fast. According to Maneka, she did nothing to provoke Mrs Gandhi. Almost as if to spite Mrs Gandhi — with good reason as Mrs Gandhi had herself sanctioned the use of the journal to malign adversaries when it suited her — Amteshwar negotiated the sale of *Surya* to Mrs Gandhi's sworn enemy, Vijay Raje Scindia, operating through Dr J.K. Jain, an erstwhile member of the R.S.S. In fairness to Amtesh the only choice that Mrs Gandhi left her and her daughter was either to close down *Surya* or sell it. Industrialists like the Modis who had helped it had been told by Rajiv that Mrs Gandhi did not approve of their giving ads to the journal. Others like Charanjit Singh of Campa Cola refused to clear arrears due from him. It was a very smooth operation performed in secrecy. Even I, who had been persuaded by Sanjay to take over the journal, knew nothing about the deal (and to this day do not know how much money, and in what form, changed hands). It was on the day that the deal was finalized that Amtesh brought Dr Jain to my apartment to have it announced in the papers (February 1982). It was clear to everyone that Maneka's days in No. 1, Safdarjung Road were numbered. The only speculation was how and when she would leave. Mrs Gandhi, who had never known matters to be decided by anyone except herself, was in for a nasty surprise. Once having decided to part company with her mother-in-law, Maneka decided that this time she would determine the terms and time of her departure. She told me several weeks ahead of the exact day on which she would be 'thrown out'.

Maneka chose the time very carefully. Mrs Gandhi was in London for the India Festival and had taken Sonia with her. Rajiv was too involved in building himself up and avoided being at home to spare himself meeting Maneka at meals.

Maneka and Akbar Ahmed decided to launch the Sanjay Vichar Manch. Mrs Gandhi did not know how to express her disapproval of an organization professing to propagate her son's ideals. The text of Maneka's speech at the inaugural function (which Maneka claims had been approved by Mrs Gandhi) was telegraphed to London by Rajiv. Mrs Gandhi decided she had got the opportunity she had waited for all these months to get rid of her turbulent daughter-in-law.

Mrs Gandhi returned from London on the morning of 28 March 1982 — determined to call the shots. When Maneka came to greet her, she dismissed her curtly: 'I will speak to you later.' Word was sent to her that she was not expected to join the family for lunch and the food would be sent to her in her room. About 1 pm another message was sent to her that the Prime Minister would like to see her. Maneka was prepared for a dressing down. She was in the sitting room when Mrs Gandhi walked in barefoot. She ordered Dhawan and Dhirendra Brahmachari to come in as witnesses to what she had to say to Maneka. According to Maneka she was fuming with rage and was barely comprehensible as she screamed, wagging her finger at Maneka. 'You will get out of this house immediately.' Maneka assumed an air of innocence and asked, 'Why? What have I done?' Mrs Gandhi screamed back, 'I heard every word of the speech you made!' Maneka added, 'It was cleared by you.' This caused another outburst. Mrs Gandhi accused her of disobeying her wishes, and for good measure added, 'There was venom in every word you spoke. Get out this minute. Get out!' she shrieked. 'The car has been ordered to take you to your mother's house.' Maneka stood her ground. She did not want to go to her mother's house and needed time to pack. 'You will go where you are told. Your things will be sent to you later,' said Mrs Gandhi and again used strong words for Amteshwar. Maneka started sobbing and left for her room shouting back that she would not allow her mother to be insulted. Mrs Gandhi followed her barefooted on the gravel road shouting within the hearing of the staff and sentries outside: 'Get out! Get out!' Meanwhile, Feroze Varun had been taken to Mrs Gandhi's room.

Maneka's friends got busy spreading the word round to the press. Before going to the Prime Minister's house Ambika rang me up to tell me what was happening to her sister and to spread the information. By 9 pm a crowd of photographers and reporters, including foreign correspondents, began assembling outside the gates. Mrs Gandhi always had a healthy dread and hatred of the foreign press. The police, which had been amassed at different points of approach to the house, had not been fully briefed about whom to stop and whom to let through.

Ten minutes later Ambika and her brother arrived at the house. For the first time in eight years they were stopped. Word of their arrival was sent to Mrs Gandhi and she was told that Ambika was talking to the pressmen. Their car was allowed to enter and the two went into Maneka's room. They found Maneka in tears, trying to put whatever she could into her trunks. Mrs Gandhi suddenly walked in and ordered Maneka to leave without taking anything. Ambika spoke out, 'She won't leave, it is her house.' Mrs Gandhi's dislike of Ambika was tinged with fear of the girl's sharp tongue. 'This is not her house,' shouted Mrs Gandhi, 'this is the house of the Prime Minister of India. She cannot bring people here without my permission. In any case, Ambika Anand, I don't want to speak to you.' Ambika was not the one to be cowed down. 'You have no right to speak to my sister like this. This is Sanjay's house and she is Sanjay's wife. So it is her house. No one can order her out of it.' Mrs Gandhi began to fumble for words and to cry. 'I did not tell her to get out; she is leaving on her own,' she said at one stage. 'I have never told a lie in my life,' she protested. 'You have never told the truth in your life,' retaliated the two sisters now emboldened by each other's presence. The fight went out of Mrs Gandhi; she began to cry hysterically and had to be escorted out of the room by Dhirendra Brahmachari. Thereafter, messages had to be conveyed through the hapless Dhawan who received his share of tongue-lashing from the two girls — as well as being rewarded for his pains by being bitten by Maneka's Irish Wolfhound Sheba, who had been upset by the excitement.

Left to themselves, the two sisters planned their strategy and time-schedule for departure. They ordered lunch and watched a film starring Amitabh Bachhan on their VCR at full blast so that Mrs Gandhi who was in the neighbouring room could know they did not give a damn. Every time Dhawan came in to plead with them to leave, they presented him with a new demand. The dogs had to be fed. The dogs were fed. When

Dhawan failed to dissuade the girls from taking away anything, Mrs Gandhi came in with Brahmachari to order a search of everything they had packed. Maneka insisted that if there was going to be a search of her belongings it would take place on the road for all the press to see. The trunks outside the room were deliberately opened for pressmen to see and photograph by cameras outside the gate fitted with telescopic lenses. Another round of accusations and counter-accusations followed.

By now Mrs Gandhi was no longer mistress of the situation. Rajiv accompanied by Arun Nehru took over. They summoned the security officer, N.K. Singh, and ordered him to throw out the two sisters. Being a shrewd man, N.K. Singh asked for the order to be put in writing. Neither Rajiv nor Arun Nehru would commit themselves on paper. Verbal requests by N.K. Singh were turned down by the girls who wanted their luggage, dogs, and now also Feroze Varun who had a fever, to be sent ahead of them. Mrs Gandhi knew she had been beaten and gave in down the line.

The girls and their brother took their time eating a sumptuous lunch. The luggage and the dogs were sent ahead in a taxi. A very sleepy Feroze Varun was handed over to them at 11 pm. Instead of a taxi, the Prime Minister's car was ordered to take Maneka and her son wherever she wanted to go. The last thing Mrs Gandhi did, as was her habit, was to dictate a letter to Maneka spelling out her misdeeds which had made her expulsion necessary. Maneka sat down and wrote her reply which she released to the press. A few minutes after 11 pm, a very tearful Maneka, bearing a bleary-eyed and bewildered Feroze Varun, came out of the room to explosions of press-camera flash-bulbs. Maneka had won this round against the Prime Minister of India with a knock-out.

My close relationship with Amtesh and Maneka came to an abrupt end a few months later. A journal had interviewed me about some allegations levelled at Maneka. My comments obviously displeased her because a couple of days later, she stormed into my apartment and flung a copy of the magazine in my face and stormed out. An hour later I received a registered

AD letter from Amtesh accusing me of telling lies about the family. My association with the Gandhis and the Anands had ended. I heaved a sigh of relief. Another chapter in my life was over.

13 1980–86, Parliament and The Hindustan Times

O GO BACK slightly in time: the December 1980 General Elections swept Mrs Gandhi back to power. I had predicted her victory in a 'quickie' entitled *Indira Gandhi Returns!* which I wrote some months before the election. I had done my bit for her and her family. I defended them when they were being reviled by everyone. I was the only journalist to refute baseless calumnies spread against Sanjay Gandhi's Maruti car project, I helped Maneka and her mother Amteshwar edit and get advertisements for their monthly magazine *Surya* when it was just launched. For six months I edited *The National Herald*, without drawing a salary. I was with Sanjay when he appeared before the Shah Commission and kept in touch with him when he was put in jail. I enthusiastically supported his birth-control programme, his slum clearance drive, and was primarily responsible for his interest in tree-planting. I confess I expected some kind of recognition or reward for what I had done for them.

Though Mrs Gandhi became Prime Minister again, the real ruler of the country was Sanjay. Since I saw a lot of him and Maneka in their days of trouble, we developed an affection for each other. He was a man of few words but a go-getter. Unlike other politicians who, in order to keep their supporters happy, make promises which they have no intention of fulfilling, when Sanjay promised to do something, you could be sure he would do it. He also had the guts to say 'no' if he felt the request was unreasonable.

As I said, I expected to be rewarded by the Gandhi family. Sanjay asked me if I would be interested in a diplomatic assignment. He had the post of High Commissioner in London in mind. I turned it down without hesitation as I did not want to leave India. Then he offered to get me a nomination to the Rajya Sabha and the editorship of *The Hindustan Times*. I accepted the alternative. I was in the *New Delhi* office when one afternoon Giani Zail Singh, then Home Minister, rang me up and told me that he was going to see the President with the list of nominees for the Rajya Sabha. My name was among them. I behaved like a child who has been given a whopping big birthday present. I yelled out to my colleagues in *New Delhi:* 'Hooray! I've become a Member of Parliament.' I ran down the corridor of the PTI building shouting the news to everyone whose face was familiar to me. I drove to my mother's home and broke the news to her and my sister. I went over to Sanjay Gandhi to thank him and came home to celebrate. Early next morning I left for Kasauli to avoid callers with garlands and the flood of congratulatory letters and telegrams which would inevitably follow.

I spent a week in Kasauli exulting over the turn in my fortunes. They had been low ever since I had been fired from *The Illustrated Weekly*. A few weeks after the announcement of my nomination to the Rajya Sabha, K.K. Birla asked me to see him. He offered me the editorship of *The Hindustan Times*. I knew beforehand that he would do so, but was not sure what he would do with Hiranmay Karlekar who was then editing the paper. It was a very awkward situation for me. I had worked under and been a friend of Karlekar's father-in-law, Ashok Chanda, when he was Deputy High Commissioner in London. I had been local guardian of Chanda's elder daughter, Anju, during her final year at school and first year at Oxford. Knowing my close friendship with the family, my father had gone out of his way to give the Chandas a flat in Sujan Singh Park. The very evening that Birla had offered me the job, Monica Chanda dropped in for a chat. As usual she told me how much Birla relied on her son-in-law and how well he was doing as editor of *The Hindustan Times*. I felt it was time to tell her the unpleasant truth. 'Monica, I don't know where you've got all these stories from! Birla is not happy with Ronu and means to sack him.'

'How can you say this kind of thing!' she exclaimed. 'How do you know?'

'I know because I have been offered his job this afternoon and will be taking over next week.' A very dejected Monica Chanda left my apartment to return to her own.

I took over the editorship of *The Hindustan Times* in 1980. Hiranmay Karlekar had left a note recommending promotion for some members of his personal staff who were to join me. I decided to honour his recommendations. I also received a note from Sanjay Gandhi giving me a longish list of assistant- and sub-editors whom he knew to be communists: I was to get rid of them as soon as possible. I kept this note in my pocket to check whether his 'inside information' was reliable. I had no intention of victimizing anyone for his political views. I found that Sanjay's information was correct. Three men on his list sought voluntary retirement; others continued to do their jobs. The one man who made no secret of his being a card-holder of the Communist Party was Chand Joshi. He spent most of his time in Union activities. He drank hard and rarely turned in more than one piece every three or four months. His name was not on Sanjay's list; nor did Birla or the management ever try to fire him or transfer him out of Delhi. I often wondered how Chand Joshi, whom I got to know well and whose second wife Manini Chatterji I found very likeable, could afford to spend his afternoons drinking at Five-Star Hotels. His salary could barely keep his two families in comfort. It was some years after I had left *The Hindustan Times* that Chand was forced to give up alcohol on medical advice. The one-time Marxist atheist also became an ardent worshipper of the goddess Durga.

*T*he Hindustan Times was started during World War I by a group of Sikh revolutionaries belonging to the Ghadr party in Canada and the United States to propagate nationalist views. Its first editor was Sardar Mangal Singh. The paper was unable to pick-up a viable circulation, and being anti-British was often threatened with closure. Its owners were forced to sell it to J.N. Sahni who, with his brother-in-law, Kohli, was able to establish it as Delhi's leading daily paper. They too found the going very difficult and were often victims of the government's displeasure. The paper was in the red when Pandit Madan Mohan Malviya persuaded the industrialist G.D. Birla to buy it and run it along business lines. The Indian National Congress was keen to have a daily paper in the capital to project its views. G.D. Birla bought it more as a favour to the Congress than as a commercial venture. Mahatma Gandhi's son, Devadas, was appointed editor. The Editorial offices and the printing press were housed in a few rooms in the outer circle of Connaught Circus. Within a few years the paper acquired a respectable circulation and became, as it were, the daily habit of Dilliwalas: their bowels would not move till they had the paper spread before them when they went to the loo. It became the paper in which to advertise eligible progeny and announce the departures of loved ones 'to their heavenly abodes'. Despite its circulation being confined to the capital and its neighbourhood, the paper's revenue from advertisements far exceeded those of daily papers published in other cities with much larger circulations.

On the division of G.D. Birla's assets amongst his sons, *The Hindustan Times* came to the share of the eldest son, K.K. Birla. It was the least important of his legacies. But having political ambitions, he set about modernizing and expanding it. He acquired land on Curzon Road (later Kasturba Gandhi Marg) and raised a multi-storeyed building of marble and plate glass. The first three floors were earmarked for *The Hindustan Times* printing press, advertisement section, editorial and managerial offices. The other floors were rented out. From the time he took over the paper, K.K. Birla used it to keep the government on his side and forward his political and business interests. He did not intend it to be an independent paper. He obliged ministers by giving their sons and daughters jobs, or agreeing to transfer them to places recommended. He could not afford to offend anyone except the Opposition — that, too, mildly lest the Opposition one day become the government. As a result, more than two-thirds of the paper theoretically reserved for editorial matters was filled by what it received from the wire services; of the remaining space, one-third was taken by reports sent by State Correspondents, almost invariably favourable to the State's governments. It carried very little foreign news save what was put out by the wire-services. It had only two foreign correspondents, one in London and the other in Washington. Despite these drawbacks, nothing could shake *The Hindustan Times'* near monopoly circulation in the capital. Its Sunday editions carried five to six pages of matrimonial ads; its daily edition had almost half a page devoted to obituaries and *in memoriams*. It was the first and perhaps the only paper for announcements of *uthalas, antim ardasas, bhog* ceremonies and *keertans* for the departed. It was generally admitted that *The Hindustan Times* was the worst paper in the capital with the largest circulation. The much more readable, *Statesman* had the lowest. The *HT's* only challenge came from *The Times of India* which was as complete a daily paper as any in India. However, its attempts to overtake *The Hindustan Times* proved an abysmal failure.

The Hindustan Times had had some eminent editors, notably Sri Mulgaonkar and B.G. Verghese. Sri Mulgaonkar, though he enjoyed K.K. Birla's respect, preferred to write for B.D. Goenka's *The Indian Express*. B.G. Verghese proved too straight and unbending for K.K. Birla's liking and was fired. The very young and inexperienced Hiranmay Karlekar, an Assistant Editor with *The Statesman* was then pressed on K.K. Birla by the then Bengal Chief Minister, Siddhartha Shankar Ray, and remained Editor till Ray lost clout with the government. His services were dispensed with in favour of one who Mrs Gandhi and her son Sanjay felt would serve their purpose better, myself.

I had no illusions about the amount of editorial independence I would enjoy. On the day I took over, K.K. Birla handed me a typed document mounted on cardboard spelling out the editorial policy of the paper. It read like the introductory part of the Indian Constitution dealing with objectives. It could be interpreted anyway one liked. I read it cursorily and nodded my head. I noticed a small table in Birla's sitting room, beside the sofa he sat on. On it were three items which mattered most to him: his private telephone to pass instructions and receive reports, a pocket calculator to compute gains and losses, and a small picture in a silver frame of Lakshmi, the goddess of wealth. I liked the little I got to know of him. He was frail of build, always dressed in a dark suit and tie, and, like other members of the Birla clan, extremely courteous in his speech and behaviour. He served tea, coffee and biscuits to every visitor with his own hands and saw them to the door when they left.

I spent my first day going over lists of names of the assistant- and sub-editors. I glanced over the editorials and articles which were to go on the editorial page. What improvements could I make in the paper? I knew something of magazine journalism but, except for the short and fruitless stint with *The National Herald*, had no experience of running a large newspaper employing a staff of nearly 1,500 men and women. I did not know where to begin.

I resolved to do the best I could. As was my habit I rose early, listened to the BBC, Radio Pakistan and All India Radio and made notes on what they had to say. I came to the office an hour earlier than anyone else and cleared any correspondence that remained unanswered. I held an editorial meeting with my assistant editors and questioned them on why we had missed out items which other papers had carried, and assigned the three edits for the day to them, asking them to have them on my table by early afternoon. I did the rounds of the office to see that everyone was at their desks. There were always far too many visitors, most of them time wasters. During parliament sessions I spent a couple of hours in the Rajya Sabha. After lunch and a very short siesta at home I returned to the office. I went over the editorials and articles for the centre page — and often rewrote the text. And once again I did the rounds of the office. It was seldom that I went home before dark. I returned to the office after dinner and stayed there to get the latest news and see the contents of the first page. There were times when I returned home after midnight. At no other job had I worked such long hours, or to so little purpose. I soon discovered that there is very little an editor of a daily paper can do to improve its quality with a staff not chosen by him. What is expected of him are balanced but not scintillating editorials. In any case, few people bother to read editorials. I left them largely to my assistants and only made sure that they did not transgress the policy directive that Birla had given me. My only real contribution to *The Hindustan Times* was my Saturday column 'With Malice Towards One and All'. Much as my fellow journalists and editors scoffed at my brand of journalism, it became (and remains to this day) the most widely read column in the country and was reproduced in over a dozen English papers published in State capitals and in translations in regional languages all over the country. There were many people who took *The Hindustan Times* only on Saturdays to read what they called the 'Malice column.' Amongst them was K.K. Birla who was very particular that no other paper carried it till after it had appeared in his *Hindustan Times*.

It didn't take me long to sense the intrigue and corruption that went on among the staff. The main trouble with *The Hindustan Times* was that it was grossly over-staffed by people Birla had hired to please powerful politicians. Hiring was easy; firing them virtually impossible. The State Correspondents sent in stories favourable to Chief Ministers and received favours in return. Sometimes stories were planted in the paper after I had left the office around midnight. I could do little beside asking for explanations. In a few instances I was able to persuade Birla to punish erring correspondents by ordering their transfer to inhospitable regions. They approached Chief Ministers and Cabinet Ministers to speak to Birla, who then changed his mind and asked me to give them another chance. I was also overburdened with administrative work and had no deputy to act as editor in my absence or who could be groomed to take my place when I retired. In sheer desperation I asked

Birla to let me get N.C. Menon, our correspondent in Washington, to return and be my deputy. He had done the job before and was known to hammer away editorials on his typewriter within a few minutes. Birla agreed. I had to rue my decision — so, without admitting it, did Birla. Perhaps I am prone to Meningitis. I had heartily disliked Krishna Menon; I learnt to loathe N.C. Menon even more heartily.

As soon as I took over as editor, it got bruited around that I would fill the place with Sikhs. As it happened, I recruited only four men and a woman in senior positions; not one of them was a Sikh. For what was going on in the office, I relied on only one man, my personal secretary, Lachhman Dass. He proved to be a rare combination of efficiency, integrity, loyalty and discretion. His association with me continued long after I retired from the paper.

Let me go back several years to say something of my last days in *The Hindustan Times.* My contract was for three years. I expected that, when the time came, it would be renewed. My relations with K.K. Birla were cordial and I had every reason to believe he thought well of me. Once he asked me, 'Sardar Sahib, *aap kaa retire honay ka koee idea nahin hai?*' — Haven't you thought of retiring? I replied, 'Birlaji, *retire to main Nigambodh ghat mein hoonga*' — I will only retire in the cremation ground. He smiled and made complimentary references to my physical and mental fitness and the number of hours I spent in the office.

Three months before my contract was due to expire, I asked him whether he wanted to give me an extension. He was surprised. 'I did not realize you had only three months left. Let me think over the matter. I will send for you in a few days.'

I had already apprised Birla of what I thought of my deputy, N.C. Menon. I did not like the way he sponged off people, including me. But what bothered me most was his habit of going to the homes of Ministers, including the Prime Minister, and telling them about what was allegedly going on in *The*

Hindustan Times. Dhar and a few other members of the staff had told me about this. I did not believe them till I had evidence of it myself. He had written an editorial in which he castigated Maneka Gandhi and her mother. I scored out the lines, adding in the margin that the remarks were unwarranted. He passed on the information to the PM's office. By then anyone known to be friendly to Maneka was regarded as an enemy of Mrs Gandhi. Elections to the Delhi Metropolitan Council were due in a few months. The Congress party could not afford to have a man known to be critical of it as editor of the city's most important paper.

When I went to see Birla the next time, he looked somewhat dejected. He told me that he had decided to make a change in *The Hindustan Times* and was considering N.C. Menon as my successor. 'I have lots of reports against him about money matters and his morals but I want to give him a chance,' he said. 'But I hope you will continue to write your "Malice column". You can ask for whatever you like. And I hope we will remain friends.'

I was disappointed. I had no doubt he had succumbed to pressure put by Mrs Gandhi. Some time later *Probe* magazine interviewed me. I repeated my uncharitable view of *The Hindustan Times* being Delhi's worst paper with the largest circulation and how it was overstaffed with illiterate journalists because Birla could not say no to people in power. The interview created a furore in the Indian media. Menon wrote an editorial roundly abusing me as an editor who did no work, was a free loader in the habit of running down his successors, and that I did not know how to write correct English. With him in full cry was Promilla Kalhan, whom I had saved from lending money to Menon and who had earlier been most sycophantic in her attitude towards me. I sent a notice to *The Hindustan Times* that I would not be writing the 'Malice column' for them anymore.

A month after my column ceased appearing, an emissary from K.K. Birla came to see me in my home with the request that I resume writing my column for *The Hindustan Times*. I agreed, provided an announcement to that effect was carried on the front page, that Menon would have no right to meddle with it and my payment would be raised. All my terms were agreed. So I began to reappear in a paper whose editor did not wish my name to be mentioned anywhere.

About the time I took over as editor of *The Hindustan Times* I was sworn in in 1980 as a Member of the Rajya Sabha. Being an agnostic, I did not swear in the name of God and instead made an affirmation in the name of my conscience. I was allotted a seat next to the film star, Nargis Dutt. We were much sought after by other members: she for her looks and charm; I because I was the editor of the paper that mattered the most in the capital. I looked forward to making my maiden speech. I was confident that I would make my mark. That was not to be.

On the second day I went to parliament I was summoned by Mrs Gandhi to her office. She told me that after I had left the House the day before, the leader of the Communist Party, Bhupesh Gupta, had said nasty things about my nomination and described me as Mrs Gandhi's *chamcha* (hanger on). She gave me the book of rules with a clause marked by her which entitled members to speak if they had been personally attacked by another member. 'Send in your request to the Chairman in writing, quoting this clause. He will allow you to make your submission. We must not allow this kind of insinuation to go unchallenged,' she told me. As directed, I put in my request to Chairman Hidayatullah in writing that very day. I was informed that I would be given the opportunity to speak after the Question Hour on the following day.

I spent the afternoon preparing points in my defence. I could not very well indulge in self-praise and talk of the books I had written, or the papers I had edited and written for. I thought it best to emphasize that, although I had supported the Emergency when it was first imposed, I was virtually the only journalist to plead for its abrogation, asking for leaders of the Opposition to be released and the lifting of censorship on the press. L.K. Advani in his book had made favourable references to my efforts in these directions. I hoped that after I had my say Bhupesh Gupta would be gentleman enough to withdraw his insulting innuendos.

The next morning after the Question Hour Hidayatullah called on me to make my statement. I spoke in slow, measured tones in as dignified a manner as I could and appealed to Bhupesh Gupta that, having made the offending remark when I was not present, he should, as a seasoned parliamentarian and a gentleman, withdraw it. I was loudly applauded by the treasury benches. Hidayatullah asked Bhupesh Gupta if he had anything to say. He stood up and said, 'I stand by every word I said; I have nothing to withdraw.' I lost my temper and shouted, 'You are no gentleman; you are a bastard.'

'Bastard is unparliamentarian,' interposed Hidayatullah, 'it will be struck off the records, "no gentleman" can stay.'

The next morning's paper had the *chamcha* business on their front pages. This was not how I wanted to begin my career as a member of the House of Elders. My father had sat in the same House many years before me. He came to it in a white turban, black coat, striped trousers and spats on his brightly polished black shoes; he made no more than two speeches in the years he was a member, but they were carefully worded and read out. I felt I had let him down by an intemperate outburst and using unparliamentary language.

My years in the Rajya Sabha coincided with the beginnings of the Akali agitation in the Punjab rising to a crescendo with the storming of the Golden Temple by the army (code named 'Operation Blue Star'), which caused havoc to the sacred precincts, the loss of thousands of innocent lives, and that of the not-so-innocent Jarnail Singh Bindranwale. Six months later came the assassination of Mrs Gandhi and its fiery aftermath in which over 5,000 Sikhs were knifed or burnt alive in cities all over northern India. The situation in the Punjab came up in both Houses with nauseating regularity. To begin with the Rajya Sabha had three Akali members, Gurcharan Singh

Tohra, president of the S.G.P.C., Jagdev Singh Talwandi and Bibi Rajinder Kaur, daughter of Master Tara Singh; two Sikhs, H.S. Hanspal and Amarjit Kaur, sat on the Congress benches. Tohra and Talwandi rarely came to the House and the once or twice that Tohra stood up to speak in Punjabi what he said made no sense even in translation. Rajinder Kaur never bothered with issues or reasoned arguments. She could only shout and accuse the government of anti-Sikh bias.

Circumstances forced me to become the spokesman of the Sikh and Punjabi point of view. At first I had to contend with Amarjit Kaur who read out her speeches in clipped convent accents, and the anemic, barely audible whining of Hanspal. Then the Congress benches were reinforced with Darbara Singh, ex-Chief Minister of the Punjab, and the elephantine young man with a name as long as a giraffe's neck — Vishwajeet Prithvijeet Singh, a clean-shaven Sikh related to the Kapurthala family. He could match anyone in the Rajya Sabha in oratory; he also did his homework. Willy nilly I found myself at variance with the government which had pushed me into becoming the mouthpiece of the Akalis.

The Akalis were a bunch of narrow-minded bigots, single-minded in their pursuit of power in the Punjab. I had supported their demand for a Punjabi-speaking state because I felt that denying Punjabi what had been conceded to all the other regional languages was morally wrong and fraught with dangerous consequences. Once the Punjabi Suba was granted (in 1966), with the Sikhs forming 60 per cent of the population, I felt that the Sikhs had no right to ask for more than minor boundary adjustments, equitable distribution of river waters and more autonomy. I was opposed to the Anandpur Sahib Resolution which described the Sikhs as a nation apart from other Indians and thus germinating the seeds of a demand for a separate Sikh State — Khalistan. I felt passionately that Khalistan would be fatal to the interests of the Sikhs and to India.

The only Akali leader I had got to know reasonably well was Master Tara Singh. He had publicly denounced my first short history of the Sikhs without having read it. After he had done so, he came round to the view that my forecast that, if young Sikhs continued to renege from Khalsa traditions at the prevalent rate, the Sikhs would lose their distinct identity and become Hindus believing in Sikhism by the turn of the century. Whenever he came to Delhi, Masterji sent for me. I spent many hours with him in his small room in the dusty compound of Gurdwara Rakab Ganj. What his Akali colleagues were like I discovered fairly early. At one closed meeting there were only three others, besides Master Tara Singh and myself. One of them was Kapur Singh, ex-M.P., ex-I.C.S. officer, whom they regarded as their political mentor. We drafted the resolution demanding a Punjabi Suba. When I drove home, the police took down the number of my car; this was a routine practice which did not bother me. That evening my uncle Ujjal Singh who was then Governor of the Punjab, came to dine with my father. Before he had left Chandigarh he received a long telegram from the C.I.D. giving details of the discussion that had taken place in Master Tara Singh's room and what each of the other four had said. This was classified information but my uncle blurted it out to warn me against the consequences of mixing with Akalis. The next day when I told Masterji about this, he wrung his hands and said, 'There is no one I can trust; they are all in the pay of the police.'

I wanted to get better acquainted with Punjab politics and decided to go to Amritsar on the day the Akalis launched their *Dharma Yudh Morcha*. I had strong reservations about it. In the morning I had met leaders of the Congress and the B.J.P. groups. In the afternoon I walked up to Manji Sahib Gurdwara adjoining the Golden Temple to listen to Akali leaders and take in the scene. There must have been over 20,000 Sikhs sitting on the ground and another five to ten thousand standing around. On the dais, beside the Granth Sahib, sat the elite of the Akali party: Sant Harcharan Singh Longowal, Jathedar Tohra, ex-Chief Minister Prakash Singh Badal, ex-Finance Minister Balwant Singh, ex-Members of Parliament Balwant Singh Ramoowalia and Nirlep Kaur, as well as the sitting MP, Rajinder Kaur. The shining star of the galaxy was Jarnail Singh Bhindranwale. Tohra spotted me standing in the crowd. He sent two men to fetch me. Very reluctantly I allowed myself to be dragged along and found myself seated in the front row between the Granth Sahib and the microphone. Most of the speeches that followed were directed at me. Bhindranwale had never seen me. I heard him turn to one of his cronies and ask, '*Eh kaun hai?*' — who is he? I heard my name mentioned. He knew about me and what I had written against him. I had issued instructions that the prefix Sant (Saint) was not to be used with his name in any reference to him in the paper I edited. An Australian pressman had also told him that I thought that Bhindranwale was aiming to become the eleventh Guru of the Sikhs. 'If that fellow really said that,' Bhindranwale replied, 'I will have him and his family wiped out.' The Australian quickly recanted, to save our lives.

I find it very painful to sit on the ground and had to keep shifting my position to give relief to my aching knees and bottom. One fiery speech followed another. The crowd became restless and clamoured for Bhindranwale. At last he came to the microphone amid thunderous cries of '*Boley So Nihal — Sat Sri Akal*'. He was a tall, lean man with an aquiline nose, fiery eyes and a long, flowing beard. In his left hand he held a silver arrow, the sort seen in pictures of Guru Gobind Singh and Maharaja Ranjit Singh. A bandolier charged with bullets ran across his chest. He had a pistol attached in its holster and held a four-foot-long kirpan in his right hand. His speech was also addressed to me. 'I don't know this Sardar Sahib sitting near my feet,' he started. 'They tell me he is the Editor of some English paper called *The Hindustan Times*. I can't speak English. I am told he writes that I create hatred between the Sikhs and Hindus. This is a lie. I am a preacher. I go from village to village telling Sikhs to come back to the path of the tenth Guru. I tell them to stop clipping their beards, to refrain from taking opium and smoking tobacco, I baptise them into the Khalsa panth.' There were loud cries of *Sat Sri Akal* to express approval. He warmed to his theme. 'If I had my way, you know what I would do to all these Sardars who drink whisky-shisky every evening? I would douse them in kerosene oil and set fire to the bloody lot.' The announcement was greeted with prolonged cries of

'*Boley So Nihal — Sat Sri Akal*'. It was ironical that the vast majority of the audience applauding him were Sikh Jats notorious for their addiction to hard liquor. I turned to Badal and Balwant Singh, both of whom had taken Scotch in my home and said, 'What Chief Minister Darbara Singh has been unable to do with all his police, this chap will do with one matchstick.' They sniggered.

I had an exchange of views with retired General Shahbeg Singh. He was another tall, lean man with a long, grey beard. He had been clean-shaven when he trained and led the Mukti Bahini in the liberation of Bangladesh. He had been cashiered on charges of corruption and was very bitter with the government. I discovered that, without a single exception, all the army officers and men who joined the Akalis had been dismissed or superseded in service and had personal grievances for the way they had been treated. At one time there were over 10,000 with the Akalis.

I followed the Akali procession through the narrow streets of Amritsar to the police station, where a fleet of buses was lined up to take those who offered themselves for arrest to different jails in the Punjab. Amongst them were Tohra, Badal and General Shahbeg Singh. It was a well-organized affair. The men sat down in the police station's courtyard to be served a sumptuous evening meal brought from the gurdwara. Then at their leisure they boarded buses and were driven away. This 'sacrifice' was a charade of the *morchas* of the 1920s when Akali volunteers were beaten with steel-tipped staves and dragged by their long hair to be put in handcuffs and leg irons.

I returned to my hotel late in the evening. A mood of depression overtook me. Much as I felt emotionally involved with my community, I could not regard this agitation, launched entirely to get the Congress government in the State out of power and put Badal, Balwant and company in its place, as a battle for righteousness — *Dharma Yuddha*. It was selfish power-seeking by the Akalis, an exploitation of the emotions of the common mass of Sikhs against the State government. I know of only one way of getting over depression: a couple of stiff pegs of Scotch.

Bhindranwale was not the only man whose ire I evoked. I had also to cross swords with S.L. Khurana who, after having served as General Manager of *The Hindustan Times*, was appointed Lt Governor of Delhi. He had been on very friendly terms with me, and whenever I had a pretty visitor I rang him up to come over to take a look. It was after he was named Lt Governor of Delhi that one of my most trusted reporters, Prabha Dutt, came and told me, 'I have a scoop, I will only give it to you if you promise not to kill it.' I gave her my promise. Her story was of Khurana wangling the admission of his son to a medical college by transferring a seat reserved for a foreign student to another university and pressurizing the Principal into taking his son instead. I had no doubt the story was correct. That evening Khurana rang me up and said he would like to drop in for a few minutes on his way to the airport where he was to receive some dignitary. He requested me not to use the story about his son's admission. I promised to do my best. When I went back to the office after dinner, I had the story killed. It was published by another Delhi paper. The next morning I had to face a very angry and tearful Prabha Dutt. She accused me of breaking my word and succumbing to pressure. I did my best to assuage her hurt feelings and, since the story had already been published, allowed her much more detailed version to be carried in *The Hindustan Times* the next day. Khurana was extremely angry with me because *The Hindustan Times* had a much wider circulation than the other paper and he, as one-time Executive President, felt let down. Besides being angry with me, he became vindictive against K.K. Birla. He went out of his way to reject some business project of the Birlas which had been sanctioned by his predecessor. Then Khurana was transferred as Governor to Tamil Nadu. In my 'Malice' column I wrote about Delhi's gain being Tamil Nadu's loss and illustrated it with the way he had misused his clout as Lt Governor to get his son admitted to a medical college and thus deprived a more deserving candidate of his rightful opportunity. I also referred to the vindictiveness he had shown towards his erstwhile employer. Khurana promptly took the matter to the Press Council, acquired the services of the Attorney-General of the

State, and a string of senior lawyers of Madras, all at government expense, to present his case. I was represented by Siddhartha Shankar Ray who was a standing counsel for the Birlas. The case dragged on for many months. Ultimately, like most cases before the Press Council, a compromise was arrived at: *The Hindustan Times* published a few lines to the effect that it did not intend to hurt the feelings of Governor Khurana.

Gopal Singh Dardi's case against me also arose from my comments on his being appointed Lt Governor of Goa. Dardi was the kind of person I could not come to terms with. I first heard of him as the editor of a weekly paper, *Liberator*, in which he ventilated the grievances of the Sikhs. Next, he and his close friend at the time, Kapur Singh, were cited as correspondents in a divorce case filed by a one-eyed English editor of an automobile journal. Dardi divorced his first wife and married the Englishman's Sikh wife and adopted her daughter. After I had refused to appear before the Das Commission constituted to go into the grievances of the Sikhs (Master Tara Singh had asked Sikhs to boycott the Commission), Dardi agreed to tender evidence to prove that Sikhs were not discriminated against. Pratap Singh Kairon, Chief Minister of Punjab, rewarded him by having him nominated to the Rajya Sabha. He made very little contribution to its proceedings but went on to translate the Granth Sahib, had it published in four volumes and sold to State libraries and universities. I was asked by All India Radio to review his work. After conceding the amount of labour that must have gone into translating nearly 6,000 hymns, I ended the talk by saying that now it was time somebody took upon themselves the task of rendering them into English. The AIR officer did not notice the last damning sentence and let it go on the air; Dardi was furious. But undaunted by adverse criticism, he sent his translation to the Nobel Prize Committee and to the King of Sweden. His Majesty courteously acknowledged receipt of the volumes. This was good enough for Dardi to inform All India Radio and P.T.I. that he had been awarded the Nobel Prize for literature. I heard the announcement in the 9 pm news. A few minutes later somebody rang me up from the radio station and asked me if I would care to pay a tribute to Dardi. I told him that the story was a canard as the Nobel Prize was never given to a work of translation. The P.T.I. release was not taken seriously by any paper, but it was published with the introductory 'it is reliably learnt' nevertheless. Dardi's reputation as a man of letters had received a boost: it was spread around that he had *almost* won the Nobel Prize.

At the end of his six-year term in the Rajya Sabha Dardi managed to get appointed as ambassador to an East European country. During this assignment he called on the Pope and presented him a copy of a poem he had composed on Jesus Christ. He had his photographs with the Pope widely publicized. The only one who did not take Dardi seriously was myself! But whatever I said about him was dismissed as envy for a man who had done better in life than I had. After retiring from his foreign assignments Dardi bought a lot of real estate in Chandigarh, where he set up a printing press, and a large house in Delhi. He had done well for himself. He wrote a series of articles on the important role he had played in the negotiations between Mr Jinnah, the Congress leaders, and the Akalis on the eve of Partition. This was a figment of his imagination, as records of the Partition discussions have nothing to say about him. He approached Giani Zail Singh and Mrs Gandhi to appoint him as a governor. The Giani had strong reservations against him. Mrs Gandhi gave in. She told Gianiji that though she had many adverse reports about Dardi, he could be made a governor since there was no Sikh governor. So Dardi found himself in the beautiful Raj Bhavan on the sea-shore of Goa. In my 'Malice' column I traced Dardi's career and added that only in a sick society like India could a bluffer bluff his way into positions of importance. I quoted Sheikh Saadi's memorable lines:

Sana-e-khud bakhud guftan
Na Zebad Mard-e-daana ra
Choon Zan pistan-e-khud maalad
Kuja lazzat shavad Baakee?

(It does not behove a man of wisdom
to use his tongue in praise of himself.
What pleasure does a woman beget
If with her own hands she rubs her breasts?)

Dardi rang up Birla. Birla was abroad. Dardi sent me legal notice claiming one and a half crore rupees in damages for maligning his character, and threatened to take me to court. Instead, he took me to the Press Council. He knew he couldn't get round the self-generated story of having won the Nobel Prize. As in the Khurana case, so with that of Dardi. After many hearings, Justice Grover, Chairman of the Press Council, drafted a compromise formula and the case was withdrawn.

I thought Dardi would have liked to see me dead. I didn't know the man. I happened to be in Goa for a meeting of Orient Longman's Board of Directors. Two fellow directors who made it a point to call on local dignitaries wherever they went, called on Dardi and were invited for dinner. From them he learnt that I was in Goa. The next morning, while I was in the hotel lobby awaiting transport to take me to the airport, there was a call for me from Raj Bhavan. I told the receptionist to say that I had left. When I got to the airport, the airport manager had the V.I.P. lounge opened for me and asked me to ring up the Governor. I said I felt happier sitting in the public lounge and would ring up as soon as I could. A few minutes later the Governor's A.D.C. arrived at the airport and begged me to sit in the V.I.P. lounge and speak to the Governor. 'Otherwise I will lose my job,' he pleaded. I spoke to Dardi. He asked me why I had stayed in a hotel when Raj Bhavan was like my own home, etc., etc. I didn't know how to respond to a person who could turn so sugary towards a man who had criticized him without mercy.

It was much the same when he was transferred as Governor of Nagaland. My wife and I were invited by Chief Minister Jamir to spend Christmas with them at Kohima. He had a large Christmas-eve dinner for us. I hoped Dardi would not be there. He and his wife were the first guests to arrive. Both embraced us. Mrs Dardi sat next to me and said how much she had looked forward to meeting me. They insisted we have coffee with them before we left for Dimapur on our way back to Delhi. We did. They were most cordial. He made arrangements for us to travel to Dimapur on an undamaged part of the road, normally only meant for use of the army, and for our stay at Dimapur. The last I saw of Dardi was at a function organized by the Foundation for Freedom of Information, where Prime Minister V.P. Singh gave away cheques of Rs 25,000 to five media people, including myself. Dardi came to tell me that he was there only to see me get the award. A few weeks later, I read of Dardi's sudden death from heart failure. I was then at my wit's end about what to write for my column 'This above all' which appears every week in *The Tribune* of Chandigarh. I wrote a long obituary on Dr Gopal Singh Dardi. He belonged to the tribe which always come up as winners.

The article that really put me in a spot as editor of *The Hindustan Times* was not written by me but by my colleague B.M. Sinha. It was on corruption in the judiciary. It was a well authenticated article on how many judges of different high courts patronized some lawyers, discriminated against others, helped their relations in the legal profession to build their practices, and had their own sons of mediocre ability elevated to the bench. There was no doubt that the article was contemptuous of the way our judiciary conducted itself. I was assured by everyone, including eminent lawyers like Nani Palkhiwala, Soli Sorabjee and retired Chief Justice R.S. Narula, that things were much worse than portrayed in the article and that it was time somebody brought it out in the open. I was served with a notice to appear before the Punjab and Haryana High Court. Dozens of lawyers offered their services to me free of charge. I was asked by the Chief Justice whether I knew that in cases of contempt of court, truth was no defence. I said I knew, but wider public interest had compelled me to publish the article. I refused to purge my contempt through an apology and asked the court to adjourn the hearing to another date when Nani Palkhiwala would appear for me. Another date was fixed. Nani's name made the judges have second thoughts on convicting me. They decided to withdraw the case against me on some technical ground.

Then the Allahabad High Court summoned my presence along with B.M. Sinha and the acting General Manager of *The Hindustan Times*, Dr Rajhans (later Member of the Lok Sabha). We had Siddhartha Shankar Ray to defend us. The court-room was packed with lawyers. Justice Katju (B.M. Sinha's article had hinted at him) and a judge recently appointed comprised the Bench. Katju told Ray in no uncertain terms that, unless we tendered an unqualified apology, he would send us to jail. The lawyers standing behind me urged me not to give in. Ray asked the court to give us time to think over the matter. We were told to appear next morning: it had to be an unqualified apology or some days in Naini jail till Ray could have us bailed out by the Supreme Court. It was mid-summer and the thought of spending time in a mosquito- and rat-infested cell did not appeal to me. B.M. Sinha stuck to his guns and said he would rather go to jail than apologize. Ray told us that the court would not accept the apology of one and that all three would have to act in unison. Rajhans and I prevailed on Sinha not to martyr us along with him. Next day we tendered an unqualified apology, but with a firm conviction that the judiciary stank with corruption and needed to be exposed.

Let me return to the Rajya Sabha, because it dominated the three years (1980–3) when I was editor of *The Hindustan Times* and three further years after that. These six years witnessed rising insurgency in Punjab and I had more than the normal share of speaking expected of a nominated member.

I was dismayed to see how lightly most members took their responsibilities. There was usually a full House when the proceedings began at 11 am with Question Hour. Some questions appeared with monotonous regularity. One that never missed a session was about soft drinks: members took up cudgels on behalf of their patrons — Ramesh Chauhan's Limca versus Charanjit Singh's Campa Cola. No one had any doubt as to which member was beholden to one or the other. Some members were congenital raisers of supplementaries, and if they were disallowed, they raised points of order which were inevitably ruled out. And there were members like the portly Piloo Mody who kept up a running commentary on the proceedings. However, he was a man of ready wit and raised more laughter than anyone else. He held pronounced conservative, pro-American views and was often accused by members of the ruling Congress party as being a 'Washington patriot'. Once he came to the House wearing a placard reading 'I am a C.I.A. agent'. The Chairman ordered him to remove it. He did so, remarking 'I am no longer a C.I.A. agent'. The one member who took it upon himself to heckle Piloo Mody was J.C. Jain, a very loud-mouthed member of the Congress. Once, when he kept needling him, Piloo lost his temper and shouted, 'Stop barking!' Jain was up on his feet yelling, 'Sir, he is calling me a dog. This is unparliamentary language.' Chairman Hidayatullah agreed, and ordered, 'This will not go on the record.' Not to be outdone, Piloo Mody retorted, 'All right then, stop braying.' Jain did not know what the word implied. It stayed on record. When India put its first satellite in orbit there were rounds of speeches to congratulate Prime Minister Indira Gandhi and the Indian scientists. Piloo Mody also paid fulsome compliments to both. He then turned to Mrs Gandhi and said, 'Madam Prime Minister, we know our scientists have taken great strides in technology. I would be obliged if you could now enlighten us as to why our telephones don't work.'

Quite a few back-benchers regarded shouting at the top of their voices and gesticulating wildly as an essential part of their parliamentary obligations. The noisiest among them were lady members quick to take umbrage at the remotest hint of discrimination against their sex. Once the Delhi police was being pilloried over the gang rape of a gangsters' moll, Maya Tyagi. A lady member of the Communist Party, who was short, fat and wore thick glasses, went for the government. 'Every day we hear of a rape here or a rape there. It is rape, rape, rape all the time. What is the government doing about it?'

Nargis Dutt, sitting beside me, shot up from her seat and

shouted, 'Why are you so worried? No one is ever going to rape you.' It was an unkind remark addressed to an uncommonly plain-looking woman. No one protested.

Question Hour was always lively and covered a wide range of subjects, though not always of national importance. What followed is something unique to the Indian democratic tradition: Zero Hour. This is a kind of free for all. A dozen members are on their feet shouting about what is uppermost in their minds. Chairmen often retire to their chambers and let their deputies deal with the pandemonium. While the shouting is going on, he or she will call on ministers to place papers on the table of the House. By the time this is over, members are allowed to raise issues for special attention. Few members stay to listen to them. The House empties quickly. So does the press gallery. Everyone who has nothing against his name in the proceedings of the day adjourns for tea or coffee in the Central Hall. Here political differences are put aside for far more serious business — gossip and spreading scandal. The private lives of ministers and lady members of the House are exposed. Mrs Gandhi, who never came to the Central Hall, had informers to let her know what members were saying about her behind her back.

After Darbara Singh's government was dismissed in Punjab and the State put under President's rule, debates on Punjab became a regular feature of Parliament. Terrorism began to spread its tentacles over the State and beyond its borders. Bhindranwale's speeches became more acerbic and contemptuous of Hindus. He would refer to Mrs Gandhi as *Panditan di dhee* or *Bahmani* — that Pandit's daughter or the Brahman woman. Hindus were *dhotian, topian walley* — those who wear dhotis and caps. In one speech he exhorted every Sikh to kill 32 Hindus, not 31, not 33 — only 32 he said (in that way the entire population of Hindus would be accounted for). I do not know why more Sikhs did not denounce him as a homicidal maniac. During the days when he was making these hateful utterances I called on Sant Longowal, who was nominal head of the *Dharma Yuddh Morcha*, in his room in the offices of the S.G.P.C. This meeting with Longowal did not yield much copy: I sensed that he was unhappy with Bhindranwale but was unable to do anything about him. Bhindranwale was entrenched in the Akal Takht, his armed bodyguards had the run of the Golden Temple complex and were more than eager to bump off anyone their leader wanted out of the way. I asked Longowal why he allowed Bhindranwale to say nasty things about the Hindus from the sacred precincts of the Akal Takht. Longowal replied, *'O tay saada danda hai'* — he is our stave [to hit the government with].

As tension mounted in Punjab and the killing of innocent people by terrorists at the behest of Bhindranwale increased, the government realized that its options were closing; it had to somehow get hold of Bhindranwale again (he had been arrested earlier on charges of murder and released at the time and place of his choosing). By now Bhindranwale and his military adviser, General Shahbeg Singh, had converted the Akal Takht into a fortress and a variety of arms had been smuggled in with trucks bringing in rations for the gurdwara kitchen. The government had left it too late, and a violent confrontation was fast becoming inevitable. On many occasions I warned the government against sending the army into the Golden Temple because it would rouse the wrath of the entire Sikh community, most of which was unconcerned with Bhindranwale or the Akalis. 'You don't know the Sikhs,' I once told the Home Minister P.C. Sethi, a peace-loving Jain. 'They can be like a swarm of hornets. You put your head in their nest and you will be stung all over your face.' He assured me that the government had no intention of sending the army into the Temple. So did Mrs Gandhi, more than once.

It is not known when Mrs Gandhi came round to the view that she had no option but to order the army into the Golden Temple, and who her advisers were at the time. The names of Rajiv Gandhi, Arun Nehru, Arun Singh and Digvijay Singh were mentioned. It is also unknown who chose the date when operations should commence. There is no doubt that President Zail Singh was kept in the dark. When Mrs Gandhi persuaded him to put Punjab under military rule, she did not tell him that she had decided to order the army to clear the Temple of Bhindranwale and his armed followers. When it came to Punjab or Sikh affairs, she did not trust Gianiji. And none of her advisers had the foggiest notion of Sikh traditions. They chose 5 June 1984 as the day to launch the operation. It was the death anniversary of Guru Arjun, the founder of the Hari Mandir, a day when hundreds of thousands of Sikhs were expected to come on pilgrimage from remote areas. Nor were alternative methods of getting at Bhindranwale considered seriously. He could have been overpowered by a band of commandos in plain clothes; the Temple complex could have been cordoned off; the people inside deprived of rations and access to potable water and forced to come out in the open to surrender or be picked up by snipers. It would have taken a couple of days longer, but would have been comparatively bloodless.

However, the army stormed the Golden Temple with tanks, armoured cars and frogmen, with helicopters hovering overhead to give directions. The battle that ensued lasted two days and nights. In the cross-fire almost 5,000 men, women and children perished. The Akal Takht was reduced to rubble by heavy guns fired from tanks; the central shrine which both parties had declared *hors de combat* was hit by over 70 bullets. The entrance (*deohri*) had a large portion blasted off; archives containing hundreds of hand-written copies of the Granth Sahib and *hukumnamas* (edicts) issued under the signatures of the Gurus were reduced to ashes. Even Mrs Gandhi, who had been assured that the operation would not last more than two hours, was horrified at the extent of damage caused to sacred property and the horrendous loss of lives. Instead of admitting that she had blundered, she decided to cover up the whole thing with a barrage of lies.

Despite my indifference and even hostility to religion, I had no doubt in my mind that I should re-affirm my identity with my community. I regarded Bhindranwale as an evil man who deserved his fate. But 'Operation Blue Star' went well beyond the slaying of Bhindranwale: it was a well-calculated and deliberate slap in the face of an entire community. I felt strongly that I must register my protest. I did not consult anyone: my wife was away in Kasauli, my daughter in office, my son in Bombay. I rang up Tarlochan Singh, the Press Adviser of President Zail Singh, and asked for an appointment with the latter. I was asked to come straightaway. I took the framed citation awarding me the Padma Bhushan under the signature of President V.V. Giri. Tarlochan had anticipated that I had come to return it to the government. Giani Zail Singh was in a state of acute depression. 'I know how you feel,' he said to me, 'but don't be hasty. Think over the matter for a few days and then decide what you should do.' I held my ground. 'No Gianiji. I don't want to give myself time to change my mind. I had sworn that if the army entered the temple I would renounce the honours bestowed on me by this government.' He asked Tarlochan to put aside the citation and continued talking to me. 'I don't think my *qaum* [community] will ever forgive me for this,' he said. He was looking for some kind of assurance to the contrary. 'No Gianiji, I don't think the Sikhs will ever forgive you for Blue Star.' He was in the depths of despair. 'Do you think it would serve any purpose if I resign now?' I told him it was too late: whether or not he resigned, the Sikhs would hold him responsible for the desecration of their holiest shrine.

I knew Gianiji would keep my returning the Padma Bhushan to himself. I did not give him a chance. From Rashtrapati Bhavan I drove straight to the P.T.I. office on Parliament Street and handed over the short text of my letter of protest and about returning the award. 'To kill a rat you don't have to bring down your house,' it read. The evening papers carried the news; the morning papers had it on their front pages.

What followed was a painful discovery to me. Overnight I became a kind of folk hero of the Sikhs: the first to openly denounce the government. And a villain for Hindus. I, who had always preached secular ideals and condemned Bhindranwale, had come out in my 'true colours' they said. I was flooded with letters and telegrams: Sikhs applauding me for having shown how a Sikh should act; Hindus denouncing me as an arch enemy of the country. Even Girilal Jain, a man I had regarded as being above communal prejudices, wrote an editorial against me. Every pressman who came to interview me asked why I had not resigned from the Rajya Sabha as well. I told them that I was not going to deprive myself of the one forum from which I could tell the government and the people what grievous wrong it had done to the Sikhs and the country.

A few days later I visited Amritsar. Entrance to the Golden Temple was still restricted. But they could not very well keep me out. I was met at the railway station by an army officer who told me that he had been deputed by General K.S. Brar, who had played a leading role in Operation Blue Star, to be by my side for the sake of my safety. In fact he had been deputed to keep an eye on my movements.

I went round the *parikrama* and saw the devastation caused by the army. (Workmen were hastily filling in dents left by bullets and cleaning up the marble floor of blood-stains.) Soldiers were still about in considerable strength. Near the rubble that once was the Akal Takht stood a signboard in English and Hindi reading, 'Smoking and drinking in these premises is prohibited.' This is what our jawans had been doing after taking over the Temple. When I drew my escort's attention to it, he ordered the board to be removed. I saw clusters of peasants gazing at the ruins of the Akal Takht with tears running down their cheeks. Doordarshan had hauled up a very frightened head-priest, Kirpal Singh, and made him read out a statement that very little damage had been caused to the buildings: *'O Kirpala annha see?'* — was that Kirpal Singh blind? people asked. In the central shrine I counted the number of fresh bullet marks. In front of each there were peasant women in tears of anger, their mouths full of curses. *'Inhaan da beej naas hoey!'* — May their seed perish! *'Kuttian dee aulaad!'* — Progeny of dogs, etc. From down below the balcony came the strains of Gurbani. It sounded utterly out of place.

For many days parties of Sikh men and women came to call on me unbidden and without appointment to condole with me. They included well-dressed ladies who spoke in English. A day earlier, Jathedar Rachpal Singh, at the bidding of Home Minister Buta Singh, had called a press conference at Hotel Imperial to explain the government's point of view. The press, including foreign journalists, had turned up in full force. The Jathedar read out a statement and, before allowing questions, asked guests to stay on after the conference was over and be his guests for lunch. A lady strode up to the platform and slapped him across the face, knocking off his turban. 'You shameless creature! Our Temple has been destroyed and you want to celebrate it with a luncheon party?' The press conference was hastily concluded. This lady, a school teacher, was among those who called on me.

Asad Farooqi, Station House Officer of Tughlak Road Police Station which included Gurdwara Bangla Sahib, rang me up and asked if he could see me. When we met he told me that he was at the gurdwara every afternoon to hear the speeches being delivered there. My name came up frequently and it was often announced that I would be coming to the gurdwara to address the congregation. We talked for quite a while and I told him of the death and destruction caused in Amritsar: *'Zara see baat peh aap Sarkar say itney khafaa ho gayey'* — On such a small matter you have become so cross with the government, he exclaimed.

'Zara see baat! Do you know upwards of 5,000 Sikhs were slain in this single operation? You call it *zara see baat!'* I replied.

'Itney Mussulman yeh har saal maar daaltey hain' — They kill as many Muslims every year, he maintained. I could not resist retorting *'Aap Mussalmanon ko to maar khaaney kee aadat par gayee hai'* — You Muslims have got used to being beaten regularly; *'Inshallah, Sikkhon ko bhee par jayegee'* — If God wills Sikhs will also get habituated to it.

In my articles and speeches I pleaded with Mrs Gandhi to go to the Golden Temple as a pilgrim and ask for forgiveness. I assured her that Sikhs were an emotional people and the gesture would assuage their feeling of hurt. She allowed herself to be guided by her Home Minister, Buta Singh. They decided to have the Akal Takht rebuilt exactly as it was and in as short a time as possible, so that the Temple complex could be handed back to the S.G.P.C. Money was no problem. A firm of Sikh contractors, Skipper & Co., owned by Tejwant Singh, was given a blank cheque to do the job — including getting the gold to recover the domes.

Buta Singh was aware of the Sikh tradition of building temples through voluntary labour, *Kaar Sewa*. Failing to get anyone respectable to lead it, he hired the services of a fat Nihang who described himself as Sultan-ul-Qaum, ruler of the community, to do the job. This Falstaff-sized man, known to be addicted to hashish, arrived with a motley bunch of followers who went through the motions of taking bricks and mortar to the site of the building. Evening after evening Doordarshan dutifully showed them on the screen. When the matter was raised in the Rajya Sabha I had to face the ire of three Sikh members sitting with the Congress: Amarjeet Kaur, Hanspal, and the new entrant, ex-Chief Minister Darbara Singh. When I described Santa Singh Nihang as 'a fat old buffoon', they were on their feet to protest that my language was unparliamentary and should be struck off the records. Darbara Singh followed it up by saying, 'Mr Khushwant Singh, Baba Santa Singh is a much better Sikh than you are!' I acknowledged that his observation was correct and added, 'I have never claimed to be a good Sikh. But let me tell all three of you who claim to be such devout Sikhs that today what I say matters to the Sikhs; Sikhs like you have become irrelevant.'

The main debate on Operation Blue Star had to await the publication of the White Paper. I stayed back in the House till the first copies of the book were released and spent long hours going over it again and again. I knew I would be the only one to speak against it, as by then the Akali members had resigned. The whip of the Congress party had lined up his henchmen to heckle me and put across the official point of view. When I was called on to speak the House was full. Right from the start, cronies of the Congress party tried to barrack me. Jayalalitha, who had been recently elected to the House, rose to my defence and asked the Chairman to let me have my say without interruption. I let loose whatever oratory I had at my command and roundly denounced the government for what it had perpetrated. I criticized the army for the ham-handed way it had done the job and quoted an Urdu couplet to illustrate the outcome of serious errors of judgement,

Voh waqt bhee deykha taareekh kee gharion nay
Lamhon nay khataa kee thee
Sadiyon nay sazaa paayee

(The ages of history have recorded times
when for an error made in a few seconds
centuries had to pay the price.)

Only members of the Opposition applauded my speech. Mrs Gandhi, sitting in the Lok Sabha, was kept informed of what I was saying; she described my speech as anti-national.

All the speakers who spoke after me had something to say on what I had said. Narasimha Rao, who had replaced P.C. Sethi as Home Minister, jibed at me for trying to pose as a military expert who could advise the army command on how to go about its job.

I also did the best I could in defending Pakistan against biased and unverified propaganda fed to the press through government hand-outs. Whether it was about Pakistan's alleged involvement in maintaining training camps for Sikh terrorists, or supplying arms, or fomenting communal riots, it was left solely to me to question the government's contentions. An issue that came up in Question Hour was the future of Jinnah House in Bombay. After Jinnah had left for Pakistan, his mansion on Malabar Hill had been leased to the British as the residence for their Deputy High Commissioner. When the lease was due to expire, our government agreed to let it out to Pakistan for its consulate. It was a solemn undertaking given by the Government of India in writing. Pakistan's Consul-General had arrived and was staying in a hotel awaiting the day he could move in.

Suddenly the Indian government decided to go back on its word and cancelled the lease. This was Mrs Gandhi's personal decision and based on the fear that the house would become a place of pilgrimage for Pakistanis. Why she had not thought about this earlier or what was wrong if Pakistanis did in fact regard it as a semi-sacred monument was not clear to me. Muslim M.Ps were understandably shy of saying anything which might give the impression that they harboured pro-Pakistani sympathies. I had a field day roundly condemning my own government for breaking a commitment made in writing. When Home Minister Narasimha Rao had no answer, he descended to insinuation. 'Why do you get so emotional and excited about everything that has to do with Pakistan?' he asked.

As a litterateur of sorts, I was allowed in the Rajya Sabha to have my say on book publishing and the three cultural Akademies subsidized by the government. Having at one time been a member of its committee, I had some personal knowledge of the way the Sahitya Akademi functioned. The giving of annual awards had become a racket. At one time I had reported against a professor who approached me to get him the prize. He was hauled over the coals by Dr Radhakrishnan, then President of the Sahitya Akademi. Some years later, a lady who was the wife of the officer in charge of the President's household, drove up to my home in a Rashtrapati Bhavan car and asked me to propose her name for the prize. She told me that President Radhakrishnan had assured her that, if the proposal came from me, he would see it through. I told her that canvassing was forbidden, and of what I had done to the professor the year before. She retorted: *'Eh taan gallaan karan diyaan nay'* — This is just talk — everyone has to have an approach to get anything. I rated this lady's poetry highly and felt she deserved the award, but I also felt she deserved to be blacklisted for canvassing. I wrote to Krishna Kripalani, Secretary of the Akademi. The same Radhakrishnan who had read a moral sermon to the poor professor saw that the lady got the award that year and her husband the year after. I resigned from the Akademi's committee.

When the Sahitya Akademi came up for discussion in the Rajya Sabha, I quoted the Khosla Committee report on its functioning. It had indicated that the worst form of skullduggery was practised in the giving of awards for Punjabi. Every single member of its Executive Committee had got the award. At one meeting a lady member had cast the decisive vote in her own favour! The House was rocked with laughter. I pleaded with the government to abolish awards and relinquish state patronage over literature. Giving money to writers and poets was like sprinkling fertilizer over a patch of weeds. Creative writers should fend for themselves and those who could not survive should be allowed to perish in oblivion. Publishing their works at government expense, and buying stocks to place in government-controlled libraries, only encouraged the second rate. They heard what I had to say, they were amused by the examples I cited, then they passed the grants asked for by the Akademi.

Equally light-hearted was my response to allegations about several MPs going on free trips to Taiwan and South Korea at the invitation of one Ram Swarup, who was an agent of the Taiwanese and the Israelis and of pronounced anti-communist views. Ram Swarup was arrested on charges of espionage. I had known him since the days I had set up the Indian Friends of Israel. I found him an uncouth and unsavoury character who tried to make the organization into a right-wing Hindu body with a marked anti-Muslim bias. I had not seen him for many years when he asked me if I would care to visit Taiwan as a guest of its government. My travel and hospitality would be taken care of. I agreed and decided to take my wife along at my own expense. We had a wonderful time watching parades, visiting beauty spots and nuclear installations, and spent an afternoon in underground bunkers on an island facing mainland China. The question of MPs accepting the hospitality of a government that India did not recognize through a man of doubtful antecedents was raised by the communists. Two ministers who had visited Taiwan resigned. Others named were allowed to make statements. They made angry speeches denouncing those who had cast aspersions on their patriotism and pleaded ignorance of Ram Swarup's background. When it came to my turn, I admitted that I knew Ram Swarup and his connections with South Korea, Taiwan and Israel; that I was happy to have visited Taiwan: it was a beautiful country with beautiful women. Furthermore, I had given the Taiwanese government and the C.I.A. classified information to which they had no access, viz., the exact location of the Qutub Minar and the Red Fort, Delhi's beautiful mosques and mausolea. The House enjoyed this light-hearted confession, and the communists were made to look silly.

Needless to say, I became a thorn in the side of the government. Over the years that I enjoyed the privileges of being an MP (a spacious bungalow, free telephone, free travel and much else) I also felt that it achieved very little because members did not take their jobs very seriously. I read a very amusing article in *The Spectator* written by their columnist Auberon Waugh on British parliamentarians. He described them as semiliterate and useless 'dogs bodies' — nothing had happened to him. In my 'Malice' column I rested my gun on Waugh's shoulders and fired the same kind of buckshot at members of the Rajya Sabha, adding at the end of each paragraph 'dare I write the sort of thing Waugh has written about his MPs about members of our Parliament?'

Unknown to me, Satpal Mittal of the Congress who had once professed fraternal affection for me, got 71 members to move a privilege motion for contempt of the House against me. When I heard about it, I was not unduly worried. If the matter was brought to the House, I would get another opportunity to say what I thought about my fellow MPs. That opportunity did not come. One morning, as I sat in the House during Question Hour, I got a note from the Secretary to say that the Chairman wanted me to stay on as he had an important announcement to make concerning me.

After Question Hour, Chairman Hidayatullah rose to draw attention to a privilege motion moved against me. He read out my article and the charge of contempt made by Mittal and 71 others. He criticized my knowledge of Latin (I had fabricated some words) and proceeded to cite precedents of the British Parliament. Then he dismissed the privilege motion. After he retired from Vice-Presidentship and Chairmanship of the Rajya Sabha, he said in a speech delivered in Bombay that the moment he had enjoyed most as Chairman of the Rajya Sabha was dealing with the privilege motion against me.

There is a lot more I could have written and said about my fellow MPs which would not be flattering. Many only signed their names to get their monthly allowances, without even coming into the House. Many came because in the heat of summer it was the coolest place to be in; the eminent Hindi novelist who for a time sat next to me was fast asleep within five minutes of taking his seat. He had been there for several years. Whenever I asked him for the names of members who were speaking he would answer with a beatific smile *'Naam vaam to main kisee ka naheen jaanta'* — I don't know anyone's name or anything about anyone. After his death he was replaced by an elderly Muslim who always suffered from a bad stomach. His silent farts stank. Every time he took his seat, I would move to another place till he left. There was also a portly member from Assam with a similar problem. Whenever he had too much wind in his belly he would let off a loud fart that echoed in the hall. I was often tempted to move a privilege motion against loud farters.

More annoying than snoring or farting was the nauseating sycophancy displayed by members towards the Prime Minister and those in the cabinet. Every Thursday, when Mrs Gandhi came to the Rajya Sabha, the Congress benches were full. As soon as she got up to leave, half a dozen Congress MPs would run after her to the corridor. It was the same with senior ministers. A change in status brought a sea-change in their behaviour. The obscenely fat Kalpnath Rai, who was often pulled up for bad manners (snoring, reading papers, talking to his cronies during debates), became arrogant when he was made a minister and would beckon lady members with the crook of his index finger. When I first became an MP it was generally believed that I was very close to Mrs Gandhi (which was not true) and her son Sanjay. Ministers and MPs were always coming over to chat with me. When it got known that I no longer enjoyed her favour, they kept their distance from me.

By sheer coincidence, three members who sat next to me died in quick succession. The first was the beautiful Nargis Dutt; then the Hindi novelist; then the elderly Muslim. On my last session their place was taken by the eminent ornithologist, the nonagenarian Salim Ali. He died a few months later. Perhaps the seat bore seeds of mortality; or being next to me speeded their departure.

I was still a Member of Parliament when Mrs Gandhi was assassinated on the morning of 31 October 1984. Despite my differences with her I was deeply distressed to hear of her dastardly murder at the hands of her own security guards, both Sikhs. If circumstances had allowed, I would most certainly have gone to condole with the family and pay my last tribute to her when her body was cremated. I had no great admiration for her as Prime Minister and am convinced that all that has gone wrong with the country emanated from her. She could be petty and vindictive, as she showed herself to be in her dealings with her widowed daughter-in-law, Maneka. She could be very discourteous to senior officials like Kewal Singh (retired Ambassador to the United States), and Jagat Mehta (retired Foreign Secretary, whom she suspected of having let her down). She particularly enjoyed snubbing people who assumed she was their friend. She was nasty to Dom Moraes after he had written her biography; she accused Akbar Ahmed (Dumpy), a regular visitor to her house, of plotting her murder and issued orders that he was not to be allowed in. There were several occasions when I could have met her, as on the release of Sanjay Gandhi's biography by his wife Maneka, which I had helped edit. She expected me to be present on the occasion. I sensed she would be rude to me. I did not attend the function. She did not spare Maneka. It was the same at the release of the translation of her autobiography from French to English, to which I had written a preface. Mrs Gandhi had agreed with the publishers, Vision Books, to release it in her own home. She expected me to be there. Again I sensed she was waiting for an opportunity to be nasty to me. I did not go for the release. She had to vent her spleen on the publisher. She told him before the assembled crowd that she would have nothing whatsoever to do with the book. It bore her name on the jacket.

I was unable to pay homage to Indira Gandhi in person because anti-Sikh violence, instigated by local leaders of her party, broke out all over the city. They spread false stories of Sikhs celebrating Mrs Gandhi's murder and distributing sweets and lighting up their houses; of Sikhs having poisoned Delhi's water supply, and of trainloads of Hindu corpses massacred by Sikhs coming to Delhi. Gangs of hired hoodlums were armed with iron rods and cans of gasoline to burn down gurdwaras, Sikh homes, shops and taxis, and to burn Sikhs alive. I was a marked man. The next morning I was warned that a mob was on its way to get me. In the nick of time Rolf Gauffin of the Swedish Embassy, whom I had never met before but who was a close friend of Romesh Thapar, came in his embassy car and took my wife and me away to his home in the embassy compound. I watched Mrs Gandhi's funeral on TV. I am pretty certain that, had she been alive, she would have gone round the city like her father, and stopped the carnage of thousands of innocent people. Her son, Rajiv Gandhi, stayed by his mother's body receiving V.I.Ps. If he was not the author of the order to 'teach the Sikhs a lesson', he did nothing to countermand it.

Before the opening of the next parliamentary session, I called on Vice-President Venkataraman (who had succeeded Mr Hidayatullah) with a request that I be allowed to pay a tribute to Mrs Gandhi. The first day of the session was devoted to tributes by leaders of all parties. I was among the last to be called. I think I delivered my best speech, paying unqualified tribute to one of the most important women of our times. It got very brief references in the papers because, by the time I spoke, the press gallery was empty.

About the last important thing I did as an MP was re garding the money and winter clothing sent by Sikh communities living abroad to help families who had suffered in the November 1984 pogrom. The money (nearly Rs 8 lakhs) I handed over to the Peoples' Relief Committee run by George Fernandes. Since most of the gift parcels were addressed to me, I had to have them released from the Customs. Jaya Jaitley, who was working with Fernandes, went from one official door to another, but failed to get clearance from the Delhi Administration. The entire winter passed with woollen blankets and sweaters in Customs sheds and destitute Sikhs shivering in their hovels. On the other hand, I was served with a notice demanding Rs 75,000 as demurrage for not having the goods cleared on time. Somebody raised a question about the fate of those parcels. I raised my hand to ask a supplementary. I waved the paper containing the demand for demurrage made on me, and let loose a vituperative attack on the government's callousness. Fortunately, several Congress MPs, notably Prithvijeet Singh, joined me with cries of 'shame! shame'. And fortunately, it being a Thursday, both Prime Minister Rajiv Gandhi and Finance Minister V.P. Singh were present in the House. I saw V.P. Singh having a whispered consultation with Rajiv. Then he asked his deputy to sit down and announced that the entire stock of garments would be released within twenty-four hours. He expressed his government's regret at the time taken. A few days later I was also able to get Charanjit Singh's new machinery released from the Bombay Customs to replace that wrecked by rioters.

I hoped against hope that I would get a second term in the Rajya Sabha. Many nominated MPs had more than one term and I felt I had done more than my share of speaking in the House. I wrote to Rajiv Gandhi to consider my re-nomination. When Narasimha Rao took the names of new nominees to President Zail Singh, he sent the list back asking for my name to be included in it. Prime Minister Rajiv Gandhi did not agree. Zail Singh asked a second time for my name to be included. It was turned down again, but this time with the assurance that I would be offered something worthwhile. H.Y. Sharda Prasad, whom I met at a private party, and Siddhartha Shankar Ray told me the same thing. I was offered the Chairmanship of the National Book Trust. Without a second thought I turned it down.

I was disappointed that I did not get a second term in the

Rajya Sabha. My farewell speech was spiced with anecdotes which raised much laughter. I still hoped that the Punjab MLAs would have me elected as a member from that State. I will write of that experience later.

Let me pause a while in the narration of my political ambitions to digress on a personal tragedy — the death of my mother.

Of my parents, I felt more relaxed with my mother than with my father. None of her children were as scared of her as we were of our father. When we were small, she often threatened to slap us, but it never got beyond raising her hand and threatening *'maaraan chaat?'* Nothing followed. She was frail, short, with little confidence in herself. Whatever little she may have had as a girl was squashed by her overbearing husband who would not trust her to run her home. He even prepared menus for his dinner parties — they hardly ever varied from tomato soup, fish, chicken, pilaf, followed by pudding — and he kept all the accounts except the dhobi's. There were other reasons for her willing subservience to her husband — her father and two brothers were in our employment; of her three sisters' husbands, two depended on my father's patronage. She had never been to school and only learnt enough Gurmukhi to be able to write letters and read the headlines of Punjabi newspapers. She didn't waste time on books and preferred to gossip with her sisters and maid servant, Bhajno, who was an inveterate carrier of tales against her sons' wives. However, when I was abroad I got more news from the few lines she wrote to me in Gurmukhi than the two pages of typescript my father dictated to his secretary. He wrote about the government, political wranglings and the budget; she wrote about births, liaisons, marriages and deaths. She often grumbled that she could not read or write English. Despite the instructors my father employed to teach her the language, she stubbornly refused to go beyond 'yes, no, good morning, good night, good-bye and thank you'.

When the Punjabi translation of my novel *Train to Pakistan* was published, I gave her the first copy. I did not expect her to read it. When I went to see her next morning, my father told me that she had been reading the novel late into the night and was down with a severe headache. I went to her bedroom. She was lying covered from head to foot in her shawl. I shook her by the shoulder and asked how she was feeling. She peeped out of the shawl with one eye and made a one-word comment: '*Beysharam!*' — shameless creature.

My mother was somewhat of a hypochondriac. The only thing she really suffered from were migraine headaches. The attacks could be so severe that she had to stay in bed for two days and only felt better after she had thrown up a few times. But whenever she caught a cold she was sure it was her last moment. Whenever she felt a pain in any part of her body she was sure it was cancer. She had heard that cancer was incurable. Therefore what she had could be nothing except cancer. When my father died in his ninetieth year, she was in her early eighties and in good health. Instead of being shattered by his going, as everyone expected, she came into her own as a very domineering *mater familias*. Nobody dared to address her except as Lady Sobha Singh. Like Queen Victoria, she held court every day. At eleven she presided over the mid-morning coffee session; in the evening, over drinks and dinner. I persuaded her to have a little alcohol in the evenings. At first she consumed it surreptitiously. When bearers came round with tray loads of soft drinks for the ladies at parties she would tell them that her son was bringing her orange juice. I initially spiked her glass with a little gin, and then I introduced her to Scotch. Again she made a mild protest. 'What will people say! An old illiterate woman from a village drinking whisky?' She began to like her sundowner and became discerning enough to tell good Scotch from bad *desi*.

In her ninetieth year she began to sense that she did not have very much longer to live. She never said anything about it but started giving things away. My father's sweater, his ebony walking-stick with a silver knob, and his gold watch came to me; jewellery and a gold watch went to my sister; jewellery, watches, gold pens, gold buttons, and sovereigns were distributed amongst sons, daughters-in-law and their progeny. There was seldom a morning when I went to see her when she did not give me a shirt, a pair of socks or shoes that my father had worn. We knew that she meant to give these things away with her own hands.

Without there being anything specifically wrong with her, she began to wither away. Dr I.P.S. Kalra, who was married to my cousin, also a doctor, came to see her twice a day to take her blood pressure and temperature. She began to spend a longer time in bed. My sister slept in her bedroom to help her go to the bathroom. Then a night maid was hired to clean, sponge and help change her clothes. Her appearances at coffee sessions became rarer and rarer. But even when half conscious, she would send for her servant, Haria, and mumble, 'Coffee.' He would assure her that visitors were being served coffee. Many times my telephone rang to tell me that she was sinking. We would hurry over. Dr Kalra was there giving her a shot of something or the other. She rallied round and we returned to our homes. One evening, when all her children, grandchildren and a number of great-grandchildren were there, she went into a coma from which she never came out.

We spent many hours of many days sitting by her supine body, assured by the rise and fall of her sheet that she was still alive. More than once we asked Dr Kalra not to persist in injecting her with life-saving drugs and to let her go in peace. He refused to listen to us and said that he was determined to keep her alive as long as he could. Back in my flat, I dreaded the ringing telephone. The final call came on the afternoon of 9 March 1985. It was my sister's anguished voice crying, 'She's gone.'

By the time we got to her she looked peacefully asleep. Beside her pillow, incense spiralled upwards to the ceiling. My elder brother sat by her bedside reading out from a small prayer book. Others embraced each other in tears and sat in chairs in the garden, only to break down again and again as people came to condole. As in earlier happenings in the family, it was my younger brother, Brigadier Gurbux Singh, who took control of the situation. He made me draft the obituary notice, corrected it and sent it off to all the Delhi papers. He fixed the time of her cremation and the day the Akhand Path would commence and terminate with *bhog* and *kirtan*. He ordered us to return to our homes for the night. He, his wife and my sister would stay with the body. My elder brother sat by her making the *japs* over and over again throughout the night, as he had done years earlier by our father's body.

The next morning we took our mother's body to the same electric crematorium where we had earlier taken our father and uncle. My brother, Gurbux, took her ashes to Hardwar as he had our father's ashes and those of my grandmother, to be immersed in the Ganga. Thus ended the days of Veeran Bai, Lady Sobha Singh, my mother.

Having failed to get the nomination for a second term in the Rajya Sabha I toyed with the idea of seeking election to it from Punjab. My equations with Punjab's Sikhs and Hindus were good. I expected the Akalis and the B.J.P. to support me and hoped to steal a few Congress MLA votes as well. But my main support had to come from the Akalis who were beholden to me for presenting their point of view for six years in Parliament and the press. I did not wish to join their party, and those who I met agreed with me that I would be more effective as an independent member. Two Akalis who assured me full support were Balwant Singh, the Punjab Finance Minister, and B.S. Ramoowalia, M.P. My friend Charanjit Singh invited Balwant Singh for lunch at Le Meridien and asked him bluntly whether or not he would support my candidature. If any money was required, he would look after it. Balwant Singh was much the most cunning man in the Akali party. He had risen from a Block Development Officer to being one of the richest men in the State. 'As far as I am concerned,' replied Balwant Singh, 'you can take my word for it that I will lend my full support to him. But he should come to Chandigarh and meet other Akali leaders.'

Ramoowalia's assurance was even more emphatic. He came to my home and, when asked by Charanjit whether we could rely on him, he slapped his chest as Punjabis do when giving a pledge: 'Once Ramoowalia gives his word, he never breaks it.'

I got my son, who was then in Chandigarh, to have my name enrolled as a voter in Punjab. As advised by Balwant Singh, I went to Chandigarh and attended a large luncheon given by him in his house. I was informed that there was another aspirant for the Akali ticket, a semi-literate Jathedar with the incredible name of Tota (Parrot) Singh. I couldn't think of him as a serious rival. Balwant Singh warned me that I should not dismiss him lightly as theirs was a tribal society where clan loyalties mattered more than learning or competence. Every Akali leader I spoke to assured me that it would be an honour for them to have me as their candidate.

I was the first to file my nomination papers. Balwant Singh said that it would not be right for him to propose or second my name. But once again he assured me of his support. I called on the leader of the B.J.P. in the Punjab Assembly and was assured that he would instruct his party M.L.As to support me if the central leaders like L.K. Advani so desired. Advani had already assured me of support. I even approached the President of the State Congress Committee. She told me that, if there were any Congress votes to spare, she would have them cast in my favour.

I had to go to Chandigarh three times in the heat of the summer to assure myself that nothing would go wrong. I spent the hot afternoons reading Christopher Fry's plays and listening to *papeehas* calling interminably. The place is infested with them. I understood why the English loathed the bird and interpreted its call as 'brain fever'. I sensed that things had begun to go wrong. Ramoowalia would not answer my phone calls. Balwant Singh became even more elusive. Came the last day for withdrawing candidates. I was back in Chandigarh. By now I was pretty certain that even if the Akalis backed out, I had a fair chance of getting enough votes to win. Balwant Singh also recognized that possibility.

The Akali leaders met in a conclave that morning. In the afternoon, Balwant Singh came to see me in my hotel. He regretted that he was unable to secure Akali support for me and that I should withdraw my name. He laid on a lot of flattery about how proud the community was of me and how much the Akalis meant to honour me by entrusting me with responsibilities. What he really wanted was to have me out of the running so that his candidate could romp home. I assumed it was Jathedar Tota Singh. I was foolish enough to withdraw my candidature. The man they elected came as a great surprise to me. It was Lt General Jagjit Singh Aurora. Some years later an Akali leader who was present at the conclave told me that most of the top leaders like Barnala and Badal had supported me. It was Balwant Singh who carried the day for General Aurora. He also mentioned the large sum of money that had gone into Balwant Singh's pocket.

I was asked by the editor of *Sunday* to write of my years in the Rajya Sabha. I mentioned my experiences with the Akalis. A few days later, Balwant Singh wrote to me saying that I had not been fair to him, as he had always told me there was another candidate. A month later, when I happened to be in Chandigarh to participate in a meeting of the States' Integration Council, he did his best to attract my attention. I scrupulously avoided catching his eye. Unfortunately for me, during the tea-break I found him standing alongside me in the urinal. He was as unabashed as ever and invited me over for a drink. I told him that I was staying with the Governor and didn't know what had been fixed up for the evening. I told Maya Ray, the Governor's wife, that I did not want to see the man's face and would be grateful if she got me out of the invitation. Balwant Singh came to the Ray's car as we were about to leave and repeated the invitation to her. He had a nervous tic in one eye and sniffled when he spoke. As he was talking to Maya Ray, he had a fit of coughing. 'Sardar Sahib, you have been smoking too much,' remarked the Governor's wife within the hearing of a dozen people around us. She was innocent of the *faux pas* she had made. I felt she had slapped the minister on my behalf. That was the last I saw of Balwant Singh. A few months later, when on his way home from somewhere, he was shot dead in broad daylight. The group that claimed responsibility for the crime stated to the press that they meant to rid the community of all corrupt leaders, and Balwant Singh was known to be the corruptest.

Ramoowalia's change of face was equally dramatic. Having ditched me he tried to make up to me by blatant flattery. He said he wanted me to spare him a little time every week so that he could draw some inspiration from me! After his tenure in Parliament was over, he managed to wangle a safer assignment as Member of the Minorities' Commission. He once came personally and pleaded with me to come to dinner at his home, and persuaded Charanjit and his wife to come as well. We all went.

Like most people, I didn't put much trust in the promises of politicians. Because of their past record of sacrifice in Punjab, I nevertheless harboured illusions that the Akalis were different. But more than half a century of controlling gurdwaras and their incomes has corroded their consciences. All they had to do was wear dark blue turbans and sport long, flowing beards to become acceptable as spokesmen of their community. Once addicted to parasitism, they were unable to kick the habit. The succession of *morchas* (fronts) they launched were aimed at keeping their hold on gurdwara coffers and grabbing political power. There was little pain or sacrifice involved. Volunteers were given regular salaries while they were in jail. Going to jail involved no hardship, and they came out as heroes who had fought for a cause. Ultimately, it was not the gullible peasantry which became wise but the terrorists who felt that the Panth had been taken for too long a ride and for too long a time. They tried to kill Talwandi and Tohra, but only succeeded in injuring them. They succeeded in killing Balwant Singh. A few innocent men and women, like the venerable Sant Longowal and Bibi Rajinder Kaur, fell victims to bullets. The party ceased to exist except in name. Real power passed into the hands of militants who elevated their mascot, Simranjit Singh Mann, to the top position. One only had to listen to what Mann had to say and the moves he indulged in to know that the Akalis, who were a legend in the history of India's freedom movement, had been succeeded by a bunch of bearded buffoons bereft of the power of thinking and vision. Giani Zail Singh used to pun on their name to say *'Akali aql tay khaalee'* — the Akalis' heads are empty of brains.

14 Pakistan

I AM AMONGST the few Indians fortunate enough to have visited Pakistan many times. Only once did I sense hostility towards myself. This happened to be soon after Partition when feelings against Indians, particularly Sikhs, ran very high.

I was passing through Karachi on my way to London. I had a few hours to spare and hired a taxi to see the sights of the city I had never visited before. I asked the driver to take me to Mr Jinnah's grave. As soon as I stepped out of the cab, a crowd began to collect. I heard someone shout, 'What business have these people to come to Pakistan?' The taxi driver took me by my arm, put me in his cab and drove away.

Anti-Sikh feelings had spread throughout the Muslim world, where wildly exaggerated stories of Sikhs massacring Muslims were circulated. I sensed this at Cairo when I stepped out of my hotel to take a stroll. I heard people shout, 'Sikh' and, realizing that they did not mean to be friendly, retraced my steps to the hotel.

I never experienced this animosity against Sikhs in Pakistan again. On my subsequent visits, I was singled out for a special welcome. Tongawallas and cab drivers refused to take money from me, shopkeepers gave away things free, plied me with tea and cold drinks. I recall my visit to Murree with Manzur Qadir, who was then Pakistan's Foreign Minister. We happened to pass by a shop selling walking sticks. Manzur wanted one for himself, I thought I would take one as a memento. After we had selected what we wanted, Manzur asked for their price. On being told, I remarked to Manzur in English that you could get them cheaper in Shimla. Manzur translated my remark to the shopkeeper. *'Aap durust farmaatey hain'* — You must be right, replied the shopkeeper. 'This one is a gift from me to our Sikh visitor; you pay me half for the other.' I asked him if he knew who the person with me was. 'I do,' he replied. 'I see his pictures in the papers. He is our Foreign Minister. He pays for what he buys; you don't pay for anything in Pakistan.'

Besides the general goodwill towards Sikhs, whom they had once hated, educated Pakistanis also knew how often I had stuck my neck out in their support. For Jinnah's birth centenary celebrations they invited two Indians to read papers in their seminar. The other delegate failed to show up. I was the sole Indian amongst a galaxy of European and American scholars on Indo-Pak affairs. When my turn came to speak, I referred to my father's friendship for their Qaid and his being the chief guest at my wedding. I went on to quote Jinnah's first speech as Governor-General of Pakistan in which he assured Hindu and Sikh minorities of equal treatment and exhorted them to regard Pakistan as their motherland. He had never wanted the two-way migration of religious minorities. I stated categorically that Indians accepted the right of Pakistan to be a sovereign, independent state; what we did not, nor ever would accept, was the two-nation theory of Muslims being a nation apart from Hindus and Sikhs. My speech was applauded. But soon Pakistani delegates began to heckle me. 'If you don't accept the two-nation theory, you don't accept Pakistan,' they maintained. I stood my ground, argued that we conceded Pakistan because the majority of the population of the regions concerned wanted to have independent states of their own and not because they were Muslims. If we accepted the two-nation theory what were we to do with the 90 million Muslims who remained in India? I got a second round of applause from college students in the audience. They invited me to their campus to speak to a selected number of students on Indo-Pak affairs. 'You have been saying nice things about Pakistan, now tell us the truth. Do you really think Pakistan is going the right way and is doing as well as India?' they asked me.

I told them, 'Pakistan Standard Time is 30 minutes behind the Indian. You are 30 years behind us in development.' I had seen a large number of fancy cars on the road, all imported from Japan, Germany, England or the United States — not one manufactured in Pakistan. In India foreign automobiles were a rare sight. 'However *rat-khatia* our cars may be, they are made in India,' I said with *rat-khatia* pride. Even matchboxes and the lavatory paper in my hotel room came from China. They were talking of having colour TV when they could not produce simple items like bicycles in their own country.

'Why do you think this is so?' they asked.

'You can either build new mosques or make motor cars,' I replied. 'You can't do both at the same time.' I told them of the dozens of modern mosques I had seen going up in every new quarter in Islamabad. Of course, what I said was somewhat of an exaggeration, but they understood that I was doing so to drive my point home. And they knew I was a friend.

Once I happened to be in the Karachi International Hotel. I had been out for a late dinner and wanted a little sleep before catching the morning flight to Bombay. A tall, dark young man accosted me on my way to the elevator. 'A Sardarji from nowhere,' he said jovially, grabbing my arm. 'Come and have a drink with me.' I protested that I had already had enough and wanted to retire. 'You will have one with me before you go,' he said as he dragged me into the bar. He was a powerful man. There was no escape. I ordered a Drambuie. 'You some kind of businessman? You from Iran or Afghanistan?' he asked. I explained I was from Bombay and was the editor of a paper. 'In that case you have to have another,' he insisted, and ordered a second Drambuie. I didn't know how to escape from his clutches. Every time I tried to get up he pulled me back on my chair. 'You may be an editor or something bigger,' he said aggressively, 'I write the names of the likes of you on my *laura* [penis].' I couldn't resist asking him, 'Do you write them with a ball point pen?' He didn't catch the pun. Fortunately for me, his bladder was full and he had to go to the loo. 'Don't you run away when I am emptying my bladder,' he warned me as he staggered out. That is exactly what I did. Instead of taking the elevator, I ran up the stairs to the security of my room.

I have visited Pakistan almost every alternate year for the past several years. Once I specifically went to attend the wedding of my friend M.A. Rahman's son, and on another occasion it was to deliver the Manzur Qadir Memorial Lecture.

I wandered about freely and unescorted in the streets of Lahore. I made it a point to pay homage at the graves of my departed friends, Manzur Qadir, his uncle Sleam and Mohammad Anwar. My association was not restricted to the past: every time I went I made new friends, was invited to new homes; they come to mine when in Delhi. Amongst my latest acquaintances are the publisher-bookseller Najam Sethi and his moon-faced beauty of a wife who edits *Friday*, her cousin the poetess Hina Feisal Imam and her sister's husband Aijazuddin of the Hakeem family, three of whom were among Maharaja Ranjit Singh's closest advisers.

Many years later, I was invited to a media seminar in Islamabad on Indo-Pak relations. Amongst the other invitees were Prem Bhatia, editor of *The Tribune* and Kuldip Nayar. Despite the tension prevailing between the two countries, the atmosphere in the seminar was most cordial. I had no idea that I was being treated as the leader of the Indian delegation till at a lunch hosted by their Foreign Secretary, Nawabzada Yakub Khan, I found myself seated on his right. After lunch he delivered a long and lucid oration analysing Indo-Pak tensions and proposed a toast (in plain water) for future good relations. I was expected to respond. I insisted that Prem Bhatia, being the seniormost amongst us, should reply. I only had to raise my glass of water and wish Pakistan prosperity. Bhatia made a short, dry speech.

That evening there was a farewell banquet for us in the hotel where we were staying. Our host was Pakistan's Minister for Information and Broadcasting. The evening before I had seen him in a panel discussion on TV. He was being heckled by three Moulvi-looking types and a lady draped in a burqa with its flap thrown back to reveal her dour face. They complained that Pakistani electronic media was not doing enough to inform the people of the beauties of Islam and the validity of the two-nation theory. He was having a hard time convincing them that he was doing his best. I came to the banquet well-oiled with Scotch. At that time there was strict prohibition in Pakistan. Once again I found myself seated on the right of the host. Bhatia told me, '*Bacchoo* [son] this time you have to make your own speech.' A printed copy of the Minister's speech was handed over to us. I didn't have the foggiest notion of how to respond. It ruined my appetite for food and soured the whisky inside me. When I stood up to speak, I referred to the Minister being pilloried on TV the previous evening. I told the audience that, despite prohibition, I had my quota of Scotch and if they wanted to do anything about it they better do it fast because in a few hours I would be flying back to India. I said that before leaving Pakistan I would make an offering of an Urdu couplet to the Minister, which might come in handy when he next faced the *thekedars* of Islam. It ran:

> *Mullah, gar asar hai dua mein*
> *To Masjid hila kay dikha*
> *Gar nahin, to do ghoont pee*
> *Aur Masjid ko hilta deykh*

(Mullah, if there is power in your prayer
Let me see you shake the mosque!
If not, take a couple of swigs of liquor
And see the mosque shake on its own.)

The audience burst out in full-throated laughter. My host was most amused and took down the couplet. He then told me how fed up he was of the prevalent bigotry and religious fanaticism. 'You know, they objected to our showing the Chinese women's table-tennis team playing in T-shirts and very short shorts. If they had their way they would insist that our women's hockey team play in burqas.'

I don't know how the Pakistani press reported my speech because I left Islamabad in the early hours of the morning for Lahore en route to Delhi. I had my last laugh at the expense of the Pakistanis at Lahore airport. After passing through customs and immigration I had to face Security. The man ran his metal detector over my turban and body. As he was taking it over my middle there was a loud beep of protest. He paused. What could I be hiding in the front of my middle? He tried again. Again a loud beep. '*Janab, fauladi hai*' — sir, it is made of steel, I told him. It was my zip fastener which was made of steel, but he understood what I had alluded to and ran round telling his fellow security officers what I had said. They came beaming with smiles to shake my hand.

In April 1994 I received a letter from the Pakistan Forum inviting me to a seminar on Kashmir. I had nothing very new to say on the subject, but I readily accepted the invitation. I thought it might be my last chance to visit Pakistan and meet old friends who were dearer to me than my relations. In Islamabad was Asghari Qadir (Manzur's widow), close to 85. She had had two major surgeries performed on her. And there were her two sons, Basharat and Asghar with their families. In Lahore there was M.A. Rahman, who had taken over my friendship from where Manzur had left it by dying in London some years earlier. There was also Jameela Anwar and her daughter Naheed, recently married. In Lahore there were others, like the Noons, who had been close friends of my wife's parents.

So I took the P.I.A. flight from Delhi to Lahore. I had barely one hour at Lahore airport to take the connecting flight to Islamabad. By the time I was cleared through Health, Customs and Immigration my onward flight had been called. I had only a few seconds to greet Rahman and Bapsi Sidhwa. Both thrust currency notes in my hands to pay the porter. It was hullo and goodbye in the same breath. Half an hour later I was in Islamabad. Minoo Bhandara (Bapsi's brother), owner of Murrie Breweries, and Basharat (Manzur's elder son), were there to receive me. After a late dinner given by Minoo, I retired for the night. I had reserved the next day for the Qadirs.

The next morning Minoo's driver dropped me at Asghar Qadir's house in Islamabad. Asghar, whom I had known from the day he was born in Lahore, has become Pakistan's top physicist and mathematician. I was told by Suladesh Mahajan, who teaches physics in the University of Austin (Texas) that, after Dr Abdus Salam, he expected that the next Pakistani to win the Nobel Prize would be Asghar Qadir. Asghar is currently head of the department at the University of Islamabad. Besides his academic pursuits, he has a passion for flowers. Larger and more fragrant roses I have not seen in Delhi. His garden was ablaze with varieties of ivory-whites, pinks and reds, his rooms full of fragrance. The professor and his wife were at their jobs, their children at school. I had three hours to spend with Asghari. It was a very emotional embrace, which seemed to take in more than the half-a-century we had known each other. I was choked with emotion and was unable to say anything for a few minutes. I am very prone to making a fool of myself in such situations.

Basharat joined us for tea and then took me out shopping. Except for onyx, there is not very much one can buy as gifts in Pakistan that cannot be got in better craftsmanship in India. I bought some plates and cups with verses of the Quran inscribed on them and some pieces of hand-woven textiles with patterns painted in vegetable dyes, and a couple of onyx bowls. Basharat did not let me pay for them. He took me to two of the best known bookstores in town, London Bookshop and Mr Bookshop. Both were larger and better stocked than any we have in Delhi, Bombay or Calcutta. I do not know whether Basharat had tipped them off or whether they had seen my name in the papers, but my books were prominently displayed near the entrances of both the stores. Indian publications outnumbered the Pakistani. During the couple of hours I spent in the shopping centres of Islamabad, I did not see a single woman in a burqa.

There was another interesting thing I picked up about the women of Pakistan. Divorces and remarriages are much more common among their upper classes than in India. While coveting another man's wife or having intercourse with her is frowned upon, persuading her to leave her husband and become your wife is no longer a rare phenomenon. It is also surprising that in the Islamic Republic of Pakistan, where drinking can get you the lash, my creative friends of the past like the poet Faiz Ahmed Faiz and the painter Sadqain were hard drinkers. So are my friends of today, the poets Ahmed Faraz and Qateel Shifai. When they have problems in replenishing their stocks, they come over to India for a few days and drink like camels setting out on a long, dry desert journey.

They fill their human tanks to last them their sojourn in their fatherland.

My only contribution to the seminar on Kashmir organized by the Pakistan Forum was that, instead of putting across the official Indian point of view or contradicting what the Pakistanis had to say, I stated the point of the Kashmiri Muslims, whose future is the real bone of contention between India and Pakistan. The Pakistani press gave full coverage to my speech and one paper even wrote an editorial supporting me. Pakistan TV gave me half an hour to elucidate my proposals for an amicable solution. The Indian press blanked me out.

After bidding farewell to my closest Pakistani family, I took the afternoon flight to Lahore to spend three days with the Rahmans. Rahman had suffered a heart attack a few months earlier but he was nevertheless at the airport to pick me up. When we arrived at his home Rehman showed me to the bedroom his son had vacated for me. On the bed lay four sets of cotton Awami suits newly stitched and, on the carpet, a couple of brand new Peshawari chappals. 'You and I are of the same size; I think our feet are also of the same size,' said Rahman. 'I have had these made for you. Try out the chappals and wear the Awami suit hanging in the bathroom. We will be dining with my daughter Sameena and her husband Aurangzeb.' I was dumbstruck. All I had brought for the Rahmans were packets of cashew nuts, one packet of tea and two of my books. Before I could protest, he changed the subject to brief me on recent events in the family. A fortnight before I arrived there was an armed robbery in his house. The Rahmans were returning from dinner at 11 pm. While their old chowkidar was opening the gate for his wife to drive in, Rahman stepped out of the car. A man approached him and asked for a job as a driver. 'I have a driver,' replied Rahman, 'and this is no time to go to people's homes asking for jobs.' The man pulled out a gun and held it against Rahman's head. Three other men, all armed, came behind them and warned them that if they tried to shout for help they would be shot. 'Now hand over whatever you have in the house,' said the gang leader. Rahman had cashed a cheque for Rs 10,000 that morning. He handed over the bundle of currency notes. He asked his wife to take off her gold bangles and rings and hand them over. The gangsters were not satisfied with the haul and ordered the Rahmans to open the house door. They did. The gangsters woke up their two sons and daughters-in-law. They handed over all their cash and jewellery. Rahman's Bangladeshi servant, who lived in the out-house, sensed something wrong was going on indoors. He ran to a neighbouring house which had a police guard. Four men with guns came to Rahman's house. The gangsters realized the game was up. They tried to run away. The gang leader jumped into the canal to cross to the other side. By then some people had got together on the other side of the canal to catch him. The gang leader was nabbed and given a hammering before being handed over to the police. The cash and jewellery was recovered from him. He disclosed the names of his accomplices. Three were arrested in Gujranwala. The fourth was still absconding.

At dinner with Sameena and Aurangzeb, the only talk was of the increasing incidence of crimes of violence in Lahore. On an average six or seven dacoities took place every night. They told me that the situation in Karachi was even worse. I was given a sample of that the next morning when I went to call on the Noons.

Akbar Hayat Noon is the younger brother of Sir Feroze Khan Noon. He was over six feet tall, handsome as a film star and an all-India athlete before Partition. After taking a degree in engineering from England he joined the Central Public Works Department. He married Asghari's younger sister Akhtari (both daughters of Mian Sir Fazl-i-Husain) and settled down in Delhi. They became favourites of my father-in-law, Sir Teja Singh Malik. Being from our part of the Punjab, they were often invited for meals by my parents. In their time Akbar and Akhtari made the handsomest couple in Delhi.

Partition took the Noons to Pakistan. When Akbar retired from the P.W.D. the couple settled down in Karachi. One night armed robbers broke into their home. After collecting all the loot they could, they ordered Akbar to hand over the keys of his car. He did so. They were unable to unlock the door and suspected that Akbar had deliberately given them the wrong keys. They ordered him to unlock the car. Akbar's hands were shaking and could not fit the key in the keyhole. One of the gangsters shot him in the arm, shattering his arm bones. The gangsters were never traced. After some months in hospital the Noons migrated to Lahore. As soon as I had greeted all the members of the family, Akhtari took me aside and begged me not to bring up the subject of dacoity either in their home or at the Rahmans'. 'He has become paranoid with fear,' she told me. 'As soon as it gets dark, he gets nightmares of dacoits prowling about. He keeps the TV on all night watching tennis, cricket or hockey. Somebody has to be with him all the time.'

Before I left, Akhtari gave me a large painting made by her son. Then a cousin of Akbar's, Ata Mohammad Noon, who had been in the same class as I at Government College, breezed in. He had joined the Police and was living in retirement in Lahore. Although in poor health he was the same thin, cadaverous looking man, now sporting a small grey beard. We were meeting after sixty-one years.

One more social call remained for the morning: Jameela Anwar and her newly married daughter. Jameela's husband, Mohammad Anwar, had been a friend and drinking companion before Partition. Every time I came to Lahore to spend a few days with Manzur he joined us in the evenings. After Partition he and Jameela and we had travelled by the same Polish boat, the *Batory*, from London to Karachi. We were together all the time. Anwar had fallen foul of Z.A. Bhutto and suffered persecution at his hands. He had stood his ground. Then he suddenly died. He was only in his fifties. On an earlier visit Jameela had taken me to his grave and recited the *Fateha*. They had no children of their own and had adopted Anwar's niece. She had agreed to marry a married man much older than her, a Wadero landlord who was absorbed in Sindhi politics. Jameela gave me a warm embrace, as did her daughter. A few minutes later, her son-in-law came out of the bathroom where he had been hiding let there be policemen with me. Wanted for some case of abduction, he was on the run from the Sindh police.

Like a dutiful son-in-law he touched my feet to invoke my blessings. Before I left, Jameela put a heavy pen-and-ink holder made of green onyx in my hand. 'Anwar used this all his life. I know he would be happy if it was with you,' she said. During my last meeting with Anwar, he had in fact given me a large bowl of the most expensive variety of onyx.

In the afternoon Rahman's daughter Sabeena took me out shopping. I picked up several books, music tapes and old textiles. She would not let me pay for them. In the evening I accompanied Rahman to a department store from where he wanted to get provisions for dinner. The store was larger than any in our big cities and stocked with foreign cheeses, biscuits, sauces, jams, cosmetics and medicines. I thought I'd take some bars of English and Swiss chocolate for my grand-daughter. I put them on the counter and asked for the bill. A young man strode up, took the piece of paper on which the salesman was adding up my total and put it in his pocket. 'Pack them up for the Sardar Sahib,' he ordered the salesman. He was the proprietor of the store. He did not know me. I was recognizably a visitor from India. That was good enough for him. I discovered that his family, the Chaudhuries, had migrated from Ambala in 1947. It reminded me of the sports store in Glasgow where I had picked up a pair of sneakers worth £35. The shopkeeper refused to let me pay for them. I was a total stranger, but obviously from India. He was a Pakistani Punjabi.

In my entire life I have never encountered another people as reckless in their generosity as Punjabi Mussalmans. The trait is not to be found in Punjabi Hindus or Sikhs, nor to the same extent in Pakistanis of the Frontier Provinces or Sindh. It is unique to the people living between the Indus and the Sutlej, down to the confluence of Punjab's five rivers. They have other traits unique to them. They are not a humble people and share much of the pride common to most Punjabis. Being Muslim adds to their self-esteem. Their logic is simple: Punjabis are the world's elite; Islam is the best of all religions. Put the two together and you get the best people in the world. When puritanical, they can be insufferably narrow-minded and fanatical. A call to *Jehad* brings out all their macho, militant zeal

to do or die. Then it is best to keep out of their way. I have a
simple rule: avoid making friends with a Punjabi Pakistani who
prays five times a day, who fasts during Ramadan — and does
not drink.

Rahman used to be a healthy drinker: after developing a heart
problem he occasionally takes half a peg of whisky to keep
others company. Our common friend, Ejaz Batalvi, has never
been much of a drinker and will fondle his first glass of Scotch
all evening. Their attitudes towards religion are also different.
Rahman, though otherwise very liberal-minded, conforms to
the spartan traditions of the Wahabis and has no use for Sufism
and paying homage at the tombs of saints. Batalvi, on the other
hand, believes that the true spirit of Islamic tolerance is best
seen in the teachings of Sufi saints. My last afternoon in Lahore
was reserved by him to visit the dargahs of Hazrat Mian Meer,
who is believed by most Sikhs to have laid the foundation stone
of their Harimandir in Amritsar, and the tombs of Madho Lal
Husain in Baghbanpura near the Shalimar gardens. In the years
when I lived in Lahore as a student and a lawyer, I had never
visited these places.

A strange, unearthly peace pervades the enormous courtyard
around the modest-sized mausoleum of Mian Meer. At the
time I went there it was almost deserted. A cluster of women
and children sat bunched together on a corner of the platform.

Two beggars sitting a distance from each other were
chanting something I could not catch. Ejaz bought a leaf-bowl
of rose petals to strew on the peer's tomb. A couple of old men
were at prayer. Ejaz recited the *Fateha*, came out and gave
money to the beggars. We drove through the bazars of
Baghbanpura and parked our car a good distance away from the
mazar of Madho Lal Husain. The lanes were narrow, winding
and smelly. Once again I noticed hardly any women wearing
burqahs. We arrived at the *mazar*. A man with bells round his
ankles and on his hands was dancing and singing. A group of
children followed him dancing in circles. Their mothers

watched them. The mausoleum was not very impressive: just two tombs side by side. One was of the Muslim Husain, the other of the Hindu Madho Lal. They were poets who formed a corporate personality, Madho Lal Husain. Maharaja Ranjit Singh used to pay homage at their tombs every Basant Panchmi day, dressed in yellow silk and accompanied by his bodyguard of Kashmiri women, all likewise dressed in yellow silks. To me, more interesting than the mausoleum was the cemetery surrounding it. Among the graves was one of the Punjabi poet Chiragh Deen, better known as Ustaad Daaman. He had been put in jail by the Martial Law regime for reciting a poem:

> *Pakistan deeyan maujaun ee maujaun*
> *Chaarey paasey faujan ee faujan*

> (Pakistan is having a wonderful time
> whichever way you look there is the Army.)

On a visit to Delhi he recited another poem regretting the partition of the country.

> *Akhiyan dee laalee pay dasdee*
> *Tusee vee roey ho, roey asee vee haan*

> (The redness in our eyes has no secret
> If you have cried, we too have wept.)

Daaman died about ten years ago and composed his own epitaph which is engraved on the marble headstone of his grave. Ejaz copied it out for me on a piece of paper:

> *Sarsaree nazar maaree jahaan andar*
> *Zindgi varg utthalya main,*
> *Daaman koee na miliya rafeeq mainoo*
> *Maar kafan dee bukkal tay challiya main*

> (I gave a cursory glance at the world,
> I turned a few pages of the book of my life.
> I Daaman could find no companion — so
> I fling my shroud over my shoulder. And I go.)

15   Oddballs and Screwballs

ANYONE IN THE public eye attracts a variety of odd people towards himself. I have had more than my share of them because I am a patient listener. Something about me makes strangers open up and unfold their private lives to me in the firm conviction that I will keep their confessions to myself. Although I am a great advice-giver, I have never been able to keep peoples' secrets. On the contrary, I usually betray confidences reposed in me by telling them to everyone interested in hearing them. I make fun of people who confide in me and, when confronted, totally deny having done so. As a result I have hurt a lot of people.

Oddballs who have come into my life fall into three categories: compulsive talkers, women who want to reveal their innermost secrets, and those on the border line dividing sanity from mental derangement.

Being, as I said, a patient listener, I have had to suffer a lot of compulsive talkers. I don't enjoy listening to them and often let my mind wander to more interesting things, but lend one ear to hear what is being said lest it contains questions I might be expected to answer. For the most part, I keep up an appearance of being deeply interested by periodically making monosyllabic noises like 'Yes' or 'I see' or just nodding. I have never been able to cut short long-winded people. The best I can do is to evade them. At times I have suffered acute discomfort in trying to do so. One very hot summer evening in Lahore, as I returned to my first-floor apartment, I saw my cousin crossing the road to come over to see me. I ran to the kitchen and told the cook to tell him that I had not returned from the club. I then locked myself in the lavatory, hoping he would leave. Instead, I heard him tell my cook that he would wait till I returned; he sat in my sitting room to read the morning paper, while I sat on the lavatory seat with nothing to read or do. It became dark but I could not switch on the light lest it be noticed. I had to sweat it out for over an hour till my cook had the presence of mind to tell him that I often came home very late.

My communist friend Danial Latifi, whom I liked and respected, was another compulsive, long-winded talker. He never modulated his voice and would drone on and on till I was almost lulled into sleep. He also had no sense of humour. Once I told him of running into his wife Saramma in Bombay while strolling along Chaupatty. A meeting of the All India Cow Protection Society was going on by the seashore. I made some remark to Saramma about how absurd the whole thing sounded in the twentieth century. She replied that the American meat industry was financing cow-protection so that it could sell tinned beef to India. Instead of laughing at his wife's naivete, Danial said very earnestly, 'You know, there could be some truth in it. I don't put anything beyond cunning American capitalists.'

Danial and Saramma moved into an apartment in Sujan Singh Park in Delhi for a while. Dodging Danial became a problem. It was easy enough when I saw him from my window coming towards our flat. I drew the curtains and told my cook or bearer to go from the backdoor and tell the Sahib that I was not in and not expected back for several hours. But there was no escape when I answered the doorbell myself and found Danial standing there. I told him that I had a lot of unwelcome visitors and didn't know what to do about them. 'Why don't you get a spyglass fixed in your door?' he asked. 'All Bombay apartments have them. You can see the visitor from your side without his being able to see you,' he explained. It was the kindly Danial who got one for me from Bombay. We had it fixed in our door. The first victim of the contraption was none other than Danial. When the doorbell rang, I peered through the glass, saw him standing outside and tiptoed back, and asked the bearer to tell the Sahib I was not in. I think Danial sensed I was in but did not want to see him. He never dropped in again without first ringing me up. However, that did not bring about any change in his desire to buttonhole me at parties and bore me to tears. The last I saw of him was at a reception in the French Embassy. After filling my plate I wanted to find somewhere to sit (it was a standing buffet) and enjoy the Brie, Camembert and glass of wine. I ran into Danial holding a glass of whisky. I had never known him to drink alcohol and was foolish enough to ask him how he had taken to consuming something forbidden to Muslims. Danial proceeded to quote chapter and verse from the Quran and Hadith to prove that liquor was disdained but not forbidden as *haram*. While he was expounding the sacred law people came to introduce themselves to me, shake my hand and ask me questions. Undeterred by these interruptions, Danial continued to cite fatwas delivered by Caliphs and opinions given by theologians and Muslim jurists justifying the intake of liquor.

The most long-winded, compulsive talker I met was the retired Lieutenant-General Nathu Singh of Dungarpur. He often stayed with my parents. Since my parents had lots of visitors he had no problem finding victims for his monologues. And if no one was around, he got people on the telephone in Delhi or distant towns. While he was there the line was always engaged; office work (there was only one line) was disrupted and the bills for long-distance calls mounted. After some visits, whenever the General wrote from Dungarpur to ask whether he could stay with him, my father had to cook up names of people he expected as guests around the same time. After my parents died, Nathu Singh decided to honour my elder brother's home by considering it his own. They had to make excuses and go out, leaving their telephone at his mercy. He would get me on the line and ask if he could come over. Like the rest of the family, I had respect and affection for this doughty old Rajput warrior with a handle-bar moustache and martial swagger. Even in his eighties he stood ramrod straight and walked like a soldier. I was then a member of the Rajya Sabha, and spent the mornings going over Parliamentary papers. Nathu Singh wanted full attention. His monologues covered a wide field: his days at Sandhurst, his postings with British regiments, the battles he had fought, the women he had bedded, his views on the state of the nation, his contempt for politics and politicians, and what he would do if he were Prime Minister of India. There were no breaks in his oration to give me a chance to say that I had other appointments to keep. After his first visit I rang up my brother's wife Amarjeet to protest that I had wasted almost two hours politely listening to their house guest. 'Share and share alike,' she responded cheerfully. 'He is a family friend and we must bear the burden equally.' But thereafter she was kind enough to warn me, 'General Nathu Singh is in town. So look out.'

My brother also soon began making excuses about why they couldn't have the General stay with them. Old Nathu was compelled to stay with his son (or perhaps his son-in-law). They happened to live close to Sujan Singh Park. The General would stroll up to my apartment ostensibly to spend a few minutes with me. Minutes stretched into hours. I tired of his frequent visits and even thought of writing to his relations to keep him at home. One morning he waylaid me as I was leaving for Parliament. I had to shake him off with the lie that I had a question tabled and had to be punctual. 'Why don't you take me to the Rajya Sabha one day? I would like to know what you Johnnies talk about all day,' he said. I promised to get him a pass for the next day and insisted on picking him up as I did not want to risk his coming over before time. He spent an hour in the visitors' gallery. He was not allowed to talk with the people around him and had to suffer MPs doing all the talking. When I joined him at the appointed time in the lobby he looked very dejected. 'What a lot of *buk buk* you fellows talk!' he said. 'Instead of all this *buckwass* why don't you do something positive?'

I wrote a nasty little piece in my 'Malice' column on compulsive talkers being crashing bores. General Nathu Singh got the message and did not bother me any more.

A close second, and perhaps even topping my personal list of compulsive talkers, was Nazar Hayat Tiwana, son of Sir Khizr Hayat Tiwana, one-time Chief Minister and the wealthiest landowner of pre-Partition Punjab. Nazar had fallen out with his father, married a Hindu woman and migrated to the States. He got a job as an assistant librarian in Chicago University and retired with a handsome pension. His obsession was friendship between India and Pakistan and amicable relations between the different religious communities of India. The first time he came to visit me in Delhi I received him and his family very warmly. I immediately sensed that Nazar had been bitten by the talking bug. 'My wife tells me I talk too much,' he repeated many times in the course of his endless monologue. And he went on relentlessly with half-sentences breaking off into other half-sentences and back to the need of setting up an Indo-Pak Friendship Society which would also propagate inter-communal harmony in India. All this was for the peace of his father's soul, who had opposed the partition of India. Fortunately, everyone Nazar met in Delhi or Lahore (where he came to attend the Manzur Qadir Memorial Lecture delivered by me) realized that Nazar could not control his loquaciousness and didn't mind being snubbed: *'Bas vee kar!'* — Please stop talking.

It is best to deal with a compulsive talker as soon as you realize he is one. If you can't dodge him, then face him squarely. This I did to Mahinder Kapur, Principal of Modern School for many years. I had engaged him to conduct my American students round Delhi and Hardwar and arrange lectures for them. I discovered that what could be said in two minutes took Kapur twenty minutes to put across. When he got me on the phone, he would hum and haw from one irrelevant point to another. I wondered how he ran his school: he had the reputation of running it very efficiently. He was easy to handle. Every time he rang, I started by telling him I had exactly five minutes to spare and would he be as short as possible? He got the message.

I do not know whether compulsive talking is a psychiatric, congenital, inherited or acquired disease. It progresses with age and ends in senility. It is a malaise which has been allowed to grow unchecked. It needs to be taken more seriously.

Of women who repose confidences in me, I will say no more

than it baffles me as to why they do so without having the least desire to have a liaison with me. I have known total strangers ring me up to discuss their personal problems. They tell me of their inhibitions, their love affairs, their extra-marital relationships. When it comes to women, I am a patient as well as an interested listener because I love to hear tales of marital discord, the number of times married couples had sex, how and where they met, their married paramours and the precautions they take against being discovered and becoming pregnant. I encourage them to reveal more and more. I have had young, unmarried girls telling me of their trysts with married men and spending nights with them when their wives are away. Once an unmarried woman whom I had never known arrived at my doorstep with her baggage. She sent me a note saying that she expected her child to be born within the next three days and wanted its birth to take place in my apartment so that the newcomer could open its eyes to the world in my 'benign presence'.

I have always been fascinated by the mad and the slightly mad. Whenever the opportunity came my way I visited the mental asylums in Lahore, Ranchi, Agra and Poona. I was surprised to find the number of people whom I had known earlier undergoing treatment. It was difficult to communicate with them. But the slightly mad had the faculty of talking sanely for some time and then going off on a tangent where I could not follow them.

As Editor of *The Illustrated Weekly*, I sometimes published articles which, without my realizing it, hurt some people. I had published something about the Parsees, who usually take things in their stride. But not all of them. One day a Parsee sent in his visiting card and desired to see me on urgent business. The visiting card read 'Atom Bomb', with the visitor's designation, address and telephone number on it. I sent for him. He was a puny little fellow with an explosive temper. 'How dare you make fun of the Parsees?' he thundered. 'You know who I am? I am the Atom Bomb. With one look of my eye I can reduce you to *bhasma* — ashes.' I thought it best to apologize and save myself from untimely death.

More amusing was my meeting with a man called Raheja. In his lucidly written letters he described himself as a retired army officer running a gas station somewhere in Haryana. He claimed to have invented an internal TV through which a person could see past and future events. I was intrigued. Being one to encourage inventors, I wrote back asking him to see me and bring his invention with him.

Raheja turned out to be a harmless little man with a gentle, soothing voice. I could not see his internal TV because it was indeed inside him. He talked of his premature retirement due to ill-health and his need to be given recognition for his invention. 'I am not going to accept any *aira-ghaira* job,' he said. 'The least I deserve is the Chief Ministership of Haryana or being made a senior minister in the central cabinet.'

'How do you propose to get one or the other without being elected to the Haryana Assembly or the Lok Sabha?' I asked.

He gave me a condescending smile to indicate that I did not understand the inscrutable workings of destiny. 'I consulted Punditji [Nehru]. He advised me to see you as you were the only one who could fix me up as a Chief Minister or in the central cabinet,' he said.

'Punditji?' I asked with surprise. 'But Punditji has been dead for over twenty years.'

Raheja gave me another understanding smile and remarked, 'So what? It is my internal TV through which I communicate with him.'

'Where and when did you establish communication with Panditji?' I asked.

'Only this afternoon, as I was leaving the psychiatric ward of the All India Institute of Medical Sciences.'

I realized I had to be gentle and understanding with Raheja. I let him talk on for an hour or more; I promised to do my best to fix him up as Chief Minister of Haryana or Minister of Information and Broadcasting in the central government.

I led him to the door and bade him godspeed. I told my security guard that, if he came again, he was to be told that I was not at home.

I forgot about Raheja; even his name had disappeared from

my memory when he rang up six months later and said he had some very important information which would shake the entire country. A journalist is as hungry for a scoop as a man-eating shark is for a juicy piece of human flesh. I asked him to come over at once. It was only after he sat down that I realized the person was Raheja, inventor of the internal TV I was less patient with him this time and asked him what it was he wanted to tell me.

'You were a close friend of Sanjay Gandhi, weren't you?' he asked.

'I had met him several times, but I couldn't describe him as a close friend,' I replied.

'Never mind!' he assured me, 'To this day no one knows how he died.'

'He died in an air crash. And with him was Captain Saxena.'

'That everyone knows! The two were killed when their plane crashed on the Ridge. But who caused the crash?'

'I don't know. Pilot's error or some defect in the machine.'

'No,' he maintained. 'The crash was deliberately contrived.'

'By whom?'

'Churchill.'

'Churchill? He died long before Sanjay. In any case, why would Churchill want to kill Sanjay?'

'I will tell you why,' he replied with a patient smile. 'You know Sanjay liked women. He was particularly fond of white women. Churchill didn't mind that very much, but when Sanjay set his sights on the Queen of England, Churchill got very upset. He told him, "Sanjay, I don't care how many English girls you sleep with, but you must lay off our Queen. That is not proper." But Sanjay wouldn't listen to Churchill and was about to seduce the Queen when Churchill had his spies tamper with Sanjay's plane so that it would crash.'

Raheja looked at me for a long time hoping to see me deeply impressed with his inside knowledge. I feigned to ponder over the matter and promised to write about it in my column. This time Raheja's name remained imprinted on my mind. I stopped answering his letters and telephone calls. A year later I read in

The Hindustan Times that Raheja had 'proceeded to his heavenly abode,' as death is so frequently referred to in India.

Equally interesting and baffling was the case of a young Sikh. He sent me a closely typed letter in English soliciting my help in having some foreign exchange he held in a German bank cleared by the Reserve Bank of India. He said he was a Sikh born in Iran and had a large export-import business with West Germany. He had migrated to India with his wife and children when the Iraq-Iran war broke out. He repeated that he had several million Deutschmarks in German banks but was unable to get the money transferred to India. It did not make sense to me because India would welcome Deutschmarks flowing in; perhaps there was some hitch on the German side. I asked him to see me.

He turned out to be a tall, strapping man with an excellent command of English. When I asked him who was preventing him from his drawing his own money, he evaded my question and went on to explain his domestic problems. 'My wife has taken a job as a stenographer with a businessman in Jalandhar,' he said. 'Is it right for the wife of a man of my status to be working as a stenographer?' he asked.

'No,' I conceded. 'But have you been providing her with the money she needs?'

'How can I? It is held up in Germany.'

'How is she to live then without earning something herself?'

He seemed to comprehend his wife's dilemma. 'It is okay if she earns something; but she is also sleeping with her employer.'

I sensed his wife's infidelity had upset the young man more than the millions he imagined were locked up in German banks. 'Don't you agree it is a disgrace for the wife of a Nehru to work as a mere steno and sleep with her boss?'

'Nehru? How does she become a Nehru?'

'You didn't read my letter carefully,' he explained. 'Perhaps you didn't see my name at the end of the letter.'

I quickly glanced at his letter. He had indeed signed himself as something Singh Nehru.

'Are you related to the Nehrus? I didn't know there were any Sikh Nehrus.'

'I am Pundit Jawaharlal Nehru's son,' he said.

'Oh! I didn't know he had a son,' I replied. 'What proof do you have that he was your father?'

'I consulted the archives in the Golden Temple. There it is recorded that I am Punditji's son.'

'Does Indira Gandhi know this? Have you met her?'

'Yes,' he affirmed. 'I went to call on her. She was convinced I was her brother. But she told me not to tell anyone else about it till the right time.'

I promised the young man I would speak to the German ambassador about his bank account in Germany. 'Yes, please do. I am also seeing Giani Zail Singh and Charanjit Singh this afternoon to solicit their help.'

I don't know how Giani Zail Singh handled the young man. I asked Charanjit who dropped in for a drink that evening. 'He is a nut case,' replied Charanjit. 'I threw him out of the office within two minutes. I don't have as much time to waste as you have.'

I warned Charanjit that what often appears to be a harmless eccentric on the surface can turn out to be a dangerous case of schizophrenia easily provoked to violence. One has to be gentle when dealing with oddballs and screwballs.

16   *Wrestling with the Almighty*

AS CHILDREN WE were not encouraged to ask too many questions about religion. The last Guru had ordained that Sikhs must never cut hair on any part of their bodies, not eat Kosher *(halaal)* meat, smoke or consume tobacco in any form. And that was that. Men who clipped their beards or moustaches were automatically ostracized as *patits* (renegades). The observance of ritual and prayer were also laid down. If you recited the five prescribed prayers *(nitneym)* you were a good boy; if you did not, you were an urchin. Since I could recite my morning and evening prayers by rote and at times sang a *shabad* or two in the gurdwara, I was my grandmother's favourite grandchild.

Till I was fifteen I liked wearing my hair long. There was nothing effeminate about it. Ours was a macho creed of the Khalsa and our warrior Guru had ordained that long hair was sacred. When hair began to sprout on my face and genitals I began to question its sanctity. I used depilatory cream to remove my pubic hair and thought women without it and hair in their armpits, as portrayed in marble statuary, looked more fetching than those with bushy growths between their thighs in dirty picture-postcards. Thus the first dogmas I began to question were these external emblems of Sikh separateness: they appeared to me to be as superfluous as superfluous hair on the body; they had no spiritual content. I continued to retain the outward emblems of the Khalsa not because of any conviction but out of a wish to remain a part of the Khalsa fraternity. The sense of belonging gave me a sense of social security, as it does to this day.

As noted earlier, anti-Muslim prejudices were also a part of our religious upbringing. Apart from eating different kinds of meat, the different attitudes to circumcision, etc., we were fed on stories of Muslim tyranny against the Sikhs: two of our

Gurus had laid down their lives rather than convert to Islam; four sons of our last Guru were slain by Muslims: two fighting them, two by being buried alive. Their father had exhorted his followers never to trust Muslims: '*Turk meet tab keejeeye, jab aur jaat mar jaaye*' — only befriend Muslims when other castes are dead. Consequently, much as we addressed Muslim elders of our village as uncles and their women as aunts, we did not rid ourselves of the deep-rooted prejudices ingrained in us. Over the years I made several Muslim friends, but most of all it was Manzur Qadir, whom I came to respect and admire above any other human being, who turned me into a Muslim lover. By the time I befriended the Zakarias in Bombay, I was thoroughly cleansed of my anti-Muslim prejudices and had come round to the naive belief that Muslims could do no wrong.

Prejudices were easier to uproot than overcoming the habit of ritual and prayer. I gave up the latter off and on, but returned to them when in physical pain, when frightened, under emotional stress or in need of help. When my relations with my wife once came to a breaking point and she told me bluntly that she meant to leave me, I spent the whole night at Gurdwara Bangla Sahib praying for strength to face the crisis. Many a time in Tokyo, when I got up at 3 am to work on translations of the hymns of Guru Nanak, I felt the hand of the Guru on my shoulder. I knew it was make-believe, but I found it very comforting. What ultimately put me off rituals were *akhand paths* — non-stop readings of the Granth Sahib by relays of granthis hired at different rates. Recitations went on throughout the night when members of the family who organized the *path* slept. More disturbing to me was the way the holy book came to be treated as an idol. It was 'woken up' in the mornings (*Prakaash*) and put to bed (*Santokh*) in the evenings. In the home of my wife's parents, who were irrationally devout, the prayer-room in which the Granth was kept had an air-conditioner going on throughout the summer months. A Sikh who suddenly came into wealth went further: alongside his prayer-room (*Babaji da kamra*) he built a lavatory of white marble — Indian or European style I do not know.

Kirtan, which I loved, also got commercialized: raagis demanded different rates per hour ranging from a few hundred to a few thousand, depending on their popularity. Granthis, raagees and jathedars became *thekedars* (contractors) of ritual, with vested interests in perpetuating them. This was no better than in the Hindu temples, where gradations of fees were prescribed for the *darshan* of deities. What I saw and experienced in Hindu places of pilgrimage like Hardwar, Varanasi, Jagannath Puri, the Kamakhya Temple in Guwahati, Madurai and elsewhere in south India was enough to turn anyone against them. But Sikhs had also taken the same path in commercializing their religion.

The rejection of ritual was not very painful; rejection of the basics of religion proved harder as it required searching within myself and questioning beliefs on which I had been nurtured. I asked myself, does God really exist? Were his prophets, messiahs, messengers and avatars worthy of being equated with God and worshipped? Were scriptural texts really divinely inspired? Did places of worship deserve the sanctity we accorded them? Did prayer really improve a human being? If I rejected these five pillars of religion, how would I fill the vacuum? How explain the Universe, life on earth and the laws of nature? Reason and logic helped me to demolish much I had been brought up on, but they did not give me all the answers I was looking for. So began the quest for a personal religion. Iqbal echoed my sentiments:

> *Dhoondta phirta hoon main, ai Iqbal, apney aap ko*
> *aap hee goya musaafir, aap hee manzil hoon main.*

> (O Iqbal, I go about everywhere looking for myself
> As if I was the wayfarer as well as the destination.)

The process began in earnest in long discussions with Manzur Qadir. He went along with me in admitting that we do not know where we have come from, what the purpose of our existence on earth is, and what happens to us when we die. There are no plausible reasons for us to accept the existence of God. However, Manzur did not categorically reject the possibility of there being a divine power which governed the cosmos. It was during one of these discussions that the incident of the red ball took place. I converted it into a short story entitled 'The Agnostic'. We were playing with our children in Lawrence Gardens (now Bagh-e-Jinnah) in Lahore when a red ball I tossed into a tree got caught in its branches. We tried in vain to knock it down with stones and sticks. We gave it up for lost and proceeded to the club to treat our children to ice cream. On our way back we saw the ball still lodged where it was. I exclaimed somewhat rashly, 'If that ball drops down, I will believe there is a God'. A gentle breeze shook the branches and the ball dropped right into my hands. 'That should teach you a lesson!' said Manzur. 'You must not treat subjects like the existence of God so lightly.' Although the incident shook me, it did not teach me any lessons. For me it was pure coincidence.

No one has seen God. No one has been able to define God besides investing him with innumerable attributes. He is seen as the creator, preserver and destroyer; benevolent and helpful; father, mother, etc. Also wrathful as well as just. The Upanishads avoid giving a positive description by resorting to the formula *neti, neti* — not this, not this. An Urdu poet admitted defeat.

> *Too dil mein to aataa hai*
> *Samach mein nahin aata*
> *Bas jaan gayaa teyree pahchaan yahee hai*

(You come into my heart,
But my mind cannot comprehend you.
I understand this is the only way to know you.)

I was not much impressed by the Voltarian argument that if there is a watch there must be a watchmaker. I knew a few watchmakers. I do not know any world maker. Why is there not a simple answer to a simple question — if God created the world, who created God? As long as the primary cause of creation remains unknown it is more honest to admit that we do not know, rather than accept fairy tales of God creating the world in six days or in a self-generated, unending cycle of

births, deaths and rebirths. Shaad Azimabadi put the dilemma
in a couplet:

Sunee hikayat-i-hastee to darmiyaan say sunee
Na ibtida kee khabar hai, na intiha maaloom

(All we have heard of the story of life is its middle;
We know not its beginning, we know not its end.)

I have had the opportunity to discuss reincarnation in some
detail with His Holiness the Dalai Lama in Dharamsala. While
he conceded that, as a Buddhist, he had an open mind about
the existence of God, he believed in rebirth after death. When I
asked him to give me proof to substantiate his belief, he gave
me examples of children who recalled events in their previous
births. I protested, 'Surely, Your Holiness cannot accept these
childish fantasies as convincing evidence! How is it that stories
of previous births are current only among Hindus, Jains,
Buddhists, and Sikhs who are brought up on these notions?
Have you ever heard of a Muslim child talking of his previous
life? And even with us, it is mainly children before their teens
who are cited as examples of recognizing their parents or
spouses in their previous lives. When they grow up, all is
forgotten.'

The Dalai Lama laughed uproariously — he is an incarnation
of the Laughing Buddha — and replied candidly, 'If I did not
believe in re-incarnation I would be out of business.'

An interesting answer to my questioning the existence of
God came from Supriya, the twelve-year-old daughter of
Rajmohan Gandhi. I wrote an article spelling out my views on
God and religious beliefs. It was published in *The Indian Express*
of 13 December 1987. Supriya's father was then its resident
editor in Madras. I was in Washington. Supriya wrote to me:
'Dear Uncle, I read your article in Daddy's paper. So you don't
believe in God? You are wrong! Let me tell you God exists. He
visits our garden every day. He talks to my Mummy and my
Daddy. He also talks to me and my little brother. So there!' I
was charmed by the child's outburst and wrote back to her:
'Dear Supriya, I am glad to hear that God visits your home every
day. And that He talks to your Mummy, Daddy, you and your

little brother. But He does not talk to me. Please send me his telephone number.' Supriya did not write back. Three years later I met her parents in Delhi. They told me ruefully: 'Supriya no longer believes in God.' I was delighted I had won a convert in the great-grandchild of two great believers in God, Mahatma Gandhi and C. Rajagopalachari.

There are people who quote what is described as the 'unseen hand' as evidence of the existence of God. Most people will know of incidents of miraculous escapes — of narrowly missed planes which crashed, of being outside their homes when an earthquake brought down the roof that killed other inmates. Such coincidences do puzzle one but can scarcely be treated as positive evidence to prove that the unseen hand was the hand of God.

What should finally clinch the argument about God is that belief in His existence does not make the believer a better human being or the disbeliever a rascal. It could be proved by statistics that the vast majority of black-marketeers, tax-evaders, liars and thugs believe in God, while a fair proportion of non-believers are saintly, try avoiding hurting others, and do not tell lies or cheat.

There is an amusing saying ascribed to the Sikh trading community once settled in Pothohar (now in Pakistan), which was known for its rigid adherence to religious ritual as well as its sharp trading practices:

> *Jhooth vee aseen bolney aan*
> *Ghut vee aseen tolney aan;*
> *Par Sacchey Padshaah*
> *Teyra naa vee aseen lainey aan.*

> (We admit we tell lies,
> We also give short measures;
> But O True King of Kings,
> We also take your name.)

I came to the conclusion that the concept of God is like a gas balloon which will burst on contact with the pin of truth. Or perhaps it is a bunch of gas balloons of different colours floated by different religions and given different names. The one thing these coloured balloons have in common is that they have nothing in them except hot air. In the religion I have evolved for myself and recommend to my readers God has no place.

The Holy Quran promises dire consequences for those who question the existence of God. 'Surely for those who reject the signs of God there is punishment most severe; and God is a mighty avenger' (Surah Imran 2–7). So be it.

Even those who believe in God have little justification for describing Him as omnipotent and just. Whatever evidence we have is to the contrary. Some children are born blind, spastic or mentally retarded; God-fearing parents who never harmed anyone in their lives are punished by the loss of their innocent children.

Next I come to the founders of different religions. I have found that while many people are open-minded about the existence of God, few will tolerate anyone questioning the divinity of the founder of their religion. This is understandable as, while we know nothing about God, we claim to know something about the founders of different faiths. They were humans born to women; they ate, broke wind and defecated; they fell sick and died. Or were murdered or executed. Undoubtedly they were remarkable men with extraordinary powers that swayed the masses and so changed the course of history. Though enough to entitle them to important places in history, this does not justify our investing them with the magical powers we ascribe to an unknown God. We are asked to believe that these vice-regents of God on earth could bring the dead back to life, heal the sick by the touch of their hands, fly to heaven and back in the blinking of an eyelid, stop avalanches by stretching their hands, and walk on water. And, of course, all had hot-line communications with the Almighty. Most of them were illiterate or semi-literate but had the gift of words and were able to rouse deep emotions among their followers. It is not surprising that the religious-minded are very touchy with people questioning the divinity of their human gods: '*Ba Khuda diwana basho, Ba Mohammad hoshiar*' — Say anything you like about Allah, but beware of what you say about Mohammad — applies to all religious communities. It is time we made more mature estimates of the roles of the founders of our religions: give them their due as moulders of public opinion, but worshipping them is neither fair to them nor to ourselves.

And what about the various scriptures? We do not judge them with the same yardstick as we judge works of prose or poetry. Instead we treat them as sacrosanct and invest them with magical powers. They are not meant to be studied as works of religious philosophy but chanted or recited. The less we understand their meaning, the greater is the potency we ascribe to them. Those in ancient languages like Pali, Sanskrit, Greek, Latin, Arabic or Santbhasha have a stronger appeal because few people know their meanings. Their translations into languages which we can comprehend robs them of much of their potency. Read in translation, the Gayatri Mantra, the Psalms, verses from the Quran like the Ayatul Kursee or Sura Yaseen, and the Sikhs' Sohila seem to lose their vaunted powers of healing and dispelling fear. Some passages in all scriptural texts are good prose or poetry, but by and large they are repetitive, banal and often illogical. Personally, I would prefer to read the works of great writers, poets and dramatists — Kalidas, Shakespeare, Goethe, Tolstoy, Tagore, Iqbal, Eliot and Faiz — than any religious scripture. Secular prose and poetry can be read with joy and prove instructive; religious prose and poetry is largely an exercise in self-hypnosis.

There is little that can be said in defence of places of worship. Without exception they have become places of commerce from which parasites like priests, pandas, pujaris, mullahs, mujawars, granthis and ragees draw their sustenance. All they give in return for offerings made at places under their care are palmfuls of prasad paid for by worshippers. When people acquire vested interests in places of worship, these places become bones of contention and subject to litigation and, far too often, attempts are made to seize them by force. The Kaaba has witnessed many bloody battles. So has the Sikhs' Golden Temple. The managements of most Hindu temples and ashrams are periodically before the courts. It can scarcely be contested that the only legitimate place for worship and prayer is one's home. Some religions like Islam enjoin congregational prayers in mosques to engender fraternal feelings amongst the faithful, but there can be little justification for any religious group to impose its presence on others by organizing meetings in public places, taking out processions and broadcasting its beliefs over loudspeakers. A growing aberration are all-night *jagratas* which disturb the sleep of entire localities, including the sick and the aged.

Lastly, I come to prayer and meditation, which are basic to every religious creed. It cannot be disputed that we Indians, whether we be Hindus, Muslims, Christians, Sikhs, Jains or Parsees, spend more time in prayer, pilgrimage and the performance of ritual than any other people in the world. The Hindi adage *'saat vaar aur aath tyohaar'* — there are seven days in the week but eight religious festivals — is not an overstatement. Count the number of religious holidays and the number of hours we spend mumbling prayers, visiting places of pilgrimage, attending *satsangs*, listening to *pravachans, kirtans, bhajans, qawalis*, etc. — it will make a staggering total. Then ask yourself, can a poor, struggling nation like ours afford to expend so much time on pursuits which produce no material benefit? Also ask yourself, does strict adherence to the routine of prayer or telling the beads of a rosary make a person a better human being? These are not always performed for good ends. Robbers, dacoits and thugs are known to pray before embarking on their nefarious errands. Prayer, though outwardly addressed to God, a deity, prophet or a Guru, is essentially addressed to oneself to boost self-confidence and will-power.

The latest fad of the educated Indian is meditation. He will tell you with an air of superiority *'Main mandir-vandir nahin jaata, meditation karta hoon'* — I do not go to temples or such places, I meditate. The exercise involves sitting in the lotus pose, regulating one's breathing and emptying the mind to prevent it 'jumping about like a monkey' from one thought to another. Tall claims are made for rousing the *Kundalini* from the base of the spine through *chakras* to the cranium, till the she-serpent within one is fully roused and the practitioner achieves his goal of self realization. They say it gives them peace of mind. If you ask them 'and what does peace of mind give you?' you will get no answer because there is none. Peace of mind is a sterile concept which achieves nothing except peace of mind, and can only be justified as therapy against hypertension and disturbed minds. There is no evidence that it enhances creativity. On the contrary, it can be established that most great works of art and literature, all the great discoveries of science, were made by highly agitated minds. Allama Iqbal prayed:

> *Khuda tujhey kisee toofaan say aashna kar day*
> *Keh teyrey beher kee maujon mein iztirab naheen*

(May God bring a storm in your life.
There is no agitation on the waves of your life's ocean.)

A word he often used was *talaatum*, restlessness of the mind, as the *sine qua non* of creativity.

It was after much effort of will that I abandoned prayer and worship. I coined the slogan 'work is worship but worship is not work'.

Having discarded the bases of all accepted religions, I felt that the vacuum so created had to be filled because people do need a religion of some sort. The most sensible compromise I can suggest is that we nominally stick to the religions we have been brought up on because they have taken deep emotional roots, but discard what is manifestly irrational or superfluous about them. Most of us have reduced our religions to what we should or should not eat or drink. To many Hindus vegetarianism is an article of faith. There are innumerable variations of vegetarianism, including veganism which forbids eating anything produced by animals, birds and insects: no milk or milk-products; no eggs or honey. There are those who will eat non-fertilized eggs but refuse to eat vegetables grown under the earth like carrots, radishes, potatoes or garlic. This makes as little sense as selective non-vegetarianism. To the Hindu and Sikh, beef is taboo but pork is okay. To Jews and Muslims eating pig is *haraam* but eating cows is okay. Most religious codes forbid consumption of liquor or tobacco. Ask yourselves, what has eating or drinking to do with religion? Diet is a matter of health not of faith.

India's new religion must be based on a work-ethic. It should provide leisure time to recoup one's energy to resume work but discourage uncreative pastimes. We must not waste time. There is a *hadith* of Prophet Mohammed which says: '*La tasabuddhara; Hoo wallahoo*' — Don't waste time; time is God. Every practice that is not productive of material wealth should be discouraged. The religious sanction accorded to asceticism, *vanprastha* and *sanyas* must be withdrawn. If people wish to earn merit, they will not do so in the seclusion of caves or sitting by the banks of the Ganga, but by working amongst the poor and the handicapped. For me, Mother Teresa, Bhagat Puran Singh, Ela Bhatt and P.K. Madhavan are worth more than a hundred Shankaracharyas, Chinmayanandas and other godmen and godwomen put together. The only form of meditation that I recommend is to see your face in the mirror every night before retiring — looking into your own eyes is a very difficult thing to do — and ask yourself, 'Have I wronged anyone today?'

The only religious principle I subscribe to is *ahimsa* — non-violence. It is indeed *paramo-dharma* — the supreme faith. The rest is of marginal importance.

There are many other irrational beliefs which enjoy religious patronage. On top of my list are forecasting the future through astrology, palmistry, numerology and the use of ancient texts like the *Bhrigu Samhita*. All Hindu children have horoscopes cast. Marriages are arranged after matching horoscopes. Despite centuries of experience that there is no scientific basis for equating worldly events to movements of the stars, our belief in astrology remains unshaken. The third battle of Panipat was lost by the Marathas who outnumbered their Afghan adversaries ten to one because their commander gave ear to his Rajya Jyotishi instead of using his common sense. In 1962 when eight planets were in conjunction (*ashta graha*) our astrologers proclaimed that on 3 February at 5.30 pm the world would come to an end. Trains, planes and buses went empty. People stayed in their homes with their families. Tonnes of ghee were burnt in performing hawans to propitiate the gods.

Nothing happened, but India was made to look very foolish and backward in the eyes of the world. Not a single astrologer forecast the assassination of Indira Gandhi or her son, Rajiv. Many claimed, as is their practice, to have done so after the event. All the horoscopes my friend Charanjit Singh had cast for himself promised him over seventy years of life. He died at fifty-one. The daughter of a well-known astrologer whose forecasts I published in *The Hindustan Times* and who is consulted by the Prime Minister and members of the Cabinet had her marriage arranged after matching her horoscope with that of her husband-to-be. The marriage broke up within a month.

Belief in the occult persists. Mrs Gandhi had Tantric rites performed in her home to combat evil forces; Rajiv Gandhi was persuaded by Home Minister Buta Singh and Speaker Balram Jakhar to seek the blessings of Deoraha Baba who sat naked aloft a tree. He touched their foreheads with his big toe! A few weeks later Rajiv lost his Prime Ministership, Buta Singh and Jakhar were defeated in the parliamentary elections. Many Chief Ministers, including Janaki Ballabh Patnaik of Orissa and N.T. Rama Rao of Andhra Pradesh, practise black magic. Jayalalitha of Tamil Nadu has an astrologer to advise her every day. Most Indian politicians, including Prime Minister Narasimha Rao, subscribe to *Rahu Kalam* — the inauspicious hour. Astrological magazines enjoy wide circulations and the top astrologers earn huge incomes. Nothing more approximates to *haram ki kamaaee* (illicit earning) than that made out of the cupidity of the gullible. I would recommend religious censure against the practice of astrology.

Every religion was a creature of its times and evolved to meet prevailing social and economic needs. To describe them as eternal truths for all time to come is sheer bunkum. When the world was sparsely populated and wars, famine and epidemics wiped away large sections of the population, there was reason for religious teachers to tell people to go forth and multiply. When women outnumbered men because men were killed in battle, there was justification for sanctioning polygamy. Today many parts of the world, most of all India, are grossly overpopulated and the male-female ratio is about the same. There must be religious sanction to forbid bigamy and couples having more than one child. More important than their taking vows to remain faithful to each other is trying to make them swear that they will voluntarily submit themselves to sterilization on the birth of their first child. No concession should be made for religious communities which regard birth control as irreligious. Indians with no thought for the future of their country continue to have large families irrespective of their religious affiliations. President Giri had sixteen children, Prime Minister Narasimha Rao has eight; the Chief Minister of Bihar, Laloo Prasad Yadav, still virile as ever, has nine. None of them were or are Catholics or Muslims who are accused of breeding recklessly.

I would not only make the one-child norm an integral part of the marriage vows, but encourage the parents of a bride to make the supply of condoms a part of her dowry and blessed by the priest performing the marriage rites.

Another tradition which has the sanction of religion and needs drastic change is the Hindu, Sikh, Jain and Buddhist manner of disposal of their dead. Two forms were practised in olden times: burning dead bodies with wood and casting them into rivers (*jal parwaah*). Throwing half-burnt bodies into rivers continues to be surreptitiously practised to this day. But the commonest form is to burn them on funeral pyres. Only a few large cities have gas or electric crematoria. They are almost entirely used by the educated rich or to dispose of the unclaimed corpses of beggars. On an average a funeral pyre requires two quintals of wood to be burnt with every dead body. Over one hundred Hindu-Sikh-Jain or Buddhists die every day in Delhi. In other large cities like Bombay and Calcutta mortality is much higher. It has been calculated that two crore quintals of wood are destroyed annually to dispose of human corpses. Entire forests go up in flames every day in a country already dangerously short of forest cover and therefore subject to soil erosion and the silting of dams. The answer is not more gas or electric crematoria — we do not have the means to make them — but Hindu-Sikh-Jain-Buddhist burial grounds near every village, town and city. There is nothing in these religions requiring cremation by wood. Many Hindu communities in south India bury their dead. Annadorai and C. Ramachandran were buried. Swami Chinmayananda, MP and a great propounder of the Gita was buried seated in his chair. Many Jain Munis are also buried. These cemeteries should not be like the Muslim or Christian ones with *pucca* tombs. The dead should be stood up in the ground to save space and no memorial tablets raised above them. Instead, the site should be marked by planting a tree, or the land be ploughed back for agriculture every five years. People living along the coast should immerse their dead in the sea at some distance from the shore.

In my will I have provided that I should be buried in the Bahai cemetery without any religious ceremony. The Bahais have acceded to my request, provided they can say their prayers for my soul. Since I do not believe in a soul I could not care less.

We have to revive the worship of trees — not as objects of religious adoration but as things to be preserved for posterity. The Chipko movement should be given religious backing, and the use of wood for furniture or building forbidden and replaced by synthetic material now available in plenty. There are communities like the Bishnois of Haryana and Rajasthan which forbid cutting trees and killing animals. Their practice should be made universal. There should be religious sanction against killing animals for sport. Animals live off each other but humans have other resources of food and should be discouraged from making their bodies tombs for beasts.

Planting trees should be made an integral part of religious ritual and our educational system. At every *mundan*, sacred thread or marriage ceremony, a certain number of trees should be required to be planted. Students should not be given their degrees or diplomas unless they provide evidence of having planted and nurtured to health a specified number of trees. In charities left by the dead, tree planting should be given top priority — above building temples, mosques, schools or hospitals. Tree planting must become a nation-wide peoples' movement. Only then will we succeed in making our country as green, salubrious and healthy as it was in the times of our earliest forefathers. The state alone cannot do it. If religion has to have any meaning today, it has to lend its moral authority to such movements.

Most of what I have written in this chapter recapitulates what I have written and spoken about in dozens of articles and public speeches. However, I felt that my life story would not be complete unless I spelt out my beliefs in greater detail.

17 On Writing and Writers

I HAVE ALREADY touched on circumstances which turned me from law to public relations, teaching, and, finally, to journalism and writing. I have been persuaded to say something about the writers I got to know, those who have influenced me, what it takes to become a writer, whether writing is fun and if one can make a good living out of it.

Despite my poor showing in school and college, I have harboured the ambition of becoming a writer since my infancy. Even while at junior school, I once acquired a notebook to write a novel. In bold letters I wrote its title on the first page: 'Sheilla', by Khushwant Singh. At that age the name Sheilla sounded ultra-modern and more impressive than the commonplace Sheila, with only one 'l'. I was enamoured of athletic girls who wore their hair in pigtails tied with red ribbons, who wore shorts and exchanged smart words with boys. I carried the notebook with me for several days and perhaps scribbled a few lines on my heroine. 'Sheilla' was never written.

In my five years in college and the Inns of Court in England the desire to try my hand at writing took more concrete shape. I was bored by law books but enjoyed reading fiction and poetry. Fortunately, being endowed with a reasonably good memory, I added to the repertoire of poems I had learnt in India. I also vaguely sensed that, while poetry was something that gushed out of a poet, prose writing needed a background of wide reading and a larger vocabulary. I began to keep a dictionary by my side and marked every word that I did not understand. I went back to the Bible, to which I had been introduced at St Stephens College. I found the New Testament somewhat pedantic, the Old Testament more poetic. The Song of Solomon, the Psalms, Proverbs and the Book of Job I read over and over again and memorized passages from, some of which remain with me to this day. At the same time, I read a lot of nonsense verse; limericks, clerihews, nursery rhymes, Lewis Carroll and the operas of Gilbert and Sullivan. From a Punjabi rustic I tried to make myself a middle-class English gentleman. I even took to solving *The Times* crosswords, an addiction on which I have wasted many precious hours of my life. Of the many novelists I read, the two who impressed me most were Aldous Huxley and Somerset Maugham. I wished I could evolve the Huxleyan turn of phrase and malicious wit with Maugham's ability to hold the reader's attention. But, to be quite honest, what inspired me to write were not great authors but the second-raters, mainly Indians, who had been published in England and the United States. I read Mulk Raj Anand, Raja Rao and R.K. Narayan. I felt that I could write as well as they, and if they could be published abroad, so would I. I was not far wrong in my self-estimate.

During my second posting in England I seriously contemplated taking up writing as a career. Like many aspiring writers, I tried to befriend famous men and women of letters and get them to autograph their books for me. I got autographed copies of Francois Mauriac's novels as well as his photograph. I got a hand-written note by André Gide to his lady secretary; I shook hands with Stephen Spender, Mary McCarthy, Norman Mailer, Compton Mackenzie, Sacheverell Sitwell, Dylan Thomas, Rosamond Lehmann, Samuel Beckett and some others. This juvenile worship of authors lasted a few years before I realized that knowing authors does not help anyone to become one. Writing is a solitary profession in which no one can help you except yourself. There is no such institution as the *Guru-chela*, mentor-guide, relationship in the writing world. A writer has to be his own mentor-guide and ultimate judge.

The second posting in London saw the publication of my short *History of the Sikhs* and a verse translation of Guru Nanak's morning prayer. By the time I returned to Delhi I had more than a half of my novel *Mano-Majra* (*Train to Pakistan*) in my baggage. It took me another month by myself in Bhopal to finish it. I have already referred to all this in an earlier chapter.

It was in the following two years, working in the External Services of All India Radio, that I got to know Nirad C. Chaudhuri, Ruth Jhabvala and Manohar Malgaonkar. All three became close friends. Nirad Babu's *Autobiography of An Unknown Indian* had just been published. It had created an uproar in Indian government circles because its dedication was to the British Empire, to which Nirad Babu ascribed all that was worthwhile in India. I was charmed by his command of the English language, his descriptions of the Bengal countryside and his unusual analysis of the country's problems. I sought his friendship at a time he had been declared a social outcaste. He needed friends and accepted the hand of friendship I extended him.

Nirad Babu was diminutive in size, he wore a suit and tie and an incredible khaki sola topee that was a size too large for him. He looked a comic figure. When he strode out of his house, street urchins followed him chanting 'Johnnie Walker, Johnnie Walker'. He also had an explosive temper. Once his room-mate in the office made some uncharitable remark about his being a bootlicker of the British. Nirad Babu took umbrage and shouted at him, 'You cur, withdraw that remark or I will hammer your skull'. The man refused to retract. Whereupon Nirad Babu walked across to his table and hit him savagely with a heavy glass paperweight till he drew blood. The two of them went to the head of the department, Mehra Masani, to lodge complaints. Poor Mehra could do little except reprimand them for behaving like children. She had a soft spot for Nirad Chaudhuri and, like most other open-minded Indians, admired his guts and scholarship. The Minister of Information and Broadcasting, Keskar, was not one of them. When his attention was drawn to the dedication he ordered Nirad Chaudhuri to be dismissed from service and threatened to black-list papers which carried Nirad's articles. Nirad, who had no private means, and a family to support, was in dire straits. A few friends comprising Mehra Masani, Ruth Jhabvala, her husband, and I rallied round him. We made it a point to invite him and his wife to our homes. There he met many foreign admirers. One book had made him a celebrity. Amongst his admirers was my father

Sobha Singh who had not read him, but only heard of him from me. Every time he came to our house, my father took him round his garden to show him his exotic varieties of roses. Nirad had exaggerated regard for people with British titles, and my father was a Knight. My father in turn sensed that Nirad Babu was much sought after by his English friends and was the centre of attraction at every party. They got on very well.

Nirad could be very provocative. Once when dining with the Jhabvalas he told Jhab's mother that Indians did not regard Parsees as fellow Indians. Mamma Jhabvala, whose husband had been jailed in the Meerut Conspiracy Case, lost her cool and exploded: 'You British toady, how dare you question our patriotism?' She left the party to retire to her room. Nirad remained unperturbed and repeated his assertion.

The trouble with Nirad Babu was that he knew more of everything than anyone else I have ever met. His knowledge was encyclopaedic. Whether it was history, literature, science, natural phenomena, or whatever, he knew it. Once at a party at the house of Henry Croom Johnson, then head of the British Council, I told Henry's wife, Jane, that I had spent the morning listening to a learned lecture on someone called Wittgenstein and his theory of hydro something or the other. 'I don't think any member of the audience had heard of Wittgenstein,' I said, without realizing that Wittgenstein was a legend in philosophical circles. 'I bet no one in this room except perhaps Chaudhuri knows of him,' I continued somewhat brazenly. My bet was taken.

Jane announced it to her guests, all of whom were scholars. No one had heard of Wittgenstein, but Nirad Babu proceeded to pronounce on Wittgenstein's theory. Even more incredible was another performance in my home. I had asked Sillanpie, the Icelandic Nobel Prize winner to dine with me and invited a few Indian authors to meet him. Nirad Chaudhuri hogged the evening lecturing to the Nobel Prize winner on Icelandic literature.

Nirad Babu had his eccentricities. On his roof garden he grew a variety of cacti which bloomed for an hour or two at sunrise. He invited people to his flat in distant Mori Gate to watch the spectacle. Fleets of cars would wind their way through the city to be present at the bewitching hour. He rarely invited people for a meal because his wife had to do the cooking. When he did, it was an unforgettable experience. At home he was always in his Bengali kurta-dhoti and did his writing sitting cross-legged on the floor. At every dinner he had a selection of vintage wines. First he subjected his guests to a lecture on the region from which the particular wine came, the best vintage years and its special bouquet. Then he poured out thimblefuls in small cut-glasses with more information on the cut-glass industry of Europe. There was never enough wine to refill the glasses. The food served was Bengali. The Chaudhuris had no hang ups about eating beef or pork but preferred *maachher jhole* — fish curry.

My friendship with Nirad Babu was a one-sided affair. He was the guru, I his humble disciple. Whenever he disagreed with me, he called me a fool. His wife often protested, 'If you behave like this you will lose the only friend you have.' I had no intention of losing him. I have reason to believe neither did he. In many of his books there are references to me, and to no other of his Indian admirers. I knew he loved India but could not stomach Indians. When he left for England to write Max Muller's biography I sensed that he would never come back. He stayed in Oxford all his life.

With Ruth Prawer Jhabvala it was very slow-going at first. She was a shy, demure young woman of Polish Jewish origin. When she came to India as a bride, she was enamoured of everything Indian, including her architect husband. The story going round was about her mother's strong disapproval of her marriage. She was alarmed when Ruth started dating the young Parsi student of architecture in England. When Ruth announced her decision to marry him, her mother is said to have remarked, 'But he is not even a Goye!' They were deeply in love with each other. One evidence of this was that Ruth was pregnant every second year: they had three lovely daughters.

I got to know Ruth when I was in charge of the English section of All India Radio's External Services. I invited her to record talks for us. She wrote good scripts and rarely had to repeat passages she recorded. In the few minutes when she came to my room to be escorted to the studio and for a cup of coffee I was able to gain her confidence. She was extremely reticent. I suspect it was my strong pro-Israeli feelings (I had set up the Indo-Israel Friendship Society) that made her thaw towards me. She was strongly Zionist.

The first time she and her husband came to dinner along with the Chaudhuris and Mehra Masani, the two clung to each other most of the evening. He was an edgy person and could only relax with people he knew well. Thereafter, whenever we invited them for dinner we had to be careful about our other guests. Ruth's first couple of novels had won her many foreign admirers and people in the embassies in Delhi wanted to meet her. I discovered that, no matter how anti-Nazi a German had been, Ruth found it difficult to talk to him or her. Most of our parties when the Jhabvalas were present were restricted to a small coterie of close friends: Mehra Masani, the Nirad Chaudhuris and, later, Catherine Freeman, the wife of the British High Commissioner.

Ruth was very short-sighted and even after many years of living in Delhi her Hindustani remained very elementary. Her readers wondered how she was able to portray Indian characters so accurately and get their dialogue right. She did not personally know many lower middle-class Indians, the people she wrote about. Her husband was a good raconteur and an excellent mimic. She saw Indians through his eyes and heard their talk through his ears.

Many summers the Jhabvalas came up to Kasauli and stayed at the Alasia Hotel, a stone's throw below our bungalow, Raj Villa. They were in and out of our home every other day. Once I accompanied them down to Delhi in their large station wagon. One of the girls was sick most of the way and the car began to give trouble. Jhab stopped at a mechanic shop in Panipat bazar to have it mended. Soon we were surrounded by curious onlookers. Jhab was a handsome, debonair looking young man. His *mem* and three pretty girls made a nice family picture-postcard. I was probably taken to be their driver. Jhab started getting irritated with the crowd and pleaded, '*Bhai, yeh koee tamasha hai?'* — Brothers, is this some kind of show? Some turned away, others took their places. Jhab's voice got louder. Then someone remarked *'Koee actor maaloom hota hai'* — He seems to be some kind of an actor. That touched Jhab to the quick and he exploded, *'Actor teyra baap, actor teyree maan, actor teyree bhain, actor teyree beti'* — Actor your father, mother, sister and daughter. It worked. The crowd melted away.

Reading Ruth Jhabvala's novels in chronological order, the reader will sense her growing disenchantment with India and Indians. The process is complete with her best novel *Heat and Dust*, which won her the Booker award. I sensed that it was a matter of time when, like Nirad Chaudhuri, she too would quit India to settle in Europe or the United States. By the time it came for her to decide, some of her novels had been made into films by the Merchant-Ivory team. More were on the sets. Her film-makers lived in New York. So Ruth opted for New York. By then her husband discovered he could draw as well as design buildings. His sketches of Delhi's ancient monuments were an instant success.

Ruth introduced me to Anita Desai, the half-Jewish, half Bengali wife of a business executive. She was a frail, good-looking girl with two small children. I suspect she was inspired by Ruth and their Jewishness brought them closer. There was a certain similarity in their writing, and Anita too enjoyed more esteem among foreigners than she did amongst her own countrymen. She spent one summer in Kasauli. That year there was a terrible forest fire which devastated an entire hillside covered with inflammable pine-needles. Some houses were also burnt down. Anita's novel *Fire on the Mountain* was based on this experience. Like Ruth, Anita remained conscious of her Jewish heritage. Her novel *Baumgartner's Bombay* is based around a Jewish family.

During my two years with All India Radio I was able to nurture an ambition to write in one man who was later to be recognized as the John Masters of India. Like Masters, Manohar (Mack) Malgaonkar had served in the army. He was a very good shikari and took assignments from travel agencies to take out foreign visitors on tiger shoots. He soon sickened of the slaughter of these beautiful animals and gave up this job. He showed me a short story he had written on how he had saved the life of a particularly large, handsome but stupid young tiger who was in the habit of stretching itself in the middle of the road. It could have been a sitting duck for anyone armed with a rifle. Mack fired shots close to it to warn it that humans were dangerous animals and should be kept at a distance. The tiger stopped displaying itself. I had the story broadcast. Thereafter there was no stopping Mack Malgaonkar. A stream of novels poured out of his pen — fast moving, macho and with a strong sense of the dramatic. They were very well received in England and the United States. Being Maharashtrian, he also wrote several historical novels on Mahratha heroes. In the course of churning out books, Mack discovered that he was sitting on a gold mine; manganese was located in his ancestral estate not far from Goa. He now lives like an English country gentleman in a large house with a large garden and his own private bathing pool. He has his Scotch, Feni and wine while writing books and columns for newspapers.

I was still in the phase of my life when I believed that anyone who wrote well was worth knowing. So I went out of my way to befriend Sasthi Brata. That was not his real name, but an abbreviation of the Bengali Brahmin name, Bhattacharya. I read Brata's autobiographical novel *Confessions of an Indian Woman-eater* which had been published in England. I had not read anything as explicitly erotic and well written as these adventures of a Casanova on the rampage. I praised it in my columns in *The Illustrated Weekly of India*. I also read pieces written by him in prestigious English journals like *The Spectator* and *The New Statesman* — very lucid and well-worded. Later I learnt that Sasthi Brata had worked for *The Statesman* (Calcutta and Delhi) and most of the girls he had written about were well-known to Delhi's coffee house circles and easily recognizable. They were understandably very upset at Bratas's *Confessions*. He was then living in London, working for some kind of engineering or chemical firm and probably married to or living with an English girl.

Sasthi Brata rang me up from London to tell me that he planned to visit India and, if I commissioned him to write a series of articles for *The Illustrated Weekly*, he would be able to pay for his stay in India. I readily agreed to do so. He asked me to book a room for him for a week at the Taj Mahal Hotel. I did so.

On the evening of his arrival I asked him over for a drink at my apartment. I invited my son Rahul and an attractive Parsi girl, Dina Vakil, who was with one of the journals published by the Times of India group of papers. Sasthi turned out to be a very short man with a small goatee and a torrent of words — a very engaging conversationalist. While we were still trying to get to know each other, he abruptly turned to Dina Vakil and asked her, 'Are you a virgin?'

Dina did not blush with embarrassment. She did not bat an eyelid and replied with a smile, ' That's for men to find out.' Sasthi, I discovered, wanted to shock people to attract attention.

Sasthi spent over a week at the Taj and lavishly entertained his friends. At the end of his stay he signed his name in the bill with the noting that it should be sent to the editor of *The Illustrated Weekly of India*. I refused to pay it as Sasthi had given me no articles and I had only booked the room for him in his name not in the name of the *Weekly*. The triangular correspondence between the hotel, Sasthi and myself went on for several months. Camelia Panjabi, Director of the hotel, finally wrote off the bill.

A year or so later Sasthi turned up in India again. I refused to see him. He stayed some days with my son, borrowed money from him and, to the best of my knowledge, never returned it.

I have not seen any more books or articles written by Sasthi Brata for many years. A great pity, because the fellow had so much to him.

Of contemporary writers I rate V.S. Naipaul amongst the best. The first novel written by him that I read was *A House for Mr*

Biswas. Although I have never been to the Caribbean I could tell this was an authentic account of the community of Indian origin settled there. All the characters came alive and their dialogue was very funny. Some time after Naipaul had been acclaimed as the rising star in the English world of literature, he came on a visit to the land of his forefathers. With him was his wife, a very unhappy looking English woman. By the time they arrived in Delhi both seemed very disillusioned with what they had seen. Naipaul expected to be acclaimed as a son of India and perhaps show his wife how admired he was. At the time only the *cognoscenti* — anywhere a very small minority — had read Naipaul.

I became their guide. I took them round to my friends' homes: few of them had read him. To restore his self-esteem I took them to the local bookshops to show him how much his novels were in demand. I took the couple to Suraj Kund. It was late February and the valley close to the ruins of this ancient city of Delhi was ablaze with the Flame of the Forest in full flower. We had a breakfast of sandwiches and hot coffee beneath the massive walls of the Tuglakabad fort. Children from a nearby village came to gawp at us. They were in tattered clothes, noses running and flies glued to their dirty eyes. In his *Area of Darkness* Naipaul dismissed the spectacular scene at Suraj Kund in just four words, but dealt in great detail with grimy village children. He did the same describing the saffron fields in Kashmir — a passing reference to the autumn crocuses in bloom, greater detail about Kashmiri women raising their long phirans to defecate. Naipaul seemed to have an obsession with filth and squalor.

He was also very edgy. He shrank from physical contact and repulsed anyone who wanted to greet him with an embrace. He was also allergic to being photographed. On his subsequent visits he had all the acclaim he deserved. He was quite eager to be invited out: it gave him material for the book he was writing. I took him along to a party to which I had been invited by one of the Modis. We were amongst the first to arrive. Lined along the wall were a bevy of attractive young women. We made a bee line for them, only to discover that they spoke no English and were call girls brought in to entertain bored businessmen. But it was not always the same. I took him and his companion to Anees Jung's, where Ram Niwas Mirdha, the Cabinet Minister, was present. Mirdha had read each of Naipaul's books. The evening went very smoothly.

On at least two occasions I was rung up by the literary editor of the *New York Times* to get ready to do a profile on V.S. Naipaul, as he expected Naipaul to be given the Nobel Prize for literature that year. I brushed up my notes. The coveted and much deserved prize did not go to Naipaul. At that time it seemed they would never give it to a coloured man writing in English. The British government made amends by conferring a knighthood on Naipaul, but it was not the same thing as getting the Nobel Prize. Naipaul never prefixes his name with 'Sir'. And strangely enough, once he realized he would not get the Nobel Prize the quality of his writing went into decline.

Through Vidya Naipaul I got to know his mother and his younger brother, Shiva. I sensed that V.S. had not much time for either. We had his mother over for meals many times. It was evident that Shiva was her favourite son. I took her to some of Delhi's bookstores. There were rows of books by V.S. Naipaul on display but rarely one by Shiva. 'Why don't you have more of my Shiva's books?' she would ask the shopkeepers. She had few friends and I suspect did not much enjoy her visit to India.

Although I met Shiva a few times (my son saw much more of him), he seemed to be more relaxed in Indian surroundings than his brother or mother. He was more outgoing and made friends easily. I suspected that he would prefer to make his home in India rather than in London or Trinidad.

One Christmas my American publisher Barney Rosset of Grove Press sent me Ginsberg's poem *The Howl* as a gift. I was impressed with its explosive power and in my letter of thanks asked him more about the poet. A few months later I was in New York staying with my friends Professor John Hazard of

Colombia University and his wife Susan. Rosset asked me to dine with him in a restaurant in Greenwich Village. Alan Ginsberg was his other guest.

Ginsberg was a very semitic type, deliberately made up to look unkempt and grimy. He proceeded to try and shock me. 'Do you masturbate? Are you a homosexual? Do you smoke cannabis?' I found it very childish. He proceeded to roll himself a cigarette, inserted some white powder in the tobacco and took a few long pulls and exhaled through his nostrils. 'Would you like to try it?' he asked. 'I would,' I replied, 'but I don't know how to inhale smoke. Give me some and I'll try it out at night before I go to bed.'

Back home with the Hazards I tried out the hash-laden cigarette Ginsberg had given me. It only produced a violent fit of coughing — no hallucination of any kind. I did not know how to inhale.

A couple of years later Ginsberg and his boyfriend Peter Orlovsky arrived at my doorstep in Delhi — both in khadi shirts, lungis and sandals, both unshaven, uncombed and looking very untidy. Ginsberg, being short and dark, could pass off as an Indian; Orlovsky was tall and ash blond and could only be a Scandinavian in Indian garb. I lost sight of them for many months as they travelled to Varanasi, Patna, Calcutta, visiting as many Hindu places of pilgrimage as they could. They lived with sadhus, smoked ganja in chillams, slept in the open on riverside ghats with corpses burning close by, wrote poetry and fucked each other. They had not had their fill of India and their visas were due to expire. They turned up at the American embassy to ask for help in having their visas extended. The Consulate official advised them to get letters from an Indian citizen certifying their good character. They came to me. By now Ginsberg was more hirsute than ever, his hair was very long, his beard was wild and there was much growth on his body. Orlovsky was a blond version of his friend. They told me of all they had seen and done — none of it deserving certificates of good character. However, I wrote down whatever they wanted me to write. The Indian government granted them their extension of visas. I never saw Ginsberg or Orlovsky again.

Ginsberg came to Princeton when I was teaching there. He had become a cult figure by now and drew large crowds of students at his recitations. I rang him up in his hotel. He was most effusive in his greetings, but I could sense that he had not placed me.

Recently, the poems he had written in India were offered to Penguin (India). My colleagues David Davidar and Zamir Ansari were for accepting them as they were being offered at a throwaway price by Ginsberg's American publisher. They gave the American edition to me for approval. By sheer chance (and good luck) I came across a passage written at Kalighat. Ginsberg had let himself go with great gusto about what he would do to Hindu goddesses because 'they were all prostitutes'. I rang up my colleagues. 'Oh, my God!' they exclaimed. 'We must take the passage out at once.' We did. This was at a time when the ire of Muslim fundamentalists against Penguin-Viking was at its height for publishing *The Satanic Verses*. Ginsberg's references to Hindu goddesses were far more offensive than Rushdie's to the Prophet Mohammed's wives. I have little doubt that, had we published the unexpurgated verses of Ginsberg's poems on India, it would have been the end of Penguin India, its Indian proprietors the Sarkars of *Anand Bazar Patrika*, David Davidar, Zamir Ansari and myself.

Not many writers come to Kasauli. However, one summer two well-known Hindi novelists, Upendra Nath Ashk and Rajendra Yadav, who were staying at Kalyan Hotel, called on me. I was familiar with their names but had not read anything by them. Both of them were eager to tell me of their achievements in Hindi literature. Yadav was somewhat reserved in praising himself and referred to his wife, Manu Bhandari, who was also into writing; with one novel *Mahabhoj*, Manu achieved stardom. It became a bestseller and was filmed. One morning at breakfast Ashk told my wife that he was only a child of seven when he realized he was destined to be a *maha likhaaree* — a great writer. He was a good storyteller; his tiffs with his first wife, whom he wanted to be rid of, were as cruel as they were comic. Ashk wrote a large number of novels and set up his own publishing house in Allahabad. Despite his eminence he remained in dire need of money. Once he dramatically announced that he would stop writing because there was no money in it, and instead that he would set up a vegetable stall because there was more money in vending potatoes and cauliflower than in churning out novels. The gimmick earned him a lot of publicity.

Modesty is little known in the writing world. Indian writers, perhaps because many are less sophisticated than Europeans, do not consider self-praise to be a form of vulgarity. Writers in the regional languages can be blatantly eulogistic about their achievements. Ghalib, the greatest poet of the Urdu language, boasted that while dozens of others wrote poetry, his style and thought marked him out as someone unique. Modern writers organize celebrations for their birthdays, get their cronies to chant their praises and have *abhinandan granths* (commemoration volumes of praise) published and distributed.

Some Indians writing in English, too, are not above indulging in self-praise. Since not many people read books, least of all politicians and civil servants, and public memory is short, beating one's own drum pays handsome dividends. Second-rate writers receive literary awards judged by people who have not read their works. They get diplomatic assignments and are nominated to the Upper House of Parliament. Those who protest against recognition of the second-rate are dismissed as being envious. Canvassing for awards has become common practice. More bizarre are the claims periodically made by Indian writers that they have been short-listed for the Nobel Prize for literature. The first to aspire for this highest literary award was my friend Govind Desani. He had written just one novel, *All About H. Hatter*, and a short lyrical play, *Hali. Hatter* was undoubtedly an astonishingly good piece of writing but I could hardly think of anyone aspiring for the Nobel Prize on so thin an output as Desani's. Nevertheless, dear Govind cajoled me (I was then Press Attache in London) into recommending his name to the Selection Committee as a nominee of the Indian Government. The matter was referred to Dr Radhakrishnan, then Ambassador in Moscow. He gave me a round ticking off.

One year all Delhi's papers carried the news on their front pages that the Hindi writer Vatsayan, who wrote under the pseudonym Agyeya, had been informed that he was to be that year's Nobel Laureate. For the next few days the papers were full of the great honour done to Hindi, and interviews with his then wife Kapila. A few days later came the announcement that the prize had gone to the Israeli writer, Agnon. When questioned on how the misinformation had spread the Vatsyayans gave the naive explanation that the telegraph clerk had misread Agyeya for Agnon. Which telegraph clerk, which post office, no one was clear.

The most brazen attempt to bolster his self-image was made by Dr Gopal Singh Dardi. I have already written about the canard he spread about himself and the benefits he reaped out of it.

A few years later, there were reports that the Malayalam poetess Kamala Das had been short-listed for the prize. This also made front page news in all the papers. Kamala has quite a reputation as a poet in her own language and had written an autobiographical novel with explicit portrayal of her marital sex life. It was not a good novel but received wide publicity. I wrote about Kamala spreading the story about being short-listed and regretted that a nice woman like her should have succumbed to the temptation of building herself up thus. She was furious. She rang me up and cried on the phone. Her son sent me a legal notice demanding an apology. Or else. Nothing followed.

As an editor of various journals, newspapers, and as an honorary editor of Penguin-Viking in India I have done whatever little I can to encourage young talent. Those who had anything in them made it; among them, one is M.J. Akbar, who rose to be editor of *The Telegraph* of Calcutta, then a Member of

Parliament and the author of several books on politics and social affairs. Another is Bachi Karkaria, whom I picked up as collaborator on a book on the Wadias of Bombay Dyeing. (The Wadias did not like the text and it was not published.) I suggested her name for a biography of the hotelier M.S. Oberoi, which was published by Penguin-Viking. As a reviewer of books for magazines, radio and TV I have been able to project many up-and-coming authors like Amitav Ghosh, Upamanyu Chatterjee, Githa Hariharan, Shama Futehally, Allan Sealey, Rukun Advani, Ramesh Menon, Mukul Kesavan and, above all, Vikram Seth. In my review of *The Golden Gate* I wrote that at long last India had produced a writer of international calibre who would win the highest laurels for his country. The success of his novel *A Suitable Boy* confirmed that my prediction had not been wrong.

Encouraging young hopefuls has its hazards. Among those whom I brought into the writing world with fatal consequences was Indrani Aikath-Gyaltsen — a Bengali girl from Bihar and married to a Tibetan tea-planter managing an estate near Darjeeling. We were introduced to each other by the wife of the German Ambassador who had stayed with her in the Glen Burn tea estate. We started writing to each other. She sent me some of her poems. I wrote to her admitting candidly that I knew very little about poetry but that if she wrote a novel or short stories I could be of some help. She had her poems published at her own expense and dedicated them to me. I was flattered and pressed her to turn to writing fiction. She started sending me chapters of her novel *Daughters of the House*, which was promptly accepted by my colleague David Davidar for Penguin-Viking and sold to publishers in England and the United States. Indrani was launched on a new career. But she was impetuous and impatient for success; she wanted instant recognition. Once, when she was with me at the Calcutta Book Fair, she asked me, 'Why doesn't anyone ask me for my autograph?' I assured her that people would do so after she had written some more novels. It was in the last few days of the Book Fair that her second novel *Cranes Morning* (also dedicated to me) was released. It got excellent reviews in India and was also accepted by foreign publishers. That was not good enough for her; she wanted to be recognized and talked about. She was commissioned to write a weekly column for *The Statesman* of Calcutta. She was very excited by that assignment because most of her friends read *The Statesman*. She did not put in the work required of a columnist. More than once I warned her that churning up whatever came to her mind was not good enough. After a couple of months *The Statesman* stopped taking her column. This came as a severe blow to her *amour propre*. Her relations with her family members deteriorated at the same time. She left Darjeeling to be by the side of her ailing father in Chaibasa (Bihar). He had suffered a stroke and was paralysed. She was by his bedside when he died. She had never got on well with her mother and sister. There were differences between them over the division of her father's mining estates and the house in Chaibasa. But something far more serious was gnawing her inside. Her letters to me became shorter and she complained of being in deep depression. Penguin-Viking had accepted her third novel but this did little to get her out of the mood of despair. By strange coincidence this third novel was entitled *Hold My Hand I am Dying*. One morning she was found lying unconscious on the floor by her bed. A doctor was summoned. Her husband was sent for from Calcutta. The next day she died with no one holding her hand.

Indrani wrote me a brief letter the day before she died. It reached me two days later. It indicated that there was something bothering her. I had reason to suspect she had taken her own life. When everything seemed to be going her way why would she put an end to her own career?

A possible answer came some months later when Penguin-Viking received a legal notice that portions of *Cranes Morning* had been lifted from an American novel published twenty years earlier. I suspect Indrani had received letters from readers accusing her of plagiarizing before the attention of the publisher of the American novel was drawn to it. Indrani must have felt it was only a matter of time when the plagiarism would blow up in her face and her dreams of becoming a celebrated writer turn to dust. I examined the relevant passages in both the novels. There was no doubt that she had lifted them from the other novel, with minor variations. It was equally clear that she need not have done so as she could handle the language as well as anyone. It was simply her anxiety and impatience to get on with the novel and finish it that made her take this foolish risk. I cannot forgive myself for keeping the pressure on her because I became dearly fond of her. She was my protege, my daughter and my sweetheart all in one. I keep her framed photograph in my study.

What does it take to become a writer? First, a compelling passion to become one. The motivating force is not money (there is much more money in running a food or paan stall, a gas station or in law and medicine), nor the quest for recognition or fame: you can get it easier in politics or in the films. As a matter of fact, most writers have no clear idea why they took to writing except for some kind of inner urge which compelled them to do so. In most cases the urge abates when they discover that it takes a lot more to translate desire to become a writer into actually becoming one. The urge comes up again and again, some find outlets writing short articles, unfinished short stories or novels before accepting defeat and accepting that they do not have it in them to become writers. Most sensitive people have a fund of poetry in them which gushes out in their adolescent years. This subsides quietly in later years. Writing prose is much harder. It requires wide reading of classical and modern literature, a larger vocabulary and above all else stamina to persevere till the task is done. In short the ability to slog, the ability to sit for hours if need be facing a blank paper, a determination not to get up until it is filled with writing. What you fill the paper with is perhaps a lot of rubbish, but the discipline will prove worthwhile. Soon the writing will improve, soon the best that a writer has in him will come out. I believe writing a daily diary is a useful exercise. Writing long letters to friends is also good practice. Writing regular columns for newspapers and meeting deadlines imposed is good discipline.

Give up writing even for a few days, and its resumption becomes somewhat painful.

What have I got out of writing? Quite a lot of money from newspapers and magazines which carry my columns. Not quite as much from my books. But the income from the two puts me in the top bracket of tax payers. My problem is not income but income tax. More than money is the satisfaction that many people read me and seek me out wherever I am in India. Being lionized can be a very heady experience. But more than money or recognition, it is the sense of fulfilment that writing gives me. I did not get it practising law, diplomacy or teaching; I get it in ample measure scribbling away every day. I hope to do so till the pen drops out of my hand.

18 The Last but One Chapter

IN THE FIRST chapter of this autobiography I spelt out the
reasons why I felt I should get down to writing it. I was
doing it at a leisurely pace when the sudden deaths of three
friends, all younger than I, warned me that I should get on, or it
may remain half-written. Since I am also on the hit list of
Khalistani terrorists, my end may come sooner than I
anticipate. As it is, I had two narrow escapes from Harjinder
Singh Jinda. After killing General Vaidya in Pune, he returned
to Delhi to get me. He came to my apartment, asked for a glass
of water from my cook and had a look at my sitting room. He
then followed me up to Kasauli. There he felt he was being
shadowed and turned back and awaited my return to Delhi. He
was captured and later hanged for murdering Vaidya. A plan of
my apartment was found on his person. On interrogation, he
admitted that he had been instructed to kill me as an enemy of
Khalistan. I was a soft target and getting me would give the
terrorists some publicity they badly needed. Allama Iqbal put
the unpredictability of life in a beautiful couplet:

> *Row mein hai raks oer umar*
> *Kahaam deykheeye thamen,*
> *Na haath baagh par hai*
> *Na pa nakaali mein*

(My life runs at a galloping pace
who knows where it will come to a stop
The reins are not in my hands
my feet are not in the stirrups.)

The three friends died in 1990. The first was Satindra Singh.
As the cliché goes, he was in every way a man larger than life.
He was a six-footer, bulging from his puffed out, sparsely
bearded cheeks to his middle. He had a very loud voice and was
full of bawdy jokes. He had a computer-like memory for facts,

dates and figures, and an incredibly large repertory of Urdu
poetry. He was a hard drinker, and if his exploits could be
believed, also a champion fucker. I can vouch for his drinking;
he could put down a bottle and a half of rum in a few hours. Of
his fucking, I have only his word to go by. He was loud,
garrulous, quarrelsome and prone to violence. Also extremely
soft-hearted and sentimental. All these traits got accentuated
after his wife, a very pretty woman, walked out on him with
their two daughters following a beating he had given her. He
was crushed. He became morose and vindictive. I had to
persuade him to give her a divorce. But I could not persuade
him to cut down on his drink. I encouraged him to have affairs
and abetted some liaisons to ease the hurt he caused himself.
The last time I saw him was at a party given by Roli Books for
the release of my book *Nature Watch*. He came to my home to
get a lift to the hotel. He was reeking of alcohol. I had to switch
off the air-conditioner and put down the glass panes of my car
windows to get some fresh air. At the party I saw him moving
from one group to another, emptying glasses of Scotch and
embracing women he knew. When it was time for us to leave, I
asked him to come along. 'No,' he said categorically, 'I will get a
lift from Ravi and Mala.'

The next day we left for Kasauli by the early morning train.
And the following day I read of his death in *The Tribune* of
Chandigarh. I got details from my daughter Mala when I
returned to Delhi. After the party, he was too drunk to be able
to walk out unaided. She and Ravi had to help him into his
apartment. The next morning, when his servant knocked on his
bedroom door with a cup of tea, he got no response. The door
was bolted from inside. He tried two or three times and became
apprehensive. The only friends of his master's he knew were
us. He turned up at our apartment, and fortunately found my
daughter there. She rang up Satindra's brother-in-law, Inder
Malhotra. The two got the police to break into Satindra's
bedroom. He was lying dead. A half-empty bottle of rum lay
beneath his bed. Satindra left a deafening silence in our lives.

Charanjit was an altogether different kind of character. He
had inherited a sizeable fortune from his father who was a

furniture maker, builder and had Coca Cola's franchise for India. Charanjit was short, fond of dressing in expensive suits tailored in London and wearing scents. He owned a fleet of cars — Toyotas, a Mercedes and a Rolls Royce. His friends called him Baby. He married an extraordinarily pretty girl, Harjeet Kaur. She was nicknamed Bubbles as she always bubbled with laughter. They had no children. Though the younger of the two sons of his father, it was he who took command of the family business and began to expand it. He also had political ambitions. After becoming President of the New Delhi Municipal Committee, he befriended Mrs Gandhi and her family. He provided them with cars and cash whenever and for whatever purpose they needed it. He was given the Congress ticket to fight the South Delhi Parliamentary seat and became an M.P. Our families had known each other since they had settled in Delhi. We regarded them as upstarts, they disdained us as they had outsmarted us in making money.

My personal relationship with the Charanjits began in the autumn of 1984 after the anti-Sikh violence in Delhi following Mrs Gandhi's assassination. The worst sufferer was Charanjit: three of his Campa Cola bottling plants were wrecked by rampaging Hindu mobs. There was clear evidence that the vandals had been hired by a rival manufacturer of soft drinks. Charanjit had to start all over again. He got licences to import new machinery. When it arrived in Bombay, the Customs people raised one technical objection after another to delay its release. Once again, it was his rival who had bribed officials to delay clearance so that he could have time to capture the northern Indian market from Campa Cola. Charanjit's efforts to get the new Prime Minister, Rajiv Gandhi, to order clearance were not successful. He happened to be in the Rajya Sabha when the question of release of blankets, sweaters and other warm clothing sent by Sikh communities living abroad for the families of victims of the November 1984 pogrom came up. I have mentioned in an earlier chapter how these articles were released.

After the debate Charanjit came to speak to me in the lobby.

'Why don't you help me get my machinery released?' he asked. I promised to do my best.

By coincidence a couple of days later the Prime Minister called a meeting of senior members of his cabinet, some MPs and leaders of the opposition parties to review the steps taken to rehabilitate Sikh victims of the violence. After the others, including Unnikrishnan who was known to be a friend of Charanjit, had expressed satisfaction with the arrangements, I demanded to be heard. I contradicted whatever Home Minister Buta Singh had said and cited documents demonstrating the complicity of government officials in thwarting justice being done to Charanjit. That afternoon Charanjit got clearance for his machinery. He came to see me in the evening carrying a massive bouquet of gladioli. 'I am told you pay other MPs large sums of money to do your work, but you fob me off with a bunch of flowers,' I said. 'If I knew you accept money, I would have given it to you a long time ago,' he replied.

Thereafter the Charanjits became regular visitors to our home. He liked good food and drink; in my home he got both. He returned our hospitality by inviting us to parties at his house or at the new hotel, Le Meridien, he had raised. He was lavish with his gifts: Cartier pens, gold watches and hand-made cut-glass glasses with our names inscribed on them. He was a fussy man: he sat in the same chair whenever he came to dine with us. It faced the bathroom, and if the door was open and the loo visible he would not take a drink till the door was closed. I became a sort of father figure (he was twenty-five years younger than I); he turned to me whenever he was in trouble. Although I knew nothing of hoteliering, finance, or company law, he put me on the Board of Directors of Le Meridien.

It was in the last year of his life that I noticed that he was getting irritable and short tempered. I told him so. While spending weekends at his farmhouse near Chattarpur, I noticed the number of medicines he took for blood pressure, diabetes and uric acid, plus a variety of multi-vitamin tablets. 'Why don't you read books?' I asked him once. He replied, 'To read books you need to have peace of mind. I don't have any.'

That was true; he was a restless man. When in trouble he consulted astrologers, palmists and wore lucky stones. He also sought solace in religious ritual and regularly visited his favourite Sant near Ludhiana. My joking about his irrational beliefs did not make the slightest difference to him.

In the summer of 1989 Charanjit had a stroke. He was saved in the nick of time. I went to see him in the Escorts hospital. The doctors assured me that the clot travelling towards his heart had been dissolved before it could get to a fatal destination. Being assured that he was out of danger, I left for Glasgow to attend a literary seminar. When I returned three weeks later, Charanjit was at home but advised not to receive visitors. We were the only exceptions and allowed to see him every evening. After a stroll in his garden he lay in bed watching video cassettes. On the last evening he asked me when I intended to go abroad again. I told him I had no plans. 'You come with me next summer. From England we will go to the States: I will have a second check-up. These johnnies here don't know much about the heart.'

The next morning, as I returned from tennis, my wife quietly informed me, 'I've just had a call from Charanjit's house. He is dead.'

It happened to be my son's fiftieth birthday (4 October 1990). Charanjit was only fifty-one.

The third death was of my wife's cousin Ujjal. He was more a relative than a friend. We had little in common. He was golf-obsessed. He had won the Delhi championship. His son Vikramjit was the youngest man at eighteen to win the Asian amateur golf title. Ujjal talked of nothing besides the matches he had played against world celebrities and the compliments he had received for his stylish swing and accurate putting. I used to dread his visits because I found him a crashing bore. Otherwise he was a good chap with excellent taste. He built himself a lovely farmhouse near the Qutub Minar and invited me to use it whenever I wanted to get away from Delhi. I accepted his invitation and said we would spend a week-end after we returned from Calcutta. As we were about to get into the car to leave for the airport, Ujjal's daughter rang up to say that her father had died in his sleep. My wife cancelled her visit.

I had much to ponder over during the three days I was in Calcutta. Would I go the same way as these three men, without prior warning?

There is a passage in the *Mahabharat* which says that the greatest miracle of life is that, while we know that death is inevitable, no one really believes that he too will die one day. Death comes to others; we expect to go on living forever.

Concern with death and dying has always been a human obsession. I tried to come to terms with it but found myself, as the Dhammapada says, like a fish thrown on dry land and thrashing about trying to free itself from the power of death. I put my fears to Acharya Rajneesh the one time I met him in Bombay. The only prescription he gave me to overcome my phobia was to expose myself to the dying and the dead. I had been doing this on my own for many years. I sat by dead relatives, attended funerals (I rarely attended weddings), and often went to the cremation ground at Nigambodh Ghat to watch corpses going up in flames. It acted like a catharsis: it cleansed me of petty vanities, helped me to take setbacks in life in my stride. I returned home at peace with myself. But it did not help me overcome the fear of dying. On the contrary, my nights' sleep was often disturbed by nightmares set off by what I had seen.

What exactly is death? I do not have a clue, except that I have dreaded it ever since becoming conscious of it. Basically it is because I have no idea of where I will be after it takes place. The deaths of relatives yielded no answers. They simply dissolved into nothingness. Tom Stoppard echoed some of my frustration when he wrote, 'Death is the absence of presence, nothing more . . . the endless time of never coming back . . . a gap you can't see. And when the wind blows through it, it makes no sound.' Or, as Paul Valery put it, 'Death speaks to us with a deep voice but has nothing to say.'

Only those who have experienced death are entitled to speak about it. I have not experienced it. As far as I am concerned I am willing to accept it as the final full-stop beyond which there is a void that no one has been able to penetrate. It has no tomorrows. 'What is the world to a man when his wife is a widow?' asks an Irish proverb. I will try to answer the question as best I can.

The process of dying begins from the time we are born. It takes us bit by bit before it finally swallows up what remains. As the *Good Book* says, we have made a covenant with death and on our eye-lids lies its shadow. Why then are we scared to death of it? Would it be any better if we knew exactly when it would occur? I don't think so. When people suffering from terminal diseases or under sentence of death are told how long they have left to live, they are unable to come to terms with it.

Most of my fears are due to my inability to accept the existence of God, life hereafter or the possibility of rebirth. The Bhagvad Gita assures us, 'For certain is death for the born, and certain is birth for the dead; therefore, over the inevitable thou shouldst not grieve.' I accept the first part of the assurance because I know it to be so; I am unable to accept the second part because there is no convincing evidence of it.

Having decided that I have only one life to live, and not knowing when it will come to an end, I want to get as much out of it as I can. I will indulge my senses to the full; see all that is beautiful in the world; its mountains, lakes, its sea-shores and its deserts; I will gaze with wide-eyed wonder at rain clouds rolling by and marvel at rainbows spanning the horizons; I will savour the delicacies of different countries and sample their vintage wines; I will listen to good music, Western and Indian, and go into trances watching beautiful ballerinas dancing on the stage; I will inhale the fragrance of flowers, herbs, perfumes and of the dry earth when the first drops of rain fall on it; I will ogle at lovely women, make passes at them and, if they are responsive, make love to them.

I am not a hedonist who indulges himself in the sensual for the sake of indulgence. The good things of life can only be enjoyed by people who have put in an honest days' hard work which gives them a sense of fulfilment. I got fulfilment out of journalism and creative writing. It was only then that I really began to relish the bounties of nature as my just and due reward for the work I had put in.

I am fully aware of the brevity of life: there is so much to do and so little time to do it in. Fairly early in life I cut out time-wasting pastimes such as prayer, meditation, religious ritual, *gup-shup* with friends, cocktail parties and dinners (unless assured of Scotch and good food served exactly on time). I began to value the classics of literature above religious scriptures, which I found invariably tedious, repetitive and uninspiring.

I do not understand people who complain about time hanging heavily on them. I don't understand boredom; it is a self-inflicted, time-wasting disease which afflicts people who are congenitally lethargic. And yet it is these very people who dread death more than people too busy to think about it. People who belong to the 'You-can't-take-it-with-you' school may well ask, if you can't take the money you have earned or any of your worldly goods with you when you die, what's the point of sweating it out while you are living? True, the shroud has no pockets, but there are things which do survive death. Money does. So do your children and bequests you make to charitable institutions. A man's learning, the wisdom he has garnered from books die with him, but what he puts on paper lives on after he is gone. There is also his reputation, good or bad, that survives his death.

The Talmud says, 'When death summons man to appear before the creator, three friends are his: the first, whom he loves most, is money. But money cannot accompany him one step. The second is relatives. But they can only accompany him to the grave, and cannot defend him before the judge. It is his third friend, whom he does not highly esteem, his good deeds, who can go with him, and can appear before the King and can obtain his acquittal.' This kind of argument makes sense only to those who believe that there is something incorporeal which survives the body. For want of a more precise word, they call it the soul. No one has the foggiest idea of what the soul really is. I concede that there is more to a human being than his flesh, blood and bones. He is a talking, thinking animal with a character uniquely his own. Is his collection of non-corporeal attributes what they call the soul? If it is, it vanishes as soon as a person dies. The soul is yet another figment of the human imagination created to buttress notions of an afterlife. The same applies to concepts like the kingdom of heaven where the rainbow never fades. It is strange that, although everyone aspires to go to paradise, no one is over-eager to quit the hell he regards his life on earth.

For me, if there is a paradise, it has to be a paradise on earth. I have been to many places in many climes which more than answer my notions of paradise. The Rockies, the Thousand Islands, Muskoka and the awesome grandeur of the Niagara Falls; the Lake District and the Cotswolds in England; the Italian lakes, Garda and the Maggiore; the subterranean caves lit by myriads of glow-worms in New Zealand. The prehistoric magnificence of Ayers Rock in Australia; the plethora of wild life at Murchison Falls on the Nile running out of Uganda; the beaches at Rio de Janeiro, Kovalam and Goa; the mountains and streams of Kashmir; the ethereal beauty of the Taj Mahal at all hours — with the blush of pink at dawn, its dazzling brilliance under the mid-day sun, the soft amber glow at twilight and its cool, silken beauty in the light of the moon. There are hundreds of other paradises scattered over the world. I would be happy to accept their earthly reality in place of the fevered dreams of fast-running streams of limpid water and houris capable of renewing their virginity. Who wants virgins anyhow? Good looking women with experience, vivacity and brains make much better lovers and companions.

What does all this amount to? Not very much. I don't know where I came from, I don't know the purpose of my existence; I don't know where I will go when I die. Since I do not know the date of my birth, I can't even have a horoscope cast to indicate how long I will live. Once in Bombay, a swamiji who had a copy of the *Bhrigu Samhita* came to see me. He told me that he had a page with my name and future on it. Also the date and time I would receive him. It ran somewhat as follows: 'In a city beside the ocean beginning with the letter B on the fifth day of the fifth month of the Vikkami era at 11 am a man named

Khushwant Kesri [meaning Singh] will ask questions about himself.' It continued to read that, in my previous birth, I had been a disbeliever in the occult and suffered because of a lack of faith. Some of that lack of faith had persisted as a kind of hangover into my present life. The sage Bhrigu warned me against persisting in my error. He also 'foretold' that much of my life would have to do with pen and paper. He predicted the exact time, day, month and year of my demise. According to him I would live up to 1999 and die a few months before the turn of the century. That has not happened. It is odd that Nostradamus also predicted that life on earth would end on July 31, 1999. Had his prediction come true, then you, my readers, would also have departed about the same time as I.

I fear I may make an ass of myself at the time of my death — most people do. I don't want to cry for help, or ask God to forgive me my sins and make any display of weakness. Like my father who died a few minutes after he had his evening Scotch, I would like to have one before embarking on the long road. I would like to go as Allama Iqbal exhorted strong men to go.

> *Nishaan-e-mard-e Momin ba too goyam?*
> *choon marg aayad, tabassum bar lab-e-ost*

(You ask me for the signs of a man of faith?
When death comes to him
He has a smile on his lips.)

Postscript: November 2001
The Harvest Years

I FINISHED WRITING this autobiography over six years ago and handed over the manuscript to my publisher. Ravi Dayal had it typeset, the jacket design was prepared, and he was poised to have it printed and published. To gain advance publicity he offered a chapter each to *India Today*, *The Telegraph* and *The Hindu*. In its issue of 31 October 1995 *India Today* published the chapter dealing with Maneka Gandhi's expulsion from the house of her mother-in-law, Indira Gandhi, when the latter was Prime Minister of India. I had based it on what had been published earlier by *India Today* when the event took place and on Pupul Jayakar's and Ved Mehta's biographies of Mrs Gandhi, with additional details given to me by Maneka Gandhi and her sister, Ambika, who was present at the final showdown. Nevertheless, Maneka took me and my publisher to court but left *India Today* out. On 12 December 1995, she obtained an ex parte Order of injunction in the Delhi High Court restraining publication of the book. We appealed against this Order immediately. Justice K. Ramamoorthy of the Delhi High Court heard arguments from both sides several months later. After almost a year and a half he ruled that I had infringed on Maneka's right to privacy and upheld the injunction on publication of the book. Once more we filed an appeal. It took over four years for that to come up for hearing in the High Court.

The long delay cannot be entirely attributed to the lethargy of our legal system. First, my Senior Counsel Soli Sorabji was made Attorney General: he could no longer appear for me. Then his assistant M. Mudgal was elevated to the Bench: he could no longer appear for me. Kapil Sibal agreed to take my case. He was elected to the Rajya Sabha and had little time left for legal practice. Only Sridhar Chitale, who had been our junior counsel, was left to handle the appeal. Our case was argued by C.A. Sundaram, assisted by Chitale. My daughter and I sat through the arguments in the Division Bench comprising Justices Devinder Gupta and Sanjay Krishan Kaul. We heard Maneka's counsel Raj Panjwani argue at tedious length, hour after hour, going over what he had said before Justice Ramamoorthy. Our counsel C.A. Sundaram spoke no more than half an hour twice. I have rarely heard such forceful arguments in favour of freedom of expression. Perhaps I was biased because he was speaking on my behalf. I could sense he was carrying the judges with him. The judgement was pronounced three weeks later. My daughter and son-in-law were away in Ranikhet. I was accompanied by my son Rahul and my granddaughter. The judgement was pronounced by Justice Kaul. The injunction against publication of my autobiography was vacated and Maneka ordered to pay Rs 10,000 in costs to us. We had spent rather more than that to vindicate the right of freedom of expression against Maneka's charge that I had infringed her right to privacy. Now you can judge for yourself.

The news of the judgement spread like the proverbial wildfire. My telephone rang every few minutes with people calling to congratulate me. Media-men, including TV teams, invaded my privacy to get my reaction. My granddaughter bought me ice-cream to celebrate the occasion.

Maneka has appealed against the High Court judgement in the Supreme Court and may still take me to court on charges of defamation. In that case she will have to face detailed cross-examination on her own part on being thrown out from the Prime Minister's residence. That may prove embarrassing. In any event, by the time the case is decided I will probably be well beyond her reach. I am now getting on to eighty-eight.

My chief grouse against Justice Ramamoorthy's judgement against me is the gratuitous advice he renders to writers. He pronounced: ' . . . as a matter of common knowledge he [i.e. myself] is a learned person with wide experience, having moved with great personalities in India and abroad. Any person would expect from him materials useful to the society which would inspire the younger generation. . . . Generally, people would expect from great writers high thinking, higher living and high learning. The law in India does not permit scrawly writing by individuals just for the purpose of satisfying their impulses arising out of personal animosities.' Thanks, Justice Ramamoorthy, for telling me what I should write about and how. I choose to ignore your advice, as any writer worth his salt would, with a smile on my lips and contempt in my heart.

When I began this autobiography, I believed it would be the last book I would write in my life. I was wrong. In the last six years I have churned out more books than I had done in any six years in the past. Most of them were reproductions of articles kept by my readers and collections of jokes I append at the end of every column I write. There are now six such collections of joke books in the market, each going into over a dozen reprints. Their royalties provide me premium brands of Scotch whisky, an item I value most in my old age. I also wrote a novel, *The Company of Women* (Penguin-Viking). I was not very eager to see it published as it was about the sexual fantasies of an octogenarian (i.e., myself). But Ravi Singh of Penguin-Viking spent a week with me in Kasauli to put the disjointed pieces in order and to make them into a book. Without exception, all the critics panned the novel. Nevertheless, it became a bestseller and remained on the top of India's bestseller list for over six months. It earned me more royalties than any of my other books. So much for the critics! They can stew in their own juices.

A few other books made the bestseller list: *Unforgettable Women* (Penguin); a reprint of my biography of Maharaja Ranjit Singh (Penguin); the coffee-tabler *The Sikhs* (Roli Books), with excellent photographs by Raghu Rai. I also had a collection of translations of love poetry, *Declaring Love in Four Languages* (Penguin), published with Sharda Kaushik. I have two more books in the pipeline: *Among the Sikhs* with Dr Surjit Kaur of

Washington D.C., which will be about Sikh communities in foreign countries and their men and women who have earned money and fame. It is likely to be published by Roli Books. A translation of the Sikhs' evening prayer, *Rehras*, done in collaboration with Reema Anand, is with Penguin. I have no reason to complain.

In the past six years I have also redefined my equation with religion and God. Without making any conscious compromise with agnosticism, I began to listen in to the morning service *Asa Di Vaar* relayed from the Golden Temple every day. I found it very soothing and felt hearing it would help my ailing wife who had at one time been very devout. Every evening I listen to the recitation of the evening prayer, *Rehras*. This certainly helped me in translating it with the help of Reema Anand. We decided to call it *Evensong*. More than the revival of interest in religious texts, my sense of belonging to the Sikh community, which I regard as more important than subscribing to its ordinances, received a boost. My name was included among those to be honoured with the *Nishaan-e-Khalsa* at the 300th anniversary of the foundation of the Khalsa Panth. Then Guru Nanak Dev University conferred an honorary doctorate on me for my services to the community. Displayed on the walls of my home are the citation of the honorary doctorate and a replica of a copper plate with coins of the Sikh Darbar containing the lettering *Nishaan-e-Khalsa*.

Another award that came my way was given by the Punjab Arts Council in Chandigarh. There were dozens of recipients, Indians and Pakistanis. Also dozens of long-winded orations. I came down with a heavy cold and returned to Delhi. No sooner had I dumped the packet of currency notes in my grand-daughter's lap than my cold mysteriously disappeared. I understood why money is called filthy lucre.

Perhaps the most significant event for me, and certainly the most lucrative, in the past six years was the conferment on me of 'The Honest Man of the Year' award by Sulabh International. If I was really an honest person, I should have turned down the award, but the sum of ten lakh rupees tax free proved too much for me to quibble about my honesty. It was a huge event. The FICCI auditorium, the largest in Delhi, was packed to overflowing. To prove how dishonest I could be, I stole the ballpoint pens from the portfolios of Chandrababu Naidu, Chief Minister of Andhra Pradesh, who handed me the cheque, and Jaswant Singh, Foreign Minister, who presided over the function. My sleight-of-hand received louder applause than any of the speeches delivered by the eminent personalities present.

Other events now coming into my memory that were important landmarks in my life: my novel *Train to Pakistan* was at long last made into a film, by Pamela Rooks. She did it on a shoestring budget but made a splendid job of it. It was shown on TV and then for a few months in cinemas all over the country. It took me on a free jaunt to London and was shown to a mixed audience of Indians, Pakistanis, Bangladeshis and the Brits. The money went to a hospital in Pakistan.

My novel *Delhi* was translated into German. My German publishers invited me over and I was taken around different cities of Germany and Austria to be present at readings of extracts in English and German. *Train to Pakistan* won the Mondello Award. I got yet another free trip to Italy, and flew to Sicily to collect my cheque of Rs 2 lakhs from the Mayor of Palermo.

And finally I spent four days in Karachi at the invitation of Rotary International. I was the main speaker at the Convention. What I said went down very well with both Indian and Pakistani participants. They put me live on TV channels. All I said was, if we go to war again (this was after Kargil), it will be our last. Neither you nor we will survive, and this region will have the peace of the graveyard.

Overshadowing these years of minor triumphs was the gradual decline in my wife's health. She had always been in better shape than I. She never had problems with her bowel movements and every morning exclaimed triumphantly, 'Clean as a whistle'. And often an hour or two later in French, *'Deuxieme fois'* — a second clearing. I, on the other hand, had to coax my sluggish liver with laxatives, glycerine suppositories and enemas. She rarely fell ill. I was constantly catching colds and often suffered from headaches. Whenever we went for a stroll, she would walk ahead of me and I had to remind her that Indian women walked behind their husbands, not in front of them. In our early years of marriage, she played tennis vigorously. In middle-age we played golf; she always got the better of me. After she gave up games, she took to walking. She drove to the Lodi Gardens and did the rounds of the park without talking to anyone. All the regulars recognized her.

She was always house-proud, ordering the servants around till everything looked spick and span. She provided me tastier food than any five-star hotel. Every morning she read out some recipes from cooking books and instructed our cook, Chandan Singh, how the food was to be made. So we had French, Chinese, Italian and occasionally desi food, invariably gourmet-class. She looked after our little garden and had vegetables planted at the turn of seasons. She watched over them like a hawk and drove off urchins who entered the garden to steal ripening fruit or vegetables. She spent an hour or two teaching the servants' children Hindi and English. And always found them jobs after they had finished with schooling.

She had a zest for life; she could put down more whisky than I. Unfortunately, she had a poor memory and a short temper. She had no sense of direction. At times, after dropping me at the Gymkhana Club, on her way back home she found herself on the road to Palam Airport. Our married years were full of quarrels which clouded our otherwise reasonably happy married life. I had the great advantage of being in a profession which required my being left alone for several hours in the day. She left me alone.

Suddenly things began to change. She gave up all exercise. She also gave up drinking and reading. I always looked up to her to make some comment on my columns which appeared in the papers every Saturday. She stopped reading them, nor did she care to read my books as they appeared with tedious regularity. Most of all, she turned into a negative personality. To every suggestion I made her immediate response was no. It caused me a lot of irritation because I did not realize that something within her was changing, over which she had no control. It dawned on me after she started falling ill. The first time was in Kasauli, when she went into a depression and stopped talking. I cut short our holiday and returned to Delhi. She was barely able to board the train at Chandigarh. The following Christmas at Goa, she fell ill on the third day of our vacation. Shivani Rarki, manager of the hotel, had her meals sent to her in her room and looked after her as if she was her mother. I had to cut short this holiday as well and return to Delhi. Our family doctor, I.P.S. Kalra, suggested I consult a psychiatrist and employ a whole-time nurse. She was indignant and turned down both suggestions. She became unsteady on her feet and began getting attacks of vertigo. Twice she fell off her bed, while trying to get up, and badly bruised her forehead. The wound had to be stitched and she was given an anti-tetanus injection. She felt no pain because she had lost the sense of pain. I have had to employ day and night nurses to be with her at all hours. My daughter got a friend, Dr Ravi Nehru, a handsome Kashmiri bachelor who is a specialist in such ailments, to meet my wife. He spent an hour talking to her, and made her walk a few steps with him. After she had retired, he told me in plain words: 'This is Alzheimer's. We have no cure for it. The best we can do is to stabilize her condition.' He prescribed Exelon, a drug which is also being given to the former US President Reagan. It is murderously expensive. That, the nurses and the doctors (Ravi Nehru does not charge me anything) cost more than a precious paisa. I am more than happy to shell out the cash for somebody who has been with me more than sixty years of my life. But it is hard for me to sit all day watching a person who was so lively and full of zest for life become a non-person. Failing memory, little speech, reduced to a skeleton and gradually withering away. I was always certain she would outlast me by many years. I am no longer so sure that she will. But I have a gut feeling that if she goes before me, I will put away my pen and write no more.

Index

A

Abbas, Khwaja Ahmed, 255
Advani, L.K., 310, 342
Ahmad, Fakhruddin Ali, 258, 259
Aikath-Gyaltsen, Indrani, 399, 400, 401
Akbar, M.J., 256, 398
Aman, Zeenat, 261
Anand, Ambika, 282, 293, 297-99, 413
Anand, Amteshwar, 281-84, 286-88, 292-96, 299-301
Anand, Chetan, 44, 260
Anand, Dev, 260, 262
Anand, Tejinder Singh, 282, 287, 292
Ashk, Upendra Nath, 396
Azmi, Shabana, 263

B

Babi, Parveen, 262-63
Badal, Prakash Singh, 313, 315, 343
Bannerjee, Subroto, 232-34
Bans, Rama, 263-64
Bansilal, 284
Bedi, Protima, 263
Begum Para, 249-51
Bhagat, Usha, 281, 294
Bhindranwale, Jarnail Singh, 313-14, 316, 323-26
Bhutto, Zulfiqar Ali, 249, 252, 277-78, 355

Birla, G.D., 304
Birla, K.K., 295, 302-09, 316, 319
Biswas, Roma, 24, 48, 52, 57-58, 67
Booth, Lillian, 65-67
Bose, Kamala, 13, 14, 16, 18, 19, 40
Brahmachari, Dhirendra, 281, 294, 297-99
Brata, Sasthi, 391-92

C

Chand, Kishan, 259
Chaubal, Devyani, 260-61
Chaudhuri, Nirad C., 162, 200, 201, 386-90
Chopra, B.R., 44, 260

D

Dardi, Dr Gopal Singh, 172, 268-69, 317-20, 398
Das, Kamala, 398
Dayal, Mala, 2, 148, 173, 188, 191, 224, 275, 404
Dayal, Naina, 289, 356, 414
Desai, Anita, 390
Desai, Kanti, 272, 273
Desai, Morarji, 235, 271-73, 285, 289, 292
Desani, Govind, 149, 397-98
Dhar, Sheila, 193, 196
Dharmendra, 260-61
Dhawan, R.K., 281, 294, 297-99
Dhingra, Baldoon, 175-76

Dutt, Nargis, 262, 310, 322, 335

F
Farooqi, Asad, 328
Fernandes, George, 258, 336

G
Gandhi, Feroze, 280
Gandhi, Indira, 103, 249, 254,
  255-56, 257-59, 271, 276,
  280-99, 301, 305, 309-11,
  318, 322-25, 328, 330-31,
  334-36, 368, 380, 405, 413
Gandhi, Mahatma, 13, 34, 122,
  222, 304, 374
Gandhi, Maneka, 279-80,
  282-84, 286, 288-99, 301,
  309, 335, 413-14
Gandhi, Rajiv, 280-81, 287-88,
  293-94, 296, 299, 324, 336,
  337, 380, 405
Gandhi, Sanjay, 257, 271-72,
  277, 279-91, 293-96, 298,
  301, 302-03, 305, 335, 336
Gandhi, Sonia, 287, 288, 293,
  294, 296
Gandhi, Supriya, 373-74
Ghosh, Sudhir, 117-22
Ginsberg, Allen, 394-96

H
Haksar, P.N., 145, 268
Haq, Zia-ul, 278
Hyder, Qurrutulain, 256

J
Jain, Ashok, 271, 273
Jain, J.C., 202, 204, 231, 322
Jaspal, Kamla, 120-22, 131, 134,
  137, 145-46, 149
Jayalalitha, 329, 380
Jha, L.K., 54, 57, 60
Jha, Prem Shankar, 274

Jhabvala, Ruth Prawer, 200, 386,
  388-90
Jinnah, M.A., 85, 116, 244, 255,
  318, 330
Joad, C.M., 141-42
Johar, I.S., 263-64
Joshi, Chand, 303
Jung, Ali Yavar, 256
Jung, Anees, 242-43, 245, 394

K
Kapoor, Raj, 261-62
Kapoor, Yashpal, 276
Karkaria, Bachi, 399
Karlekar, Hiranmay, 302-03, 305
Khan, Tikka, 249, 252, 255
Kidwai, Jamal, 131, 135, 152, 193
Kirpal, Prem, 163-64, 171, 179,
  186, 191
Krishnamachari, T.T., 195, 200
Kumar, Dilip, 249, 256
Kumar, Suresh, 277, 292
Kumari, Meena, 262

L
Laise, Carol, 164, 203, 205-06
Lakshmi Bai, 3, 5, 6, 8, 31
Lall, Arthur, 33, 96, 103,
  117-20, 131-32, 142
Lall, Sheila, 33, 103, 117, 120,
  131-32, 152
Latifi, Danial, 99, 360-61
Laxman, R.K., 236-37
Lewis, Primila, 259
Longowal, Sant Harcharan
  Singh, 313, 324, 344

M
Malgaonkar, Manohar, 386,
  390-91
Malhotra, Inder, 257, 274, 404
Mangeshkar, Lata, 171, 256
Mann, Simranjit Singh, 344

Matthai, M.O., 136, 138, 277, 280
Menon, Krishna, 116, 118-22, 130-31, 133-38, 141-49, 162, 240, 308, 340,
Menon, N.C., 308, 309
Miranda, Mario, 237
Mody, Piloo, 322
Moraes, Dom, 177, 335
Mountbatten, Lady Edwina, 114, 130, 133, 135, 137-38
Mountbatten, Lord Louis, 130, 133, 136

N

Naipaul, V.S., 392-94
Narayan, Jayaprakash, 256-57, 285
Nehru, Arun, 299, 324
Nehru, Pandit Jawaharlal, 13, 35, 96, 114, 118, 121, 134-39, 162, 172, 277, 280-81, 283, 365
Noorani, A.G., 242-45

P

Palkhiwala, Nani, 290-91, 320
Patel, Rajni, 119, 142, 243, 254, 257
Patel, Vallabhbhai, 116-17, 121
Patnaik, Biju, 131-32
Paul, Swraj, 293

Q

Qadir, Asghari, 100, 116, 351, 354
Qadir, Manzur, 100, 101, 105-08, 112-13, 207, 252, 346, 349, 351, 355, 363, 370-72

R

Radhakrishnan, Dr S., 90, 164, 172, 173, 175, 176, 331, 398

Raghav, Raman, 231-33, 246
Rahman, M.A., 348, 351
Rai, E.N. Mangat, 32-33, 37, 39, 41, 76, 78, 94-96, 101-03
Ram, Bharat, 20, 78, 84, 159-60, 174, 196-97
Ram, Charat, 20
Ram, Babu Jagjivan, 292
Ramoowalia, B.S., 313, 341-42, 344
Rao, Narasimha, 330, 331, 337, 380, 381
Rao, U.S. Mohan, 192, 194, 196
Ray, Maya, 343
Ray, Siddhartha Shankar, 257, 305, 317, 321, 337

S

Sahni, Balraj, 44, 260
Sarkar, Aveek, 277
Shergil, Amrita, 96-99
Shraddha Mata, 277
Shukla, V.C., 290, 293
Shungloo, Krishen, 162-63, 213
Simba, 188-91
Singh, Balwant, 313, 315, 341-44
Singh, Bhagwant, 25
Singh, Buta, 328, 329, 380, 406
Singh, Charanjit, 276, 296, 321, 337, 341-42, 344, 368, 380, 404-07
Singh, Daljit, 174, 265
Singh, Darbara, 312, 315, 323, 329
Singh, Dr Tarlochan, 171-72, 173, 205-06, 326
Singh, Giani Zail, 302, 318, 325, 326, 337, 345, 368
Singh, Gurbux, 340-41
Singh, Kaval, 14, 24, 76-79, 83, 84-86, 94, 95, 96, 98, 124,

130, 149, 202, 232, 266, 271, 289, 417-19
Singh, Khushwant, birth and childhood in Hadali, 3-9; schooling, 12-20, 22, 25; college in India, 32-4, 37, 39, 40-45, 50-51; at Shantiniketan, 46-9; college in England, 57-61, 65-82; courtship and marriage, 72, 76, 77-9, 83-6; as lawyer, 87-90, 106-7, 108-10, 116; experience of Partition, 104, 105, 106-7, 107-14; as diplomat, 116, 117-22, 124, 125-8, 130, 131, 133, 134, 135-8, 144-8; as writer, 101-3, 128, 149, 150, 151, 158, 159, 161-2, 180, 187, 202, 205, 206-7, 215, 228, 274, 278, 384, 385, 401-2, 415, 416, 417; with AIR, 162-3; with UNESCO, 164, 165-74, 175, 176, 177-80, 182, 183-7; with *Yojana*, 192, 193-5, 202; with *The Illustrated Weekly*, 202, 204, 228, 231-4, 236-7, 245-9, 254-9, 263, 271, 274, 275, 276; with *The National Herald*, 276, 277, 301; with *New Delhi*, 277-8; with *The Hindustan Times*, 302, 303, 304-9, 316, 317, 320, 321; as MP, 302, 310-11, 312, 321-3, 329-35, 336-8, 341, 343; travels to Pakistan, 9, 249-54, 346-58; relationship with wife, 77-9, 83-6, 94, 95-6, 149, 275, 417-9
Singh, Tara, 312-13, 317
Singh, Raghubir, 12, 13, 14, 16-17
Singh, Rahul, 130, 148, 232, 242, 270-71, 281, 392, 414
Singh, Satinder, 67
Singh, Sobha, 1, 3, 12, 26-7, 39, 40, 51, 83-4, 87, 89, 93, 141, 148, 160, 192, 213, 264, 265, 266, 267, 289, 311, 339, 387
Singh, Sujan, 3, 4, 11, 20
Singh, Ujjal, 5, 12, 21, 41, 86, 265, 270, 313
Singh, V.P., 320, 337
Sinha, B.M., 320, 321
Stokes, Hazel Marie, 69, 70, 216

T
Tagore, Rabindranath, 13, 18, 44, 46-48, 125, 376
Tohra, Gurcharan Singh, 311-13, 315, 344

V
Veeran Bai, 3, 21, 28, 63, 148, 265, 338-41

Y
Yadav, Rajendra, 396
Yunus, Mohammad, 103, 280, 283

Z
Zakaria, Fatma, 234-37, 241, 243, 254, 266, 274-75
Zakaria, Rafiq, 234, 254, 262